Experiments with

Documenta11_Platform2

Experiments with Truth:
Transitional Justice and the Processes of Truth and Reconciliation

Documenta11_Platform2

Edited by
Okwui Enwezor
Carlos Basualdo
Ute Meta Bauer
Susanne Ghez
Sarat Maharaj
Mark Nash
Octavio Zaya

Hatje Cantz

This volume contains all contributions to Documenta11_Platform2, "Experiments with Truth: Transitional Justice and the Processes of Truth and Reconciliation," a conference held in New Delhi, India Habitat Centre, May 8–12, 2001, accompanied by a film and video program, shown at the India Habitat Centre's Visual Arts Gallery, May 7–21, 2001.

Managing Editor: Gerti Fietzek

Editing: David Frankel

Proofreading: Michelle Piranio

Translations: Linda Phillips, Diana Reese, Miranda Robbins

Visual Concept and Typography: Ecke Bonk

Typesetting: Weyhing digital, Ostfildern-Ruit

Printed by Dr. Cantz'sche Druckerei, Ostfildern-Ruit

Photo Credits:
pp. 159, Courtesy South African National Gallery; pp. 166, 167 Copyright: The Argus; pp. 283–287 Courtesy Eyal Sivan; pp. 290, 292–310 Courtesy Alfredo Jaar; p. 354 Luftbild & Pressefoto Berlin.

Published by
Hatje Cantz Publishers
Senefelderstrasse 12
73760 Ostfildern-Ruit, Germany
www.hatjecantz.de

Distribution in the USA
D.A.P., Distributed Art Publishers, Inc.
155 Avenue of the Americas, 2nd Floor
New York, NY 10013, USA
www.artbook.com

ISBN 3-7757-9080-2

Printed in Germany

Die Deutsche Bibliothek – CIP-Einheitsaufnahme
A catalogue record for this book is available from Die Deutsche Bibliothek.

Platform2 was organized in collaboration with the Prince Claus Fund for Culture and Development, The Hague, and in cooperation with the Visual Arts Gallery of the India Habitat Centre, New Delhi.

Project Advisor and Research: Charity Scribner

Organization: Markus Müller

New Delhi Coordinator: Alka Pande
Assistants: Poornima Backliwal, Malika Das, Priya Kumar, Mala Panjwan, Anushree Somany

Film and Video Program Coordinators:
Stephanie Mauch, Karin Rebbert

Thanks to:
Els van der Plas, Director, Prince Claus Fund, The Hague
Geerte Wachter, Policy Officer, Prince Claus Fund, The Hague
Heimo Richter, Ambassador Federal Republic of Germany, New Delhi
Heike Dettmann, Counsellor Cultural Affairs, Embassy of the Federal Republic of Germany, New Delhi
Peter Sewitz, Program Director, Max Mueller Bhavan, New Delhi
Tilmann Waldraff, Director, Max Mueller Bhavan, New Delhi
Ronit Avni, Program Assistant, Witness, New York
Ranjit Hoskote, Bombay
Geeta Kapur, New Delhi

Platform2 was realized with the generous support of the
Prince Claus Fund for Culture and Development, The Hague
and with the assistance of the India Habitat Centre, New Delhi

This volume is made possible through a generous grant from the Prince Claus Fund for Culture and Development, The Hague.

Fonds

Contents

Uncivil Conduct: State Violence, Ethnic Conflict, Civil Society

Crimes against Humanity: Truth Commissions and the Pursuit of Justice

The Immersive Spectacle: Historical Testimony and
the Limits of Representation

The Politics of Witnessing: Trauma, Memory, and the Narration of Truth

It is now commonplace to declare that the world changed with the spectacular and traumatizing events of September 11, 2001. What the change represents, however, is still hard to define, given how deeply such change is also seen to be caught in the proliferating processes of globalization. A teleological reading of September 11 positions it in a sort of flawed cause-and-effect representation. That it marks a deep cleavage in the ways one thinks of political Islam is certain, but whether this should mean that all responses to it should be understood from the point of view of the pre- and post-syndrome that has overtaken all discussions around it, especially in the United States, is quite another matter.

Even if we cannot deny that the events of September 11 and its aftermath in the war in Afghanistan have significantly widened the political horizon of democratic and juridical discourses of our time, they could hardly be pronounced the central ground on which the struggle to overcome Westernism and imperialism is being waged. September 11 represents one of the most radical and terrible visions of the conflict of values that has attended the slow dismantling of imperialism. It is also a sanguine lesson for late modernity, and has launched debates worldwide – from Palestine, Pakistan, Saudi Arabia, Iran, and the rest of the Islamic world to the United States, France, England, the North Atlantic Treaty Organisation alliance, and Russia – on themes of fundamentalism (religious and secular), concepts of governance and political participation, juridical interpretations of civil society, ethical principles of terrorism as a tool of radical political struggle, peace, security, and other secular and theocratic themes. Whatever the outcome of these debates, the commonplaces we all share are to be found in the very features of global instability and insecurity that explode the triumphalist conceit of "a new world order." Not since the end of World War II and then the collapse of communism in the Soviet Union have there been such demands for such radical rearticulations and reinterpretions of the basic principles of universal political rights.

What is to be done? This popular refrain, heard so often in these tense times, is a measure of the incertitudes that have suddenly arisen to make deeper

demands on the sunny projections of globalist progress. Such incertitudes mark
another kind of critical procedure, namely the analogous idea that globalization
and the political discourse of terrorism have a common root in fundamentalism,
whether secular or theocratic, in that they respectively hegemonize the markets
and religion with limited participation from other sources.

The series of conferences, public debates, and film and video projects from
which the first four books of Documenta11's five Platforms are drawn were
planned and begun more than two years before the events of September 11
brought a new urgency to the political and philosophical debates that form the
focus of our wider project – debates on democracy, justice, cultural and religious
difference, and new spatial arrangements. Nonetheless, the contributions to
these volumes share a common assumption in the fact that each is an attempt by
the author to illuminate the epistemological texture and complexity of the present political and cultural climate.

Beginning in Vienna on March 15, 2001, and ending in Kassel on Septem-
ber 15, 2002, the Platforms, based on the conceptual initiative of Docu-
menta11, unfolded over the course of eighteen months. The first four Platforms
were constituted as collaborations between Documenta11 and the Prince Claus
Fund for Culture and Development, The Hague; the India Habitat Centre,
New Delhi; the Academy of Fine Arts Vienna; the House of World Cultures,
Berlin; DAAD (Deutscher Akademischer Austauschdienst – German Academic
Exchange Service), Berlin; CODESRIA (Council for Development of Social Sci-
ence Research in Africa), Dakar; and the Goethe Institute, Munich and Lagos.
For the present volume, Documenta11, the Prince Claus Fund for Culture and
Development, and the India Habitat Centre have worked closely at every stage
of the realization of the New Delhi conference and film and video program.

These collaborations not only highlight the larger scope of Documenta11's
intellectual project based on the principle of shared research interests, they
inscribe within Documenta11's exhibition project a critical interdisciplinary
methodology that is to be distinguished from interdisciplinarity as a form of
exhibitionism. The interdisciplinary dimension that forms part of our common
association is also a manifestation of a central concern of Documenta11 from
the very beginning, namely, the idea that the space of contemporary art, and the
mechanisms that bring it to a wider public domain, require radical rethinking
and enlargement.

Such an enlargement has both spatial and temporal consequences. In a kind
of counterprocedure, it represents a limit and a horizon. The limit specifies the
point of Documenta11's beginning, that is, the articulation of the exhibition
dimension of the project; while the horizon points to the intellectual and artistic
circuits that make up aspects of the exhibition project's drive toward the pro-

duction of knowledge, through a gesture of open contestation, debate, and transparent processes of research. The framework within which this takes place has both political and aesthetic objectives. But rather than subsume the concerns of art and artists into the narrow terrain of Western institutional aesthetic discourses that are part of the current crisis, we have conceived of this project as part of the production of a common public sphere. Such a public sphere, we believe, creates a space whereby the critical models of artists, theorists, philosophers, historians, activists, urbanists, writers, and others working within other intellectual traditions and artistic positions could productively be represented and discussed. The public sphere imagined by these collaborations is to be understood, then, as a constellation of multifaceted Platforms in which artists, intellectuals, communities, audiences, practices, voices, situations, actions come together to examine and analyze the predicaments and transformations that form part of the deeply inflected historical procedures and processes of our time.

If there is a politics of any kind to be deduced from the above, it is a politics of nonambiguity, and the idea that all discourses, all critical models (be they artistic or social, intellectual or pragmatic, interpretive or historical), emerge from a location or situation, even when they are not defined or restricted by it. In proposing the five Platforms that make up our common public sphere, we have above all else been attentive to how contemporary artists and intellectuals begin from the location and situation of their practice. The objective of all five Platforms has been to bring all the forces emanating from these disciplinary departures and conjunctions into an enabling space of productive intellectual and artistic activity.

Okwui Enwezor
Artistic Director, Documenta11

Els van der Plas
Director, Prince Claus Fund for Culture and Development, The Hague

Alka Pande
Consultant, Art Advisor, and Curator, Visual Arts Gallery, India Habitat Centre, New Delhi

Introduction

In the last two decades a series of juridical inquiries and political and social assessments have been initiated all over the world to consider the nature of the wanton violence inflicted by various states on their own people and others, and of the ensuing questions of impunity or else of guilt and punishment arising out of cases of genocide and gross violations of human rights. Until recently, juridical bodies, empowered by the overwhelming evidence of such violence and violation, have been the primary means of addressing these cases within the social context of societies in transition and undergoing political reorganization. The trauma of loss, however, and its debilitating impact on the collective psyche, have increasingly called for other mechanisms that could build a credible bridge between on the one hand the juridical form of justice and on the other the personal need of victims to have their stories be heard and entered into the historical record.

One answer to this search for a bridge has been the establishment of numerous "truth commissions" in different countries around the world. But what happens when neither truth commissions nor juridical inquiries are able to heal the rifts that so often divide the societies in which they have been implemented? Scholars, nongovernmental organizations, museums, and the media are currently showing an overwhelming historical interest in the work of these commissions, and a category has emerged in the humanities that is dedicated to the study of memory and its ethical and aesthetic implications within representation.

A problematic central to this interest, especially for philosophers, is to answer the question, "What constitutes truth?" But it is often the case that the largely secular endeavor of juridical truth, when counterposed to the quasi-religious dimension of "truth and reconciliation," may produce unsatisfactory answers for victims and their families, as well as resistance from the individuals and institutions whose record of abuse it spotlights. Skepticism from the victims and resistance from the perpetrators have repeatedly called the efficacy of this transitional endeavor into question, and the results of the inquiries have also been disputed. Even so, the broader implications of the work undertaken by these various bodies of inquiry, juridical and otherwise, have called for new assessments of them, even as many of the decisions that have accompanied their findings have continued to be debated within the structures of civil society. It is the aim of this conference to analyze and produce a debate around the historical work that has emerged from the study of these commissions, and around not only the artistic and cultural responses that have accompanied them but the philosophical and political theories as well.

Concerning Violence   The catastrophic fate of European Jewry during the years of National Socialism – the calamity of the Holocaust for the Jews, and also for other minorities, under the Third Reich – continues to press contemporary thinkers, legal practitioners, institutions, and historians to address the difficult task of coming to terms with its features. But while the Holocaust or Shoah remains representative of a form of criminal violence enacted by the state upon its own people, as well as upon others it considers its opponents, the notion of that terrible event as overwhelmingly singular has repeatedly been tested by other examples of systemic state violence and repression, as in the cases of South Africa, Argentina, Cambodia, Rwanda, Chile, Guatemala, Chad, Algeria, Bosnia, Kosovo, Belgium, France, Kurdistan, the United States, and Haiti.

The modern emergence of a human-rights-based law and its system of justice is an inheritance owed to the Nuremberg Trials of 1945–46, in which the allied powers prosecuted former officers of the Nazi regime for their actions under the Third Reich. Prompted by the destructive premeditated violence of the Nazi state, the trials and their various verdicts defined a notion of accountability that drew from an emerging theory of human-rights law. Such law repudiated the legality of regimes that violated the rights of their citizens; more important, this universal theory of rights criminalized a host of behaviors by the state, its institutions, and its agents. More recently this evolving concept of law has been extended to civilians acting outside the organized structures of the state, as was generally the case during the genocide in Rwanda.

As was made clear by the extradition case brought by Spain against the former Chilean leader Augusto Pinochet, the discourse around state violence and state impunity is a contentious one. The details of violent state actions over the past decades have been confronted and engaged by two assumptions: one centered around the secular issue of law, the other emerging from an ambiguous, quasi-religious ethic of "truth and reconciliation," that is, those moments when violations on the part of the state and its agents are brought to light. The expressibility of the law is mostly concerned with the legality of actions by the state and by individuals acting on behalf of the state (a central thesis of the Nuremberg trials and of Adolf Eichmann's trial in Jerusalem), but for "truth commissions" – a recent emergence in the lexicon of the search for answers to genocide and state repression – punitive justice has proven inadequate. Because of this inadequacy, truth commissions seek to engage the dimension of the social and political space, a space of collective bargaining within civil society to spotlight terrible crimes and abuses, but also to animate public discussions and opinions.

As has been noted by many observers, the methods of the law and of truth commissions are not symmetrically aligned – in fact they are diametrically opposed to each other. The example of South Africa makes this disalignment patently clear. For many victims the unaccountable power and violence of the state are so overwhelming that their representation and narration require the grain of the victim's voice to counter the narrow construction of the law, and to bring the lucidity of truth into the public imagination.

Experiments with Truth   Mahatma Gandhi titled his autobiography *The Story of My Experiments with Truth*. In conceiving this expression – "experiments with truth" – he touched upon the complex intersection between truth, justice, and representation that presented itself at the time of the postcolonial transition in India and South Africa.

Over the past half century Gandhi's critical inquiry into the notion of truth has grown even more salient, encompassing other conflicts such as ethnic, religious, and sectarian violence. Today the search for "truth" proliferates into an array of perspectives. Politics in Algeria, Argentina, the Basque region of Spain and France, Chile, India and Pakistan, Northern Ireland, South Africa, the former Yugoslavia, and beyond expose truth as variously constituted, as does the Romany people's demand for justice and recognition. Truth is a governing principle in the search for justice and reconciliation, but it is also an ontological, ethical, juridical, and philosophical problem. As a result, such notions as juridical truth, narrative truth, experiential truth, ontological truth, performative truth, and so on, have variously emerged, each with their own pressing demand for precision.

Just as historical contingency brings each of these truths into convergence with one another, it also brings them into contest. In the most adverse cases, this contestation over truth materializes as fundamentalist polemicism and political violence; in other cases it represents a sober reassessment of the fabric of civil society. For philosophy the notion of truth is in itself an aporia, while for jurisprudence it merely works to situate culpability relative to testimony, evidence, and provability. In general terms, and theoretically, reconciliation works as a mechanism to bring the two together. It has its roots in neither philosophy nor jurisprudence but is situated somewhere between cultural and religious logic. Therein lies the paradox of what truth must express: is it principally forensic or ineluctably abstract and contingent?

Transitional Justice   Confrontations with colonial, ethnic, racial, gender, religious, and civil violence, and the spate of nationalisms that have risen in their wake, today press liberal reformers to produce new concepts of justice. This challenge is further complicated by the end of the cold war, the dissolution of the Soviet Union, and the emergence of new democratic regimes in Eastern Europe, as well as by the dismantling of dictatorships in a number of Latin American countries. Wherever these transitions are occurring, new juridical principles have been theorized to examine the nature of justice and accountability. Thus the legal category of transitional justice has been instituted in a number of countries to deal with crimes committed under now-defunct regimes and states.

The case of the former East Germany, and the changes in South Africa over the last decade, have brought matters of truth and transitional justice to crisis. The struggle to dismantle the legacies of both communism and the apartheid state, and to implement liberal democracies in their place, has entailed a confrontation with the state's violent history. As liberal democracies work to come to terms with this violence, they also reconstitute the relationship between the state and its citizens, as the case of the former Yugoslavia has revealed. But in cases of extreme violation, does the mere repudiation and discredit of former repressive regimes square properly with the logic and concept of justice? This reconfiguration poses new challenges with regard to representation, in both its political and its cultural modes, and forces a further rift between the ideals of liberal reformers and institutions and the nature of the justice that they claim to administer in the name of a larger global ethic.

Memory, Narration, and Representation   How to bear witness and ensure democratic representation? How to remember and represent the past and historicize its reality? As many countries and cultures have been confronted by the legacy of their past and history, a great desire has emerged to commemorate that past and history around broadly accepted themes that unite various polities within the nation. This desire constitutes another area in the search for truth, which it calls for mechanisms to represent and narrate. The need for commemoration has generated a spate of monuments, memorials, museums, and archives intended to address questions of memory and history and to represent a nation's heritage. The cases of South Africa, Argentina, Israel, Germany, Rwanda, and so on have only amplified the tensions between collective memory and official history that have subtended the cultures of other regions in recent decades, most notably Latin America and Central Europe. In this search for an ethical space of historical narration the spectral voices of the politically disenfranchised, the disappeared, and the exterminated come into accord, if only for a moment.

Where law and scholarship convene around the aporias of trauma and testimony, works of art and literature have emerged that give form to the remnants of these histories. Whereas each of these cultural fields offers a singular perspective on the limits of witnessing and of representation, recent investigations in philosophy have drawn upon these perspectives to enable a larger critique of universal truth. If Western humanism and rationality always rest upon some agency of exclusion, what are the limits of their application to contemporary crimes against humanity?

At this crux modern philosophy meets the postcolonial struggle that Gandhi set into motion. *Experiments with Truth: Transitional Justice and the Processes of Truth and Reconciliation* seeks to animate the intellectual and creative methods that underpin the social, cultural, political, juridical, religious, and philosophical confrontation with one of the central preoccupations of the twentieth century. It is our intention that this conference and book should not only examine the central arguments that form the core of the juridical and social methods of truth commissions as they pertain to state crime and violence, it should also argue for a sober reflection on other complex conflicts (ethnic, racial, religious, and sectarian) that are seen as extraterritorial and marginal to the discourse of the search for truth and reconciliation.

Okwui Enwezor
Carlos Basualdo
Ute Meta Bauer
Susanne Ghez
Sarat Maharaj
Mark Nash
Octavio Zaya

**Experiments with Truth:
The Burden of Gandhi's Moral Philosophy**

Making Sense of Political Violence in Postcolonial Africa

Mahmood Mamdani

We have just ended a century replete with violence. The twentieth century was possibly more violent than any other in recorded history – just think of world wars and revolutions, of colonial conquests and anticolonial resistance, and, indeed, of revolutions and counterrevolutions. Yet even if the expanse of this violence is staggering, it makes sense to us. For the modern political sensibility sees political violence as necessary to historical progress.

Ever since the French Revolution, moderns have come to see violence as the midwife of history. The French Revolution gave us terror and it gave us a citizens' army. The real secret behind Napoleon's spectacular battlefield successes was that his army was comprised not of mercenaries but of patriots, those who killed for a cause, who were animated by sentiment, by what we have come to recognize as a civic religion: nationalism. Reflecting on the French Revolution, Hegel thought of man – in the generic sense – as different from animals in that he was willing to die for a cause higher than life. Hegel should have added: man is also willing to kill for a cause higher than life. This, I think, is truer of modern man and woman than it is true of humanity in general.

The modern political sensibility is not horrified by all violence. Just put millions in the wrong uniform: a body of citizens and patriots will celebrate their deaths as the end of its enemies. The world wars are proof enough of this. What horrifies the modern political sensibility is not violence per se but violence that does not make sense. And the violence that appears senseless to us is violence that is neither revolutionary nor counterrevolutionary, violence that cannot be illuminated by the story of progress. Not illuminated paradigmatically, nonrevolutionary violence appears pointless.

Unable to explain such violence, we turn our back on history. Two such endeavors are worth noting: the first turns to culture, the second to theology. The cultural turn distinguishes modern from premodern culture and then offers premodern culture as an explanation of political violence. If revolutionary or counterrevolutionary violence arises from market-based identities such as class, then nonrevolutionary violence is said to be an outcome of cultural difference.

On a world scale, it is called a clash of civilizations.[1] Locally – that is, when it does not cross the boundary between the West and the rest – it is called communal conflict, as in South Asia, or ethnic conflict, as in Africa.

Faced with political violence that arises in a modern context but will not fit the story of progress, theory has also tended to take refuge in theology. The violence of the Holocaust is branded as an evil that can only be understood outside historical time.[2] Rather than understand the Holocaust as a clue to the debased and grim side of humanity, this kind of thinking turns this horror into a question mark against the very humanity of its perpetrators. There is a huge resistance, moral and political, to thinking through this violence by locating it in a historical context.

Thinking through the Holocaust: The Violence of the Settler   In the corpus of Holocaust writing, Hannah Arendt stands apart. Rather than talk of the uniqueness of the Holocaust, Arendt insisted on locating the Holocaust in the history of genocide. The history she sketched was that of the settler genocide of the native. It was the history of imperialism, and specifically of twin institutions – racism in South Africa and bureaucracy in India and Algeria – forged in the course of an earlier European expansion into the non-European world.[3] Not only did genocide have this history but modern genocide, Arendt wrote, was nurtured in the colonies: the "elimination of Hottentot tribes, the wild murdering by Carl Peters in German Southwest Africa, the decimation of the peaceful Congo population – from 20 to 40 million reduced to 8 million people and ... worst of all ... the triumphant introduction of such means of pacification into ordinary, respectable foreign policies."[4]

Of the two main political devices of imperialist rule, race was discovered in South Africa and bureaucracy in Algeria, Egypt, and India. The former was originally European man's barely conscious reaction to tribes of whose humanity he was ashamed and frightened, whereas the latter was a consequence of that

---

1 See, for example, Samuel Huntington, *The Clash of Civilizations and the Remaking of World Order* (New York: Simon and Schuster, 1996).

2 For a discussion of group violence as evil see Ervin Staub, *The Roots of Evil: The Origins of Genocide and Other Group Violence* (Cambridge: Cambridge University Press, 1989). On the relationship between evil and historical time see Paul Ricœur, *The Symbolism of Evil* (New York: Harper & Row, 1967), Alain Badiou, *Ethics: An Essay on the Understanding of Evil* (London and New York: Verso, 2001), Georges Bataille, *Literature and Evil* (London: Marion Boyars, 2001), Malcolm Bull, ed., *Apocalypse Theory and the Ends of the World* (Oxford: Blackwell, 1995), and Alenka Zupancic, *Ethics of the Real* (London and New York: Verso, 2000). I am thankful to Robert Meister of the University of Calfornia, Santa Cruz, for suggesting this latter set of readings.

3 Hannah Arendt, *The Origins of Totalitarianism* (New York: Harcourt Brace), 1975, p. 185.

4 Ibid.

administration by which Europeans had tried to rule foreign peoples whom they felt to be hopelessly their inferiors and at the same time in need of their special protection. Race, in other words, was an escape into an irresponsibility where nothing human could any longer exist, while bureaucracy was the result of a responsibility that no man can bear for his fellowman and no people for another people.

The idea "that imperialism had served civilization by clearing inferior races off the earth" found widespread expression in nineteenth-century European thought, from natural sciences and philosophy to anthropology and politics.[5] When the British Prime Minister Lord Salisbury claimed in his famous Royal Albert Hall speech on May 4, 1898, that "one can roughly divide the nations of the world into the living and the dying," Hitler was but nine years old, and the European air was "soaked in the conviction that imperialism is a biologically necessary process, which, according to the laws of nature, leads to the inevitable destruction of lower races." The paradigmatic example of the destruction of lower races was Tasmania, an island the size of Ireland where European colonists first arrived in 1803, the first massacre of natives occurred in 1804, and the last original inhabitant died in 1869. Similar fates awaited the Maoris of New Zealand, the Native Americans, the Hereros of Southwest Africa, and so on.[6]

By the time the twentieth century dawned, it was a European habit to distinguish between civilized wars and colonial wars. Laws of war applied to wars among the civilized, but laws of nature – that is, of biological necessity, expressed in the extermination of the lower races – applied to colonial wars. In World War II, Germany observed the laws of war against the Western powers but not against Russia. Among English and American prisoners of war, 3.5 percent died in German captivity, but 57 percent of Soviet prisoners – 3.3 million people in all – lost their lives. The gassings of Russians preceded the gassings at Auschwitz: the first mass gassings were of Russian prisoners of war in the south-

---

5 Herbert Spencer wrote in *Social Statics* (1850), "The forces which are working out the great scheme of perfect happiness, taking no account of incidental suffering, exterminate such sections of mankind as stand in their way." Charles Lyell pursued this train of thought in *Principles of Geology* (1830–33): if "the most significant and dimunitive of species … have each slaughtered their thousands, why should not we, the lords of creation, do the same?" His student, Charles Darwin, confirmed in *The Descent of Man* (1871), "At some future period not very distant as measured in centuries, the civilized races of man will almost certainly exterminate and replace throughout the world the savage races." "After Darwin," comments Sven Lindqvist in his survey of European thought on genocide, "it became accepted to shrug your shoulders at genocide. If you were upset, you were just showing your lack of education." See Lindqvist, *"Exterminate all the Brutes": One Man's Odyssey into the Heart of Darkness and the Origins of European Genocide* (New York: The New Press, 1996), pp. 8, 107, 117.

6 This paragraph is based on Lindqvist, *"Exterminate all the Brutes,"* pp. 119, 141, 149–51.

ern Ukraine.[7] The first to be gassed in Auschwitz were Russians, beginning with intellectuals and communists. The Nazi plan, writes Sven Lindqvist, was to weed out some 10 million Russians while keeping the remainder alive as a slave-labor force under German occupation. When the mass murder of European Jews began, the great Jewish populations were not in Germany but in Poland and Russia, where they formed 10 percent of the total population and up to 40 percent of the urban population "in just those areas Hitler was after." The Holocaust was born at the meeting point of two traditions that marked modern Western civilization: "the anti-Semitic tradition and the tradition of genocide of colonized peoples."[8] Here then was the difference in the fate of the Jewish people: they were to be exterminated as a whole. In that, their fate was unique – *but only in Europe.*

This historical fact was not lost on postwar intellectuals from the colonies. In his *Discours sur le colonialisme* (1951), Aimé Césaire writes that a Hitler slumbers within "the very distinguished, very humanistic and very Christian bourgeois of the twentieth century," yet the European bourgeois cannot forgive Hitler for "the fact that he applied to Europe the colonial practices that had previously been applied only to the Arabs of Algeria, the coolies of India and the Negroes of Africa."[9] "Not so long ago," recalled Frantz Fanon in *The Wretched of the Earth* (1961), "Nazism turned the whole of Europe into a veritable colony."[10]

The first genocide of the twentieth century was the German annihilation of the Herero people in Southwest Africa.[11] The German geneticist Eugene Fischer did his first medical experiments on the "science" of race-mixing in concentration camps for the Herero; his subjects were both Herero and the offspring of Herero women and German men. Fischer argued that these Herero "mulattos" were physically and mentally inferior to their German parents. Hitler read Fischer's book, *The Principle of Human Heredity and Race Hygiene* (1921), while

7 See Arno J. Mayer, *Why Did the Heavens Not Darken? "The Final Solution" in History* (New York: Pantheon, 1988).

8 Except where indicated, this paragraph is based on Lindqvist, *"Exterminate all the Brutes,"* pp. 158, 160.

9 Aimé Césaire, *Discours sur le colonialisme* (Paris and Dakar: Présence Africaine, 1995), p. 12.

10 Frantz Fanon, *The Wretched of the Earth* (London: Penguin, 1967), p. 75; for a discussion, see David Macey, *Frantz Fanon: A Biography* (New York: Picador, 2000), pp. 111, 471.

11 See Jan-Bart Gewald, *Herero Heroes: A Socio-Political History of the Herero of Namibia, 1890–1923* (Oxford: James Currey, 1999), pp. 141–230; Tilman Dedering, "'A Certain Rigorous Treatment of All Parts of the Nation': The Annihilation of the Herero in German Southwest Africa, 1904," in Mark Levine and Penny Roberts, eds., *The Massacre in History* (New York: Berghahn Books, 1999), pp. 204–22; Regina Jere-Malanda, "The Tribe Germany Wants to Forget," *New African* (London) no. 383 (March 2000): 16–21; and Horst Dreschler, *"Let Us Die Fighting": The Struggle of the Herero and the Nama against German Imperialism, 1884–1915* (London: Zed Press, 1980).

in prison, and later made Fischer rector of the University of Berlin, where he taught medicine. One of Fischer's prominent students was Joseph Mengele, who would run the gas chambers at Auschwitz. The Holocaust was the imperial chickens coming home to roost.

The link between the genocide of the Herero and the Holocaust was race branding, whereby it is possible not only to set a group apart as an enemy but also to annihilate it with an easy conscience. To understand the mindset that conceived the Holocaust, one would have to return to political identities crafted by modern imperialism: the identities of the settler and the native. Arendt and more recently Lindqvist focused on the agency of the settler but not on that of the native, yet the native just as much as the settler is a product of the imperial imagination. Framed by a common history, they define two sides of a relationship. Unless they are transcended together, they will be reproduced together.

The historians of genocide have sketched half a history for us: that of the settler's annihilation of the native. To glimpse how this could trigger a counter-tendency, the native annihilating the settler, one has to turn to Fanon.[12] Hailed as a humanist by most of those who came to pay him homage after death, Fanon ironically came to be regarded as a prophet of violence after Arendt claimed that his influence was mainly responsible for the growing violence on American campuses in the 1960s.[13] He was recognized as the prophet of decolonization on the publication of his monumental *Wretched of the Earth*; yet one needs to recognize that he was also the first critic of decolonization. To understand the central thesis of *The Wretched of the Earth* – summed up in a single sentence, "The colonized man liberates himself in and through violence" – one needs to put it in a triple context: the respective histories of Algerian colonization, modernist thought on the historical necessity of violence, and the postwar movement to decolonization. Put in context, Fanon's thesis was at the same time a description, a claim, and a problematization. First, it was a *description* of the violence of the colonial system, of the fact that violence was key to producing and sustaining the relationship between the settler and the native. Second, it was a *claim* that anticolonial violence is not an irrational manifestation but belongs to the script of modernity and progress, that it is indeed a midwife of history. And third – the more important for this essay – it was a *problematization* of a derivative violence – the violence of victims turned killers.

It is in Fanon that one finds the premonition of the native turned perpetrator, of the native who kills not just to extinguish the humanity of the other but to defend his or her own, and of the moral ambivalence this must provoke in

12 Fanon, *The Wretched of the Earth*. See also Macey, *Frantz Fanon*, p. 22.
13 See Hannah Arendt, *On Violence* (New York: Harcourt, Brace and Company, 1970).

other human beings like us. Although the extermination of colonizers by natives never came to pass, there were enough uprisings in which many were killed for extermination to hover in the settler imagination as a historical possibility.[14] No one understood the genocidal impulse better than Fanon. Native violence, this Martinican-born psychiatrist and Algerian freedom fighter insisted, was the violence of yesterday's victims, the violence of those who had cast aside their victimhood to become masters of their own lives.

Listen to Fanon: "He of whom they have never stopped saying that the only language he understands is that of force, decides to give utterance by force. . . . The argument the native chooses has been furnished by the settler, and by an ironic turning of the tables it is the native who now affirms that the colonialist understands nothing but force." For Fanon, the proof of the native's humanity consisted not in the willingness to kill settlers but in the willingness to risk his or her own life. "The colonized man," he wrote, "finds his freedom in and through violence."[15] If the outcome was death, natives killing settlers, that was still a derivative outcome. The native who embraces violence to safeguard his or her freedom is the victim-turned-perpetrator.

Legal and Political Identities   If we are to make political violence thinkable, we need to understand the process by which victims and perpetrators become polarized as *group identities*. Who do perpetrators of violence think they are? And who do they think they will eliminate through violence? Even if the identities propelled through violence are drawn from outside the domain of politics – from domains such as race (from biology), or ethnicity or religion (from culture) – we need to denaturalize these identities by outlining their history and illuminating their links with organized forms of power.

Just as we must locate market-based identities such as class in the history of markets if we are to understand them as the outcome of specific historical relations, so we need to turn to the history of state formation to understand the historical nature of political identities. This is particularly so with the modern state, which tries to naturalize political identities as anything but political. On the one hand the modern state enforces particular group identities through its legal project; on the other it gives depth to these identities through a history-writing project. It is by giving group identities both a past and a future that the modern state tries to stand up to time.

---

14 For a journalistic account of the specter of genocide in the White South African imagination, read Rian Malan, *My Traitor's Heart: A South African Exile Returns to Face His Country, His Tribe, and His Conscience* (New York: Grove, 1990).
15 Fanon, *The Wretched of the Earth*, pp. 33, 66, 68, 73.

The identities of settler and native may be drawn from biological discourses on race, but they need to be understood as political identities enforced by a particular form of the state. If they became politically potent, it is because they were legally enforced by a state that made a distinction between those indigenous (natives) and those not (settlers), and that turned this distinction into grounds for political, social, and civic discrimination. Where indigeneity was stigmatized as proof of lack of civilization, and taken as sufficient reason to deny the rights of those conquered; and where foreignness was valorized as a hallmark of civilization and turned into a guarantee of rights – indeed privileges – for immigrants, there settler and native were racialized as legal and political identities.

The colonial history of Africa lends itself to a distinction between two distinct modes of rule, each identified with a different form of the colonial state. In the literature on modern colonialism these modes are characterized as direct and indirect rule. The transition from direct to indirect rule is one from a modest to an ambitious project: whereas *direct rule* was preoccupied with shaping elite preferences, *indirect rule* aimed to shape popular preferences.

Indirect rule needs to be understood as a response to the crisis of direct rule, which focused on native elites, aiming to create native clones of Western modernity through a discourse on civilization and assimilation. Direct rule generated a dual crisis: on the one hand, its civilizational project tended to divide society between an alien minority claiming to be civilized and a native majority stigmatized as backward; on the other hand, the products of this civilizational project – native intellectuals and entrepreneurs – aspired to replace alien rule by self-rule as the basis of a native modernity. The demand for self-rule was the crisis of direct rule.

The colonial response was to subordinate the civilizational project to a law-and-order project. The big shift was legal: whereas direct rule aimed at introducing the rule of law as a single project, indirect rule replaced this single rule of law with a multiple construction of many sets of "customary" laws. In doing so it bypassed the modernizing native elites by championing alternate elites – said to be traditional – who would be allies in the enterprise of shaping mass preferences through a discourse grounded in tradition. But indirect rule did not accept tradition benignly, as a historical given. It treated history as a raw material, putty from which to shape "genuine" tradition. Whereas direct rule was dogmatic, and dismissed native tradition as backward and superstitious, indirect rule was analytical. The political project of indirect rule aimed to unpack native tradition, to disentangle its different strands, to separate the authoritarian from the emancipatory, and thereby to repack tradition as authoritarian and ethnic and to harness it to the colonial project. By repacking native passions and cul-

tures selectively, it aimed to pit these very passions and cultures against one
another. I wrote of this in *Citizen and Subject*,[16] and need not elaborate on that
argument here.

Unlike those who seek to explain political violence by turning to the domain
of culture, I intend to argue that even when political identities are drawn from
the domain of culture, they need to be understood as distinct from cultural
identities. Theoretically the experience of indirect rule should alert us to the
relationship between culture and politics. When the raw material of political
identity is drawn from the domain of culture, as in ethnic or religious identity,
the link between identity and power allows us to understand how cultural identities are translated into political identities, and thus to distinguish between
them. At the same time, to historicize political identity by linking it to political
power is to acknowledge that all political identities are historically transitory
and all require a form of the state to be reproduced.

Politically, indirect rule was an attempt to stabilize colonial rule by moving
away from direct rule. This created a volatile context in which the identity of
both rulers and ruled was racialized, but the former as a minority and the latter
as a majority. Indirect rule dealt with this through a legal project that fractured
the singular, racialized, and majority identity *native* into plural, ethnicized,
minority identities called *tribes*.

To understand how political identities may be defined through the force of
law, let us take an African example from any indirect-rule colony in the first half
of the twentieth century. Recall that the colonial census classified the population into two broad overall groups. One group was called *races*, the other *tribes*.
This single distinction illuminates the technology of colonial rule. To elaborate
that technology I would like to make five observations.

First, the census divides the population into two kinds of groups: some are
tagged as races and others as tribes. Why? On examination one can discern a
clear pattern: *nonnatives* are tagged as *races* whereas *natives* are said to belong to
tribes. *Races* – specifically Europeans, Asians, and Arabs – were all those whom
the colonial state defined as not indigenous to Africa. *Tribes* – called "ethnic
groups" in the postcolonial period – were all those defined as indigenous in origin.

Second, this distinction had a direct legal significance. All *races* were governed
under a single law – civil law. True, civil law was full of discriminations: it distinguished, for example, between the *master race* (Europeans) and *subject races*
(Asians and Arabs). Subject races were excluded from the exercise of certain

16 Mahmood Mamdani, *Citizen and Subject: Contemporary Africa and the Legacy of Late Colonialism*
(Princeton, N.J.: Princeton University Press, 1996).

rights considered the prerogative only of members of the master race. But this discrimination needs to be understood as internal, for the domain of civil law included all races.

The situation was different with tribes and customary law. Although all tribes were defined as one racialized group – natives – they were not governed by a single law. Instead, each tribe was ruled under a separate set of laws, called customary laws. It was said that each tribe was governed by a law that reflected its own tradition. Yet most would agree that the cultural difference between races – such as whites, Asians, and Arabs – was greater than that between different tribes. To begin with, different races spoke different languages, which were mutually unintelligible. They often practiced different religions. They also came from different parts of the world, each with its own historical archive. Different tribes, in contrast, often spoke languages that were mutually intelligible.

My point is simple: even if *races* were as different culturally as whites, Asians, and Arabs, they were ruled under a single law, the imported European law called "civil law." But *ethnic groups*, even if their languages were similar and mutually intelligible, were governed under separate laws, called "customary laws," which were in turn administered by ethnically distinct native authorities. With *races*, cultural difference was not translated into separate legal systems. Instead it was contained, even negotiated, within a single legal system, and enforced by a single administrative authority. But with *ethnicities* the opposite was the case: cultural difference was reinforced, exaggerated, and built up into different legal systems and, indeed, separate administrative and political authorities. In a nutshell, different races were meant to have a common future; different ethnicities were not.

My *third* observation: the two legal systems were entirely different in orientation. We can understand the difference by contrasting English common law with colonial customary law. English common law was presumed to change with circumstances. It claimed to recognize different interests and interpretations. But customary law in the colonies assumed the opposite: it assumed that law must not change with changing circumstances. Rather, any change was considered prima facie evidence of corruption. Both the laws and the enforcing authorities were called "traditional." Indeed, Western colonial powers were far more concerned to establish the traditional credentials of their native allies than they were to define the content of their allies' tradition. Their preoccupation was with defining, locating, anointing the traditional authority.

Most important, traditional authority in the colonial era was always defined in the singular. We need to remember that most African colonies had never before had an absolutist state. Instead of a single state authority whose writ was considered law in all social domains, the practice was for different authorities to define separate traditions in different domains of social life. The rule-defining authority thus differed from one social domain to another: besides chiefs, the definers of tradition could include women's groups, age groups, clans, religious groups, and so on. The big change with the colonial period was that Western colonial powers exalted a single authority, called the chief, as *the* traditional authority. Marked by two characteristics, age and gender, the authority of the chief was inevitably patriarchal. As David Laitin showed in his study of Yoruba-land, the practice was to look for those local elites most in danger of being side-lined, local elites that had legitimacy but lacked authority, and then to sanctify their position, enforce their point of view as customary, and reinforce their authority in law as traditional.[17]

Colonial powers were the first fundamentalists of the modern period. They were the first to advance and put into practice two propositions: one, that every colonized group has an original and pure tradition, whether religious or ethnic; and two, that every colonized group must be made to return to that original condition, and that return must be enforced by law. Put together, these two propositions constitute the basic platform of every religious or ethnic funda-mentalism in the postcolonial world.

Fourth, this legal project needs to be understood as part of a political project. The political project was highlighted by the central claim of the indirect-rule state: that natives are by nature tribal. Although this claim was first fully imple-mented in the late nineteenth century, in the African lands colonized by Britain in the aftermath of the Berlin Conference of 1884–85, it had already been made by Sir Henry Maine, Law Member of the Viceroy's Commission in post-1857 India. To quote Maine's *Ancient Law*: "I repeat the definition of a primi-tive society given before. It has for its units, not individuals, but groups of men united by the reality or the fiction of blood-relationship."[18] In time this very claim, that natives are by nature tribal, would be advanced to explain why the African colonies had no majority but only tribal minorities. This claim needs to be understood as political, not because it is not true but because this truth reflects not an original fact but a fact politically created and legally enforced.

It is not that ethnicity did not exist in African societies prior to colonialism; it did. I want to distinguish ethnicity as a *cultural* identity – an identity based on a shared culture – from ethnicity as a *political* identity. When the political authority and the law it enforces identify subjects ethnically and discriminate among them, ethnicity turns into a legal and political identity. Ethnicity as a cultural identity is consensual, but when ethnicity becomes a political identity it

17 See David Laitin, *Hegemony and Culture: Politics and Religious Change among the Yoruba* (Chicago: Chicago University Press, 1986).
18 Sir Henry Maine, *Ancient Law* (Washington, D.C.: Beard Books, 1861), p. 178.

is enforced by the legal and administrative organs of the state. These organs make a distinction between ethnic groups, between those considered indigenous and those not. The former are given access to rights considered "customary," such as the right to use land, but the latter are denied these same rights.

This takes me to my *fifth* observation. When law imposes a cultural difference, the difference becomes reified. Prevented from changing, it becomes frozen. Meanwhile, as the basis of legal discrimination – between those said to belong (whether in terms of religion or ethnicity) and those said not to belong, between insiders entitled to customary rights and outsiders deprived of these rights – these culturally symbolic differences become political.

The distinction between cultural and political identities is important for my argument. Cultural identities are as a rule consensual and voluntary, and they can be multiple.[19] All postmodernist talk of hybridity and multiple identities belongs to the domain of culture. Once enforced by law, however, identities cease to be all of these. A legal identity is neither voluntary nor multiple. The law recognizes you as one and as none other. Once cultural identity is enforced legally, it is drawn into the domain of politics and becomes political. Such an identity cannot be considered solely as a vestige of tradition, even if it has an ancient history, nor can it be dismissed as just an invention of the colonial power, because it is legally enforced. Even if they are grounded in a genealogy that precedes colonialism, popular identities like religion and ethnicity need to be understood as the very creation of colonial modernity. To distinguish between cultural and legal/political identities is to distinguish between self-identification and state-identification.

Rwanda: A Metaphor for Political Violence   Colonial Rwanda was different in an important respect from the picture I have just described: in Rwanda the census did not identify tribes. It only identified races: Hutu as Bantu, Tutsi as Hamites. The Bantu Hutu were presumed to be uncivilized, the Hamite Tutsi to be civilizing agents. We shall see that this difference between Rwanda and other African colonies – that political identities in Rwanda were racialized but not ethnicized – would turn out to be of great significance. Rwanda is today a metaphor – for political violence, but more particularly for senseless violence in politics. I recently wrote a book on Rwanda. I would like to describe the intellectual and political journey that became the writing of the book.[20]

---

19 I write this without any intent to romanticize the domain of consent or to detract from the existence of power relations in the domain of culture.
20 Mamdani, *When Victims Become Killers: Colonialism, Nativism and Genocide in Rwanda* (Princeton: Princeton University Press, 2001).

Rwanda had a revolution in 1959. On the face of it, the revolution pitted Hutu, the indigenous majority, against Tutsi, the immigrant minority who had been favored by the colonizers. The identities "indigenous" and "immigrant" came straight out of colonial history books and colonial law. Within the revolution there was debate over who was the enemy and thus over who was the people. Two tendencies contended for supremacy; those who lost maintained that the battle was not in fact of Hutu against Tutsi but of the majority against the minority, the poor against the rich, the nation against the colonizers. This tendency lost not because it lacked support but because its support eroded when the counterrevolution attempted a restoration of the Tutsi monarchy. With the defeat of the counterrevolution, the targets of revolutionary violence broadened, from those who had symbolized the local manifestations of power (such as the chiefs) to all Tutsi. When the revolutionaries of 1959 talked of justice, they didn't talk of justice for the poor or for Rwandans but of justice for the Hutu – at the expense of the Tutsi. To ensure that justice would indeed be done, they insisted that the revolutionary state continue the colonial practice of issuing cards identifying every individual as Hutu or Tutsi (or Twa, an insignificant minority). Henceforth the Hutu would be the Rwandan nation and the Tutsi an alien minority.

One can today find two kinds of writings on Rwanda. The first is preponderant in the academy, the second in the world of journalism. Academic writing on Rwanda is dominated by authors whose intellectual perspective was shaped by sympathy with the Rwandan Revolution of 1959.[21] They saw the revolution and the political violence that effected it as progressive, as ushering in a more popular political and social order. Unable to see the dark underbelly of the revolution, and thus to grasp the link between it and the 1994 genocide, this kind of writing portrays the genocide as exclusively or mainly the state project of a narrow ruling elite. In doing so it totally avoids the question of mass participation in the genocide. In portraying racism and racialized identities as exclusively state-defined and state-enforced, it fails to explain how these same identities got socially embedded and were reproduced socially. In portraying the genocide as exclusively a *state project*, its singular failing is an inability to come to terms with the genocide as a *social project*.

But this claim is not easy to make. The massacres in the Rwandan genocide were carried out in the open. Roughly 800,000 Tutsi were killed in 100 days. The state organized the killings, but the killers were by and large ordinary peo-

---

21 See for example René Lemarchand, *Rwanda and Burundi* (New York: Praeger, 1970), and
   Catharine Newbury, *The Cohesion of Oppression: Clientship and Ethnicity in Rwanda, 1860–1960*
   (New York: Columbia University Press, 1989).

ple. The killing was done mainly by machete-wielding mobs. You were more than likely to be killed by your neighbors or your workmates, by your teachers or doctors or priests, or even by human-rights advocates or your own husband. A few months ago in Belgium, four civilians stood trial for crimes against humanity in Rwanda. Among the four were two nuns and a physicist. How do we explain their participation – and the participation of other sectors in civil society – in the genocide?

In contrast, journalistic writing focuses precisely on this aspect of the geno-cide.[22] Its peculiar characteristic is to constitute a pornography of violence. As in pornography, the nakedness is of others, not us. The exposure of the other goes alongside the unstated claim that we are not like them. It is a pornography in which senseless violence is a feature of other people's cultures, in which they are violent but we are pacific, and in which a focus on their debasedness easily turns into another way of celebrating and confirming our own exalted status. In the process, journalistic accounts also tend to reinforce larger claims: that the world is indeed divided into the modern and the premodern, whereby moderns *make* culture but premoderns live by a timeless culture.

If the social science account is overly *instrumentalist*, accenting only the agency of the state and the elites, journalists tend to lean heavily on a *primor-dialist* account that tends to explain contemporary conflicts as replays of time-less antagonisms.[23] If social science accounts tend to explain mass participation in the genocide as mass obedience to rulers (for ordinary Rwandans, the most widespread reasoning goes, an order is as heavy as a stone), journalists see the masses as gripped in ancient passions and antagonisms. In the final analysis, nei-ther the instrumentalist nor the primordial account can give a historical expla-nation of agency in the genocide.

Politically, journalistic writing has given us a simple moral world, in which a group of perpetrators faces another group of victims but neither history nor motivation is thinkable because both groups stand outside history and context. When journalists did address the genocide as a social project, I thought they failed to understand the forces that shaped the agency of the perpetrator. Instead, they looked for a clear and uncomplicated moral in the story. In a con-text in which victims and perpetrators had traded places, they looked for victims distinguished from perpetrators for all time. Where yesterday's victims are today's perpetrators, where victims have turned perpetrators, this attempt to

22 The most compelling journalistic account is Philip Gourevitch's *We Wish to Inform You That Tomorrow We Will Be Killed with Our Families: Stories from Rwanda* (New York: Picador, 1999).
23 For a crossover journalistic account that strongly criticizes journalistic voyeurism but gives an unabashedly conspiratorial (instrumentalist) explanation, see Bill Berkeley, *The Graves Are Not Yet Full: Race, Tribe, and Power in the Heart of Africa* (New York: Basic Books, 2001).

find an African Holocaust could not work. Thus I called my book *When Victims Become Killers.*

How many perpetrators were victims of yesteryear? What happens when yesterday's victims act out of a determination that they must never again be victimized, *never again*? What happens when yesterday's victims act out of a conviction that power is the only guarantee against victimhood, so that the only dignified alternative to power is death? What happens when they are convinced that the taking of life is really noble because it signifies the willingness to risk one's own life, and is thus, in the final analysis, proof of one's own humanity?

I thought it important to understand the humanity of the perpetrator, as it were to get under the skin of the perpetrator – not to excuse either the perpetrator or the killing, but to make the act "thinkable," so as to learn something about us as humans. How do we understand the agency of the perpetrator? Framed by which history? Kept alive, reproduced, by which institutions? Who did the Hutu who killed think they were? And whom did they think they were killing in the persons of the Tutsi?

The History of Violence Between Hutu and Tutsi   The significance of Fanon became clear to me as I tried to understand the history of political violence in Rwanda, and specifically of violence between Hutu and Tutsi. I was struck by one fact: I could not find any significant episode before 1959 in which battle lines were drawn sharply between Hutu on one side and Tutsi on the other. It was 1959 that saw the first significant episode of Hutu being pitted against Tutsi in a political struggle, so that "Hutu" and "Tutsi" became names identifying political adversaries.

I thought this contrasted sharply with earlier political struggles, such as the Nyabingi episode at the outset of the colonial period. Nyabingi was a spiritual cult and political movement in what is today northern Rwanda, a region incorporated into the expanding kingdom of Rwanda at the beginning of the twentieth century. I thought two facts striking about this movement. First, when the Bakiga fought the alliance of German imperial power with the Tutsi aristocracy of the Rwandan kingdom, they did not fight as Hutu against Tutsi. They fought the Tutsi in power, but they fought in alliance with the Tutsi out of power. In fact they fought under the leadership of a former Tutsi queen, Muhumuza, and then under the leadership of her son, Ndungutse.

Second, these mountain people called themselves not Hutu but Bakiga (the people of the mountains). Only when they were defeated, and incorporated into the Rwandan kingdom, did they cease to be Bakiga and became Hutu. For "Hutu" was not the identity of a discrete ethnic group but the political identity of all those subjugated to the power of the Rwandan state. In Rwanda before colonialism, prosperous Hutu had become Tutsi over the course of generations. True, the numbers involved were too few to be statistically significant. Yet this was a process of great social and ideological significance. This process of ritual ennoblement, whereby a Hutu shed his Hutuness, even had a name: *kwihutura*. Its counterpart, whereby an impoverished Tutsi family lost its status, this too over generations, also had a name: *gucupira*.

Belgian colonialism did not invent Tutsi privilege. There was Tutsi privilege before colonialism. So what was new with Belgian colonialism? Not Tutsi privilege but the justification for it. For the first time in the history of Rwanda, the terms "Hutu" and "Tutsi" came to identify two groups, one branded indigenous, the other exalted as alien. For the first time, Tutsi privilege claimed to be the privilege of a group identified as racially alien, specifically as Hamitic. Only with Belgian colonialism did Hutu become indigenous and Tutsi alien, the degradation of the Hutu a degradation of the native and Tutsi privilege an alien privilege. As Belgian authorities issued identity cards to Hutu and Tutsi, Tutsi became sealed from Hutu. Legally identified as two biologically distinct races, Tutsi as Hamites and Hutu as Bantu, Hutu and Tutsi became distinct legal identities. The language of race functioned to underline this difference between indigenous and alien.

The point will become clear if we return to the difference between race and ethnicity in twentieth-century colonial thought. I have pointed out that only natives were classified as tribes in colonial Africa and as ethnic groups in postcolonial Africa. Nonnatives, those not considered African, were tagged as races. Tribes were neighbors, not aliens. In this context ethnic violence is different from racial violence. Ethnic violence is between neighbors. It is about borders. It is about transgression across borders, about excess. In the conflict between neighbors, what is at issue is not the legitimacy of the presence of others; at issue is an overflow, a transgression. It is only with race that the very presence of a group can be considered illegitimate, and its claim for power an outright usurpation. This is why, when political violence takes the form of genocide, it is more likely to occur between races than between ethnic groups.

The racialization of the Tutsi, and of the difference between Hutu and Tutsi, is key to understanding the political violence between Hutu and Tutsi. This is so for one reason: it is the language of race that defined insiders and outsiders, distinguishing those indigenous from those alien. Ultimately, it set neighbors apart from outsiders, friends from enemies.

Political Identities and the Nationalist Revolution   Colonialism is the genesis of Hutu-Tutsi violence in Rwanda. But colonialism does not explain why this violence continued after the revolution of 1959. If colonialism is the site of the origin of the Hutu-Tutsi problem as one of racialized political identities, then nationalism reproduced that problem. Here is the dilemma we must confront: race-branding was not simply a state ideology, it also became a social ideology, reproduced by many of the same Hutu and Tutsi branded as native and alien. That reproduction took place through the nationalist political project that translated the colonial identity of Hutu as the indigenous Bantu race into the postcolonial Rwandan nation, thereby translating the colonial race-branding project into the postcolonial nation-building project. To problematize the nation-building project is simultaneously to critique the revolution of 1959 and the popular agency that it shaped.

The Rwandan Revolution of 1959 was heralded as the "Hutu Revolution." As the revolutionaries built Rwanda into a "Hutu nation," they embarked on a program of justice: justice for Hutu, a reckoning for Tutsi. And in doing so they confirmed Hutu and Tutsi as political identities: Hutu as native, Tutsi as alien.

When does the pursuit of justice turn into revenge? The revolutionaries turned the world upside-down, but they failed to change it. The irony is that instead of transforming the political world created by colonialism, the world of natives and settlers, they confirmed it. Here, then, is the question for a postcolonial study of nationalism in Rwanda: why did nationalism fail to transform the colonial political edifice?

In South Asia, popular agency has been the subject of an ambitious project in history-writing called "Subaltern Studies." Taken from Antonio Gramsci, the word "subaltern" signifies popular strata as opposed to those who command. The great historical contribution of Subaltern Studies has been to rescue subalterns from victim status in world history by illuminating them as historical agents, people capable of changing things. The historical lesson of Rwanda suggests that we accept the limits of this contribution and recognize that subaltern agency too is undergirded by specific institutions. To accept the time-bound nature of subalternity – as Fanon did – is to begin to subvert it. To generate a perspective that can transform existing identities, we need to stand outside the institutions that reproduce them. We need to understand group identities as institutionally produced and thus of limited historical significance.

Is not every perspective, no matter how popular, locked in the narrow parameters of the relations that generate and sustain it? Untransformed, a subaltern identity is likely to generate no more than an aspiration for trading places, for hegemonic aspirations. This is why a subaltern identity can neither be embraced nor rejected unconditionally. Unless we highlight its historical boundaries and limitations, the subaltern struggle will be locked in a dilemma, a catch-22. Without a recognition and subversion of limits, without an institutional transformation leading to a transformation of identities, every pursuit of justice will tend toward revenge, and every reconciliation toward an embrace of institutional evil.

Lenin once chided Rosa Luxemburg for being so preoccupied with Polish nationalism that she could not see beyond it, and so risked being locked in the world of the rat and the cat. The world of the rat and the cat is the political world of Hutu and Tutsi as produced by colonialism and reproduced by the 1959 revolution. For the rat, there is no animal bigger in presence than the cat: not the lion, not the tiger, not the elephant. For the cat, meanwhile, there is nothing more delicious than the rat. Similarly, the political world set in motion by the modern state and modern colonialism generates subaltern identities endlessly, in binary pairs. For every sergeant there is a subaltern, for every settler a native. In a world where cats are few and rats are many, one way for cats to stabilize their rule is to tag rats by tapping their historicity through a discourse on origins, indigenous and nonindigenous, ethnic and racial. This is why, in a world where rats have belled cats, it is entirely possible that rats may still carry on living in a world defined by cats, fired by identities generated by institutions created in the era of cats.

My point is simple yet fundamental: you can turn the world upside-down but fail to change it. To change the world you need to break out of the world view of not just the cat but the rat; not just the settler but the native. Unless we break out of the world view of the rat, postcolonialism will remain a purgatory punctuated by nonrevolutionary violence. The genocide in Rwanda poses this dilemma more sharply than any other contemporary event.

The Civil War and the Genocide   A political analysis of the genocide in Rwanda finds three pivotal moments. The first is that of the Belgian colonization and racialization of the state apparatus in the 1920s. The second is that of nationalism and the revolution of 1959, a turning of tables that entrenched colonial political identities in the name of justice. The third is that of the civil war of 1990. The civil war was not born of a strictly internal process; it was an outcome of a regional development, one that joined the crisis in Rwanda with that in Uganda.

The Tutsi exiles of 1959 found refuge in many countries, including Uganda. Living on the margins of society, many joined the guerrilla struggle against the regime of Milton Obote that ruled Uganda in 1981–85. When the victorious National Resistance Army (NRA) entered Kampala in January 1986, roughly a quarter of the 16,000 guerrillas were Banyarwanda, who had emigrated to

Uganda throughout the colonial period. In the Luwero Triangle – the theater of the guerrilla struggle – migrants were nearly half the population. The largest group of migrants was from Rwanda.

Every time NRA guerrillas liberated a village and organized an assembly they confronted a challenge: who could participate in that assembly? Who could vote? Who could run for office? The dilemma sprang from the colonial political legacy of linking rights to ancestry: by defining migrants as nonindigenous the colonizers deprived them of political rights. The NRA's answer was to redefine the basis of rights from ancestry to residence. Simply put, every adult resident of a village was considered to have the right of participation in the village assembly. This new notion of rights was translated into a nationality law after 1986: any one with a ten-year residence in the country had the right to be a citizen. The big change was that the 1959 refugees of the Rwandan Revolution were now considered Ugandans.

This political inheritance was called into question with the NRA's first major political crisis, in 1990, triggered by an attempt to honor one of the ten points in the guerrilla program: the pledge to redistribute absentee-owned land to pastoralist squatters. When it came to distributing land among a population of mobile pastoralists, there arose the question: who should get the land? Who was a citizen?

The opposition mobilized around this question, aiming to exclude Banyarwanda as noncitizens. The magnitude of the resulting crisis was signified by an extraordinary session of parliament lasting three days. At the end of its deliberation, the Ugandan parliament changed the citizenship law from a ten-year residence to a requirement that to be recognized as a citizen you had to show an ancestral connection with the land, i.e., show that at least one of your grandparents were born in the territory later demarcated as Uganda. One month later the Rwandan Patriotic Front (RPF) crossed the Ugandan border into Rwanda. My point is that this was not simply an armed return to Rwanda; it was also an armed expulsion from Uganda.

To understand the explosive impact of the civil war on Rwanda, we need to understand the changing political position of the Tutsi from the First Republic, which was inaugurated by the 1959 revolution, to the Second Republic, which began in 1973, with the coup that brought Juvenal Habyarimana to power. We have seen that the First Republic was a culmination of the struggle between two lines in the revolution. The victorious line, associated with the new president, Grégoire Kayibanda, defined Hutu and Tutsi as two different *races*, two different *nations*: Tutsi were thus to be treated as aliens in Rwanda, the home of the Hutu nation. In Habyarimana's Second Republic Tutsi were redefined from a race to an ethnicity. In the First Republic, then, Tutsi had been resident aliens;

in the second they became a political minority. Instead of insisting on the distinction between Hutu and Tutsi, the Second Republic highlighted the distinction between Tutsi in Rwanda and Tutsi exiles outside Rwanda: whereas the former were politically elevated as a Rwandan minority that could legitimately expect minority representation in the country's political institutions, the latter were denationalized as perpetual aliens for whom there was no longer any room in Rwanda. During the Second Republic, the key political division inside Rwanda was not between Hutu and Tutsi but within the Hutu elite, between those from the north and those from the south.

It was the exiled Tutsi's military organization, the Rwanda Patriotic Army (RPA), and their entry into Rwanda, that triggered the civil war. The civil war in turn had multiple political effects. First, it allowed the Habyarimana regime to pose as the defender of the nation against what was said to be an attempt by exiled Tutsi to restore the colonial monarchy (a repeat of 1963), this at a time when the regime was under great pressure to liberalize – pressure from the predominantly Hutu internal opposition. Second, it allowed radical Hutu, hitherto marginalized in the Second Republic, to reemerge in the political mainstream. Describing itself as the defender of "Hutu Power," this tendency organized a variety of media, from radio and television to print, to claim that the gains of the revolution were under threat from Tutsi, who were cast as indeed a race, not an ethnicity – indeed as non-Rwandan aliens, not a Rwandan minority.

Third, the more the civil war grew and the RPA gained ground, the more the internal opposition was discredited as a political fifth column tied to the RPA, and its democratic program painted as an antinational agenda. Fourth, everywhere the RPA gained military control, the local Hutu population either fled or was expelled through administrative pressure. Most observers estimate that by 1994, as many as 15 percent of the Rwandan population had been so displaced, some of them as many as four times. Most now lived in camps in and around Kigali and the southern part of the country. Some of the most enthusiastic participants in the genocide came from the youthful populations of these camps. Fifth and finally, against the backdrop of the victorious march of the RPA, the plight of the displaced spread fear among those yet to be engulfed by the civil war. The "Hutu Power" media warned them of a fate that the sight of the displaced only confirmed: if the Tutsi returned to power, they would lose both their land and their freedom – in short, everything.

The civil war of 1990–94 hurled Rwanda back into the world of Hutu Power and Tutsi Power. The possibility of the return of Tutsi Power provided radical Hutu, earlier a marginal tendency in the Second Republic, with their first opportunity to return to the political center stage as defenders of the 1959 revolution. Without the civil war there would have been no genocide.

The Rwandan genocide needs to be located in a context shaped by three related moments: the global *imperial* moment defined by Belgian colonialism and its racialization of the state; the *national* moment that was the 1959 revolution, and that reinforced racialized identities in the name of justice; and the *postcolonial* regional moment, born of a link between the citizenship crisis in postrevolutionary Rwanda and its neighbors. True, the crisis of postcolonial citizenship was regional in scope, and led to civil wars in not only Rwanda but also Uganda and Congo. But only in Rwanda did the civil war unfold in a context that could and did set alight a powder keg born of a distinctive colonial legacy, *race-branding*, that was reproduced as a revolutionary legacy of *race-as-nation*. Though this outcome was not necessary but contingent, it is imperative that we draw lessons from it.

Political Power and Political Identity   My argument on the Rwandan genocide linked that violence to political identities that drove it, and the reproduction of these political identities in turn to a particular form of the state. Instead of taking group identities as a given, I have tried to historicize the process of group formation. Linking political identities to the process of state formation makes it possible to distinguish prepolitical identities – whether cultural, economic, or biological – from political identities. In addition, it allows for an understanding of the dynamics whereby binary political identities, like Hutu and Tutsi, become polarized.

The Rwandan genocide raises three important issues for those who must live in its aftermath, as well as for those who study it. The *first* concerns the link between political identities and the process of state formation. To understand how "Hutu" became synonymous with "indigenous" and "Tutsi" with "alien," I found it necessary to go beyond an analysis of the colonial state to a critique of the nationalist revolution of 1959 – a revolution that, in the name of justice, embraced political identities created by colonial power.

The *second* issue arises from the combined legacy of colonial rule and nationalist power. It is also the issue that represents the most troublesome legacy of the Rwandan genocide, and has bitterly divided those who write on it: was not the organization of genocidal violence from the summit of political power linked to mass participation on the ground? The evidence shows that this was indeed the case, which is why we need to understand the genocide as both a state project and a social project.

The *third* issue highlights the citizenship crisis in the entire region. Just as the civil war of 1990–94 joined the citizenship crisis in Rwanda with that in Uganda, so the entry of Rwandan troops into eastern Congo in 1996 joined the citizenship crisis in Rwanda with that in Congo. If the 1959 revolution and its aftermath underlined the difference between the colonial experience of Rwanda and that of its neighbors – the difference being that colonial rule in Rwanda created racialized political identities but not ethnicized ones – then postgenocidal Rwanda underlines the aspect of similarity in the regional colonial experience. I argued in my book that colonial Rwanda was like a halfway house between direct and indirect rule. Like direct rule, it generated exclusively racialized political identities; at the same time, like indirect rule, it legitimized the despotic power of local chiefs as a carryover of precolonial practices rather than a reorganization on the part of the colonial state. The discourse on custom ties citizenship (and rights) to cultural identity and historical origins.

The proliferation of political minorities in contemporary Africa is not a necessary reflection of Africa's cultural map. Rather, it is the outcome of a particular form of the state – the indirect-rule state – whose genesis lies in the colonial period. The real distinction between race and ethnicity is not that between biology and culture, with race a false biological identity and ethnicity a true and historically created cultural identity. Rather, both race and ethnicity need to be understood as a politicization of identities drawn from other domains: race a political identity of those constructed as nonindigenous (settlers), ethnicity an identity of those constructed as indigenous (natives). Africa's real political challenge, I have argued, is to reform and thus sublate the form of the state that has continued to reproduce race and ethnicity as political identities, alongside a discourse on nativism and "genuine" tradition.

Colonial power not only shaped the agency of popular strata, it also stamped itself on the agency of the intellectual. Colonial power was not only etched on the boundaries of the public sphere, it was also imprinted on the tables of contents of scholarly works. Just as it set into motion first the settler and then the native in the public sphere, so it preoccupied the intellectual imagination with the question of *origins*. How origin was understood depended on the language of power, and specifically on how power framed agency through customary law.

In the African context, customary law framed agency – and "custom" – as ethnic. In other contexts, such as India, agency was framed as religious. Is it then mere coincidence that if the postcolonial African preoccupation is with who is a native and who is not, the postcolonial Indian preoccupation has been with who is a convert and who is not? Is it any less surprising that if the native imagination in postcolonial Africa tends to absorb the immigrant into a script of invasion, the native imagination in postcolonial India seems to view the agency of the convert as veritable treason, as a transgression so subversive that the convert is seen as forever lacking in authentic agency?

Why is it that when it comes to the postcolonial political vocabulary, Hindu and Muslim in India, or for that matter Sinhala and Tamil in Sri Lanka, like Hutu and Tutsi in Rwanda, sound like political synonyms for native and settler? The challenge, I have argued, is neither to deny separate histories nor to build on this separation. It is rather to distinguish our notion of political community from that of cultural community, and, as a consequence, to separate the discourse on political rights from that on cultural or historical origins. The point of difference between cultural and political communities is sharpest when we contrast diasporic with immigrant communities. Diasporic communities share a common history but not necessarily a common future; immigrant communities, by contrast, are dedicated to building a common future, but may not necessarily share a common past. To distinguish between cultural and political communities is to distinguish between the past – several pasts – and a single future. The single uniting feature of a political community is the commitment to building a common political future under a single political roof. This recognition should be an important step to creating a single political community and citizenship from diverse cultural and historical groups and identities.

Different Kinds of Truth:
The South African Truth and Reconciliation Commission[*]

Albie Sachs

A Prologue   I was in my chambers earlier this year when I received a message from reception that somebody calling himself Henry had arrived to see me. I went to the security entrance with a measure of anticipation. Henry had telephoned a few days earlier to say that he was going to testify to the Truth and Reconciliation Commission (TRC) about the bomb that had led to my car exploding and my losing my right arm. Naturally I was keen to see the person who had the courage, or the foolhardiness, or just the interest to want to see me.

I opened the door with my security pass and a slender, youngish man came forward. He introduced himself as Henry and gave his surname. He had been, I think, a captain in the South African Defence Force, and he strode down the passage to my chambers with not quite a swagger but a military gait, and I loped at his side with what I suppose was a jaunty, judicial, ambulatory stroll.

We sat down and started talking. I am sure he was as puzzled about me as I was about him. He explained quickly that his role had simply been to take the photographs and prepare a dossier for the persons who were ultimately to put the bomb in my car. He said that he had in fact dropped out of the operational group some months before the explosion, so that he could not give any testimony directly as to what had happened. But he knew the group that was involved, he knew the structure, and he was going to go to the TRC and tell his story and ask for amnesty for his part in it.

I was not quite sure why he had come to tell me this. I wanted to know more about him. Who was this person whom I had never seen until that moment, who did not know me, who had no anger toward me, whom I did not hate, for whom I was just a figure, who had tried to extinguish my life? What had passed

* This essay was delivered as the Fourth DT Lakdawala Memorial Lecture on December 18, 1998, at the Nehru Memorial Museum and Library Auditorium, New Delhi, as well as at a seminar on Truth and Reconciliation organized by the Prince Claus Fund for Culture and Development and Documenta11, on July 6, 2000, in the Hague.

through his head, how had he functioned, how did he fit into this group that was on "the other side" ("the enemy," "the apartheid state"), which was almost as anonymous to me as I was to them?

I tried to draw him out, to get him to explain his background. He said his parents were decent people who had brought him up with a strong sense of honor, especially his mother. He had been a good student at university and on graduating had decided that the military was the career for him. He had advanced rapidly, he told me with pride, had been an excellent soldier, and then he had been recruited for special operations.

I did not wish to preempt the interrogation of the TRC; I just wanted him to say as much as he was willing to say. He would have seen the dossier on me. It would have shown that I had been in exile in Mozambique (which neighbors on South Africa) working on the reconstruction of the Mozambique legal system; and that although I had been an active member of the African National Congress (ANC), and especially of its Constitutional Committee, I was not involved in any underground activity or military or intelligence work at all. Yet they had chosen me, had tried to eliminate me. Why? Because I was an intellectual and challenged their claim that no political system could be found to enable black and white to live together as equals in South Africa? Every intellectual dreams of being taken seriously by someone, but not *that* seriously.

We spoke for about two hours. He looked at me almost with a measure of jealousy. Here he was sitting in my chambers, beautiful pictures on the walls, I was a judge of the Constitutional Court, the highest court in the country, and he was now a demobilized soldier with a torn past and a fragmented future. He had not even been given a golden handshake but a brass one, a modest sum of money compared to what the retiring generals had gotten. Yet he had been willing to invest his energies, his intelligence, maybe even his life for his country, for apartheid. And now he had been cast aside. He too had injuries, he told me, he had been shot in the leg and walked with a slight limp. He seemed petulant: I was on the court and he was unemployed. We could have gone on eyeing each other and talking forever.

I stood up, a cheap emotion surged in me, and I was tempted to say: I cannot shake your hand, you know why. Instead I said, Henry, normally if someone comes to my office, when I say goodbye I shake that person's hand, but I can't shake your hand. I can't now. Go to the Truth Commission, tell your story, help the country, do something for South Africa and then perhaps we can meet again.

When he walked back to the security door he was without the upright soldier's posture he had had before, and looked uncomfortable, uneasy, and sad. He went through the door, I said farewell, and he disappeared.

The Truth and Reconciliation Commission   Something like thirty truth commissions have been created in various parts of the world, yet none have had the impact of the South African one – neither for better nor for worse. None have been so profoundly influential in the countries where they functioned, none have attracted so much international attention. What has been so special in South Africa?

The first point to note is that our TRC wasn't the brainchild of a group of wise people sitting around a table and concluding that in order to deal with the injustices of the past the country should set up a truth commission. The pressure for the TRC in fact emerged from intense and specific internal South African needs.

The story starts with a meeting of the National Executive Committee of the ANC in August 1993, about eight months before the first democratic elections were due to be held. It was a passionate meeting, sharp, uncomfortable. The issue was how to respond to the report of a commission of inquiry set up by the ANC to investigate violations of human rights committed by ANC cadres in Angolan camps during the liberation struggle. The report stated that ANC security had captured or placed in captivity a number of persons suspected of having been sent by Pretoria to assassinate the leadership and generally create havoc; while interrogating them – this was in the early 1980s – the guards and security officials had frequently behaved barbarically.

I should mention that the organization itself had investigated the behavior, changed the whole security apparatus, and in 1985 created a code of conduct that was in effect a code of criminal law and procedure. It was probably the only liberation movement in the world that ever produced a code of that kind, with tribunals, prosecution, defense counsel all being established, offenses defined, charges being put, evidence led and challenged, and a system of appeals. By and large, though possibly not completely, the violations of human rights had stopped. Now it was 1993, ten years later, the war was over. Yet the violations had taken place. What did the ANC as a movement think about unacceptable things that ANC members had done during the course of the struggle? The report was emphatic: certain people should be called to account by the ANC. The eighty-member National Executive Committee was now discussing what to do.

Some people said forcefully: we set up the commission, it has reported, we have to follow through. Others responded with equal vehemence: how can we do that, we were fighting a freedom struggle in terribly difficult conditions in the bush in Angola, the enemy was ruthless and they stopped at nothing, we had young people quite untrained in interrogation techniques, they did their best, they protected the leadership, how can we punish them now?

The reply then came: we are a freedom movement, we were fighting for justice, if justice does not exist inside our own ranks, if we do not hold to these values, if we simply use the techniques of the enemy, we are like the enemy, we are no better than they are, the people have accepted great suffering because they believe in our cause, you cannot fight for life and be the enemy of life at the same time. Pallo Jordan, who is now the Minister of the Environment, stood up, and with his well-elocuted, high-pitched voice said, "Comrades, I've learnt something very interesting today. There is such a thing as regime torture, and there is ANC torture, and regime torture is bad and ANC torture is good; thank you for enlightening me!" And he sat down.

The house was divided on the issue. Profound moral issues were at stake, not the sort of matters that could be decided by a simple show of hands. Eventually somebody stood up and asked the simple question: what would my mother say? The figure of "my mother" represented an ordinary, decent working-class woman, unsophisticated in politics but with a good heart and an honest understanding of people and the world, a person whose hard life experiences had promoted a natural sense of honor and integrity. He then answered himself: my mother would say there is something crazy about the ANC. Here we are examining without stop our own weaknesses and faults and exposing our nakedness to the whole world, which maybe has to be done. But in the meantime all those rascals and villains on the other side who have been doing these things and worse for decades and centuries, murdering, mutilating, and torturing our people, are getting away scot-free. Nobody is examining what they did and what some of them are still doing. Are we so perverse and introspective, are we so obsessed with our own moral health, that we do not even think about the pain and the damage that was caused by the other side, by people who are now getting away completely without any kind of punishment, without taking responsibility for anything? What kind of freedom movement are we when we are so insensitive to the pain of millions of ordinary people? Where is the balance? Where is the justice?

It was at that moment that Professor Kader Asmal, who is now Minister for Water Affairs, stood up and said: what we need in South Africa, the only answer, is a truth commission. Only a truth commission can look at all the violations of human rights on all sides from whatever party. Human rights are human rights, they belong to human beings, whoever they might be. And torture or other violation has to be investigated on an even-handed basis across the board, not just by one political movement looking at itself, but at a national level, with national resources and a national perspective.

He was clearly right. That was the moment when a political decision was taken that if an ANC government came to power after the elections, and it was assumed that it would, a truth commission would be set up that would examine all abuses of human rights, from whatever quarter, in the last years of apartheid.

The second crucial ingredient also emerged from the bowels of the South African experience. The negotiators had signed the draft of a new, nonracial, democratic constitution. We thought it was all over. We had worked out a two-stage process of constitution-making involving an elected Constitutional Assembly, modeled very much on the Indian experience, which would draft a final constitution. We had agreed in the first-draft constitution on thirty-four principles that would be binding on the Constitutional Assembly. We thought that all that remained was to hold the elections. Then, at the last minute, we heard that the security forces had said to the leadership that they had been promised an amnesty by President De Klerk, they had loyally protected the negotiations process, they were fully prepared to safeguard the elections against a bombing campaign intended to destroy the whole transition process, they would defend the new government and the new constitutional order, but not if they were going to jail afterward for their actions in support of the previous government, that was asking too much.

This created a problem for the ANC leadership. The promise of amnesty had been given by President De Klerk, not by themselves. At the same time, they acknowledged that the security forces had loyally protected the negotiation process against many assaults from various right-wing sources. They were also aware that ANC security was not itself in a position to defend the election process – they just did not know who the bombers were. Generations had dreamed of elections on the basis of one person, one vote, of a new constitutional order in which everyone would be equal, in which the crimes of the past could not be repeated. If the elections were severely disrupted, the dream would be destroyed and racial violence would continue. The security forces were not themselves holding a gun to the transition process but were simply saying that they should get some recognition for enabling the democratic process to advance. At the same time, to grant them blanket amnesty because of their support for the constitutional process would negate the principle of institutional and personal accountability. It was at this stage, to reconcile these competing considerations, that the proposal was made to grant an amnesty to the security forces, but not a blanket or general one. The right to amnesty would be based on each individual coming forward and acknowledging what he or she had done, and then getting indemnity to that extent.

In this way the idea of the truth commission and the amnesty process were linked on an individualized basis. That turned out to be the foundation of South Africa's TRC, and the basis for its unprecedented success. It meant that the perpetrators of violations of human rights, the torturers, the killers, had a motive to come forward and reveal what they had done. In exchange the country would learn the truth. It was not through show trials, bribery, or torture that they would confess; it was not through using the methods that the old regime had used – keeping people in solitary confinement, making them stand for days on end, electric shock torture, getting compliant, emotionally destroyed witnesses to testify. It was through voluntary confession induced by the guarantee of amnesty.

Three elements turned out to be necessary for the process to work well. First, it was important that the TRC function within a sound legal framework in a clear constitutional setting. Thus the Constitution itself provided for a right to an amnesty for offenses committed in the course of the political conflicts of the past, but stated that the right could only be enjoyed under terms and conditions to be established by the new parliament. The new parliament then went on to provide that a truth commission would be the mechanism for determining how amnesty could be granted on a case-by-case basis. Second, although the drive for the TRC might have come primarily from the new government, the details could not be unilaterally imposed. Some measure of consensus, however incomplete and reluctant, had to be achieved. A year was spent on the enabling legislation. It was a strenuous period of consultation and debate, of trying to bring in all the different interested parties and civil society with a view to securing the best mechanisms, balance, and confidence in the process. Third, it was vital to staff the TRC with individuals of caliber, of standing, of manifest integrity, who had not themselves been directly involved in the conflicts of the past. This did not mean finding "neutrals." Anybody who claimed to have been neutral in the face of apartheid would not have been the right person; nor would a person who had been neutral in respect of torture. What was needed was not neutrality but impartiality. This required people who were passionate about justice and human rights, but impartial in terms of evaluating the roles and functions that any particular persons, groups, parties, or formations had played in supporting or undermining respect for human dignity. This meant persons who would look at what had happened in the ANC camps with the same degree of objectivity and impartiality that they would use in examining the massive violations committed over long periods of time by the security forces of apartheid. And in Archbishop Desmond Tutu, chairperson of the TRC, an outstanding individual with such qualities was found. After a complex screening process that covered individuals from a wide range of social, cultural, and religious backgrounds, other personalities of manifest capacity and caliber were selected.

The commission was divided into three sections that functioned separately with different personnel. The first was the structure that heard the testimony of victims of gross violations of human rights. One must recall that the system of apartheid itself violated human rights, and had been condemned as a crime against humanity. All the laws in terms of which people were identified by race, forced to carry passes, evicted from land, and denied access to education, public facilities, and the vote – all of these violated human rights. But they were not the subject of the TRC investigation, nor were the harsh security laws under which people were detained in solitary confinement without trial.

The TRC investigated acts that were crimes even under apartheid law. These were human-rights violations so ugly and gross that they had been hidden and denied even by those who had openly supported race domination. The tortures, the assassinations, the people who had disappeared, the cross-border commando raids where people had been kidnapped or wiped out, had all been illegal in terms of South African law, even in terms of draconian apartheid security legislation. That was the focus of the TRC. The idea was not to investigate apartheid, which as a system had been condemned by humanity and totally repudiated by the new Constitution. The objective was to examine the crimes that had been committed and hidden during the apartheid period, mainly those committed in defense of apartheid but also violations of human rights perpetrated in the struggle against it. Tutu called this section the one for the "little people." At last those in the townships, the communities, the rural areas, whose voices had never been heard, would be allowed to tell of their grief, their pain, and their loss. People like myself had been on television, had written books about our experiences, had traveled around the world and spoken to many audiences about what had happened to us. But there were thousands and thousands of people who had suffered not only the initial shock of violence to their bodies, or the pain of the loss of a son, daughter, mother, or father, but the sorrow of having had to keep the hurt secret all the time. Something like ten thousand people testified in various parts of the country as to what had happened to them and their families.

Judges do not cry. Archbishop Tutu cried. It was not a court of law in the sense of an austere institution making formalized findings. It was an intensely human and personalized body, there to hear, in an appropriately dignified setting, what people had been through. In a court of law no one is there to help the witness, to pat the shoulder, to provide water or tissues when the person weeps; in the TRC hearings there were comforters sitting next to the witnesses. The sessions would frequently start with a song in beautiful African harmony, intended to give a sense of encouragement and support to everyone present. Or it could begin with prayers. And thereafter people spoke and spoke in all the regions and all the languages of the country. The testimony was televised, the nation became witness to what had happened and heard the stories directly from the mouths of the persons concerned. Those who spoke were not complainants in a court denouncing accused persons in the dock. Nor were they litigants demanding damages for themselves, so that the greater the loss, the greater the sum they would receive. Neither punishment nor compensation were at issue, only the opportunity to speak the truth and have their pain acknowledged.

The five-volume report summarizing and analyzing their testimony was published in 1998.[1] And I might say it is a brilliant document. It has photographs and excerpts from some of the most poignant aspects of the testimony. It is not a dry governmental report but a passionate memorial that resonates with the emotion of the hearings themselves. In addition, it contains serious reflection on how evil behavior is condoned and spreads itself, and on what institutional mechanisms and what kind of culture are necessary to prevent its reappearance. That was one of the greatest objectives of the commission, not simply to let the pain come out but to explain the conditions that permitted gross injustice to flourish and so to ensure that these things do not happen again.

And no one escaped the inquiry. Business, where were you? Business was making money, business was cooperating directly with the security forces, supplying explosives, trucks, and information. The press, where were you? There were some brave newspapers and wonderful journalists, but by and large the press was racist in its structure and fearful in its thinking, and went along with the stories about these terrorists, how dangerous they were, and how they got what was coming to them. And the stories about people slipping on a piece of soap, falling out of the window, tripping down stairs, were carried by the press as if they might well be true, together with masses of disinformation that created a climate in which demonized freedom fighters could more easily be tortured or killed.

The legal profession, the judges, where were you? We judges, old and new, had hard debates in our own ranks. The strongest view was that the judiciary had contributed substantially to injustice by enforcing racist laws and showing an unacceptable lack of vigilance in the face of accusations of torture and abuse. When the executive took sweeping powers to lock up and detain people without trial, and brought witnesses from months and years of solitary confinement to court, this was treated as normal procedure. There were some judges, again, who showed outstanding poise and courage, proving that even in the most constrained of circumstances, choice always existed. They used what little space was available to them to maintain the greatest traditions of the law, and I am proud to say that some of them are my colleagues on the Constitutional Court today.

---

1 *Truth and Reconciliation Commission of South Africa Report,* 5 vols. (Cape Town: Truth and Reconciliation Commission, 1998).

The Reparations Committee is completely separate. It will receive reports from the first commission and will ensure that each victim gets monetary compensation, probably on a lump-sum basis paid over a few years. The pain and suffering of a whole generation, not just those who testified, cannot be measured. We cannot take money away from schooling, health, and land reform. But some kind of material compensation will be given to all the victims who came forward. There will hopefully also be living memorials, dignified reburials, scholarships for the children of those who died, streets renamed, gardens created, and monuments designed – not grandiose "monumental" monuments, but monuments as simple as the people themselves and as searing, sharp, and evocative as the pain they suffered.

The third section of the commission, the one with the most difficult task, is the Amnesty Committee. It has two judges in each panel, and is the one that comes closest to being like a court of law. Whereas a criminal court normally decides whether a person should go to jail, here it is deciding just the opposite, whether someone should be freed from prosecution. Because personal liberty is at stake, something like due process of law applies, but without the strict rules of evidence and formal charges of a trial. A number of spectacular, terrible matters still await decision.

Chris Hani, one of the first guerrillas who rose to be commander of Umkhonto we Sizwe, the military wing of the ANC, and then became general secretary of the Communist Party of South Africa, was a great popular hero. He went jogging during an Easter break in the period when we were still negotiating a new constitution. As he got to his home, somebody got out of a car, put a pistol to his head, and gunned him down. It turned out that his killer was an extreme right-winger from Poland who had been living for some years in South Africa, working with a far-right grouping in the country. A neighbor gave the identity of the car, the police captured him, and, almost literally, a smoking gun was found. One of the ironies of our history is that it was the ANC's opposition to capital punishment that saved him and a co-conspirator from execution and enabled them subsequently to apply for amnesty. Should they get amnesty or not?

Then there was a group that was part of the Winnie Mandela football team. Winnie, brave, isolated, combative, passionate, warm, embracing, and, some would say, capable of destroying anybody or anything in her way, gathered around herself a group of people who committed mayhem around them and created great conflict with the local ANC. People died cruel deaths. It was not Winnie who applied for amnesty, but members of the football team, claiming that Mama Mandela had been the one who had ordered them to do these things. Should they receive amnesty? These are hard, searing, painful South

African questions, requiring hard, searing, painful South African answers. Our TRC is harsh, it is raw. It has given rise to much controversy and invites deep reflections.

Knowledge and Acknowledgment   I propose to share some of my personal thoughts with you. I would like to deal with the difference between knowledge and acknowledgment. Knowledge involves possessing information, being aware of facts. There was in reality an enormous amount of knowledge about repression in South Africa, but hardly any acknowledgment of what the cost was in human terms. Acknowledgment involves an acceptance not only of the existence of a phenomenon but of its emotional and social significance as well. It presupposes a sense of responsibility for the facts, an understanding of the significance that they have for the persons involved and for society as a whole.

One way of looking at the TRC process is to see it as a means of converting knowledge into acknowledgment. First came acknowledgment of the pain of the past. The fact that thousands of people had suffered was common knowledge – that the state had cracked down, that injuries had been sustained, that people had died in detention. Yet the human and personal dimension had been extruded, the pain shut out. That bare information became transformed when you saw individuals on the television, when you gave them a name, when you heard their stories firsthand. It was also different for those who testified, going home to the support of their neighbors, seeing themselves later on television. As a result of the TRC, the private sorrow and grief of tens of thousands has been publicly acknowledged in a warm and personalized way. Another form of acknowledgment has emerged from the perpetrators themselves: they have come forward openly in front of the television cameras, owning up to their crimes. Finally there has been acknowledgment by the whole country that these things happened and can happen again, that we need to fit all these facts together into some kind of significant pattern that will enable us to understand their genesis and do what we can to minimize any possibility of their recurrence.

Four Categories of Truth   I have been profoundly puzzled, as a lawyer and a judge, by many features of the TRC. They mainly concern how we are to understand the concept of truth. The question asked in jest almost two thousand years ago still has to be answered: what is truth? I am not trained in the sciences of epistemology and ontology, so have invented four rough categories of truth that I find helpful in the situation: microscopic truth, logical truth, experiential truth, and dialogical truth.

Microscopic truth, whether in natural or social science, involves narrowing the field to a particular frame and excluding all variables except those to be measured. In a court of law we pose and answer a particular question in a defined field, such as whether a certain person is guilty of wrongfully and intentionally killing another at a particular time and in a particular manner. You identify, circumscribe, and verify. That is microscopic truth, detailed and focused.

Logical truth is the generalized truth of propositions, the logic inherent in certain statements. It is arrived at by deductive and inferential processes, and in the end, I suppose, it draws its strength from the capacity of language to reflect what is typical in nature as experienced by humanity. Much of the law is concerned with finding the connections between microscopic truth and logical truth, that is, with setting microscopic truth in a logical framework.

Experiential truth is of a different order. It is the understanding gained from being inside and part of a phenomenon. It is the truth that we are all exposed to by living through a particular experience. I first came across the concept when reading M. K. Gandhi's *My Experiments with Truth.* I was puzzled by that title. These were not experiments as I understood the term; experiments were what we did at school when testing hypotheses with Bunsen burners and flasks of liquid in controlled conditions. Gandhi started without a hypothesis. He was testing himself, not an idea or the world out there. The process was to immerse himself thoughtfully and sensitively in certain experiences, and then to draw conclusions from what he had lived through with an honest, objective eye. Central to the process was the capacity to stand objectively outside yourself and to look at your subjective experience in a truly unprejudiced way. Such experiential truth is deep and profound. Yet it embarrasses us in courts of law, we try to exclude it, we see it as subjective, irrelevant. We claim that all we want is the objective truth, what we call "the facts."

Finally there is what I call dialogical truth. This is a truth based on interchange between people. We all have different experiences of reality, and diverse interests and backgrounds that influence the meaning of those experiences for ourselves. The debate between many contentions and points of view goes backward and forward, and a new synthesis emerges, holds sway for a while, is challenged, controverted, and a fresh debate ensues. The process is neverending; there is no finalized truth.

Microscopic truth is definitive within its narrow frame; logical truth is objective, generalized, impersonal, and not dependent on external verification; experiential truth is open-ended but personal to the individual concerned; dialogical truth embodies elements of all of these, but it assumes and thrives on the notion of a community of many voices and multiple perspectives. In the case of

South Africa, there is no uniquely correct way of describing how the violations of human rights took place, there is no single narrator who can claim to have a definitive perspective that must be the right one.

The experience of the victims of violations of human rights was intense and real but was no more exclusively true than the experience of the perpetrators or the experience of the press or the experience of the judges. This is not to eliminate standards for evaluating conduct. The TRC notion presupposes measuring human conduct according to how it shows or denies respect for human dignity. It also assumes that people always have choices and must be held accountable for what they do. What dialogical truth implies is that the most pertinent description and the most meaningful evaluation of the phenomenon under question results from putting together all these layers of truth, these different experiences and this variety of voices. The TRC itself is not one homogenous entity with twelve, fifteen, or seventeen robotic heads, all thinking, seeing, and experiencing things in the same way. The narration and evaluation in the report are themselves the products of dialogue between different members of the commission. Tutu has his own particular confessional, personal, and experiential approach. His deputy has similar values but a different life experience. The other commissioners are from different backgrounds, reflecting diverse historical and cultural experiences. They composite rather than simply aggregate their different perspectives and evaluations. That is the way and the life of dialogical truth.

The strength of the TRC, and the reason why it resonated so powerfully, is that it was based essentially on dialogue, on hearing all the different viewpoints, on receiving inputs from all sides. It was not a case of people coming in as prosecutors and saying: we stand for the state, we are going to examine and get the truth out of you. The state did not get the truth out of anybody. It did not work that way. An increasingly rich and true story emerged from a multiplicity of voices and perspectives. Then the TRC, itself a variegated body, had the function of trying to find the language, mode of presentation, and way of telling the story that would be as meaningful and convincing as possible.

The problem I have is: why does so little truth come out in a court of law, when so much emerged from the TRC? It poured out in huge streams, with overwhelming and convincing force. Many of the details and some of the assessments may be challengeable, but the basic sweep is incontrovertible. One of its huge achievements has been the way it eliminated denial. Not even the most ardent defenders of the old order deny the evil that was done in its name. Court records, on the other hand, are notoriously arid as sources of information. Outside the microscopic events under inquiry, you learn little. The social processes and cultural and institutional systems responsible for the violations remain uninvestigated.

The answer to this puzzle must lie in the differing objectives of the respective inquiries. Courts are concerned with accountability in a narrow, individualized sense. They deal essentially with punishment and compensation. Due process of law relates not so much to truth as to proof. Before you send someone to jail there has to be proof of responsibility in the microscopic sense. When the penalties and consequences are grave and personalized, you need this constrained mode of proceeding. The nation wishing to understand and deal with its past, however, is asking much larger questions: how could it happen, what was it like for all concerned, how can you spot the signs, and how can it be prevented from occurring again? If you are dealing with large episodes, the main concern is not punishment or due compensation after due process of law, but to have an understanding and acknowledgment by society of what happened so that the healing process can really start. Dialogue is the foundation of repair. The dignity that goes with dialogue is the basis for achieving common citizenship. It is the equality of voice that marks a decisive start, the beginnings of a sense of shared morality and responsibility.

I think that is a great lesson for our country, and possibly for the world. We do need an international criminal court functioning according to due process of law, where virtue seeks unequivocally to trounce evil. But we also require a wide and flexible range of programs that would allow for other means of coming to terms with trauma and violence, where the format is not that of inquisitor and accused but that of interlocutors trying to find common ground. All have an equal chance to speak. Some achieve relief through being heard, others accept shame when acknowledging cruel conduct; but they are speaking to each other, not trying to kill one another.

Truth and Reconciliation   In an immediate sense there has been little direct reconciliation. Few of the torturers were forgiven directly by their victims, very few. People felt raw, angry, upset, the more so because not many of the perpetrators had been able to show much spontaneous human emotion. Yet there were exceptions. There was a man from the community who had been blinded by an ANC bomb in Pretoria. Abubaker Ismail, the person responsible for the bomb, applied for amnesty, explaining that as part of the freedom struggle his unit had put the bomb near a military target. He said he regretted very much that he had been compelled to fight with these methods, and felt especially sorry about the injuries caused to the victim. And the blind person put out his hand, shook the hand of Ismail who had been responsible for the bomb, and said: I understand why you did it, you were fighting a freedom struggle, that was your motivation, we must move forward now.

We had other cases in South Africa just like that. It was unusual, but it was not unique.

How do we prevent these things from recurring in future? Part of the answer is to convince the security forces that they cannot expect secrecy and cover-up in the future. The security forces must never feel that they can rely on being protected by the state, come what may. The TRC has achieved this, at least for our generation.

Another part of the answer is to develop a new culture in the country at large. The TRC process has sunk into the consciousness of the nation. Hopefully the report will be integrated into school curricula and its conclusions will irradiate South African thinking generally. Evil and cruelty must be seen for what they are; protecting the state against some imagined terrible evil from outside cannot justify it violating all moral norms and committing great evils itself. A third safeguard comes from having strong institutions in place dedicated to defending fundamental human rights. Our Constitution gives great significance to such institutions. One of them is the Constitutional Court, of which I have the honor to be a member.

The Constitutional Court   We have started a process of building a new Constitutional Court, which in a highly visible way will symbolize the "never again" principle in our national life. And here there happens to be a strong connection with India. We had an international competition for a new court building; 600 people bought the competition brochure and 180 entries were received, 40 from outside South Africa. The chairperson of the jury was the Bombay architect Charles Correa. He was chosen because we felt he had the right philosophy for the kind of building we wanted – not a copy of a North American building transplanted to South Africa, but an edifice that came out of our culture, located itself in our history, and responded to our light, physical texture, topography, and needs.

Geoffrey Bawa, a distinguished architect from Sri Lanka, was another member of the jury. Monika Correa, who accompanied her husband Charles, presented us with a luminous tapestry she had made showing a banyan tree firmly rooted in the ground yet floating in space. The symbol of the Constitutional Court is a large tree under which the people shelter; they protect the tree, the tree protects the people. Her tapestry will have a prominent place in our court, possibly behind the judges, and there will be a direct Indian presence there. But the connection with India is not simply a physical one. The site that we chose for the court building is the Old Fort prison in Johannesburg. We say, with mixed feelings of satisfaction and shame, that South Africa possesses the only prison in the world where both Gandhi and Nelson Mandela were locked up. And those of you who are familiar with the story of Gandhi in South Africa will know that many of his most intense experiments with truth took place in precisely that prison. If I recall correctly, his decision not to take salt – when he saw that Indian prisoners received salt with their food while African prisoners did not – was made there, and generated the idea of voluntarily giving up physical pleasures so as to understand the experience of living like those treated as the lowest in society. Sadly, we in South Africa provided him with that rich experience.

For the most part, the hurt is still there. Instead of coming forward and speaking from the heart and crying and being open, most of the perpetrators came in suits, expressing tight body language, with their lawyers next to them, and read prepared statements as though they were in a court of law. Their admissions were important, but tended to be limited to a factual acknowledgment of unlawful conduct coupled with a rehearsed apology, rather than encompassing an emotional and convincing acknowledgment of wrongdoing. I am sure there is a huge generosity, particularly among African people, waiting to come out, but it can only express itself if there is a counterpart of openness and honesty of feeling on the part of the perpetrators. Just as even in this highly marketized world we still have a right to altruism, so even in a legal and moral universe based on accountability, there is a right to forgive. The problem is that the right to forgive can only be enjoyed if the perpetrators acknowledge their wrongfulness.

Yet even allowing for all these serious limitations in the reconciliation process, I believe that the basic objective of laying the foundations of national reconciliation has been largely achieved. On an individual basis and between all communities we have a long way to go, but at the national level we now for the first time have a single narrative, a common history of the most painful moments of the recent past. You cannot have a country with different memories and expect a sense of common citizenship to grow. You cannot have a white history and a black history that have nothing to do with each other except that they coincide in time and place. You have to have a single, broad, commonly accepted narrative of South African history. In that sense, although we are still living in an unfair country, where facilities and life opportunities are not the same for black and white, we are living in a much less divided country than the one we occupied before, as inhabitants of two countries in one. As one American can put it – we are all on the same map. That has been the huge gain.

It should be remembered, too, that accountability can take many forms. Even punishment should not be seen simply as sending people to jail. The persons who appear on television and say, We cut up the body and threw the pieces to the crocodiles afterward, do not get off scot-free. They are punished by exposure, punished by shame. In conditions where they no longer exercise total power, they see the families of the victims, look into their eyes as equals. Afterward they go home and have to look into the eyes of their neighbors, their children, their families. Once upon a time they received handshakes and promotions, now they are abandoned and repudiated. Many are receiving treatment for post-traumatic stress. Their bleak faces serve as warnings to all in the future: nothing remains secret, the truth will out.

Many bodies of disappeared persons have been recovered. We now have the truth for the first time of how Steve Biko was killed, how the community leaders known as the Cradock Four were murdered – years of inquest and inquiry had produced nothing. So we have gained an enormous amount both of knowledge and of acknowledgment. The price was to offer indemnity to those who came forward with the truth. Yet prosecution without evidence would have been difficult, and we would not have known whom to prosecute for what. I think the country is stronger for the process.

We need a new building for our new court and our new democracy, but we are going to keep the old prison structures. The prisons will be there, right next to the Constitutional Court, representing not only the "never again" principle but also the theme of survival, of hope, of the triumph of courage and humanity over despair and cruelty. We wanted the new building to be a simple edifice, where justice would be accessible, friendly, and warm. If I walk into a magistrate's court in South Africa today I feel guilty, and I am a judge in the highest court in the land! There is something about standard court architecture that proclaims authority, that says, Beware, the state is on top of you. Yet our court does not express power, it restrains power. Our job is to defend the new Constitution, to ensure that all the agencies of society, all public institutions, function in terms of the processes laid down by our Constitution and respect the values enshrined in it.

It is in relation to values that so much of Gandhi comes through to us. The underlying values of our new democracy are spelled out in our bill or rights and in the very concept of equal citizenship, which presupposes not only negative protections against abuse by public power but also affirmative claims to a decent and dignified life for all. The foundation of our work is accordingly respect for the humanity of the least among us. The Constitutional Court is expressly required to promote the values of an open and democratic society. Such a society acknowledges the equal worth and dignity of each of its members and respects difference in society. These are Gandhian ideals.

Yet it is not only the spirit of Gandhi that can be found in our Constitution, but the philosophy of Jawaharlal Nehru. I am honored to be speaking in the building most directly associated with Nehru, to be living on a campus named after him. It is no accident that the title of Mandela's autobiography *Long Walk to Freedom* was taken from a phrase by Nehru: there is no easy walk to freedom. The experiences of the Indian freedom struggle and the processes used to accommodate diversity in a democratic national framework had a profound influence on Mandela's generation and are reflected in our new constitutional dispensation. So we get themes about the institutionalization of democracy from one great Indian personality and about spirit, compassion, and self-denial from another. These were two enormous inputs, communicated across the Indian Ocean not just by writings but through the experiences of struggle and jail of scores of South Africans who worked directly with two great Indian leaders. The universalism of human rights comes from the universality of struggle and idealism. In this way the aspirations of generations of freedom fighters are embodied in the Constitution that I as a judge on the Constitutional Court have sworn to defend.

Epilogue   A week before my companion and I flew out of Cape Town en route to India, I was at a party in Johannesburg, feeling quite light-headed after a heavy year's work in court. The party was at the home of somebody whose father had been one of the first to be assassinated by the hit squads; as a child she had cradled her dad as he lay dying. To this day she does not know who actually killed him, but she has got on with her life and has now become a film-maker of repute. It was an end-of-year party for the actors and crew of a gritty and intelligent soap opera of which she was one of the directors.

In the midst of the music and hilarity I heard a voice saying to me: Hello. I turned around and saw a familiar face smiling at me, looking very happy. The person spoke again: Hello, I am Henry, do you remember me? At first the name did not register. The speaker went on: Remember I came to. ... And I remembered: You came to my office, you were going to the TRC.

The music was throbbing, the people were dancing around. We got into a corner so that we could hear each other better. He was beaming. I asked him what had happened. He told me that he had written to the TRC, giving them all the information he could, and had applied for amnesty in relation to six different matters. And afterward, he said, he had spent hours with Sue and Bobby and Farook, all of whom had been in Mozambique in those hard years, answering their questions on behalf of the TRC. He was speaking on first-name terms about people I knew well, all freedom fighters who had been in Mozambique, and doing so with great affection and enthusiasm.

Then he stopped talking, looked at me and said: You told me that afterward

... maybe. ... And I responded: Yes, Henry, I said to you that afterward, if you cooperated with the Truth Commission, if you did something for South Africa, maybe we could meet again. ... I've only got your word for it, but I can see from your face you are telling the truth.

I put out my hand and I shook his hand. He went away elated. I moved away and almost fainted into the arms of a friend of mine.

Is Truth the Road to Reconciliation?*

Avishai Margalit

Truth is a good thing. Reconciliation is a good thing. To argue against truth and reconciliation is like arguing against motherhood and friendship. I am not going to argue about *that*. The question I would like to pose, and the doubt I would like to cast, is on the putative causal relation between the two, namely on the idea that truth brings about reconciliation – or, put more cautiously, that truth contributes to reconciliation.

There are excellent reasons to pursue the truth. Truth is good in and of itself. There are excellent reasons to pursue reconciliation in countries torn by strife and suffering. The issue, however, is whether truth is a good tool for bringing about reconciliation. So what I propose to put under scrutiny is the slogan of South Africa's Truth and Reconciliation Commission (TRC), "Truth, the road to reconciliation."

The issue, I believe, is of great moment, since the South African model for bringing about reconciliation through truth is regarded by many as the right model for handling transitional justice in many other troubled parts of the world. As I write this sentence, the South African writer André Brink is being interviewed on Israeli television and the first question he is asked is whether the truth-and-reconciliation format is applicable to the Israeli and Palestinian conflict. So I believe I have a great stake in probing this model, not mere academic curiosity.

Faith in the healing power of truth is half as old as time. It took a spiritual bully like Nietzsche to pose the quest for truth as a problem. The problem is whether truth contributes to our well-being, or, in Nietzsche's idiom, to "the forces of life." Nietzsche notwithstanding, the force of the traditional healing power of truth was never seriously questioned. Psychoanalysis was based on the belief in the emancipatory power of bringing repressed truth to the open. Once truth is revealed and acknowledged, its subversive dysfunctional role is supposed to stop.

* This essay was presented at a seminar on Truth and Reconciliation, organized by the Prince Claus Fund for Culture and Development and Documenta11, The Hague, July 6, 2000.

The psychoanalytic model of liberating the repressed, which was meant to serve as a model for the individual psychology, was quite naturally – yet uncritically – extended to the collective. Thus we are told, for example, that the French people, with the help of the arch-censor de Gaulle, repressed their shameful memories of the Vichy government during World War II, and that those memories continued to play unconscious subversive tricks on the French psyche – so much so that they put the whole nation into a neurotic dysfunctional state, manifest in the wars in Algeria and Indo-China. Yet brave people forced the truth on French society, so the story goes, and made it confront its shameful past of collaboration, which was buried under the myth of the French Resistance. Once the painful truth was out in the open, a healing process started to take place.

This picture of a nation on the psychoanalytic bed, crude as it is, constitutes a powerful claim for the healing power of truth. But it is a picture, not an argument. So let me expand a bit on my question about the relation between truth and reconciliation. I shall start with truth.

Already Pilate asked, in a sarcastic tone, "What is truth?" Well, by truth here I mean uncovering and disclosing shameful, painful, and distressful facts that people try hard to conceal from others or from themselves. More can be said about the practical sense of truth here, and more should be said, since the TRC cluttered the notion of truth first with "social or dialogue truth," then with the addition of "narrative truth" (which includes "stories and myths"), and on top of all that dealt with "healing truth." I believe I understand what the TRC was trying to do with these unfortunate divisions of truth, which seem to relativize truth beyond recognition. The idea, if I understand it correctly, was not only to capture the relevant past propositionally but to bring the past to life by reliving the experiences and the emotions of its victims. To enable this reliving of the past, the TRC invited first-person accounts of how the experiences of apartheid looked and felt to the victims at the time, even when these accounts were not fully accurate when viewed from a third-person perspective. The idea was to capture what it was like to be under the dark grip of apartheid – and it seems that the success of the testimonies was exactly in their ability to convey those experiences.

But then the idea of reliving the past takes its toll when the past was deeply humiliating. You cannot relive humiliation without being humiliated anew. The scars of humiliation never fully crust over, especially if humiliation has come with torture. Trauma, which is the Greek word for "wound," is a bleeding wound. The effort of the TRC to reenact the past seems to undermine the very idea of healing its wounds.

And here I come to the second term of the concept I'm dealing with, namely, reconciliation. Reconciliation, unlike repentance, is a symmetrical relation: both sides in a conflict have to settle and resolve their bitterness by accepting and admitting their shameful deeds toward each other as a way of restoring harmony. This is why no one can ask for reconciliation between Jews and Germans. There was nothing symmetrical in the blame between Nazi Germany and the Jews; it was all one-sided. When people like Ernst Nolte try to create such symmetry, accusing "world Jewry" of having declared war on Nazi Germany and of being a side in the war, this sounds morally outrageous. In the case of apartheid the issue of symmetry in the wrongdoing is a very serious matter indeed. It is true that in order to counter the evil of apartheid, black Africans resorted to violence and terror. But I can see how many of them resent the idea of symmetry that the notion of reconciliation implies. They see their violence as reactive violence, and they do not subscribe to the doctrine of original sin according to which there is an in-built symmetry among all human beings, who are all burdened by evil through the mere fact of being human.

It took the moral authority of Desmond Tutu, with his deep religious convictions, to reconcile the black community to reconciliation, with its implied acknowledgment of wrongdoing by their side too. Tutu indeed conferred a religious meaning on the act of reconciliation as an act of atonement, which requires an explicit confession of sins as a necessary condition for restoring the original relation between man and God. Atonement plays a role in Tutu's world view, and truth-telling by the perpetrators of evil is viewed as a confession within such an act of atonement. It seems to me that a community that shares this world view is a community in which truth may indeed lead to reconciliation, because even when a perpetrator receives immunity from the TRC in exchange for telling the truth, he is not immune from being accountable to God. So religion, in the case of truth and reconciliation, helps.

But what about those cases when religion does not help, because the community is not religious? We can easily see arguments both for and against the belief that truth, in a secular society, can bring about reconciliation. To start with some arguments against this belief: when people who have suffered immeasurably know all too well that their former tormentors are going to get away with murder, torture, and rape in exchange for telling their stories, even if they do so in a less than truthful way and without any sense of repentance – why believe that these people will be forgiving? Why believe that now, having been told exactly which perpetrators did what and to whom, it is easier for the victims to reconcile with the past? And as for the perpetrators, it is true that telling a dark secret can bring about a sense of relief, but it is a short-lived relief. Having told it, you and your family are tainted for many years to come. Moreover, you are bound to feel resentful toward those who were once in your hands but are now calling the shots and forcing you to tell what you were reluctant to admit even to yourself. These are powerful reasons against believing that truth is the road to reconciliation.

What then counts for this belief? One powerful argument in favor of the healing power of truth in the relevant cases is the great need that victims have for their suffering to be recognized. Denying or ignoring their suffering robs it of its meaning, making the sufferers feel as if they counted for nothing and denying their humanity. So even if victims feel a strong urge for retributive justice, their need for their suffering to be recognized is stronger still. In communities in which former victims and former perpetrators are destined to live together after a period of transition, retributive justice can be too costly, or a political impossibility. The second best possibility, from the point of view of the sufferers, is that their suffering will at least be recognized by all. "Confession first," then, makes not just religious sense but psychological sense as well.

So the question for us to debate is: Is truth the road to reconciliation?

Truth and Reconciliation Are Not What We Really Need

Boris Buden

The question seems to be simply rhetorical: now, after the war, is the process of confronting the truth and working toward reconciliation what the peoples of the former Yugoslavia most need? After ten years of violence and destruction, after, as we hope, they have finally gotten tired of hatred and mutual humiliation, what else should they want more? What could be more important to them than to face up to their recent past, to exhume the mass graves, and to examine the responsibility not only for the crimes they committed but for those they incited or tacitly agreed to? The process will certainly be long and painful, but do these peoples have any alternative if they really want to live in peace with each other? Only an overall process of reconciliation among individuals and peoples in the region can bring about the stability that is the precondition for necessary democratic reforms and economic achievement, and that alone could enable the societies of the former Yugoslavia to complete the transition from the totalitarian past toward a modern liberal democracy. If we believe that the Yugoslav tragedy can still have a happy outcome, the process of truth and reconciliation seems to be the only comprehensible way to achieve it.

Unfortunately, the real state of affairs looks neither as simple nor as promising. First, the war seems not yet to be over. As we gather here in Delhi in May 2001, there is fighting in Macedonia. The clashes between Macedonian forces and Albanian rebels that suddenly flared up two months ago resumed last week. The international public was astonished; no one expected this – at least no one outside the region. After the successful NATO military intervention in 1999, Macedonia and the whole region around Kosovo was thought to be completely under control, both politically and militarily. But the fighting happened anyway. The war broke out again, despite an excessive military presence, massive political and economical support, and – perhaps worst of all – the more than ten years of experience that the so-called international community has now had with political conflict and war in Slovenia, Croatia, and Bosnia.

We already have the evidence, it seems, to say openly that the West's engagement in the Balkans has suffered a shameful defeat. Of course it is not the West's military, economic, and intelligence powers that have failed; the debacle is in the first place political. What has been defeated is the developed, democratic, Western political mind, which has failed to deal with the political challenge of the Yugoslav crisis from its very beginning until the present moment. So we must ask: what has caused this political fiasco?

Free and Independent Illusion   First let us go back to the recent events in Macedonia. This eruption of violence was no less predictable than the outbreak of war in Slovenia ten years ago, and the beginning of the violent dissolution of the former Socialist Federal Republic of Yugoslavia. The international community was well aware how dangerous the tensions between Macedonians and ethnic Albanians were, and what incalculable consequences another Balkan war might have. Moreover, it even tried to intervene in the crisis to prevent catastrophe.

If we must choose a practical example that both typifies how the modern democratic West deals with dangerous political conflicts around the world and illustrates the inherent logic of its political failure, let me suggest the following one: shortly after the Kosovo war, the *Financial Times* reported on a joint project that the creators of the famous American television series *Sesame Street* and *The Muppets* had started with Macedonian television. The idea was to produce a forty-show TV series for children telling the story of two families, one Macedonian and one Albanian (a third of the Macedonian population is Albanian), who live in a so-called "mixed neighborhood." The series was to be geared toward ten-year-olds. The project was organized by an American nongovernmental organization called Search for Common Ground, and its goal was "conflict prevention" and, to quote the *Financial Times*, "to tackle two of the root causes of ethnic conflict in Southeast Europe: segregated education and partisan media."[1]

For many of those who are acquainted to some extent with the political and historical reality of the former Yugoslavia, the statement is strange in itself. Neither of the causes it identifies as the roots of ethnic conflict in the region is correct. The worst cases of ethnic cleansing in the former Yugoslavia happened precisely where "segregated education" is unheard of, notably in Bosnia. Bad educational practice is by no means the cause of violent conflicts and ethnic cleansing. Nor are the so-called partisan media: although it is certainly true that many newspapers, magazines, and especially television and radio stations have

---

1 Joe Cook, "Muppet Makers Try to Bridge Ethnic Divide: Creators of the Popular Children's Show Are Pioneering a Television Project to Bring Young People in Macedonia and Albania Together," *The Financial Times*, August 7, 1999.

been directly controlled by the state, there have also been independent media in the region since the very beginning of the 1990s and even earlier, during the last days of communist rule. The media have enough freedom to provide objective information and to generate a relatively independent public space. Even the country recently considered the worst dictatorship in post-1989 Europe, that is, the Serbia of Slobodan Milosevic, never suspended the basic freedom of the press. On the contrary! According to a report on the independent media in Yugoslavia published shortly before the NATO intervention began, there were in Serbia half a dozen independent dailies, several weeklies, three independent news agencies, more than forty independent local newspapers and journals, more than fifty independent radio and television stations together reaching about 70 percent of the country's territory, two associations of independent journalists, and an independent international press center.[2] Many a Western democracy could only envy Serbia its wealth of independent media.

A lack of information has never been the problem in the former Yugoslavia. The public was quite well informed – for instance, about the war crimes committed in its name. Yet this never had the consequences a democratic public usually expects. Let me take an example from Croatia. As early as 1994, an independent weekly published all the relevant facts about a war crime in which a Croatian paramilitary unit in Zagreb had brutally murdered an entire Serbian family, including a twelve-year-old girl. The magazine even published the complete confessions of the perpetrators, down to the smallest detail.[3] Yet solely on the basis of a minor error in legal procedure, the murderers were set free and lived happily ever after, neither persecuted by the law nor disturbed by the moral feelings of their countrymen.

Let us agree for the moment: everyone who was really interested in what was happening in the war had the opportunity to know it. The real mystery, though, was not the facts of the war crimes themselves – of who was killing and torturing whom, and how – but rather the political circumstances that made these crimes possible. No one had to wait for the mass graves to be exhumed to know where the 8,000 Muslim men who disappeared from Srebrenica in the summer of 1995 were dumped, and who deserved the blame. Europe's worst war atrocity since World War II happened under the eyes of an international public. More: it happened under the protection of United Nations forces. The scene of the crime, the perpetrators and the victims, were completely exposed to the public.

2 Velimir Curgus Kazimir, "Independent Media in Yugoslavia," *Open Society News: The Newsletter of the Soros Foundations Network* (New York), Spring 1999.

3 Davor Butkovic, "Suljic je djevojcicu postavio uz rub grabe, uzeo Hekler i pucao joj u glavu" (Suljic put the girl close to the pit, pulled a Heckler, and shot her in the head), *Globus* (Zagreb), May 20, 1994.

What we had been in the dark about, though, was the backstage interplay of political deals and power arrangements made either between the parties to the conflict or between them and the political representatives of the international community. This includes the whole range of actively and passively involved international political agents in the Yugoslav wars, their historical and ideological blindness, and their particular political interests. What was really obscured was the question of the political responsibility for the violent dissolution of the former Yugoslavia and all the crimes that accompanied this political tragedy. It is the political truth of the war that still waits to be disclosed, not the factual record of the crime or its moral and psychological consequences.

One aspect of the international community's blindness toward the Yugoslav political crisis and wars has to do with the extraordinary belief in the power of the so-called free and independent media. The media were thought to play a decisive role in the political reality of the postcommunist countries, especially in cases where democratic development was endangered by nationalistic conflict and revived totalitarian tendencies. It seemed to be expected that free media could correct the mistakes of young democracies and prevent their regression into dictatorship or violence, in short, could protect democracy from its enemies and show it the way to the safe haven of political stability, economic growth, and cultural progress. Yet concrete political realities never confirmed this expectation. As political events ran their course, no "free and independent media," whatever the truth they exposed, could have changed it. Many examples from the former Yugoslavia demonstrate this.

What lies hidden in this problem is an old assumption that when people get accurate information, when they hear "the truth," they will change their opinions and undertake collective action against social evil, aiming to change the existing social and political reality. In the Yugoslav case this would have meant that, having been properly informed of "the truth," they would have opposed nationalist manipulation, overthrown the evil dictatorship, restored democracy, urged their legal institutions to prosecute war criminals, and established a democratic procedure to call to account all those who had been politically responsible for these terrible crimes. But this idea obstinately overestimates the political effectiveness of the "free and independent media." The fetishism of information on which it is based typifies both the bourgeois understanding of the political role of the media in modern democracies and the leftist concept of the counterculture, as reflected in numerous alternative media projects and massively applied in the political struggles of new social movements, especially during the period of their formation in the 1970s.[4] Even then, critics recognized the problem that some information will only be received, people will only perceive it as truth or lie, if they also have the opportunity to actively change the social and political situation it concerns. Otherwise the realism of the media's reporting won't matter.[5] The information will be ignored. The decisive issue, then, is not so much freedom of information as the freedom of articulating – ideologically as well as practically – alternative political options that could challenge existing conditions.

People are not oblivious to the horrible reality around them because they lack information about it. No information, however true, will make politically aware subjects of democratic change out of passive masses. Rather, it is the political subject who generates the truth of necessary political change out of neutral information. We already know enough; the problem is that our knowledge has no political consequences. Why, then, has this concept of the crucial political role of the media, although credibly criticized in theory and never proven in reality, become one of the anchoring elements of the Western strategy in the Yugoslav drama?

Kiss of Truth   The first idea that occurs to us is that the real objective of this belief in media is to generate some sort of ideological interpellation. The relentless insistence on the importance of "free and independent media" in a situation of nationalist hatred, ethnic conflict, populist mobilization of the masses, severe violations of human rights, and ultimately war – the case in most parts of the former Yugoslavia in the 1990s – actually functions for the West as its call for the healthy forces of democracy. Those who perceive the information delivered by the "free and independent media" as the truth of their social, political, and moral reality, the truth kept hidden by the other, lying (biased, partisan, or state-controlled) media, see themselves as the addressees of the imposed democratic mandate, the historic mission, the struggle for democracy. By opening their eyes to the facts and finally seeing reality as it is, they simultaneously cast themselves as the subjects of democratic change. Beyond any kind of manipulation, they freely and rationally decide to vote for democrats over dictators, to choose peace over war, to abandon the totalitarian idea of dominating ethnic and other minorities, and so forth. Actually, what else could they have chosen?

Yet the kiss of the truth-telling media has never awoken the sleeping beauty of democracy into real political life. The masses of the former Yugoslavia have never identified with the call of the democratic West. The interpellation has

4 See Autonome a.f.r.i.k.a.-gruppe, "Bewegungsle(e/h)re? Anmerkungen zur Entwicklung alternativer und linker Gegenöffentlichkeit," in Nettime, ed., *Netzkritik. Materialien zur Internet-Debatte* (Berlin: Edition ID-Archiv, 1997).

5 See Oskar Negt and Alexander Kluge, *Public Sphere and Experience: Toward an Analysis of the Bourgeois and Proletarian Public Sphere,* 1972, Eng. trans. Peter Labanyi, Jamie Owen Daniel, and Assenka Oksiloff (Minneapolis: University of Minnesota Press, 1993).

failed. While the free and independent media were delivering their truths, the ethnic cleansing continued until it had reached its goals, and the führers retained their support until they died or lost their last battle. The masses kept protecting their war criminals until the pressure from outside finally became unbearable and threatened to destroy the very basis of their economic and political survival. Even the recent changes of regime in Croatia and Serbia, celebrated in the West as the final victory of democracy in the Balkans, were nothing but continuations of the same old opportunism that had in fact been the most reliable resource of nationalist politics. These changes have brought to power precisely those political forces whose active and passive support made nationalist rule possible, with all its tragic consequences, and who have always been blind and deaf to the truth delivered by the so-called free and independent media.

One is accordingly justified in asking, what, then, is the ultimate effect of this truth? It has obviously functioned as an agency of interpellation, but this interpellation has failed; it has never produced the political subject of democratic change. If some democratic change in the former Yugoslavia has nevertheless taken place, the truth we are discussing here was surely not among its motivations. Was this truth only an illusion, then? Yes, an illusion, though a necessary one – but the question is for whom. Certainly not for the masses in the former Yugoslavia. For them, this illusion – the truth of the political reality they had been facing in the mirror of their free media – was of no political importance whatsoever. The real effects of this illusion must be found in the democratic West, the proper place of its use. The purpose of this illusion projected on the Balkans, the illusion of the extraordinary political importance of the objective truth, was to support the political reality of the existing Western democracies.

The common belief that truth can liberate people from the chains of political manipulation to which they are supposedly exposed by their nondemocratic rulers, and by the media those rulers control, is a misunderstanding. The fact that this liberation, as we have seen, never took place in the former Yugoslavia does not make this belief dispensable; it still provides a plausible explanation of why people voluntarily support nondemocratic politics, why they vote for populist mass leaders instead of for proven democrats: namely, because they lack the truth. If only they had known the truth, we say, they would never have made the wrong choice. In its final effect, this belief makes out of the people – always imagined in democracies as mature political beings who are responsible for their decisions – a mass of passive, manipulable objects, the innocent victims of political seduction. What has been constructed here is an illusion of primal innocence as the zero level of political community. Every time the democratic system crashes upon some inexplicable internal error, that illusion makes possible a kind of political "restart."

The fantasy of primal innocence supports the reality of the modern democratic order in its most vital element. It alone enables the democratic system to rebuild its subjective precondition, popular sovereignty, after that sovereignty has been regressively dissolved in some kind of antidemocratic, mostly nationalist politics. There is always some innocent *demos* to be recalled behind the mob, and there is accordingly no democracy that could not restore itself out of its deepest regression. "We the people!" the famous call to action that constitutes the horizon of democratic politics, still functions today only if it can be instantaneously translated into "We the innocent victims!" For it is only on the ground of the victim's passivity that the political subject of modern democracy can be reactivated and recast in the role of an agent of democratic change. We are inclined, for instance, to forget that NATO bombed the Federal Republic of Yugoslavia in 1999 in the name not only of the hundreds of thousands of Albanian refugees who were victims of Serbian terror but of the Serbian people whom the international community recognized as innocent victims of Milosevic's manipulation. They were bombed precisely because of their innocence. It is the cause of the universal victim that makes the ultimate difference between war in a traditional sense and its new form, now called "humanitarian intervention."

But the fantasy of primal innocence supports our postmodern democratic reality in one more important way: it suggests that all the antagonisms conceivable in a democratic society can ultimately be represented by the relation between victims and perpetrators, which should be imagined as the only still-visible residue of the antagonistic character of the social totality. This decides, in a critical way, how a society constructs the field of politics. For the only social space in which we are now supposed to experience the real effects of social antagonism is the court, not the political arena. The truth of social antagonism no longer emerges out of collective political action but rather through a juridical procedure along the relation between victims and perpetrators. It is a juridical truth, not a political one. It does not disclose the complexity of power relations in the society, pointing at some social injustice and urging a political action to change it. On the contrary, by focusing on what has been acted out between victim and perpetrator, the truth of social antagonism mystifies social relations and obscures interests of power and domination. It will probably reveal the truth of how hatred has been made in a community, but will never ask how that community has been made out of hatred. And maybe the most important point here is: it presupposes an instance – the court – that remains neutral to the whole issue. This is the instance that makes the truth possible without being itself in any way involved in it. In this way, even the clearest and the most fully verified juridical truth may well turn out to be a dangerous political lie.

Let us take the example of the international tribunal in The Hague that has been given the task of prosecuting the war criminals of the former Yugoslavia. No doubt we can expect the tribunal to disclose the truth of these men's crimes as far as that is possible to do, and to punish, after fair trials, those who committed them or are in the juridical sense responsible for them. The tribunal will also give the victims an opportunity to have their stories heard. The international pressure put on the regimes in the region to arrest and extradite their culprits has already had positive political effects. But what will happen to the question of political responsibility for the Yugoslav wars, which is obviously shared by both the political agents on the ground and the international community that has organized the tribunal in The Hague? What if this tribunal primarily serves the democratic West as an escape from its own political trauma – the fact that it never found proper answers to the political challenge of Yugoslavia's violent disintegration? Will the tribunal enable the West to avoid facing the Yugoslav conflicts as a moment of its *own* political crisis, or give it a chance to maintain the illusion that social antagonisms can always be resolved in the courts? What if the tribunal is not a revolutionary act of global politics but just another means of an overall depoliticization? By treating the Yugoslav wars primarily as a criminal case, we are obviously running the risk of suppressing its political truth.

From Hannah Arendt we have learned that a curious relationship between truth and lie in politics does not have much to do with facts.[6] Since politics is a matter of a human action whose characteristic is that it can always change existing conditions and begin something new, a deliberate denial of factual truths is an inherent part of political activity. Facts in politics are never compellingly true. This means that the political truth of some historical event can only be grasped if the people involved in it have been recognized as political beings – that is, recognized in their ability to act and to change the existing reality.

Humans are political beings inasmuch as they can imagine that things might as easily be different as be what they actually are – inasmuch as they have the freedom to change the world and to start something new in it.[7] Otherwise they are passive marionettes of history, whether as its victims or – in the role of perpetrators – as its outlaws.

---

6 Hannah Arendt, "Lying in Politics," in *Crises of the Republic: Lying in Politics, Civil Disobedience, On Violence, Thoughts on Politics and Revolution* (San Diego and New York: Harvest/Harcourt, Brace & Company, 1972).

7 See ibid., p. 5.

Children of Transition   If the historical framework of the Yugoslav political tragedy has a name, it is surely the notion of transition. The concept of transition was invented by political scientists in the late 1960s and early '70s to explain various contemporary cases of regime change in South America and Southern Europe.[8] In its early phase, the theory emphasized uncertainty and unpredictability as the main features of politics, and attached much more importance to the actions of political actors than to various objective factors determining the particular historical situation. It was precisely the so-called subjective side of politics that most interested the early "transitologists." They considered the outcome of a transitional process completely open. Transition out of an authoritarian regime, they saw, could lead equally to the instauration of democracy or to the restoration of a new and possibly more severe form of authoritarian rule. A military junta in South America could undergo a transition not just to a Western type of democracy but to a socialist type of democracy, like Salvador Allende's Chile. Even a kind of Maoist dictatorship was at the time conceivable as well.

The revolution in Eastern Europe in 1989 radically changed the discourse of transition. The rapid and unexpected collapse of communism so surprised the transitologists that they had to modify their theory: now a set of objective factors made every outcome of the transition not only predictable but completely predetermined. To arrive at democracy was now simply to follow a set of external factors, whether economic, cultural, or institutional. Sometimes it was enough to follow geography, for "geography is indeed the single reason to hope that East European countries will follow the path to democracy and prosperity."[9] Other transitologists went a step further in their deterministic views: it was ultimately nature itself that decided the necessarily democratic outcome of transition, for democracy was "a natural tendency and therefore not difficult to achieve."[10] One of them even based his theory of democratization on the Darwinian theory of evolution by natural selection.[11] The main characteristic of the concept of transition after 1989 is historical determinism. Post-1989 transition theorists believe in a universal historical trend that inevitably leads societies in a backward phase of authoritarianism on to the developed phase of liberal democracy.

8 Here I draw on Dejan Jovic, "Tranzitologija kao ideologija" (Transitology as Ideology), *Hrvatska ljevica* (Zagreb) 11, 1999.
9 Adam Przeworski, *Democracy and the Market: Political and Economic Reforms in Eastern Europe and Latin America,* Studies in Rationality and Social Change (Cambridge, Mass.: Cambridge University Press, 1991), p. 190.
10 John Mueller, "Democracy, Capitalism, and the End of Transition," in Michael Mandelbaum, ed., *Postcommunism: Four Perspectives* (New York: The Council on Foreign Relations, 1996), p. 117.
11 Tatu Vanhanen, *The Process of Democratization: A Comparative Study of 147 States, 1980–88* (New York: Crane Russak, 1990), p. 47.

For the so-called children of communism such ideas are not unfamiliar. The system that collapsed in 1989 was strictly speaking not communism but socialism, a type of society in transition from capitalism to the classless society of communism. In that sense 1989 brought no essential change in the historical position of the masses; one type of transition was simply replaced by another. Instead of an iron law of historical progress based on the universal notion of class struggle, a law reflecting the necessity of the disintegration of capitalism and the passage to communism, we got after 1989 a universal trend of history leading every postcommunist society necessarily from totalitarianism to democracy.

How this concept of transition really works in a practical situation is shown to us, for instance, by the Stability Pact for Southeast Europe.[12] The international community worked out this pact in 1999, after the Kosovo war, in a final attempt to pacify the whole region and to integrate it into the European Union. If the countries in the region wanted to make any progress toward "European integration," they had to fulfill a double criterion of democracy and economic achievement established by the declaration of the Stability Pact. First they had to introduce a free-market economy. Such an economy does not work, however, without social and legal stability and appropriate institutional arrangements, which in turn cannot function unless supported by democratic political institutions and activities. Then of course traditional parliamentary politics alone cannot provide the security needed for normal economic development; they must be controlled and moderated by an appropriate public sphere. And there is no genuine public sphere without free media and a strong civil society, which does not function well until a democratic political culture is developed.

Since every country in the region had already introduced a free-market economy, had long ago institutionalized parliamentary democracy, and already had a functioning public sphere generated by free and independent media, the problem of their transition to democracy and integration into the European Union appeared to be ultimately cultural. Accordingly the task of the transitional project is predominantly educational. The peoples of the region must be educated in order to be able to use their preexisting democratic institutions and to follow the democratic will of their enlightened political elites. Transition means ultimately nothing but an endless process of education. A number of metaphors used in the transitional discourse only confirm this: education for democracy, exams of democracy, classrooms of democracy, democracy that is growing and

12 I draw here on Rastko Mocnik's intervention at the conference on the Declaration of the "Europa South-East" policy forum on the Stability Pact, Ljubljana, July 18–20, 1999.

maturing, and perhaps that might be in diapers, or making its first steps, or, of course, suffering from children's illnesses.[13]

The children of communism have become the children of transition – the world has changed indeed. But the general dependency of the masses on political powers and processes completely alienated from them has not changed. The moment of their maturity, again and again postponed during the communist period, has finally disappeared altogether in the bad infinity of the transitional process.

Where maturity is understood as the goal of an infinite process, the use of this notion serves to extend not "the circle of the mature, but the circle of those who are for the time being declared to be immature."[14] In that sense the process of transition does not automatically extend the space of democratic freedom. On the contrary, it extends the power of so-called objective factors that are completely out of the control of the masses and indefinitely defers the moment of their political maturity.

This regression corresponds with the move from the pre-1989 idea of transition as a contingent political process with an open, unpredetermined outcome to the post-1989, determinist idea of transition in which liberal democracy becomes not just the best possible result of the transitional process but the only natural, the only *possible* aim for all existing societies. What has changed here is not just the transitional paradigm but the very status of politics.

We often say that the East European revolutions of 1989 reinvented democracy, but what they actually reinvented was the political subject of democracy, the famous "we the people" of the democratic revolutions. In a genuine act of self-determination and self-liberation, the peoples of Eastern Europe reinstalled the autonomy of the political – the idea that politics, despite its historical conditions, is nevertheless ultimately founded upon itself. In the concept of transition after 1989, there is no place for an autonomy of the political. The truth and reality of politics are not *within itself*, in its own activity, but *outside itself*, in its external conditions.[15] This in fact resembles the situation under communist rule, where politics was considered to belong to the so-called superstructure: the general direction of history toward communism was decided not by political forces but by the economic sphere. The current concept of transition similarly does not expect politics to bring us to democracy; geography, nature, or simply the universal trend of history will do

---

13 See Jovic, "Tranzitologija kao ideologija."
14 Robert Spaemann, "Autonomie, Mündigkeit, Emanzipation. Zur Ideologisierung von Rechtsbegriffen," in *Kontexte* 7 (Stuttgart, Berlin) (1971): 96.
15 See Etienne Balibar, *Masses, Classes, Ideas,* trans. James Swenson (New York and London: Routledge, 1994), p. x.

that instead. This is also the reason why transition no longer needs a genuine political subject.

It would be wrong, however, to say that this transitional road to democracy is without a social agent. That agent is the concept of civil society, which has today become a universal answer to all crises of existing democracies, thanks to the role it played in the struggles against communist and military dictatorships in many parts of the world.[16] In that sense civil society is a genuine transitional concept, not only historically but also essentially. If there is a subject that can push forward democracy today, it should be civil society; if there is a place where democracy can still expand, this again should be the social space occupied by civil society; and if there is some utopian potential we can still imagine in today's democracies, its name is again civil society.

This is the idea behind the Macedonian Muppets project: that the solution of political conflict must be found somewhere within civil society – in the distribution of independent information, say, or in the processes of public education and cultural development. The project is actually very successful; the TV series is very popular among both Macedonians and Albanians. Unfortunately this seems in no way to have influenced the political reality in Macedonia. Whereas both Albanians and Macedonians enjoy the TV program that is supposed to reconcile them, the fighting between Albanian rebels and Macedonian government forces threatens to escalate into a full-scale civil war. No doubt the Muppets will improve cultural life in Macedonia. But as long as this and similar cultural projects are not accompanied by resolute political decisions, they will remain merely a symptom of a political failure by the West in the Balkans.

No More Auschwitz!   Nothing can replace a political solution – not TV programs for children, not free and independent media. From the very beginning of the Yugoslav crisis, at the end of the 1980s, until the present day, the international community has found no appropriate answer to the political challenge of Yugoslavia's disintegration. It has been disgusted by primitive Balkan nationalism while simultaneously recognizing that movement's political achievements: not only the newly established nation-states but almost all of its other, violently reached goals, including ethnic cleansing. The international community has passively accepted the violent disintegration of Yugoslavia as a kind of historical necessity. It counted the process's victims and to some extent took care of them; it started to prosecute war criminals and, with the fall of Milosevic, even to cel-

---

16 See Jean L. Cohen and Andrew Arato, *Civil Society and Political Theory* (Cambridge, Mass.: The MIT Press, 1992), chapter 1: "The Contemporary Revival of Civil Society," pp. 29–83.

ebrate the final victory of democracy in the Balkans and the rest of Eastern Europe. Commenting on the political turn in Serbia in October 2000, the German foreign minister, Joschka Fischer, remarked, "The last piece of the wall has fallen."

The truth is, unfortunately, that democracy has not won at all. Neither Serbian politicians nor the free democratic world have any idea how to solve, in a democratic way, the problem of the political status of Kosovo; there is still no democratic solution for Bosnia either. A military protectorate in an ethnically cleansed Kosovo ... an all-powerful governor in Bosnia, who can suspend the decisions of a parodic parliament at any moment ... so-called sovereign constitutional states (*Rechtsstaaten*) that cannot prosecute their war criminals on their own ... economies that need ten to fifteen years to reach the level of development they had ten years ago under communism ... a peace grounded only in a military threat from the outside ... and now new fighting in Macedonia. There is no reason for celebration.

The political problems that have arisen out of the disintegration of the former Yugoslavia are obviously much greater than the problems that allegedly caused that disintegration. The best example is that of Kosovo: for its future status, the international community has suggested the same political autonomy that it used to have within the former Yugoslavia under Tito's constitution of 1974. Not only does this intention show how far from reality the political mind of the democratic West is, it discloses that mind's profoundly nostalgic streak in dealing with the Yugoslav crisis. To be nostalgic for the former Yugoslavia is quite normal for the real victims of the Yugoslav wars. They have good reason to long for a better past. But why should the modern democracies, after their final victory over totalitarianism, still be politically nostalgic?

Let us remember the pictures of those identified during the war as victims. We saw all those children, women, and old men on the streets of Vukovar, expelled from their destroyed homes by the Yugoslav army and by Serbian paramilitaries in 1991; for years we watched them running for shelter under sniper fire in besieged Sarajevo, and met them again in endless columns leaving Croatia in the summer of 1995. These pictures evoked pity from the international public and induced massive humanitarian aid. The victims of political violence, ethnic cleansing, and war were treated like any other victims of some natural catastrophe or tragic accident. The fact that their tragic fate had something to do with politics was noticed for the first time when a British TV station showed pictures of emaciated figures standing behind barbed wire in the Serbian concentration camp in Trnopolje, in northern Bosnia. "No more Auschwitz!" the international public cried out, and this slogan initiated and symbolized the whole political and military engagement of the West in former Yugoslavia, including the NATO intervention in 1999 and the establishment of the tribunal in The Hague.

It was not the truth, however; it was an analogy – as if the whole political meaning of the Yugoslav breakup and war could be reduced to an already known episode of the common past, and the only political other for democracy today were an old, curiously resurrected, and already defeated fascist enemy, and any claim to the political dignity of the war's victims were actually derisory. Historical resentment seems to be the main driving force of this approach. The only history that the political mind of the developed democratic West is still able to recognize is a new version of the eternal repetition of the same. Behind its nostalgic longing for a clear, already known – and politically nonchallenging – historical situation is a deep fear of facing something new and unknown.

This is why the people of the former Yugoslavia do not need to establish truth commissions and launch the processes of organized reconciliation. It is an overall depoliticization that they have most been suffering from, and no truth of the past will help them to get rid of it. What they really need is to repoliticize their tragic experience and to seize the suppressed freedom to radically change their miserable reality. They must invent a new form of political solidarity, one that goes beyond their national, ethnic, cultural, and religious identities, if they really want to build new bridges toward each other over the mass graves and ruins. No reconciliation, however deep and thorough, can do that instead. For every reconciliation is finally a reconciliation with the status quo, with the existing power relations and ideological deadlocks that should be the first to be blamed – rather than a few political knaves and war criminals – for the Yugoslav tragedy. None of the victims need such a reconciliation, for it would be nothing but a reconciliation with the historical senselessness of their depoliticized fate.

What victims need most is not to remain mere victims. They need a political cause to be recognized in their tragic fate. It is not humanitarian aid, of whatever sort, from bread to bombs, that can help them; it is only political solidarity – a clear commitment to the cause of their emancipation – that can liberate them from the misery they have been suffering over the last ten years.

The "Melancholization" of the Witness:
The Impotence of Words, the Power of Images

Geneviève Morel

Introduction   No one has a better claim than the witness to the experience of truth. In court, before the law, he swears to "speak the truth, the whole truth, and nothing but the truth." But this experience of truth is not identical to the fact of providing evidence.

Jacques Derrida has insisted on the heterogeneity of witnessing and evidence.[1] He gives the example of the Rodney King event, in California: a witness was there with a video camera when the police were beating up King, and filmed the scene. This was a direct image of the event, something a priori, indisputable. But in the eyes of the law the film was a debatable item of evidence that would only have value when combined with the testimony of the young cameraman, who, even though he had filmed the scene, was also obliged to testify before the bench, in person, that he had actually seen it. Going without his word, his presence, and being content with technical evidence was impossible.

Clearly certain testimonies can serve as evidence in themselves, though, when it is a case of testifying to something purely subjective, and elsewhere than before the law. I became interested in testimonies because this was the way the psychoanalyst Jacques Lacan proposed that analysts should be recruited: on the basis of their own account of their relation to their unconscious, and of the real consequences on their lives of recognizing, through analysis, the existence of the unconscious. Here the evidence lies in the testimony itself, because the subject is the only one who can testify to his experience of the real of the unconscious. This implies other analysts listening and judging – a jury.

In apparent rebuttal of Derrida, also, there certainly does exist evidence that is valid without testimony: archives, documents, images of events, and now, for certain crimes, DNA. We note, however, that historians, like lawyers, always look for testimony to corroborate this evidence and allow it to be interpreted. In

---

1 Jacques Derrida and Bernard Stiegler, *Échographies de la télévision* (Paris: Galilée, 1996), p. 107.

the case of the law, we had an example in France in the case of Guy Georges, a rapist and serial killer of women. There was DNA evidence for most of his crimes, yet not just the victims' parents but all of France was waiting for his version of events, and was relieved by his public confession in court. For historians too, archival documents don't "say" enough without the support of protagonists' accounts, in written form in the case of ancient history. Georges Duby, a historian of the French Middle Ages, writes,

> I too am a positivist. In my own way. In my opinion, what is positive is not in the reality of "small, real facts": I know very well that I shall never grasp it. What is positive is concrete objects, texts that preserve an echo, a reflection of words and gestures that have been irremediably lost. In my opinion, what counts is the witness, the image that a highly intelligent man offers of the past, what he forgets, what he keeps silent, how he treats memories in order to adjust them to what he thinks, to what he believes to be true, to what those who listen to him wish to believe to be just and true.[2]

Historians and judges are not the only people to want testimonies as well as archives; a work of art, insofar as it has a function of transmission, can also turn to testimony. The film *Shoah* (1985), in order to transmit the Holocaust in the mode of an "incarnation," a "resurrection," its director Claude Lanzmann has said, uses only one archival document onscreen.[3] There is of course an immense quantity of historical data supporting Lanzmann's construction. (He has said that Raul Hilberg's *The Destruction of the European Jews* [1961] was for years his bible.) *Shoah*, however, is not a historical film but a film about witnessing. The film's most intense part is the accounts of *Sonderkommando* survivors who return to the vacated sites of the tragedy, where there remain only traces, almost completely erased: the Nazis were determined to render the extermination invisible. What is filmed and staged (locomotives and a barber shop were rented for the film) is not a historical reconstitution of the event, eradicating absence as certain fiction films do, but a present act of testifying to what is left for eyewitnesses: tenuous, fragile, incomplete, and partial remains, of which the surviving witness can only speak at risk, whether of being overwhelmed or of taking on in the process a new responsibility for his acts.

Thus the witness testifies at his own risk, implicating the future in the present. The necessary repetition of testimony implies an "iterability," in Derrida's sense: the repetition of what has already been said, but with an enunciation that is different each time, and thus with consequences that are a priori unpre-

---

2 Georges Duby, *Dames du XIIe siècle*, vol. 2: *Le souvenir des aïeules* (Paris: Gallimard, 1995), p. 77.
3 See Bernard Cuau, et al., *Au sujet de Shoah, le film de Claude Lanzmann* (Paris: Belin, 1990), p. 66.

dictable for the subject. *Shoah* shows us this, for the witnesses, their voices yet again failing, are not speaking here for the first time.

This serves to introduce our subject: the melancholization of the witness. Certain survivors of the camps, witnesses of the Shoah, such as Primo Levi – "a perfect example of the witness," according to Giorgio Agamben – or the Austrian writer Jean Améry, committed suicide after testifying to their experience of the *Lager* (camp) in their work.[4] There is no need to draw hasty conclusions. First, suicide is an act, and as Levi says, "No one has ever come back to relate their own death."[5] It is even the ultimate successful act, in the sense that there is a radical discontinuity between the action of killing oneself that it implies and the "obscure mass of explanations" that attempt, after the event, to identify the causes. This does not stop people from making interpretations, of course; Levi did not hesitate to do so for Améry, or for Paul Celan.[6] Second, can the experience of the *Lager* still be implicated when the suicide takes place thirty or forty years later? Does the fact of having testified to the experience of the *Lager* bear on the suicide? Has the subject's testimony protected him until then, or has it hurled him to this tragic conclusion? Of course we can only look for fragments of answers to these questions, answers that will be incomplete and different in each case.

Truth and the Real   Bearing witness is an experience of discourse, oral or written.[7] As an experience of truth, it implies the dimension of "making a mistake," even of lying. One can never tell "the whole truth." Trying to tell what has happened, the witness aims for the real. But if we agree that "full speech" – that is to say, speech that is identical to whatever is spoken of – does not exist, then every testimony implies a discrepancy with the real in question. Perhaps one illustration of this is the difference between testimony and evidence discussed earlier on.

4 Giorgio Agamben, *Ce qui reste d'Auschwitz*, trans. P. Alferi (Paris: Rivages, 1999), p. 16. Eng. trans. as *Remnants of Auschwitz: The Witness and the Archive*, trans. Daniel Heller-Roazen (New York: Zone Books, 2000). Primo Levi was deported to Auschwitz in 1944, as an Italian Jew. Jean Améry, whose real name was Hans Mayer, was deported to Auschwitz in 1943, as a Jew, after being tortured by the Gestapo for his resistance work in Belgium.
5 Levi, *I sommersi e i salvati*, 1986, French trans. as *Les Naufragés et les rescapés: Quarante ans après Auschwitz*, trans. A. Maugé (Paris: Arcades, Gallimard, 1989), p. 83. Eng. trans. as *The Drowned and the Saved*, trans. Raymond Rosenthal (New York: Summit Books, 1988).
6 For Levi, suicide was above all a human act, and he said that people in the camps did not commit suicide much because "human beings tended to resemble animals" and were far too busy trying to survive to think about killing themselves. Levi interpreted Améry's suicide in 1978 as the result of his defiant attitude, even in the camp, where he recounts punching back a Pole who had attacked him. Levi thinks this decision to "hit back" "led to standpoints of such severity and such intransigence that they made him incapable of finding any joy in living, and even of living." Ibid., p. 134. In the case of Paul Celan, whom he compares to Georg Trakl, he remarks that "their common destiny brings to mind the obscureness of their poetics as a readiness-for-death, a not-wishing-to-be,

Psychoanalysis posits an opposition between truth and the real. Truth has to
do with speech and language, in other words with the register of the symbolic;
the real is excluded from this. According to Lacan, the real is even "excluded
from meaning": on rereading Freud's "Negation" (1925), he shows how, on the
basis of a preliminary perception, the subject constitutes itself out of a primary
expulsion (*Ausstossung*) of the real, motivated by the pleasure principle.[8] Whatever is too bad or too good, whatever is in excess with regard to this principle of
homeostasis and equilibrium, "I" reject, although not without retaining a trace
of it in a symbolic affirmation (*Bejahung*) that constitutes my unconscious. The
real is thus rejected (*verworfen*) at the very outset by this primary judgment of
attribution, and from then on it lies outside symbolization and representation.
It is consequently linked to the logical modality of the impossible.

Reality is constituted in a second phase by a judgment in which objects in
the existing world are sought and found outside the self on the basis of a representation (*Vorstellung*) that imaginarily reproduces the perception of the first
object of satisfaction. The objects of reality never coincide with this representation, and reside side-by-side with the real that was earlier rejected. Reality, then,
is coextensive with the fantasy that masks this real that the subject will involun-
tarily encounter, and in a way that is invariably traumatic, when seeking his
objects of pleasure.

When a subject speaks, in analysis or in bearing witness, he mobilizes the
unconscious traces of the rejected real. Touching on what for him borders on
the real – the signifiers of the trauma – can make this unrepresentable real
emerge in the form of unpredictable acts, whether these be hallucinations or,
more banally, phenomena of déjà-vu. Let us consider the latter. Phenomena of
déjà-vu are accompanied by feelings of strangeness, a reluctance to speak, an

an escape-from-the-world crowned by deliberate death." Levi, *L'altrui mestiere*, 1985, French trans.
  as *Le Métier des autres*, trans. Martine Schruoffeneger (Paris: Folio, Gallimard, 1998), pp. 73–74.
  Eng. trans. as *Other People's Trades*, trans. Raymond Rosenthal (New York: Summit Books, 1989).
  He invokes each of their histories, crossed with History, but seems to think that obscure writing on
  their part is a sort of disavowal of responsibility to the reader. For Levi's relation to clear writing,
  see below.

7 When testimony is written, it is often in continuity with an oral account. This was the case with
  Levi: "And then, I chose writing as the equivalent of accounts given orally." Quoted in Ferdinando
  Camon, *Autoritratto di Primo Levi*, French trans. as *Conversations avec Primo Levi*, trans. A. Maugé
  (Paris: Le messager, Gallimard, 1991), p. 50. Eng. trans. as *Conversations with Primo Levi*, trans.
  John Shepley (Marlboro, Vt.: Marlboro Press, 1989). But it is not always so. Paul Steinberg wrote
  Chroniques d'ailleurs after fifty years of silence; Améry was silent for twenty years, until the
  Auschwitz trials, before writing *Jenseits von Schuld und Sühne* (1966).

8 Jacques Lacan, "Réponse au commentaire de Jean Hyppolite sur la '*Verneinung*' de Freud," 1954, in
  Écrits (Paris: Seuil, 1966), pp. 388–89. Eng. trans. as "Introduction and Reply to Jean Hippolyte's
  Presentation of Freud's *Verneinung*," *The Seminar of Jacques Lacan. Book I: Freud's Papers on
  Technique 1953–54*, ed. Jacques-Alain Miller, trans. with notes by John Forrester (New York:
  W. W. Norton & Company, 1998).

impression of temporal distortion. Lacan describes déjà-vu as "the imaginary echo that arises in response to a point of reality that belongs to the limit at which it has been cut off from the symbolic" – thus the imaginary echo of the real expulsed by the subject.[9] These imaginary phenomena, which he likens to Platonic reminiscence, must be differentiated from those recollections that have a relation to the subject's history, insofar as it is symbolically accepted.

Whoever wants to bear witness thus exposes himself to such phenomena at moments when something in his discourse evokes this severed and symbolically unaccepted real. In this hiatus between the symbolic and the real, the imaginary reveals itself as having affinities with the real that the symbolic does not have. The subject can be exposed to the return or creation of certain painful images that have great suggestive power over him. This is all the more true in that images, the imaginary, incite belief much more than discourse does, as is demonstrated by the experience of dreaming, hallucinating, or, more prosaically, a captivating movie.

Melancholy   In melancholy, the ethical "illness" in which the subject responds to a loss with a feeling of overwhelming guilt, the power of the imaginary can prove fatal. Melancholy, we know, can strike those who are mourning someone close, or who have suffered the loss of an ideal or who have themselves provoked such a loss (by voluntarily renouncing something that was nevertheless precious to them, say). The Freudian paradox of melancholy is that the libidinal tie with the lost object is shed in the unconscious after a long struggle – that is, the work of melancholy – even as the subject maintains a tie with the object that becomes completely formal, leading us to think that he remains fixed to it in a process of mourning that is eternal and idealized. One condition for this powerful libidinal rejection of the object is that, earlier on, the beloved object was also hated, or was at least the site of a certain ambivalence. But the remaining formal fixation on the object is completely imaginary. In fact, once the object has been rejected, it is introjected into the ego, which it splits into two: on the one hand, the part of the ego that is marked by identification with the lost object; on the other, the superego that is unleashed against this first part, and that is marked by the same hatred that the subject previously felt for the object. The superego's hatred for the part of the ego identified with the object can be so extreme as to lead to suicide. The moment at which the subject expresses self-reproach indicates the end of the work of melancholy, which is in general invisible, and the introjection of the object that has finally been rejected.

9 Ibid., p. 391.

Clinical experience teaches us that suicide is often triggered by the return of an image of the lost and idealized object that "comes to collect" the subject and leads him toward death.

A Killing Smile   "Adieu," a short story of Balzac's from 1830, shows the power of such mummified images of the lost object.[10] Let us briefly recall the story. Colonel Philippe de Sucy (P.) loves Stéphanie (S.), who has become the countess de Vandières on marrying the old general of that name. The three protagonists flee Russia in the Napoleonic war of 1812. As they are about to cross the Berezina River, the retreating French set the bridge on fire so as to halt the Russians' advance. To save S., P. has a raft built to take her across the river. But everyone rushes onto it in panic, and only two places remain for the three of them. P. gives up his place. "Adieu," says Stéphanie on leaving her lover. But the general falls into the water and is decapitated by a piece of ice before their very eyes. "Adieu," Stéphanie repeats.

In 1820, having survived to wander for pleasure through the French countryside, P. finds Stéphanie by chance. Since 1812 she has gone mad; failing to recognize him, she behaves like a wild child. Her only words are "adieu," repeated without meaning, empty returns. Her uncle has taken her in and is devotedly trying to help her get better. But P. has another idea. Two psychiatric conceptions of the time are contrasted here; it is that of Jean Etienne Esquirol that inspires P., who buys a neighboring property where he sets up a realistic re-creation of the army's retreat across the Berezina. He wants to produce a beneficial shock that will awaken S. from her madness. On the determined day, S. is brought, asleep, to the site and awoken by the sound of the cannon. Before the raft, writes Balzac, "she contemplated this living memory, this past life translated before her, turned her head toward Philippe, and saw him." Her face transformed by the beauty of rediscovered intelligence, she recognizes P., "comes alive," then suddenly "becomes a corpse" and dies, saying: "Adieu, Philippe, I love you, adieu!" Distressed, P. then notices the radiant smile that lights up the dead woman's face: "Ah!, that *smile* ... look at that *smile*! Is it possible?"[11]

Ten years later, in 1830, P. has once more taken up a busy social life. He seems comfortable and happy. A woman compliments him on his good humor:

10 Honoré de Balzac, *Adieu*, 1830 (reprint ed. Paris: Le livre de poche, 1999), p. 89.
11 Here and in later quotations the italics are added.

"Ah! Madam," he says to her, "I pay at great cost for my fun in the evening when I am alone."

"Are you ever alone?"

"No," he replied, *smiling*, with an expression that would have made anyone shiver.

Indeed, in the ten years since the death of the object S., the subject has not been alone, for he has been struggling against the lost object that he was trying to shed. This exhausting combat is the work of melancholy. The moment when he smiles at his worldly questioner indicates the end of this melancholic work; the shadow of the object falls on the ego, as Freud writes.[12] The subject introjects the smile, the sign of the lost object, S. P.' s look that "makes one shiver" evokes the avenging superego. Indeed the conversation continues briefly with the woman:

"Why do you not get married? … life is *smiling* at you."

"Yes" he answered, "but there is a *smile* that is killing me."

That very night he shot himself in the head.

If "adieu" is the signifier of trauma – here, of separation, loss, and death – the smile taken from the idealized lost object condenses love and guilt (P. feels he has killed S. with his traumatic historical reconstitution). After melancholic work lasting ten years, the lost object is introjected into the ego, as we have said, with the smile on P.' s lips indicating this introjection. But the smile is also the image of S., which still fascinates him and pushes him to suicide. "The ego is crushed by the object."[13]

Primo Levi   Let us return to the surviving witnesses of the Shoah.[14] Bruno Bettelheim described "the feeling of absolutely irrational guilt that one feels for the very fact of surviving," for having "been the absolutely powerless witnesses of the daily assassination of [one's] fellow men," "the fact of having lived for years under the direct and continuous threat of being killed for the single reason that one is part of a group destined for extermination." He transcribes the dialogue

---

12 Sigmund Freud, "Deuil et mélancolie," 1917, in *Métapsychologie*, trans. J. Laplanche and J.-B. Pontalis (Paris: Gallimard, 1968), p. 156. Eng. trans. as "Mourning and Melancholia," in *General Psychological Theory: Papers on Metapsychology*, ed. Philip Rieff, 1963 (reprint ed. London: Macmillan, 1997).

13 Ibid., p. 161.

14 My work on Levi is a continuation of the essay "Testimony and the Real: Psychoanalytical Elucidation," in Franz Kaltenbeck and Peter Weibel, eds., *Trauma und Erinnerung/Trauma and Memory: Cross-Cultural Perspectives* (Vienna: Passagen Verlag, 2000), p. 113.

between the reason and the conscience of the survivor: "A voice, that of reason, attempts to answer the question: 'Why was I spared?' in this way: 'It is purely a question of luck, of pure chance. It is impossible to answer otherwise.' Whilst the voice of conscience replies: 'That is true, but if you were lucky enough to survive, it is because another prisoner died in your place.'"[15] Levi disliked Bettelheim, on the one hand because of his relatively privileged position (thanks to relatives, Bettelheim was able to leave Dachau and Buchenwald for the United States, at a time when this was still possible[16]), on the other because of his psychoanalytic theories identifying prisoners with defenseless children and the Nazis with cruel and dominating fathers – a notion that is indeed more than questionable.[17] In Levi's last work, however, *The Drowned and the Saved*, we nevertheless find almost exactly the same debate, between a subject and a superegolike and accusatory "you," outlined by Bettelheim:

> You are ashamed because you are alive instead of someone else? … This is only an assumption or less: the shadow of a suspicion that each man is his brother's Cain. … It is an assumption, but it gnaws away at you; it has lodged itself so deeply in you like a worm, you cannot see it from the outside, but it gnaws and screams. … I could have taken someone's place, which in fact means killed someone.[18]

These lines, written forty years after Auschwitz, evoke a feeling of their author's shame, and are thus the sign of the melancholization of the subject. In Levi's case, I would like to suggest, the two processes that I described earlier, and that I have condensed in the expression "melancholization of the witness," are superimposed. On the one hand, there is an effect, specific to bearing witness, of seeing the gulf between the symbolic and the real widen, with the risk of one or more images becoming "the imaginary echo" of the real that preys upon the subject. On the other, there is an experience of death, on which we will elaborate, that provides these images with their content and their fatal power.

Levi committed suicide on April 11, 1987, by throwing himself down the stairwell of the house in which he had been born and still lived with his wife

15 Bruno Bettelheim, "Comportement individuel et comportement de masse dans les situations extrêmes," in *Survivre* (Paris: Pluriel, Hachette, 1979), p. 43. Eng. trans. as *Surviving and Other Essays* (New York: Knopf, 1979).

16 Bettelheim was deported first to Dachau, then, in 1938, to Buchenwald, as an Austrian Jew. He was able to leave for the United States in 1939.

17 Bettelheim, "Comportement individuel et comportement de masse," p. 101; Levi, *Le Devoir de mémoire: Entretien avec Anna Bravo et Frederico Cereja,* trans. J. Gayraud (Paris: Ed. Mille et une nuits, 1995), pp. 44–50.

18 Levi, *Les Naufragés et les rescapés*, pp. 80–81.

and elderly mother, who was senile and had cancer. Some minutes earlier he had telephoned the great rabbi of Rome and had said to him, "I do not know how to continue. I can no longer bear this life. My mother is suffering from cancer, and each time I look at her face, I remember the faces of the men lying on the planks of the beds in Auschwitz."[19] An image of the faces of the dying men in the camp, the "Muslims,"[20] then, is superimposed onto that of a loved one threatened with death. It seems that this image of the faces of the dying men had imposed itself for some time already on Levi, who was also trying to get over a painful operation. Indeed, in a poem of 1984, "The Survivor," we read:

> He sees the faces of his comrades again.
> Ashen, at the dawn of day,
> Cement grey,
> Veiled in fog,
> Colour of death in restless sleep:
> …
> "Back, out, shadow people
> I have not driven anyone out,
> I have taken no one's bread,
> No one is dead instead of me. No one.
> Return to your fog.
> It is not my fault if I live and breathe,
> If I eat and drink, I sleep and am clothed."[21]

We find here the same correlation between the image of the Muslims' faces and the protest against a reproach addressed to him by the dead. In an interview of that same year, Levi nevertheless said that he was hopeful and that he felt at peace with himself for having borne witness.[22] This suggests variations in mood:

19 See Myriam Anissimov, *Primo Levi ou la tragédie d'un optimiste* (Paris: Lattès, Le livre de poche, 1996), p. 735. Eng. trans. as *Primo Levi: Tragedy of an Optimist*, trans. Steve Cox (Woodstock, N.Y.: The Overlook Press, 1997).

20 Levi writes, "'Muselmann': c'est ainsi que les anciens du camp surnommaient, j'ignore pourquoi, les faibles, les inadaptés, ceux que étaient voués à la sélection" ("Muslim": this is what the elders in the camp, why I do not know, called the weak, the unadapted, those who were fated for the selection). Levi, *Si c'est un homme*, trans. Martine Schruoffeneger (Paris: Pocket, Julliard, 1987), p. 94, note 1. Eng. trans. as *If This Is a Man*, trans. Stuart Woolf (London: Bodley Head, 1966).

21 Levi, *À une heure incertaine*, trans. L. Bonalumi (Paris: Arcades, Gallimard, 1997), p. 88. Eng. trans. in *Collected Poems*, trans. Ruth Feldman and Brian Swann (London and Boston: Faber and Faber, 1988).

22 Levi, *Conversations et entretiens* (Paris: Pavillons, Robert Laffont, 1998), p. 217. Eng. trans. as *The Voice of Memory: Interviews 1961–1987*, ed. Marco Belpoliti and Robert Gordon, trans. Robert Gordon (New York: New Press, 2001).

he is the site of an intimate combat with himself, in which his testimony is what enables him to fight against guilt.

On Testimony as a Symptom   Defining the symptom as the thing that never stops writing itself, Lacan situates it as a need enveloping the drive, always on the border of the impossible, that is, of the real. In this sense the symptom supports the subject, even as it costs him dearly and causes him suffering. Bearing witness had this function for Levi: "I think that I am situated at the very extreme limit of those who tell their stories, I have never stopped telling my story," he says.[23] His decision to bear witness was rooted in a recurrent nightmare he had had in Auschwitz, a dream in which, returning home, he would tell people about his experience only to find that they neither listened to nor believed him. His compulsion dated from the moment at the camp when he for the first time held a pencil and paper in his hands. (This was at the IG-Farben factory, where the Nazis used him as a chemist.) On his return to Italy, his dream was realized when he tried to narrate his experiences to a group of Poles and quickly found himself alone, "bloodless."[24] Indeed we know that he had trouble making himself heard in Italy, and had to wait ten years for *If This Is a Man* to be reissued by a major publisher there.

Nevertheless, Levi found at least one person who would listen to him, his wife, whom he met in 1946 and married, as he later said, because she listened to him more than other people did.[25] He chose writing as "equivalent to a spoken report" with the intention of liberating himself, as though the act of writing were equivalent to "lying down on Freud's couch."[26] He felt writing had to be clear and precise, and had to attain an ideal of transmission in keeping with his chemist's dream of the written formula that is identical to experience.[27] Clear writing was perhaps also an antidote to death, to "obscure writing," a model of which was provided for him by that of Celan, which appeared to him as "a bestial groaning" heralding the "final chaos" for which the poet was destined.[28] The compulsion to "return, eat, relate" was accompanied by a violent anxiety evident in the opening poem of *The Truce*, written in January 1946, at the same time that Levi was writing *If This Is a Man*:

23 Ibid., p. 68.
24 Levi, *La Trêve*, trans. E. Genevois-Joly (Paris: Grasset, 1966), p. 61. Eng. trans. as *The Reawakening*, trans. Stuart Woolf, 1965 (reprint ed. New York: Macmillan, 1993).
25 Levi, in Camon, *Conversations avec Primo Levi*, p. 72.
26 Ibid., pp. 49–50.
27 Ibid., p. 72.
28 Levi, *Le Métier des autres*, p. 76.

We have returned home,
Our bellies are full,
Our report is finished.
It is time. Soon we shall hear once more
The foreign command:
"Wstawac."[29]

Testimony is thus torn between two types of anxiety: on the one hand, of not being heard; on the other, of finishing one's account and finding oneself back in the camp. Levi continued his testimony in *The Truce*, published in 1963, after the success of *If This Is a Man*. He published further memories of the camp in *Lilith*, in 1981, and in his last work, *The Drowned and the Saved*, in 1986. In between, having once again taken up his career as a chemist, he also wrote short stories (often based on his dreams[30]), works of fiction, and an autobiography, *The Periodic Table*, which is also an account of his work as a chemist and was written when he was about to retire. At the time he wrote his short stories, he thought he had used up his stock of testimony about the camps and felt the need to express his experience in another form, "by adopting another language" that was more ironic, strident, oblique, and antipoetic.[31] From that time on, notably in about 1977 and more so in around 1984, he gave many interviews expressing a growing pessimism – one in fact justified by the rising phenomenon of negationism, and by a certain deafness on the part of the younger generation and even of his own children, whose language he felt he could no longer speak.

Levi sometimes experienced a certain exhaustion of memory: he could only remember the camps through what he had written, which became a kind of "artificial memory" for him.[32] His first book functioned like a "'prosthetic memory,' an external memory that was interposed between [his] existence today and that of the time," like a "filter" or "barrier."[33] What was left out of what he had written was reduced to "a few details" – or else he claimed to have written only the "Technicolor," while the essential part, on the contrary, was the "everyday gray," the "disintegrated material," impossible to convey, that encircled the prisoners. He reproached himself with having described the life of the Muslims when they had not spoken; this preceded the self-reproaches in *The Drowned and the Saved* for not having taken their place.[34] In *Other People's*

29 Levi, *À une heure incertaine*, p. 20.
30 Levi, *Conversations et entretiens*, p. 205.
31 Ibid., p. 115.
32 Camon, *Conversations avec Primo Levi*, p. 22.
33 Levi, *Conversations et entretiens*, pp. 212, 252.
34 Ibid., p. 213.

Trades he says of writers that they "inevitably end up copying themselves. Silence is more dignified, whether temporary or permanent."[35] One has the impression that he himself arrives at this as the hero of his two short stories "Creative Work" and "In the Park": a writer who creates an autobiographical character, his double and himself, and who finds himself in a "park" with the heroes of all the literary works ever written, then disappears, his body little by little becoming transparent, for this inconsistent literary character has been forgotten in the world.

Back from the *Lager*, the work of memory was living, creative work, an experience of truth that interposed itself between the camp and himself. Testimony was thus a symptom, a work in progress, that supported him. Afterward, however, his books deprived him of his living memory; his literary venture failed to tie the death drive now raging in his conscience into a new sublimation. As in his poem, "The Truce" is over and he remains alone, confronted with the image of the Muslim who has come back like a reminiscence, an imaginary echo of the real.

On Seeing the Gorgon   Discussing the testimonies of the *Sonderkommandos*, Levi wrote in *The Drowned and the Saved*, "It is clear that those things that were said, and the others, countless others, that they must have said among themselves, but that did not get to us, cannot be taken literally."[36] Why, then, should we take him literally in the following much-remarked-on passage:[37]

> We, the survivors, are not the real witnesses. ... we are those who, thanks to prevarication, ability or luck, did not touch the bottom. Those who did, who saw the Gorgon, did not come back to tell us, or came back mute, but it is they, the "Muslims," those who were swallowed up, the complete witnesses, whose depositions would have had general meaning.[38]

Should we then deduce that Levi is not a "real" witness? This is not my reading, but I do read it also, between the lines.

"Seeing the Gorgon means ceasing to be oneself, ceasing to be alive, in order to become like her, the Power of death," says the Hellenic scholar Jean-Pierre

---

35 Levi, *Le Métier des autres*, p. 57.

36 Levi, *Les Naufragés et les rescapés*, p. 53.

37 Especially by Agamben, in *Ce qui reste d'Auschwitz*, p. 105. See also "Testimony and the Real," p. 113, and Anne-Lise Stern, "Passe ('Passe, du camp chez Lacan' II)," in *Essaim: Revue de psychanalyse*, no. 6 (2000): 5–19.

38 Levi, *Les Naufragés et les rescapés*, p. 82.

Vernant.[39] Staring at the mask of the Gorgon means becoming the mask, its double, one's own, in the afterlife. I think Levi experienced seeing the Gorgon, and bore witness to it from 1945 onward:

> Oh lifeless man who was once strong:
> If ever we meet face to face,
> Up there, in the sunlit tenderness of the world,
> How will we look to one another, how?[40]

At around the age of six months, the ego constitutes itself through an identification with the image of the body in the mirror. This occurs through the intervention of a third party, usually the mother, who fixes this identification with the recognition, "That is you."[41] This moment, the "mirror stage," is a moment of jubilation, for the child, who is still dependent on the other in its movements and whose experience is a chaos of different drives, experiences in it an artificial unity. The imaginary relation to other people acquires its ambivalence from this moment, made up of both presence and rivalry. Primary narcissism is constituted here. The image plays a large role in our relation to the other, especially in love; although it is deceptive, it nevertheless masks what it is in the other that fills us with either desire or antipathy, Lacan's object *a* – what we seek to attain, and sometimes to destroy, in the other's image.

Certain subjects experience in madness what Lacan called "the death of the subject." In a catastrophic return to the primordial moment in which the identity is constituted, the relation to the specular other is reduced to "its lethal side." Identity is reduced to a confrontation with the double, as though a "leprous corpse were leading another leprous corpse."[42] The inhuman conditions of the *Lager* could artificially produce a similar experience, with a dual consequence.[43]

On the one hand, on the level of the image, the Muslims appeared as "shells,"[44] men with "lifeless faces,"[45] as undifferentiated ("they disappeared

---

39 Jean-Pierre Vernant, *La Mort dans les yeux* (Paris: Hachette, Textes du XXe siècle, 1990), pp. 80–82.

40 Levi, "Buna," in *À une heure incertaine*, p. 15.

41 Jacques Lacan, "Le Stade du miroir comme formateur du jeu," 1949, in *Écrits* (Paris: Seuil, 1966), p. 93.

42 Lacan, "D'une question préliminaire à tout traitement possible de la psychose," 1958, in *Écrits*, p. 568.

43 The *Sonderkommando* witnesses who testify in *Shoah* also speak of the experience of a subjective death. See S. Felman, "À l'âge du témoignage: *Shoah* de Claude Lanzmann," in Cuau et al., *Au sujet de Shoah*, p. 78.

44 Levi, *Conversations et entretiens*, p. 91.

45 Levi, *À une heure incertaine*, p. 5.

without leaving traces in anyone's memory"), and even as men without faces: "They people my memory with their faceless presence."[46] "There are no mirrors, but our images stand before us, reflected by a hundred livid faces."[47] On the other hand, this image covers the real, the object *a* shall we say, that Levi calls "man in the process of disintegration"[48] or the "nonman," he who, on this side of injustice and murder, which are still human, "has been an object in the eyes of man," "he who allows himself to share his bed with a corpse."[49] I think, then, that Levi experienced such a death of the subject, which indeed inspired a supernatural short story, "A Serene Retirement," in which a piece of apparatus, "the Torec," allows one repeatedly to experience one's own death.[50] This experience of subjective death is expressed again and again, in many forms. "To get used to" or "to get accustomed to" the *Lager* is "to lose one's humanity."[51] Levi insists on the theme of bestiality, cherished by the Nazis to the point of using gas to kill equally people and lice.[52] He describes "the death of the soul" in the prisoners,[53] or "the nonman in whom the divine spark has gone out."[54] He refers to ghosts.[55] This experience of the death of the subject can also be induced from what he wants to say and reproaches himself for being unable to describe on behalf of "those who have been swallowed up": the abolition of space-time;[56] the time that goes mad for Mendel, a character in *If Not Now, When?*;[57] the feeling of chaos, or of "gray and cloudy emptiness";[58] and the oppressive blanks in thought.[59] There are also the references to the formlessness of Genesis and to Dante's Hell, and finally there is the title of Levi's first book, *If This Is a Man*.

---

46 Levi, *Si c'est un homme*, pp. 95–97.
47 Ibid., p. 26.
48 Ibid., p. 95.
49 Ibid., p. 85. A borderline experience that Levi and his friend Arthur almost shared after the departure of the Germans; see Levi, *Si c'est un homme*, p. 185. Jorge Semprún, who was imprisoned in Buchenwald, recounts an analogous experience in *Le Mort qu'il faut* (Paris: Gallimard, 2001), p. 43: he had a Muslim friend, of whom he writes, "This living corpse was a younger brother, perhaps my double, my *Doppelgänger*: another myself or myself as another." It had been planned that he would secretly take the place of this man after his death, in order to escape possibly being put to death by the Nazis himself. He noted down his friend's last words and spent the rest of the night with his corpse. His book is dedicated to this story.
50 Levi, *Histoires naturelles, Vice de forme*, trans. A. Maugé (Paris: Arcades, Gallimard, 1994), p. 223.
51 Levi, *Conversations et entretiens*, p. 228.
52 Ibid., p. 256; Levi, *Le Devoir de mémoire*, p. 66.
53 Levi, *Si c'est un homme*, p. 75; Levi, *Les Naufragés et les rescapés*, p. 59.
54 Levi, *Si c'est un homme*, p. 96.
55 Ibid., p. 173.
56 Ibid., p. 127.
57 Levi, *Conversations et entretiens*, p. 96.
58 Levi, *La Trêve*, p. 245.
59 Anissimov, *Primo Levi ou la tregédie d'un optimiste*, p. 580.

Levi fought with all his might against this experience of death, retaining the desire to "always see in [his] companions and in [himself] men and not things."[60] One sees this especially in the episode in the *Lager* in which he recounts a false dream to Kraus, whom he senses is lost. He tells him he has dreamt of returning to Turin and of receiving Kraus at his home. He thus attributes to him a value of desire, a human value. He himself, progressively and not without suffering, comes out of this state of nonman. First, his meeting with his friend Lorenzo, who has remained a man (he does not live in the *Lager*), makes him feel like a man himself, as though he were reexperiencing the mirror stage.[61] Then, when he regains his status as a chemist, even if a degraded one, in the Buna laboratory, he rediscovers mirrors and sees his reflection in a woman's eyes.[62] When the SS leave, the bonds of speech and exchange, social bonds, are reinstituted between himself and his companions in the infirmary where he has stayed.[63] Finally he rediscovers his childhood home, which "he inhabits like [his own] skin,"[64] and where he will remain for the rest of his life. He also finds love for his wife.

And he begins to write. I am struck by the fact that *If This Is a Man* is composed of portraits of the dead, at least one per chapter: Gattegno (chapter 1), Schlomo (chapter 2), Steinlauf (chapter 3), O18 and Piero (chapter 4), Alberto (chapter 5), etc. In fact Levi wanted to avoid speaking of the living in order to avoid doing them moral violence or giving them a negative image of themselves.[65] In his portraits of those who have disappeared "without leaving traces in anyone's memory," except perhaps his own, he tries, in several collections of writings, to re-create a face over what he saw: a face "the color of death," the mask of the Gorgon. This, he would later say, constituted the hopeless task "of clothing a man in words."[66] This colossal labor – an infinite and indeed impossible work of mourning, since it concerns people beyond number – is in fact the invisible and long work of melancholy of which we spoke earlier. Indeed, the subject has the same profoundly ambivalent relation to the Muslim that one has with one's double in the mirror: with this "*Mitmensch*," this "cohuman,"[67] he

---

60 Levi, *Si c'est un homme*, p. 214.
61 Ibid., p. 130.
62 Ibid., p. 152.
63 Ibid., p. 172.
64 Levi, *Le Métier des autres*, p. 18.
65 Levi, *Le Devoir de mémoire*, p. 24; Levi, *Lilith*, trans. Martine Schruoffeneger (Paris: Liana Levi, 1993), p. 70.
66 Levi, *Le Système périodique*, trans. A. Maugé (Paris: Biblio, Le livre de poche, 1998), pp. 58, 159. Eng. trans. as *The Periodic Table*, trans. Raymond Rosenthal, 1984 (reprint ed. New York: Knopf, 1996).
67 Levi, *Les Naufragés et les rescapés*, pp. 56, 80; Levi, *Le Devoir de mémoire*, p. 30.

was in competition for life. One senses reproach and a certain animosity against O18, who "is no longer a man," and who, indifferent to all, is the cause of a wound to Levi's foot, which has heavy consequences for him.[68] The episode in the passage for October 1944, where he thinks "without any particular emotion" that he owes his life to an error, to an exchange with someone in a better state than he, and then later to his privileged status as a chemist, also indicates this ambivalence, which is later transformed into a melancholic reproach (being "his brother's Cain").[69] One also senses animosity in his revulsion at the idea of seeing some of those who were with him at the camp again, such as "Henri," alias Paul Steinberg, who would also testify to his experience, although only after fifty years of silence.

This ambivalence prevents the subject from separating itself for good from the object *a* that is constituted by the Muslim, the lost object that he cannot abandon. And he feels its presence in the form of a "*Doppelgänger*, a mute and faceless brother" whom he is "condemned to drag" behind him when he writes.[70]

On the one hand, then, there is a dead faceless object that he introjects at the end of a work of melancholia lasting forty years, and that he is finally able to reproach with being mute, in the conscious form of the terrible self-reproach of having never really testified – this from the man everyone had come to know as the "perfect example of the witness." The Freudian superego is avid for such paradoxes. On the other hand, there is a hazy image, "a vile specter," the face of a Muslim, "a negative epiphany,"[71] the mask of the Gorgon who attacks him and kills him at a moment when he is weak and threatened with a new loss.

Conclusion   "The melancholization of witnesses" thus designates the overlapping of two processes. The first is linked to the gap created by any enunciation that attempts to express the real, and to the possibility that imaginary phenomena may arise and be evoked by borderline points between the symbolic (language and speech) and the real. This can happen to anyone who bears witness in an intense or repeated way, or to anyone who talks in psychoanalysis, as soon as

---

68 Levi, *Si c'est un homme*, pp. 44–47.
69 Ibid., p. 137; Levi, *Le Devoir de mémoire*, p. 60.
70 Levi, *Le Métier des autres*, p. 70.
71 A term invented by the photographer Susan Sontag to qualify the permanent impression produced in her by the first photos of the camps during the Liberation; cited in *Mémoires des camps, photographies des camps de concentration et d'extermination nazis* (Paris: Marval, 2001), p. 126.

the traumatic signifiers of his history are evoked. It must be understood that we all have such signifiers in our unconscious, even if we have not experienced extreme situations. The second process, melancholization, is linked, rather, to the experience of tragic loss, terrible suffering, and death in these extreme situations. We have shown that the case of Levi is paradigmatic of the superimposition of these two structures, and of the power that sinister image can acquire, despite the immense work of memory, speech, and writing that the writer undertook.

As a psychoanalyst, I am aware of the therapeutic power of speech to reconstruct and invent, but I also appreciate its limits. It is perhaps useful to draw attention to those limits in the face of the large-scale publication of works of surprising optimism that develop the concept of "resilience," a concept, apparently, that owes a lot to research on trauma undertaken since the Holocaust and the Korean and Vietnam wars. Thus Boris Cyrulnik writes in a recent book, "Resilience is the art of navigating within torrents," and, "Time softens memory and accounts metamorphosize feelings," and even, "A work of fiction that enables the expression of tragedy thereby has a protective effect."[72] To activate this "resilience," which will give meaning to one's experience, one only needs "a helping hand" and "to try to understand." What can one do about the real, though, which is precisely meaningless?

In his book *La Mémoire, l'histoire, l'oubli* (Memory, history, forgetting), "a plea for the defense of memory as a matrix of history,"[73] Paul Ricœur links two roughly contemporaneous Freudian texts, "Mourning and Melancholia" (1916) and "Remembering, Repeating, and Working Through" (1914). He deduces parallels between the "work of mourning" and the "work of memory," on the one hand, and between melancholy and passages to action, on the other. These two pairs are moreover opposed: one is either on the side of memory and mourning or, on the contrary, on the side of melancholy and passages to action.[74] This reading could be improved, it seems to me, if it took into account Freudian contributions after 1920 that pose the death drive as something inevitable and that complicate this opposition. The simple fact of speaking and trying to remember – in analytic treatment, of course, but I think one can extend this to testimony – brings to light, in the form of uncontrollable repetition, experiences that "even at the time could not bring satisfaction" and that the subject cannot remember.[75] It is indeed the account itself and the

72 Boris Cyrulnik, *Les Vilains petits canards* (Paris: Odile Jacob, 2001), pp. 259–61.
73 Paul Ricœur, *La Mémoire, l'histoire, l'oubli* (Paris: Seuil, 2000), p. 106.
74 Ibid., pp. 83–89.
75 Freud, "Au-delà du principe de plaisir," 1920, in *Essais de psychanalyse* (Paris: PBP, Payot, 1981), p. 60. Eng. trans. as *Beyond the Pleasure Principle* (New York: W. W. Norton & Company, 1990).

effort to remember that, in place of memories, can induce a passage to action linked to trauma, a real that has therefore been ejected from the symbolic, as we said earlier.

It is indispensable that witnesses and victims should speak, be heard, and transmit their historical experience, but let us not forget the risks they thereby run. We should also the fact that the German word for the "reconciliation" with the repressed of which Freud speaks in 1914 is *Versöhnung*, whose meaning has been extended to the idea of a compromise but which has the same root as *Sühne*, expiation or indeed sacrifice.

Translated from the French by Beatrice Khiara

Sagas of Victory, Memories of Defeat?
The Long Afterlife of an Indo-Muslim Warrior Saint, 1033–2000

Shahid Amin

It may seem odd to stand here, three miles from where the apostle of nonviolence was assassinated, and talk about a medieval warrior saint. For surely Gandhi's life and the brief of this conference point in the direction of forgetting and forgiveness, ministering to the aggrieved memories of the past with the balm of reconciliation and an empowering narrative. The title of my paper seems to hark back to early-medieval pillage and conquest, that unlovely period of our past when Turkish horsemen supposedly laid North India waste, looting and destroying temples as a matter of course.

The road that has brought me from 30 January Marg, the street where Gandhi was gunned down in 1948, to this conference at Lodhi Road, named after the Muslim dynasty that was snuffed out by Babur, the founder of the Mughal empire, is in a sense the same road that Hindu majoritarianism has traveled since the mid-1980s, but to a very different destination. For the Hindu majoritarian, one of whom killed Gandhi, it leads to the city of Ayodhya and to the destruction on December 6, 1992, of Babur's mosque, which a "Hindu nation" seeks to reclaim as the birthplace of their own Lord Rama. Eight years after the fact, a judicial commission is still sifting through the "truths" of that event, which in my view is as important a landmark as August 15, 1947, when India gained its independence. And if I am inserting this date from late in 1992 into our national calendar, it is not out of a gnawing sense of outrage: a nation is not only what it remembers but equally what its nationals are "obliged already to have forgotten," Ernest Renan wrote famously in the early 1880s.[1] The dictum still holds, and I am an Indian national.

Politicians at the helm of contemporary India have dubbed this day, December 6, alternatively as a "sad day" and as a "manifestation of national sentiment." Every anniversary of the demolition will no doubt bring out the customary

---

1 Joseph Ernest Renan, quoted in Benedict Anderson, "Narrating the Nation," *Times Literary Supplement*, June 23, 1986. An English translation of Renan's "What Is a Nation" appears in Homi Bhabha, ed., *Nation and Narration* (London: Routledge, 1990).

trading of charges and countercharges, while the business of running a fractured
Indian polity will continue as usual. How the interplay between remembering
and forgetting will work out in this particular case in the long run has, I suggest,
enormous consequences for India as a nation state. And that is why I wish to
invoke December 6, 1992, to help frame what I have to say about my medieval
warrior saint.

"India has a majority of Hindus" is of course a descriptive truism that does
not in itself lead to majoritarianism. It could be and in fact has been the beginning of a number of sentences that have elaborated on this ground reality so as
to produce very different statements. I could give some examples from the
1950s to the 1970s, from the first twenty to thirty years of the life of the Indian
republic, and of my own for that matter. For example,

> 1. India has a majority of Hindus, yet the Hindus themselves are internally differenti-
> ated socially, economically, linguistically, and by regions.
> 2. India has a majority of Hindus, yet there are a large number of Muslims, Sikhs, and
> Jains as well.
> 3. India has a majority of Hindus, yet at the level of everyday life here there is a great deal
> of overlapping with the other communities; the Indian national movement, the legacy of
> Gandhi, the spirit and the structure of the Indian constitution, and the very Idea of India
> are all based on the recognition not only of the Hindus but of the Others as well.

Hindu India and the Indian nation were not interchangeable in those years,
because the numerical brute force of that descriptive phrase *India has a majority
of Hindus* was mitigated by the refusal to allow it the status of a self-evident
statement. The phrase met its denouement in a "yet" or "but" to generate the
idea of a plural, nonmajoritarian India.

A crucial change has taken place over the past fifteen years or so: since the
mid-1980s, majoritarian politics has institutionalized itself by doing away with
these qualifiers and insisting on a narrow elaboration of the earlier phrase. Now
it goes something like this: *India has a majority of Hindus ...* and the reconfig-
ured Hindus have to be the subject of all subsequent sentences that follow from
this original sentence. Thus: India has a majority of Hindus who have to recon-
figure the nation; and who have been misled into forgetting this basic fact; and
who have been denied their prior due in the nation state; and who have been at
the receiving end of History for an entire millennium, from the beginning of
Turkish invasions and conquest, c. A.D. 1000–1200, to the present. In a word,
the replacement of a qualifying "but" by an insistent "and" changes a descriptive
truism into a majoritarian battering ram. It is obvious that such a move has
enormous consequences for our past, present, and future.

The logic of majoritarianism is of course to enforce the idea of the singularity of a narrowly majoritarian-national history. In this, majoritarianism shares a certain ground with nationalism, but there are important divergences as well. Both are committed to an accredited version of the past – the majoritarian and the nationalist past respectively. But while both seek to construct a sense of an uncluttered national past, the national past for the nationalist is not confined to the defeats and victories of any one community; for the votaries of majoritarianism in India, on the other hand, the past, present, and future of India belong largely to the life of the Hindus.

Revulsion against the idea of a cluttered national past is almost visceral with the majoritarian nationalist, for it disorders a history that is considered singular. It needs stressing that in a certain basic sense the majoritarian in India (as elsewhere) cannot recall a narrow "national history" without cleansing and avenging it. In the Indian case the enactment of a historical vendetta against the Muslim conquerors of precolonial India becomes simultaneously the condition for the realization of Indian history and for demarcating the natural citizens of post-Partition, independent India. According to this view, the citizens of the nation have, at the very least, to give assent to the forging of a "New Hindu History" whose positivist base is alloyed crucially with religious belief and nuggets dug out from the seams of a "common memory."[2]

I   The politics of the imagination of "Hindu India" have depended crucially on a particular reading of the oppression of the disunited denizens of India by Muslim conquerors and rulers from the eleventh century until the establishment of British rule in the mid-eighteenth century.

> Believing in four Vedas, six Shastras, eighteen Puranas and thirty-three core *devtas,* Hindus, to begin with, were differentiated according to *bhav-bhesh-bhasha* (language, beliefs and customs), and then the Mahabharata caused further havoc. The one or two germs of valor that remained were finished off by the ahimsa of Lord Buddha. ... Our ferociousness simply disappeared, our sense of pride deserted us, and as for anger, all sorts of sins were laid at its door. The result: we became *devtas, mahatmas,* or for that matter nice fellows *(bhalmanus),* but our spunk, we lost that. No fire, no spark, simply cold ash, that's what we became: *"Nihshankam deepte lokaih pashya bhasmchye padam."*
>
>   And on the other side in the desert of Arabia a soul appeared who was brave as his

---

2 See Gyanendra Pandey, "The New Hindu History," in *After Ayodhya,* special issue of *South Asia,* 17 (1994): 97–112.

word, and in whose new religion killing, slaughtering, fighting and marauding were the principal elements.[3]

Thus wrote Mannan Prasad Dwivedi, Bhojpuri poet, Hindi novelist, and writer of nationalist prose in an impressive two-part *History of Muslim Rule [in India]*, commissioned by the Hindi-nationalist Kashi Nagari Pracharini Sabha in 1920.

There are obvious continuities here with what Partha Chatterjee has called the "new nationalist history of India" written in Bengali in the late nineteenth century. These vernacular histories transmitted the stereotypical figure of "the Muslim," endowed with a "national character": fanatical, bigoted, warlike, dissolute, cruel.[4] Chatterjee writes:

> This distinct history originates in and acquires its identity from the life of Muhammad. In other words, the dynasty that will be founded in Delhi at the beginning of the thirteenth century and the many political changes that will take place in the subsequent five centuries are not to be described merely as the periods of Turko-Afghan or Mughal rule in India: they are integral parts of the political history of Islam.
>
> The actors in this history are also given certain behavioral characteristics. They are warlike and believe that it is their religious duty to kill infidels. Driven by the lust for plunder and the visions of cohabiting with the nymphs of paradise, they are even prepared to die in battle. They are not merely conquerors, but "delirious at the prospect of conquest" *(digvijayonmatta),* and consequently are by their innate nature covetous of the riches of India.[5]

"Jin javanan tuv dharam nari dhan tinhon linhaun": "You Muslim-foreigners! You have robbed us [Hindus] of [our] dharma, women, and wealth," wrote the North Indian Hindi poet Bhartendu Harishchandra in 1888, echoing the stereotypical recollection of Muslim conquest and its effect on a Hindu India.[6] Implied in this memorable couplet by one of the founders of modern Hindi is a conflation of the foreigner-Turk conquerors of North India with the entire population of Muslims in India.

There have been a series of retorts to this "communalization of history," as it is called in South Asia, the term "communal" implying an adherence to narrow reli-

---

3 Mannan Prasad Dwivedi, *Muslamani Rajya ka Itihas, pahila bhag,* ed. Shyam Sundar Das (Varanasi: Kashi Nagari Pracharini Sabha, 1920), pp. 1–2.

4 Partha Chatterjee, *The Nation and Its Fragments: Colonial and Postcolonial Histories* (Princeton, N.J.: Princeton University Press, 1993), p. 102.

5 Ibid., p. 99.

6 Bhartendu Harishchandra, quoted in Sudhir Chandra, *The Oppressive Present: Literature and Social Consciousness in Colonial India* (New Delhi: Oxford University Press, 1992), p. 123.

gio-sectarian loyalties that color and impede the development of a properly contextualized historical past and a composite cultural present.[7] The most powerful
(and very nearly the first) such critique came from Professor Mohammad Habib,
of Aligarh Muslim University, who in a series of essays penned between 1931 and
1952 sought to counter the communalization of India's medieval history from a
broadly Marxist perspective.[8] Habib's ire was directed particularly against the par-
tisan-political scholarship of British administrator-"orientalists" who had consistently projected the "Muslim India" of c. 1000–1700 as a period of oppression
and fanaticism from which colonial rule had at last liberated (Hindu) India.

Habib countered by arguing that the "real motives of the plundering expeditions" of the beginning of the eleventh century, associated with the name of the
notorious despoiler of northern India, Mahmud of Ghazni, "was greed for treas-
ure and gold. The iconoclastic pretensions were meant only for the applause of
the gallery." The Muslims of India were not so much the progeny of Turkish
conquerors, he wrote, as local converts from the artisanal classes, socially and
spatially at the margins of both Hindu society and early medieval towns; and
"an Indian Muslim had as little chance of becoming a warlord of the empire of
Delhi as a Hindu *Sudra* [low caste] of ascending a Rajasthan throne" occupied
by Hindu rajas. More important for Habib, "Such limited success as Islam
achieved in India [as a proselytizing force] was not due to its kings and politicians but to its saints."[9]

> With a new faith everything depends upon the method of its presentation; and if Islam
> in this land had worn no other aspect except the conquering hordes of Ghazni, it
> would not have been accepted even by a minority of people. But Islam had nobler and
> better representatives, who far from the atmosphere of court and camps lived the hum-
> ble life of humble people according to the *Sunnat* of the Prophet to whom "his poverty
> was his pride." And Hinduism in its cosmopolitan outlook enrolled the Muslim mys-
> tics among its *rishis,* and neighborly feelings soon developed a common calendar of
> saints. So it was in the thirteenth century and so it remains today.[10]

For Habib, one of the founders of a "scientific history" of medieval India, syncretism was an engrained characteristic of the land marked by a shared cultural

7 For an important statement of this idea, see Romila Thapar, Harbans Mukhia, and Bipan Chandra,
    Communalism and the Writing of Indian History (New Delhi: People's Publishing House, 1969).
8 See Mohammad Habib, *Politics and Society during the Early Medieval Period: Collected Works of
    Professor Mohammad Habib,* ed. K. A. Nizami (New Delhi: People's Publishing House, 1974),
    1:3–122.
9 Ibid., pp. 21, 116, and 22–23 respectively.
10 Ibid., p. 23.

space. "The Indo-Muslim mystics, without perhaps consciously knowing it, followed the footsteps of their great Hindu predecessors."[11] Habib's efforts were to blunt the "Sword of Islam" motif in the construction of the Indian past in both the colonial and the immediately postcolonial present. To trace Indian history as a sort of religious genealogy of India's present-day Muslims, he argued, was to do both the nation and its largest minority a grievous historical wrong.

> It is a grave injustice to the Musalmans of India to judge them by the character of their kings, for whom they were in no way responsible, while their religious leaders, their artists and poets, who exercised an immeasurably greater influence over them, are ignored.[12]

The colonial masters, however, had mischievously conceived the task of history primers in colonial India as disseminating dissension and "communal hatred" between the subject population. To this end,

> The peaceful Indian Musalman, descended beyond doubt from Hindu ancestors, was dressed up in the garb of a foreign barbarian as a breaker of temples and as an eater of beef and declared to be a military colonist in the land where he had lived for about thirty to forty centuries. All the opposite vices were attributed to the Hindu; weak, emaciated from the excessive heat of the Indian plain, quiet in his manners, unambitious in his outlook, he was obviously a fit object for "stratagems and spoils" and had no right to complain when conquered by more virile races from colder climes.
>
> Year after year, thoughtless school-masters have instilled these ideas into the impressionable minds of their pupils; year after year, boys who could not repeat these noxious platitudes in their examinations were ploughed [failed]. The result of it is seen in the communalistic atmosphere of India today.
>
> The Hindu feels it his duty to dislike those whom he has been taught to consider the enemy of his religion and his ancestors; the Musalman, *lured into the false belief that he was once a member of a ruling race*, feels insufferably wronged by being relegated to the status of a minority community. Fools both! Even if the Musalmans eight centuries ago were as bad as they are painted, would there be any sense in holding the present generation responsible for their deeds? It is but an imaginative [i.e., imaginary] tie that joins the modern Hindu with Harshvardhana or Asoka, or the modern Musalman with Shihabuddin or Mahmud.[13]

---

11 Ibid., p. 22.
12 Ibid.
13 Ibid., p. 12. I have broken this long passage into smaller paragraphs. Emphasis in original.

In this moving passage, written in 1931, Habib sketches the essentials of what amounts to much of the professional secular-national view on medieval India. Not that there have been no efforts to counter this perspective by discovering the existence of a "Hindu India" in the thirteenth century.[14] Not that all history primers in independent India have been free of sectarian orientation, intention, and effect. Rather, the two strands, which could loosely be termed the secular-national and the sectarian-Hindu, have come to occupy different terrains.

The result is that every time the "fact" of Turkish conquest of "Hindu India" and of a homogenous and eternal Hindu community/nation asserts itself in public discourse, as has happened over the past fifteen years, this receives a predictable riposte. First, the suppositions behind the claim for homogeneity within a segmented and hierarchical Hindu society are shown to be untenable. The second and by now equally traditional response is to stress the long trend of tolerance, mutual respect, and crossings in India's national past. In an impassioned piece written in early 1993, Amartya Sen argued for this position as follows:

> The heritage of contemporary India combines Islamic influences with Hindu and other traditions. ... The point is not simply that so many major contributions to Indian culture have come from Islamic writers, musicians, and painters, but also that their works are thoroughly integrated with those of the Hindus. Indeed, even Hindu religious beliefs and practices have been substantially influenced by contacts with Islamic ideas and values. The impact of Islamic Sufi thought, for example, is readily recognized in parts of contemporary Hindu literature. Even films on Hindu themes frequently rely on Muslim writers and actors.[15]

II   In representative accounts such as Sen's, the Turkish conquest of North India is either assimilated to the history of the establishment of a centralized agrarian state (the Delhi Sultanate, c. 1200) or it gets written over by the longer and gentler history of Indian syncretism. In most writings syncretism is posited as an innate characteristic of the people inhabiting the Gangetic heartland and peninsular India. A part of the "age-old moral and spiritual traditions of our people," it delineates a way of being-in-the-world, one marked by emotive floral, faunal, and cultural signifiers. Syncretism in such an understanding is not a historical process, a product of coming to terms with events: political conquest

---

14 See K. M. Munshi, "Foreword," in R. C. Majumdar, ed., *The History and Culture of the Indian People*, vol. V: *The Struggle for Empire* (Bombay: Bhartiya Vidya Bhavan, 1957), pp. vii–xxix.

15 Amartya Sen, "Threats to Indian Secularism," *The New York Review of Books*, April 8, 1993, p. 30.

and the otherworldly challenge posed to the indigenous *jogis* by what must have seemed like *arriviste* Sufis. Syncretism springs, fully formed as it were, from the same "sacred land where the black gazelles graze, the *munja* grass grows and the *paan* leaf is eaten, and where the material and the spiritual are organically intermixed." I take these evocative markers of India's sacred topology from Habib's powerful address to the Indian History Congress in the immediate aftermath of Independence and Partition.[16]

But we know that the medieval Sufis, though gentle in their persona, especially in archetypal opposition to the "holy warrior," had to carve out forcefully their spiritual domain against the already existent authority of Hindu *jogis*. Hagiographies constantly harp on contests between the Sufi and the *jogi* for spiritual supremacy, contests in which the *jogi* is invariably worsted: he either converts, along with his disciples, or retires, leaving the Sufi in triumphant possession of a prior holy and tranquil spot (often by a lake). One of India's most venerable Sufis, Muinuddin Chishti of Ajmer, is said to have established his *khanqah* (hospice) only after successfully overcoming ogres and warriors attached to a preexisting site commanded by a *jogi* and his entourage.[17]

Sometimes all that remains of the prepossessing *jogi* is a wisp of a name, carrying the toponymic stigma of a "historic" defeat for all to utter. Many place names in the Gangetic heartland enshrine the memory of such holy victories and defeats, though I am far from arguing that every time a local mentions, say, the name Maunathbhanjan, he or she necessarily recollects the destruction (*bhanjan*) of the lord and master (*nath*) of Mau, a thriving manufacturing town near Banaras since the seventeenth century. In other cases the worsted spiritual master is transformed into an ogre by the sheer act of transcription from one language to another. While the Sanskrit *dev* stands for a god, or the title of a revered person, when written in Persian without this gloss the word *deo* stands for a ghost, demon, or monster. Spiritually and linguistically mastered, the holyharmful figure often submits before the majestic Sufi, who grants him the last wish of his subservience being recorded for posterity in terms of a trace, either in a place name or as a visible marker of a suitably monstrous sort. At the Bahraich shrine of Salar Masaud Ghazi in northeastern Uttar Pradesh, the earrings of the subdued *deo* Nirmal are the size of grindstones.

---

16 Habib, "Presidential Address to the Indian History Congress," Bombay, December 1947, in *Politics and Society during the Early Medieval Period*, 1:113–14.

17 The best discussions of the theme of the *jogi*-Sufi contest appear in the writings of Simon Digby. For an overview see Digby, "Sufi Shaykh as a Source of Authority in Delhi Sultanat," *Purushartha* 9 (1986): 57–77; for detailed treatments see Digby, "Encounters with Jogis in Indian Sufi Hagiography," SOAS, University of London, unpublished paper, January 27, 1970, and "Jogis and Sufis," unpublished ms. I am grateful to Digby for allowing me to read this work in manuscript.

These are some of the ways in which eventful encounters between the holy men of Islam and of the Hindus get enshrined in the life histories of popular Sufi sites. And of course these shrines attract both Hindus and Muslims as devotees. Let me clarify. My point is not to deny the composite following of India's justly famous Sufi saints. All I wish to do, as I broach my argument about the warrior saint, is to create an analytic space for encounter, clash, and conquest as necessary elements of the conflictual prehistory of such cultic sites as that of Nizamuddin Auliya, medieval and modern Delhi's greatest Sufi saint. Wrathful, hypostatical, miraculous events and encounters, I am suggesting, not simply a longstanding Indian spirit of accommodation, go into the making of India's vaunted syncretism. Or, to put it sharply: accommodation is predicated necessarily on a prior clash of two opposing wills. The hermetically cloistered figures of rosary-fondling Sufis and saber-rattling *ghazis* (saints and warriors), even when yoked to the cause of good pluralistic politics, produce bad history. And I say this because, faced as we are with an insistence on the clash between Islam and Hinduism in India's medieval past, historians need to fashion newer histories of this encounter, never mind if our best Delhi Sufi turns out to be not so gentle after all.

III   The shared worship of worthies – heroes, warriors, saints – by a multireligious populace is rightly portrayed in most writings as evidence of the remarkable composite "religiosity" of the Indian masses. Muinuddin Chishti of Ajmer, Nizamuddin Auliya of Delhi, Khwaja Khizr, the patron saint of boatmen after whom the Kidderpore docks at Calcutta are named – all have received their fair share in most scholarly accounts on Indian Islam.[18] These personages continue to have their importance in the uncertain India of today. But the focus on syncretism *sans* conflict amounts to taking only half a step. And this is so because our concentration on intercommunal goodwill and harmony, though necessary, leaves the field of sectarian strife as the special preserve of sectarian and "communal" historians. Mine is a plea for essaying nonsectarian histories of conquest and conflict.

My plea for nonsectarian histories of the Turkish conquest is not an effort to produce a "historically correct" solution to the recent rise of Hindu majoritari-

18 See Garcin de Tassy, *Mémoire sur des particularités de la religion musulmane dans l'Inde d'après les ouvrages hindoustani* (Paris, 1831), Eng. trans. and ed. M. Waseem as *Muslim Festivals in India and Other Essays* (New Delhi: Oxford University Press, 1995); William Crooke, *The Popular Religion and Folklore of Northern India* (2nd ed. London, 1896, reprint ed. New Delhi: Munshiram Manoharlal, 1978); and Mohammad Mujeeb, *Indian Muslims* (London: Allen & Unwin, 1967), chapter I.

anism in India. Rather, it is to introduce some nuance into the relationship between "facts of history," popular remembrance, and matters of belief. Only by this means can one mount a historiographic challenge to the natural-and-necessary connection between mutilated memories (of the past) and cathartic violence (in the present) made by the votaries of majoritarianism.

My argument is fairly simple, and goes as follows. If the sites of the martyrdom of Islam's holy warriors in India are equally the sites of long-lasting, syncretic, multireligious cults, then clearly this is attributable neither to popular amnesia nor to the triumph of thaumaturgy over "facts and history." The narratives of Muslim warrior saints retailed by balladeers, which bear a complicated relationship with the more standard hagiographies, are evidence of the refashioning of sagas of "religious" conflict in order to create communities in the past and in the present. To focus exclusively on the syncretism of such cults, without taking on board the narrative refashionings of conquest that these invariably entail, is to miss out on the creation of India's vaunted composite culture as a process. It is also to hitch popular remembrance to the temporal career of superstition, while remaining impervious to the literary, cultural, and mnemonic devices through which popular assent is generated across religious divides.

IV   There are many Muslim warrior saints and saintly shrines scattered over India. Numerous place names with the prefix "Ghazi," humble shrines of "manly martyrs" (*shaheed mard*), mass graves (*ganj-i-shaheedan*), folklore, and genealogies of camp followers testify to the widespread memorialization of Ghazis and Shaheeds (warriors and martyrs) in both North and South India.[19] We are concerned here with the most popular and intriguing of such warrior saints: Syed Salar Masaud Ghazi, also known as Ghazi Miyan – the nephew of Mahmud of Ghazni, the notorious early eleventh-century despoiler of northern India.

There is little dispute that Mahmud's seventeen incursions into northern and western India resulted in widespread plunder and destruction. Writing in the train of his conquest, the great eleventh-century astronomer and savant Al Beruni also seems to have uncannily predicted the path of the memories of Mahmud Ghazni's invasions:

> Mahmud utterly ruined the prosperity of the country, and performed there wonderful exploits, by which the Hindus became like atoms of dust scattered in all directions, and

---

19 For a recent overview see Sanjay Subrahmanyam, "Before the Leviathan: Sectarian Violence and State in Precolonial India," in Kaushik Basu and Subrahmanyam, eds., *Unravelling the Nation: Sectarian Conflict and India's Secular Identity* (New Delhi: Penguin Books, 1996).

like a tale of old in the mouth of the people. Their scattered remains cherish, of course, the most inveterate aversion towards all Muslims.[20]

This sentiment has been echoed in every British and consequently nationalist "History of India," beginning with Tarinicharan Chattopadhyay's *Bharatversher Itihas*, written in Bengali in 1858. "Of all the Muslims," wrote Chattopadhyay, "it was [Mahmud's] aggression which first brought devastation and disarray to India, and from that time the freedom of the Hindus has diminished and faded like the phases of the moon."[21] Mahmud is the familiar conqueror-villain of history books just as he is the idealized supreme iconoclast of Indo-Islamic Persian chronicles, panegyrics, and treatises on governance.[22]

Paradoxically, in Abdur Rahman Chishti's Persian hagiography, assiduously translated and commented upon in the late nineteenth and twentieth centuries as well as in ballads sung over large stretches of the Gangetic plain, Ghazi Miyan is made to stand in place of Mahmud as the premier Muslim conqueror saint of North India. Martyred at the young age of nineteen in 1033, at Bahraich in northeastern Uttar Pradesh, bordering Nepal, Ghazi Miyan is absent from all standard chronicles and histories of the Sultan of Ghazni. Officially absent from History, Masaud Ghazi, Ghazi Miyan, Bale Miyan, or Ghazi Dulha (the Ghazi Bridegroom) nevertheless has an overwhelming popular presence. The cultic gathering of "commoners" at his tomb in Bahraich has remained an annual affair ever since the great North African traveler Ibn Battuta visited the shrine in 1341, along with the Sultan of Delhi, and found it too crowded for comfort.[23]

20 Al Beruni, as quoted in Edward C. Sachau, ed., *Alberuni's India*, 1888 (reprint ed. Delhi: Low Price Publications, 1993), p. 22.

21 Tarinicharan Chattopadhyay, quoted in Chatterjee, *The Nation and Its Fragments*, pp. 103–4.

22 See Richard H. Davis, *Lives of Indian Images* (Princeton, N.J.: Princeton University Press, 1997), chapter 3.

23 See *The Rehla of Ibn Battuta*, trans. and ed. Mehdi Husain (Baroda: Gaekwad Oriental Series, 1953), pp. 109–11; M. Hedayet Hosain, "Ghazi Miyan," *Encyclopaedia of Islam* (Old Series, 1927), 2:152; Nizami, "Ghazi Miyan," *Encyclopaedia of Islam* (New Series, 1991), 3:1047–48, and Digby, "Mas'ud," *Encyclopaedia of Islam* (New Series, 1991), 7:783–84; Kerrin Schwerin, "Saint Worship in Indian Islam: The Legend of the Martyr Salar Masud Ghazi," in Imitiaz Ahmad, ed., *Ritual and Religion among Muslims in India* (New Delhi: Manohar, 1981), pp. 143–61; and Tahir Mahmood, "The Dragah of Sayyid Salar Masud Ghazi in Bahraich: Legend, Tradition and Reality," in Christian W. Troll, ed., *Muslim Shrines in India: Their Character, History, Significance* (New Delhi: Oxford University Press, 1989), pp. 44–43. For a detailed consideration of the cult of Ghazi Miyan in Nepal and in North India generally, see the following writings by Marc Gaborieau: "Légende et culte du saint musulman Ghazi Miyan au Nepal Occidental et en Inde du Nord," *Objets et Mode* 15, no. 3 (1975): 289–312; "The Cult of Saints among the Muslims in Nepal and Northern India," in S. Wilson, ed., *Saints and Their Cults: Studies in Religious Sociology, Folklore and History* (Cambridge: Cambridge University Press, 1983,) pp. 291–308; and "Les Saints, les eaux et les récoltes en Inde," in Mohammad Ali Amir Moezzi, ed., *Lieux d'Islam. Cultes et cultures de l'Afrique à Java* (Paris: Autrement, 1996), pp. 239–54.

There is little dispute about the popularity of Ghazi Miyan over the past 650 years. Visits by the Delhi Sultans of the Tughlaq dynasty, attempts by the Lodhis in the early sixteenth century to control the free mixing of the sexes at the huge summer fair in Bahraich, anecdotes about the personal interest of the Mughal emperor Akbar in the large contingents undertaking the long 500-kilometer journey from the imperial capital Agra, near Delhi, to Bahraich are all on record.[24] The attempt by a prominent Sufi savant recognized by the Mughal court to pen an authoritative hagiography can be read, as I shall presently argue, as an attempt to rein in and canalize the legends about the youthful warrior saint into an orthodox "Sword of Islam" story. Popular proverbs, nineteenth-century geography primers and children's encyclopedias, census records about the religious affiliation of the humble folk, historical novels set in the eastern Uttar Pradesh countryside abutting the Hindu pilgrimage cities of Banaras and Ayodhya – all refer as a matter of course to the ubiquitous presence of Ghazi Miyan in popular consciousness.[25] Tulsidas, the great sixteenth-century Awadhi poet and "author" of the popular rendering of the Rama legend, wryly commented on the blind popular belief in the healing and redeeming powers of the shrine of Ghazi Miyan:

lahi aankh kab aandhre, baanjh puut kab biyaae;
kab korhi kaayaa lahi, jag bahraich jaaye

[Who has seen the blind regain sight, and which barren woman has been delivered of a son; which leper has regained his limbs – yet the entire world keeps heading for Bahraich][26]

24 See Iqtidar Husain Siddiqui, "A Note on the Dargah of Salar Masaud in Bahraich in the Light of Standard Historical Sources," in Troll, ed., *Muslim Shrines in India*, pp. 44–47.
25 See entry for *ghazi* in S. W. Fallon, *A New Hindustani Dictionary*, 1879 (reprint ed. Lucknow: Uttar Pradesh Urdu Akedmi, 1986); Mannan Dwivedi Gajpuri, *Ram Lal: grameen jeevan ka ek ssmajik upanyas* (Prayag: Indian Press, 1917), pp. 15–16; Qurratulain Hyder, *Chandni Begam*, Hindi trans. Wahajuddin Ahmed (Nai Dilli: Bhartiya Gyanpeeth Prakashan, 1997), p. 201; *Awadh Deshiya Bhugol, jismein awadh desh ki prithvi aur sthan aadi ke vritant nutan anveshan ke anusar atyant sugam bhasha mein chote-chote vidyarthiyon ke liye sanyukt hain*, Urdu original by Shiv Narain, *ultha* (translation) in Hindi *bhasha* by Pandit Magan Lal (Lucknow: Naval Kishore Press, 1872), p. 37; *Shishubodh* (Lucknow, 1878), a children's encyclopedia – published under the authority of the Director of Public Instruction, Awadh – containing fifty-eight lessons ranging from Pronouns to the British Museum, from Galileo to Newton Sahib, and describing Bahraich in lesson thirty, an account of the Province of Awadh; *Census of North Western Provinces & Oudh Report*, 1891, pp. 216–18; *Census of North Western Provinces & Oudh Report*, 1901, part III: *Provincial Tables and Appendices*, table VI, cols. 8 and 9 (worshippers of Panchon Pir); and *Araish-i-Mahfil, Being a History, in the Hindoostanee Language of the Hindoo Princes of Dihlee from Joodishtur to Pithoura. Compiled from Khoolasut-ool-Hind and Other Authorities by Meer Sher Ulee Ufsos, Head Moonshee in the Hindustanee Department of the College* (Calcutta: Hindoostanee Press, 1808), pp. 97–98.

Such was the popularity of Ghazi Miyan into the twentieth century that "small Bahraichs" were created in several Uttar Pradesh towns where either the Ghazi himself or one of his lieutenants had seen action in the early eleventh century! Identical fairs were held here, spread over huge grounds dedicated for the purpose. It was rare indeed for such sites to be let out for another public use. When Gandhi reached the sprawling district of Gorakhpur to address a mammoth nationalist meeting on February 8, 1921, just a year and fifteen miles away from Chauri Chaura, it was at the huge Ghazi Miyan fairground that the Mahatma was welcomed and heard.[27]

My argument is not dependent on establishing a proven thaumaturgy, an authentic genealogy, or a credible chronology for Syed Salar Masaud Ghazi; it is the construction of his figure as India's premier Muslim warrior saint that concerns us here.[28] The central text is Abdur Rahman Chishti's *Mirat-i-Masaudi* (c. 1611), which retails the military exploits of this *Sultan-us Shuhda* (King or prince of martyrs) in the cause of Islam in northern, western, and northeastern India, ending with his untimely death at Bahraich in A.D. 1033.[29]

In this Persian hagiography, written by a prolific Sufi savant of central Uttar Pradesh, Salar Masaud appears as the nephew of Mahmud of Ghazni. Conceived in the holy city of Ajmer, Masaud grows up as a youthful holy figure with a Jesus-like countenance, destined to "take possession of a country which has not fallen into the hands of any Musalman." He "excelled in all the arts" at a very young age, was "pure of body and mind," and had a preference for chewing the betel nut, something particular to India:

26 Tulsidas, *Dohavali*, quoted in Abdul Bismillah, *Madhyakalin Hindi Kavya mein Sanskritik Samanvaya* (Allahabad: Hindustani Akedmi, 1985), p. 59. For a contemporary echo of this couplet see Hyder, *Chandni Begam*, p. 185.

27 Shahid Amin, "Gandhi as Mahatma: Gorakhpur District, Eastern Uttar Pradesh, 1921–22," in Ranajit Guha, ed., *Subaltern Studies* (New Delhi: Oxford University Press, 1984), 3:1.

28 Commenting on the historicity of these claims, Subrahmanyam has observed, "Historians today largely reject any connection between Masaud and Sultan Mahmud, arguing that at the date given for his death in the hagiographies (A.D.1033), Muslim warriors simply could not have penetrated as far as the Bahraich region. Such arguments … must be treated with a little caution, since stray expeditions over even several hundred kilometers are not totally out of the realm of possibility." See Basu and Subrahmanyam, eds., *Unravelling the Nation*, p. 68. See also Siddiqui, "A Note on the Dargah of Salar Masaud in Bahraich," pp. 44–47. Nizami seems to imply that Salar Masaud may have made his raid into the Nepal foothills from one of the pockets of Muslim settlement that existed outside the fortified Gangetic valley towns in the eleventh to twelfth centuries. See Nizami, *Some Aspects of Religion and Politics in India during the Thirteenth Century* (Aligarh: Department of History, Muslim University, 1951), pp. 76–77.

29 I have used the English translation of *Mirat-i-Masaudi* in *The History of India as Told by Its Own Historians: Posthumous Papers of the Late H. M. Elliot*, 1896 (reprint ed. Calcutta: Sushil Gupta, 1953), 2:103–45, and the slightly fuller English manuscript translation by R. B. Chapman, Additional Manuscript, no. 30776, British Library, London.

He was constantly performing ablutions, though if he had prayed
without bathing, so pure was he in body and mind, it would
not have been wrong. He had clean carpets spread where
he was wont to sit, he wore pure garments and delighted in
fragrant essences and eating betel nut.[30]

While Masaud Ghazi is pious and virtuous, the Hindu rajas he subdues are
treacherous. The raja of Rawal tries to poison him with all manner of food.
Masaud spurns the raja's offer to "eat the food he had prepared for his party"
with a retort: "The Prophets never ate food prepared in the house of a Hindu,
nor will I!" Satgun, the raja, then entreats him to "take sugar, rice and all things
necessary, and have his food prepared by his own cooks," thereby maintaining
both his own Islamic as well as Hindu notions of purity, but even this offer is
turned down. Satgun then brings huge quantities of sweets – which are commonly acceptable across caste barriers – but Masaud "with divine perception
suspects the truth" and offers them to some dogs, who instantly die. Masaud
turns back and attacks the raja in the town of Rawal: "unable to withstand …
the brave youths" led by the twelve-year old Masaud, "the unbelievers … were
routed, and the Faithful scattered their heads in every street."[31]

Masaud's forays into the foothills of Nepal are in the nature of hunting expeditions during which he encounters a famous sun temple and a holy tank where
"every Sunday the heathen of Bahraich and its environs, male and female, used
to assemble in thousands to rub their heads" under the stone image of Bala
Rukh "and do it reverence as an object of peculiar sanctity." It was Masaud's
wish to "destroy that mine of unbelief, and set up a chamber for the worship of
the Nourisher of the Universe in its place, rooting out unbelief from those
parts." The local chiefs of the country around Bahraich present him with an
ultimatum: "You come from the Upper Country [*mulk-i-bala dast*], and know
nothing of these parts. This is the land of nobles; never shall the inhabitants of
the Upper Country remain here. Think more wisely of this matter."[32] Masaud
confers, gauges the strength of the enemy, and prepares for battle. Several
engagements ensue. Masaud issues orders "to bring the bodies of the Faithful
slain and cast them into the Suraj-kund [the sun-god tank], in the hope that
through the odor of their martyrdom the darkness of unbelief might be dis-
pelled from that spot."[33] Masaud now has a premonition of his martyrdom:

---

30 *Mirat-i-Masaudi*, Chapman trans., pp. 3, 5.
31 *Mirat-i-Masaudi*, Elliot volume, pp. 113–15.
32 Ibid., p. 133.
33 Ibid., p. 141.

before the final engagement he distributes all the money and property he has to those around him and tells them to spend it quickly, saying, "Jesus found no use for even his woolen cap and needle, what good shall I get from all this wealth." "He then dismissed the people … [and] retreated to occupy himself with religious exercises: from that time he abjured food and water, eating a large quantity of betel nut and rubbing himself with perfumes."[34]

In the final engagement, on Sunday, the 14th of the month Rajab in the year 424 Hijri (June 15, 1033), Sahar Deo and Har Deo, with several other chiefs, "seeing that the army of Islam was reduced to nothing, unitedly attacked the bodyguard of the Prince [of Martyrs]."

> As the time of evening prayers came on … a chance arrow pierced the main artery in the arm of the Prince of the Faithful. His sunlike countenance became pale as the new moon. Repeating the text in praise of martyrdom, he dismounted. Sikandar Diwana, and the other servants of the loved-one of God, carried him to the shade of the *mahua* tree [by the Suraj kund, a favorite resting spot of Masaud's], and laid him down upon a couch. Sikandar Diwana, taking his honored head upon his lap, sat looking towards Mecca, weeping bitterly. The Prince of Martyrs opened his eyes but once, then drew a sigh, and committed his soul to God. …
>
> A sound of woe and lamentation broke from the people; they wept aloud, and brandishing their swords, rushed upon the enemy of the unbelievers, and gave up their lives. … By the time of the evening prayers not one was left. All the servants of Masaud lay scattered like stars.[35]

The story told here is clearly an elaboration of the "Sword of Islam" motif in India, with its characteristic hyperbole, for the language of medieval conquest and warfare is necessarily one of excess: here we are centuries before today's "smart bombs" and clinical descriptions of "collateral damage." The comparisons with Jesus are intriguing, but the character of the Islamic hero is built within Indian referents: restrictions on the acceptance of cooked food, the chewing of betel nut (and perhaps the betel leaf), etc. It is the centrality of Indian tropes that opens up the possibilities of telling an Islamic tale to a wider audience of "unbelievers."

V   A detailed analysis of the structure of this hagiography must await another occasion. For the moment I wish to draw attention to the way the hagiography

---

34 *Mirat-i-Masaudi*, Chapman trans., p. 29.
35 *Mirat-i-Masaudi*, Elliot volume, pp. 113–15.

is authenticated (a difficult task in every case) with reference to two very different "histories" that predate the literary endeavors of a *mauteqid* – one who has a
firm belief in the larger-than-life deeds of a warrior saint. Abdur Rahman
Chishti claimed to have based the *Mirat-i-Masaudi* on an early Ghaznavid history, which "seems to have been written to satisfy popular curiosity about Salar
Masaud at a later date." The fact that this *Twarikh* is not mentioned by any
writer before or after the writing of the *Mirat* has not exactly endeared Abdur
Rahman Chishti to the professional historians of the early Ghaznavids.[36] But
apart from maintaining that his efforts had been materially assisted by the helping hand of his long-deceased hero (almost a hallmark of hagiographies), Sheikh
Abdur Rahman took care to maintain that "his history had been corroborated
by a learned Hindu Brahman of Bahraich from his own Sanskrit sources." It was
thus that Abdur Rahman Chishti literally "believed his work to be an authentic
history of Salar Masaud."[37]

Urdu translations of the *Mirat* with poetical embellishments were printed
routinely in the late nineteenth and early twentieth centuries, and these form
the core of the chapbook literature that is sold at the shrine in Bahraich today.[38]
A more open-ended crafting of the exploits of Masaud Ghazi takes place in the
accounts of the Muslim balladeers (*dafalis*). It is difficult to establish when these
ballads first came into existence, though it is equally difficult to conceive of
devotees covering the long distance from Agra to Bahraich, as testified by the
Emperor Akbar himself, with no songs or stories to accompany them. A large
collection made by colonial ethnographers in the late nineteenth century is not
markedly different from my own field recordings done in the 1990s.[39] The story
of Ghazi Miyan is here recounted in several episodes, but the one that is com-

36 Thus Muhammad Nazim: The *Mirat-i-Masaudi* "is a history mixed with a liberal supply of pious
fiction. The author claims to have based his work on a history by Mulla Muhammad-i-Ghaznawi
who is alleged to have been attached to the court of Sultan Mahmud, but this so-called contemporary history is not mentioned by any previous writer." See his *The Life and Times of Sultan Mahmud of Ghazna* (Cambridge: Cambridge University Press, 1931; 2nd ed. New Delhi: Munshiram
Manoharlal, 1971), p. 14. Habib, in his iconoclastic study of the "great conqueror" composed during the 1924 communal riots in Lucknow, inter alia, "to give expression to th[e] longing for
humanity, justice, tolerance and secularism," does not refer to Abdur Rahman Chishti's remarkable
hagiography. See *Politics and Society during the Early Medieval Period*, 2:36–104, 389–92.
37 See the incisive discussion in Saiyid Athar Abbas Rizvi, *A History of Sufism in India*, 1975 (2nd ed.
New Delhi: Munshiram Manoharlal, 1997), 1:311–14. I quote from pp. 312, 313, 314. I have
tried to discuss the structure of the *Mirat-i-Masaudi* in somewhat greater detail in "The Long Life
of a Seventeenth-Century Indo-Muslim Hagiography" (working paper, Center for Early Modern
History, College of Liberal Arts, University of Minnesota, October 2000).
38 For example Akbar Ali ibn Mohammad Baksh, *Khulsah-i-Tarikh-i-Masaudi* (Lucknow, 1876), and
Ghazee-namah-i-Masaud (Kanpur, 1876). See also Mansur Ali Khadim, *Hazrat Sipah Salar Masaud
Ghazi* (Bahraich, n.d.), and *Aina-i -Masaudi* (Bahraich, n.d).
39 See R. C. Temple, *The Legends of Punjab*, 1884 (reprint ed. Patiala: Language Dept, Punjab, 1988),
1:98–120.

mon to most locations in North India is about the marriage of the warrior saint. In this ballad Ghazi Miyan is being ritually bathed preparatory to his marriage when Jaso Rani (Queen Jashoda, also the name of Krishna's foster-mother) arrives, not with the customary gift of milk products but with pails brimming with the blood of Nand (her husband) and his cowherd subjects, who have lost their cows and their lives to the treacherous Raja Sohal Deo. Ghazi Miyan (here Ghazi Dulha, or the young bridegroom) responds to this Gau Guhar – "Save the kine" – cry, gets up from his wedding, and is martyred in the cause of cows/Islam. The poignancy of his martyrdom lies in the tragic reversal of marriage as death, and in a Turkish warrior, born and bred in India, responding with the last drop of his blood to a "Hindu" cry of "Save the cows!" from the treacherous assault of a local king.

Devotees form marriage parties and converge on Bahraich every May/June (*Jeth*) to complete the important ceremony that got interrupted that fateful first Sunday of *Jeth* in A.D. 1033, corresponding to Sunday the 14th of the month Rajab in the year A.H. 424. Because of some untoward occurrence (*pachkha*) – a blizzard, a drizzle, thunder – the marriage will not take place. This is, as it were, written into the script. On Sunday, May 12, 1996, an usually strong wind was read as the sign that stymied the proceedings. So the unfulfilled desire to get Bale Dulha, or the young bridegroom (Ghazi Miyan), married is pushed to the first Sunday of the month of *Jeth* in the next agricultural year, "when the first mangoes expectedly ripen." And so it has gone on at least since the great medieval traveler Ibn Battuta's visit to the shrine in 1341.

In a society such as India's, where segmentation and division into castes and subcastes are girdled by marriage rules, to be a part of the wedding procession (*barat*) of Ghazi Miyan is to subvert the normal barriers in the creation of community. And this joyous community of the devotees of Bale Dulha becomes possible because popular narratives transform the Islamic notion of *Shahadat*, martyrdom, in the very telling of the story. In principle, the story of a jihad such as Bale Dulha undertakes cannot be communicated to a "nonbeliever" outside the context of the exercise and acknowledgment of just force. *Shahadat* involves both witnessing "truth" and martyrdom, and is to be anticipated and welcomed, as indeed Salar Masaud did on 14th Rajab A.H. 424. But even in the *Mirat-i-Masaudi*, a thoroughly Islamic hagiography of a shaheed, the martyrdom of Salar Masaud is in fact precipitated by a "Save the kine" cry, which invades the text so imperceptibly as to go almost unnoticed.

Let us go back to the story of the encounter with the confederacy of rajas at Bahraich. Salar Masaud has received the ultimatum to vacate his hunting ground and retire to the Upper Country (*mulk-i-bala dast*). The Prince of Martyrs confers with his commanders and it is "agreed to take the offensive rather than allow the unbelievers to attack them … so that with God's help they might hope to conquer."

> The next day they were preparing, when news arrived that the enemy were driving off the cattle. The Prince sprang like an angry lion, and beat to arms; buckling on his armor and mounting his horse, he himself put his troops into battle array, and advanced to the attack.[40]

It seems likely that this uncharacteristic passage in the *Mirat* is a measure of Abdur Rahman's inability to absorb the popular cow trope on its own terms. The marked category "cow" (which would have placed it within a specific cultural universe) is replaced by the unmarked category "cattle" in the seventeenth-century Persian text. In terms of the logic of the hagiography it would seem all the more odd that Masaud's local opponents would gird themselves for the final attack on the Prince of Martyr's contingent by making a dash for (presumably) Masaud's or his cowherds' cattle. To make the popular "save the cow" trope derivative of the *Mirat* is to privilege an awkward seventeenth-century construction over a rooted, unhistoricized folklore. Instead of taking the early-seventeenth-century *Mirat* as the originary text, with the ballads as oral variants, we should entertain the other historical possibility: that between the fourteenth and the early seventeenth centuries there were extant a clutch of popular lores and legends about Ghazi Miyan, and that the *Mirat-i-Masaudi* of Abdur Rahman Chishti was an attempt by a learned local Sufi to bleach popular memory and thereby tame this historically recalcitrant figure. When Abdur Rahman sat down in the 1610s to write the life of his warrior hero, he did so in order to fill a narrative gap. In his writing the Sufi hagiographer was neither able to engross the cow-protector motif nor, given its popularity, to discard it totally.

In folklore and local histories Ghazi Miyan appears as the protector of "his innumerable" cows and cowherds. As Zainullah Dafali of Gonda District recounted in May 1996:

> [Ghazi Miyan] had 1,600 Ahir-cowherds and 125,000 cows. He had given his cowherds the freedom to do as they pleased, what he expected of them was the present (*shagun*) of milk every eighth day. Raja Sohal Deo got annoyed at this. He said: "A Turuk like him takes the shagun of milk, and I a Kshatriya am ignored!"[41]

40 *Mirat-i-Masaudi*, Elliot volume, p. 138.
41 Zainullah Dafali, interview with the author, Chittaura, near Bahraich, May 9, 1996.

Sohal Deo prohibits the giving of such gifts to the Turkish interloper, but the wives of the cowherds disregard him. They take the gift of milk for the marriage of Ghazi Miyan, whereupon Nand, the cowherd chief and his followers, are attacked by Sohal Deo, and Rani Jaso rushes to Ghazi Miyan with the cry of "Save the cows!" In a late-nineteenth-century rendition, Ghazi Miyan begs his mother's pardon for so abruptly disrupting the marriage festivities in order to respond to the killing of his Gwala cowherds:

"O hear me, mother mine," he said,
"Great Wrong the king [Sohal] had wrought.
He hath our kine as plunder seized
And all our Gwalas killed:
Jaso hath come to me: the air
With cries for blood is filled.
O hearken, Saifuddin; the tale
To me hath Jaso told;
Who kills my Gwalas and steals my kine
A traitor King I hold."[42]

Another eponymous ballad called "Jaso" or "Jaswa," still extant, begins with Nand turning out his *banjhin* (infertile) wife. Jaso, an inauspicious, unproductive woman (paired off initially to reproduce another lineage), is unacceptable even to her mother. Forsaken and forlorn, she seeks shelter in the desolate shrine of Ghazi Miyan, in the middle of the Bahraich jungle. The saint intercedes and Nand is prevented in the nick of time from taking another wife. Ghazi Miyan ends Jaso's travails by uniting her with her husband and blessing her with a son – Kishan Kanahaiya, Krishna himself. In fact Ghazi Miyan's own mother in the ballads is herself a barren woman, a *banjh* – the ultimate ignominy for a married woman – and is blessed with a child after she agrees to an impossible condition set by a powerful Sufi saint. Other ballads rework familiar episodes from the *Ramayana* into the exploits of the young warrior saint. There is the story of Amina Sati, modeled on Rama's wife Sita after her return from captivity in Lanka, who is turned out by her husband because she serves food to a Mussalman – Ghazi Miyan, whom she regards as a welcome guest from her distant natal home.

Let us not gloss over a major transformation that is taking place here. The archetypal outsider, the lascivious *Turuk* conqueror who repeatedly penetrates a

---

42 "The Marriage of Ghazi Miyan," ballad, Eng. trans. William Hoey.

prostrate "India," is here being domesticated and made a part of common wom-
anly sorrows and concerns about marriage: alienation from the natal home, and
the demeaning state that comes with inadequate fecundity, the *raison d'être* of a
married woman. The Hindu body politic of history books, repeatedly vanquished by the Turks, and the forsaken, forlorn, and empty body of the Hindu
woman-sans-male child until filled with the grace of the Ghazi, are here worlds
apart. Understandably, the object of the ire of the anti-Ghazi Miyan tracts of the
1920s were these very Hindu women who were thronging the Bahraich shrine,
praying that the Ghazi, himself born to a barren woman, grant them their desire
to be delivered of a male offspring.

Along with married women, Ahir cowherds are central to the story, and this
suggests that we have here the establishment of a relationship between Turkish
horsemen and local pastoralists at the moment of conquest and before the setting up of an agrarian Turkish state, the Delhi Sultanate. Ahirs and other mid-
dle- and low-caste Hindus form the majority of Ghazi Miyan's followers, and
this despite the repeated attempts by Hindu publicists (especially the Arya
Samaj, from the early twentieth century) to tell "the real history" of this "vile"
Muslim conqueror and thereby wean "ignorant" Hindus away from the cult of
the warrior saint and its charlatan *dafali* officiants.[43]

But the "ignorance" argument does not work. It is implausible for so many
to have been ignorant for such an incredibly long time; and there are, besides,
enough markers to make it virtually impossible for the non-Islamic follower not
to give assent to one or the other aspect of the jihadi career of Ghazi Miyan.
Even if one does not know what a *ghazi* is, one knows he is a Mussalman, that
dafalis are not Hindu religious officiants, that the shrine at Bahraich is not a
temple. And so the story is told and appreciated from the point of view of difference. Ghazi Miyan *is* a Muslim conqueror, yet in effect if not in fact, as the
first conqueror of the Gangetic north he is unlike other Muslim conquerors —
who are yet to be or are supposed to be, or indeed were! He is the opposite of
the stereotypical Muslim conqueror in Bhartendu's cry, "You Muslim-foreigners!
You have robbed us [Hindus] of our dharma, women, and wealth!"

He is also unlike the "Turuka" of the popular imagination. Hindu kings who
conceive of his character as the debased Turuka are shown to be debased them-

43 Some of these pamphlets attacking the popular devotion of Ghazi Miyan among low-caste men
and especially women are discussed in Charu Gupta, "Hindu Women, Muslim Men: Cleavages in
Shared Spaces of Everyday Life, United Provinces, c. 1890–1930," *Indian Economic & Social
History Review* 37, no. 2 (April–June 2000): 140–48. For an incisive contrary reading of the
Mirat-i-Masaudi from a "Hindu" point of view and an impassioned plea to Hindus to desist from
worshipping the jihadi warrior saint, see Swami Vicharanandji's article on Ghazi Miyan and the
Hindu community, and a companion piece on how worshipping Ghazi Miyan is improper, both in
Swadesh (Gorakhpur), April 26, 1928.

selves. Thus, in a ballad about Ghazi Miyan's conquest of the holy city of Banaras, the chief blood-demanding idol of the city is made to drink milk, while reciting an acceptance of the Islamic creed. Certain astrologers, when consulted by Raja Banar (the eponymous ruler of the city) on how to halt the *ghazi's* advance, suggest to him that the Mussalman hero is "protected by Khuda himself." The ballad recounts how the "shameless kafirs," in order to distract and thwart Ghazi Miyan, then parade their women before him and his companions. The virginal saint is forced to act drastically to avert his eyes from this pornographic parade: *"jab aurat par pari nazar, sar kaat aapan jeb mein dhaya"* – he cuts his head off, pockets it, defeats the raja's forces while headless, and only subsequently puts his head back on. Unlike the stereotypical lascivious Turk, the first popular Muslim conqueror of North India dies an unwed virgin.

VI   To recapitulate: there is little doubt that the narrative of Ghazi Miyan is about the Sword of Islam. But its denouement – the Ghazi's martyrdom – is played out in terms of an enduring, nonexploitative relationship between Hindu herdsmen and women and a Muslim protector of their cows. The martyrdom of the conqueror then transforms the Sword of Islam motif by creating a third possibility external to itself: it is not the usual harsh choice between conversion or death. Protected by a *ghazi* in the wilds of the Nepal foothills, herdsmen do not become converts to Islam or even subjects of a new "Islamic state": they become ardent follower-devotees. In effect they give assent to the life of a young *ghazi-shaheed* which has been well lived on two very different registers: the call of Islam and the call to save cows.

This is a bald summary of an insufficiently told story, but I hope it raises issues similar to the ones I started with. The person Ghazi Miyan and his martyrdom at Bahraich in 1033 are unchronicled. Yet his exploits, as recounted in ballads and in a seventeenth-century Persian hagiography, relate to a history – that of the Turkish conquest of North India. Historically dubious, these retellings nonetheless articulate aspects of a verifiable past conflict, in the process creating communities in the present – communities based in part on a memorialized recognition of difference and conquest. And this articulation has a narrative form that subverts the dominant narratives of difference and conquest.

To write about Ghazi Miyan in the present involves grappling with more than a narrative understanding of the warrior saint as a just conqueror. It also involves being faced with fresher "fabrications" of the story of this virgin Muslim warrior in unexpected quarters. This then opens up possibilities of creating a new and unfamiliar – and defamiliarizing – historical narrative of the "Sword

of Islam" in India. To overlook the story of Ghazi Miyan's life as recounted in
the early-seventeenth-century hagiography and in extant ballads, and to concentrate instead on the well-established syncretic and thaumaturgic aspects of the
cult, is in other words to forgo the opportunity of penning an alternative history
of the Turkish conquest of northern India: neither Turkiana (the Sword of
Islam) nor Sufiana (the gentle ways of the Islamic mystics), to borrow the polar-
ity of Suniti Kumar Chatterjee,[44] but rather a history that focuses attention
upon this recalcitrant and popular figure of North India's premier warrior saint.

The alternative history that I am advocating is not a rewriting of privileged
textbook events, which might in this instance involve a reworking and contextu-
alizing of the facticities of Mahmud Ghazni's raids.[45] Rather, I am putting forward the case for alternative histories of submerged, abbreviated, straitjacketed
events – recalcitrant events and *recalcitrant lives* – whose very telling by historians is made possible by calling into question the terms in which the "Big Story"
(as the popular idiom of modern times would call it) or the Master Narrative (as
we understand it) is told and assented to both in the profession and within the
nation.[46] Alternative histories are not local histories; they are not alternatives *to*
history; alternative histories are histories written from within the profession.
Ideally they are accessible also to those outside the profession, i.e., they ought to
become, one day, the Big Story.

VII   It serves little purpose to lay down the conditions for the possibility of
such histories in advance of the actual writing. With Ghazi Miyan, it will clearly
require making narrative and historical sense of the hagiographic, sectarian,
demotic, and performative literature about this "Prince of Martyrs" that have
been refused entry into Clio's estate on the grounds of "evidential inadmissibil-
ity." Beyond the question of evidence, such a history would require a critique of
the ways in which difference, conflict, and conquest are elided in the quest for
the Indian-national. In writing such a history one would face a creative tension
with important implications for historiography. It is now widely accepted that
the political community of Indian nationals contains differences that it would
be unhealthy for the nation-state to brush aside: regional, linguistic, caste, gen-

---

44 Suniti Kumar Chatterjee, "Daraf Khan Ghazi," first published in Vishva-Bharati Patrika
    (1354 B.S.), reprinted in *Sanskriti*, vol. 1 (1368 B.S.). I am grateful to Gautam Bhadra for drawing
    my attention to this text and translating from it.
45 Romila Thapar, "Somnath: Narratives of a History," *Seminar* (New Delhi), no. 479 (March 1999):
    15–22.
46 See Shahid Amin, *Event, Metaphor, Memory: Chauri Chaura, 1922–1992* (Berkeley: University of
    California Press, 1995).

der, and community affirmations are here to stay. The question is: if one can find traces of these differences and conflicts in our history, how may one relate these to the present life of the community of Indian nationals? This is a radical and serious issue to which Indian historiography must address itself if it is to reach out from the family of like-minded historians to, so to say, the persons-in-communities who are struggling against the homogenizing currents that are constantly and dangerously seeking merely to define the "New Indian National."

I realize that I have been unable to sew a proper pouch in which to ensconce my warrior saint for posterity and history. I am still struggling with some of the questions thrown up by the long afterlife of the intractable Ghazi Miyan. Historians' history usually relates to one form of a community – the national community. Memories, hagiographies, and ballads, on the other hand, relate to very different kinds of communities. Modern history invokes the idea of a people as historically constituted, and this together with the idea of a people as sovereign is constitutive of most national histories. The triumph of the idea of self-determination in the twentieth century has meant that all conquest has come to be regarded as unjust. In that case, how can historians' history meaningfully tackle the issue of conquest? And yet, in the overbearing majoritarian India of today, practicing historians can ill afford to throw up their hands in collective positivist despair at their inability to pen alternative, nonsectarian histories of precolonial conquest. A new kind of history is required to counter effectively the challenges posed by the majoritarian constructions of the past, the Indian past, any past.

**Uncivil Conduct:
State Violence, Ethnic Conflict, Civil Society**

The Order of Truth and the Order of Society

Yadh Ben Achour

1. Rather than abandon ourselves to a limitless discussion of the meaning of truth from a scientific, moral, philosophical, or aesthetic point of view, let us immediately inquire into the *function* of truth. For in terms of function, all forms of the truth resemble each other. We always expect certain results from the truth: that it will transform the unknown into the known; that it will clear up a mystery; that it will prove or disprove a hypothesis. It is here that the judge – who demands of both witnesses and accused that they swear to tell "the truth, the whole truth, and nothing but the truth" – meets the theologian, the scientist, the philosopher, and the moralist. All share the expectation that the truth will help them to know an object that has heretofore been either partly or totally unknown.

2. Where evil is concerned, knowledge of the truth may have different effects. It may bring about scandal, shame, or pain; it may help to lessen the evil, or even to erase it; or it may reveal errors, ignorance, and lies – that is, it may reestablish the events of the past in their actual historic development.

In recent times we have experienced all these and other effects of truth. An example of truth-as-scandal: the impact of confessions made by the French General Paul Aussaresses in March 2001 concerning tortures committed by the French army in Algeria. These confessions unleashed a chain of reactions, notably on the part of the president of France. An example of the second case, truth-as-pardon: Pope John Paul II's remarks of May 5, 2001, to the Greek Orthodox Church, in which he recognized the wrongs inflicted by the Catholic Church on the Orthodox Church. Truth-as-pardon might also be called "truth-as-repentance," or, as the pope called it, a "purification of memory," and it consists of three phases: the deed, the admission of regret (in marked contrast to the admission of satisfaction or pride), and the possibility of pardon. The third case – still drawing on contemporary experience – is exemplified by recent discoveries in the United States of truths about crimes. In a number of cases, years after trial and verdict, DNA analysis has proven that a rape could not have been committed by the man who has been found guilty and sentenced to prison for it. The discovery of such a truth puts the facts back into their real, objective context by removing an erroneous opinion from them. This is an example of what I call "the truth of the truth."

3. Before considering the actual experience of commissions convened in the name of "truth and reconciliation," I would like to make a few observations about the truth in the spheres of ethics and politics.

I. Truth in the Sphere of Ethics   4. To recognize the truth of an act, an offense, or a transgression is to seek to reestablish harmony and appeasement – as much within the internal order of conscience as within the external order of law. Simply to recognize the truth is a cathartic act that at the same time relieves the conscience, purges the social relationship of its misfortunes, and soothes the memory.

5. This concept can be found at the heart of all religions, where truth takes the form of repentance and confession. Repentance is an act of self-abasement through which the believer, in admitting the truth of his sinful acts, recognizes an offense against God – recognizes that he has either transgressed God's law or wronged his neighbor. The New Testament parable of the Pharisee and the tax collector ends with the claim that "every one that exalteth himself shall be abased; and he that humbleth himself shall be exalted" (Luke 18:14). The individual abases himself in the act of repentance.

For the offender the recognition of the crime is equivalent to self-accusation. Through this gesture of humility he loses face, reveals his shame, and calls on God as a witness. Apostasy and perfidy are pardoned. We read in the Old Testament book of Jeremiah, "Only acknowledge thine iniquity" (Jeremiah 3:13), and "Return, ye backsliding children, and I will heal your backslidings" (3:22).

Here, to admit a sin is to express the truth. Again in Jeremiah we read, "We lie down in our shame, and our confusion covereth us: for we have sinned against the Lord our God" (3:25). The admission is directed simultaneously toward the conscience of the sinner (which it tends to free through regret) and that of the victim, from whom pardon is being sought: pardon – or at least non-vengeance; forgetting – or at least the appearance of forgetting; and the acceptance of the fact itself, without other consequences.

The New Testament parable of the Prodigal Son gives clear expression to this idea of pardon. Having sinned against his father, the son receives honor and recompense when he admits his error. Dead, he returns to life. Through the truth a lost harmony is regained.

6. Repentance, in religious values, may in fact have the purpose of blocking vengeance, whether that vengeance be unleashed by God or man. Repentance assuages God's fury, but it can serve to block the penal process as well: According to Islam, the Koran frequently affirms that punishment is suspended by repentance, on the condition that it be sincere. This is the case for adultery, theft, unnatural sexuality, and rebellion.

7. Conditions and degrees establish the difference between authentic repentance, which is covered by pardon, and inauthentic repentance, which is not. The first must be characterized by sincerity and disinterestedness. This is, at the same time, relative. No act of repentance can be fully disinterested, since it necessarily arrives at a positive result, be it pardon, an assuaged conscience, or the rehabilitation of esteem. It always arrives at some sort of interest.

Inauthentic repentance obviously comes in many forms. It may come late – may not come, for example, until the final stages of life, on the deathbed. So the Koran informs us, "Repentance to Allah is only for those who do evil in ignorance, then turn to Allah soon, so these it is to whom Allah turns mercifully, and Allah is Everknowing, Wise. And repentance is not for those who go on doing evil deeds, until when death comes to one of them, he says: Surely now I repent" (4:17–18).

Repentance also loses its authenticity when it is performed under constraint, or out of purely material interest. Islam, for example, dictates the cruelest punishments for banditry but makes exception for those who repent *before* they are captured and delivered to the authorities. A fortiori, it is the same with hypocritical repentance, which is merely given in order to win the pity or mercy of the victim or judge, and is made with a view toward escaping or at least softening punishment.

8. The value of repentance also depends on the gravity of the wrong committed and on the intensity of the violation. The path toward repentance is much easier for an involuntary wrong than for a voluntary one, just as it is easier for a light or indirect wrong than for an intense or direct one. According to the Gospel of Luke, when Christ arrived at the place called Golgotha to be crucified he prayed that God pardon his assassins. These men certainly acted voluntarily, but, he said, were blinded by their ignorance: "Father, forgive them; for they know not what they do" (Luke 23:34).

9. Repentance – through which one seeks to obtain divine mercy or the pardon of another person, to relieve one's own conscience, or to repair a wrong – may be accepted or rejected. The Koran, for example, affirms, "Surely, those who dis-

believe after their believing, then increase in unbelief, their repentance shall not be accepted, and these are they that go astray" (3:90). In the most serious cases, then, repentance cannot be received.

10. Repentance thus depends on two elements. The first concerns material facts: the public recognition of the event that produced the wrong, whatever that wrong's nature – an offense against life, an offense against the integrity of the body, a material loss, emotional suffering, or other wrongs. Repentance is the objective admission of a concrete fact and an individual's acceptance of responsibility for the act.

The second element regards intention, which is invisible and will thus always remain relatively secret. Effectively there can only be relative signs by which we can make judgments about intentions: the moment of repentance, the guilty person's situation and condition, his or her physical expression of regret (through tears, sobs, timbre of voice, and spontaneity of speech and gesture), his or her future conduct. Of course these signs, in the hands an actor, may become a means of supplementing lies and falsehoods. Our acceptance of penitence is thus founded on a presumption of trust, which we know in advance to be both fragile and uncertain.

Two truths are therefore essential to the act of repentance: the truth of facts and the truth of intention, which is sincerity. Both of these truths are involved in confession, particularly in the Catholic rite of confession, which consists of the sincere admission of wrongs and transgressions to the confessor and constitutes the sacrament of penance, also called the sacrament of reconciliation. Penance is one of the seven sacraments of Catholic doctrine (the others being baptism, the Eucharist, the anointing of the sick, confirmation, holy orders, and matrimony). In Catholicism, confession consists of an admission entrusted to a priest so that the pardon of the Church in Christ's name may be received. The sacrament's key principles are truth and reconciliation. Here the truth has a dimension of absolution, of expiation. In religion as in morality, the truth serves to reconstitute the link or promise that has been broken, the trust that has been betrayed, the order that has been disrupted. In doing so it blocks the usual consequences of a criminal act, which are of a vindictive character. The effect of absolution is that it reestablishes harmony and reconciliation between God and the faithful.

In the largest sense, the religious sphere's presuppositions about repentance are to be found in the moral sphere and in the political and even the legal spheres as well.

11. In the ethical sphere, the telling of the truth erases the destructive traces of dishonesty, betrayal, injury, aggression, or inaction. Through the recognition of a crime, its attribution to the guilty party, and that person's sincere expression of regret, a reestablishment of the moral order takes place. Finally the wrong is redressed by bringing about a role reversal between the offender and the offended: The dominator puts himself in the position of the dominated. He delivers himself into the hands of the offended, to whom he offers the "good role" of moral magistrate, the role of bringing about the final victory of the good and just. The offended party becomes a judge. The sentence that is his to impose consists of either granting or refusing to grant pardon. In the first case the moral order is recovered through the return of lost esteem. In the second case the offender finds himself imprisoned in his own bad conscience.

In the legal sphere, the telling of the truth does not in fact erase the punishment, since punishment in the modern penal system extends beyond the personal situation between aggressor and aggressed. Penitence can nonetheless soften the punishment by inspiring clemency on the part of the judge or of the victim. It is already clear, then, that the order of truth and the order of law operate according to two different sets of logic, since the act of repentance does not block the judicial process of punishment. Contrary to what happens in the religious and moral spheres, in the legal sphere some sort of punishment will be pronounced, regardless of the admission of guilt and repentance. It is with this example drawn from law that we enter the world of politics.

II. Truth in the Sphere of Politics   12. Within the political sphere the order of truth and the order of society find themselves in total opposition.

The order of truth, as has been shown, is founded on moral honesty and relative disinterestedness. It is per se opposed to the domination and manipulation of others. It does not use others as a means to an end; it puts a stop to the moral disorder in which the passions and instincts overcome the virtues. The order of truth enables us to choose with wisdom, faith, and confidence in a way that conforms to superior and tangible values, without regard to the play of interests. Within the order of truth, pure philosophy is not only possible but necessary. Political philosophy, on the other hand, is something completely different, since it inserts itself into a complex play of contradictory interests that must coexist with one another: order and freedom; the whole and the particular; the individual and society. These interests are not purely spiritual, moral, or symbolic, as in the religious and moral spheres. Rather, they are tangible, material, or economic, or are connected to the exercise of power and the authority of the state, which insert themselves directly into the social fabric.

13. The principle of politics is above all to prevent anarchy and avoid the disorder brought about by man's natural tendency toward the absolute affirmation of his own ego.

In the abundant analysis that political philosophy has dedicated to the human ego, authors have generally presented pessimistic views of the natural condition of man. The Muslim theologian Ghazali (eleventh to twelfth century), in several of his works of political theology, describes mankind as animated by cruelty (*sab'ia*), deceitfulness (*shaitaniya*), bestiality (*bahimiya*), and the will to dominate (*rububiya*). The great thirteenth-century North African historian Ibn Khaldoun characterized man as disposed toward aggression and misdeeds, both of which lead to anarchy. The seventeenth-century English philosopher Thomas Hobbes held that, in nature, the human passions, desires, and instincts all lead to war – the war of man against man. It is a law of nature that men will "endeavor to destroy or subdue one another."[1]

14. Social constraint springs from this natural state. A coercive, superior force is an indispensable means of holding humans together. Ibn Khaldoun analyzed this force, which he called *Wazi'*, in a way that recognized both its material dimension, insofar as it is a physical force, and its moral dimension, insofar as it is a symbolic force. Ghazali called it *Shawka* (which means, literally, the needle, the point, and, by extension, power). Hobbes elevated it to the level of the sublime: "The only way to erect such a common power ... is to confer all their power and strength upon one man, or upon one assembly of men, that may reduce all their wills by plurality of voices unto one will. ... This is the generation of that great *Leviathan*, or rather, to speak more reverently, of that 'mortal god' to which we owe ... our peace and defense."[2] This quality became known in the West as sovereignty.

15. Constraint alone is insufficient to hold the multitude, and it is on this level that the political order separates itself completely from the moral order and the truth ceases altogether to be a part of its raison d'être. It was of course the illustrious Italian thinker Machiavelli who showed, in *The Prince* (c. 1505), that the order of truth, in its moral sense, corresponds in no way to the order of politics. This is not the place to trace the origins of Machiavelli's theories, except to draw from them what is pertinent to our subject. Thus he asserts that "all armed prophets have conquered, and the unarmed ones have been destroyed" (chapter VI), that "to slay fellow-citizens, to deceive friends, to be without faith, without

1 Thomas Hobbes, *The Leviathan*, 1651, Part I, chapter 13.
2 Ibid., Part II, chapter 17.

mercy, without religion ... may gain empire" (chapter VIII), that "a prince, so long as he keeps his subjects united and loyal, ought not to mind the reproach of cruelty" (chapter XVII), that "he need not make himself uneasy at incurring a reproach for those vices without which the state can only be saved with difficulty" (chapter XV), that he "ought to take care not to misuse this clemency" (chapter XVII), that he "ought to have a mind ready to turn itself accordingly as the winds and variations of fortune force it" (chapter XVIII), that he must possess both the force of a lion and the cunning of a fox, and that he must know how to employ religious sentiment for his own ends.[3]

Indeed, this is how power is exercised nearly everywhere on earth. Hypocrisy, intrigue, espionage, false appearances, and the like are not sins in politics unless they involve errors of calculation or tactics that may provoke greater damage. The political motto is "The end justifies the means." These means may very well include sacrificing the truth.

16. There are several ways of sacrificing truth to politics. The truth may be manipulated, contradicted, countered, travestied; people may be silent about the truth, and those who tell the truth may be intimidated, imprisoned, assassinated; the sacrifice of truth may take the form of disinformation, propaganda, and pure invention. The most radical form, as we shall see, is the act of masking the past. Indeed, memory and peace are not always compatible with one another. There are circumstances in which truth must be buried in the act of forgetting.

17. All this shows quite clearly that the order of society – its political order, which is the most essential order, in that it permits all the other orders to function normally – is situated at the antipode of the logic of truth. Politics has the goal of preserving peace and public order, without which nothing is possible. Sometimes in politics it is better not to tell the truth. If theologians occasionally allow pious fibs, what of political tacticians? Would any politician maintain that one should always tell the truth? If war is the pursuit of politics by other means (the inverse of which is also true), any military strategist who held to the motto "The truth, the whole truth, and nothing but the truth" would be a strategist of singular uselessness. War tactics and ruses are the pious fibs of the military. But such lies are small compared to the tactical ruses that take place within politics itself.

---

3 Niccolò Machiavelli, *The Prince*, trans. William K. Marriott, 1908 (reprint ed. New York: Knopf, 1992).

18. It is not only in war and peace that the truth may be, even ought to be, suppressed. There are also cases in the civil, religious, and moral spheres that call on the duty of silence. This is the realm of professional secrecy and the duty of confidentiality, be it bank, medical, and legal secrecy, the discretion of the notary, or the judge's right to confidential council. In religion, confession stops at the portal of the confessional. In all of these cases truth exists but is not to be made public. It is the publicity of the truth that is forbidden.

A deferential treatment of truth thus exists. The imperative of the truth is not absolute. It may come into conflict with superior interests that deserve respect and protection: the interests of victims, the interests of families, the interest of social order. Equally it may come up against such protected rights as the rights to privacy, family, and correspondence, or the right to the protection of home and property.

One example of the fundamental conflict between truth and other rights and interests is the case of the International Committee of the Red Cross (ICRC). In the course of exercising its humanitarian mission, the Red Cross often finds itself the keeper of many cruel and painful secrets concerning such acts of barbarism as torture, rape, and other forms of degrading or inhuman treatment. The proper unfolding of penal justice would require that the ICRC testify, providing proof of the guilt of those responsible. Before the International Criminal Tribunal for the Former Yugoslavia, however, the ICRC petitioned that it be released from the duty to testify. It won its claim. Indeed, to report the truth of what it saw and heard could seriously damage the organization's humanitarian mission and bring about a loss of its credibility.

19. In politics the truth may do damage. Sometimes the obligation to remember must cede to the imperatives of peace, order, and security. In the case of civil conflicts, a thorough knowledge of the truth may awaken sadness and tears, may prevent time from bringing about forgetting, and may block the quieting of emotions. Time needs silence in order to bring about forgetting. Truth may keep alive or even reanimate the thirst for vengeance, thus preventing the return of confidence and calm, both of which require a dose of silence in order to affirm themselves. The duty of memory (which I will address presently) very much depends on place and circumstance. When it is used too vigorously it is likely to aggravate suffering. In the latter case the right to know is not essential, but the duty to forget is, unless one is willing to perpetuate the pain.

III. Truth and Reconciliation 20. The truth commissions established in Argentina (1983), Chile (1991), El Salvador (1993), Haiti (1995), South Africa (1995), and Guatemala (1996) have not had identical results and did not have the same meaning.

One point they all share, however, is that they sought to learn the truth about the past, to free memory. In each case their inquiries consisted of investigations of serious and systematic attacks on universal values committed by former ruling parties. These values include: the right to life, liberty, security of person, dignity, and equality – racial equality in particular. The commissions share the common aim of removing the gag of silence about the facts of the past. This goal conforms to what Louis Joinet, in his report to the 55th Session of the United Nations Commission on Human Rights (1999), called "the right to know." For victims, as we have seen, the right to know is the starting point for reparation. The human rights scholar Nancy Thede writes, "These public, visible acknowledgements of what happened appear to be essential elements of reconciliation. By publicly recognizing the victims, they are symbolically restituted to the status of bona fide citizenship. Their past struggle, suffering, sacrifice, is recognized as a real part of history."[4]

21. The unveiling of truth, even in cases where responsible parties are not designated by name, is nonetheless the beginning of the condemnation of the guilty. Thede continues, "it is perhaps most important [indeed I would say it is equally important] to ensure the institutionalization of memory rather than to attempt to redress the situation through judicial resource."[5] Thus the institutionalization of memory is the point that all truth commissions have in common. The political interest dictates a revelation of past events. The interest of justice seeks to prevent crime from enjoying a supplemental privilege: complicit silence. Truth may in this way become an instrument for punishment. The following can be read in the report of the national truth commission that was established in Haiti: "Reconciliation can only come into play after the truth has been established. ... Amnesty cannot for all that lead to withholding the truth or legalizing impunity. ... A state ruled by law must in no way sanction impunity."[6] Even if the traditional judicial process is halted by amnesty, the truth encompasses the two elements of the process (without formalizing or radicalizing

---

4 Nancy Thede, "'Justice, Memory and Reconciliation' in the Context of Peacebuilding," paper prepared for the DFAIT-NGO Consultations on Peacebuilding, Ottawa, March 2, 1999, available on the Web at www.cpcc.ottawa.on.ca/memory.htm.
5 Ibid.
6 Republic of Haiti, *Rapport de la Commission Nationale de Vérité et de Justice*, chapter 2: "Le Mandat et son interprétation," available on the Web at www.haiti.org/truth/chapit2.htm.

them): the denunciation of the guilty through admission and shame, and the reparation of the victim. In this respect it is necessary to rethink the path toward civil peace taken by the government of Algeria, where amnesty is granted to any and all terrorists who turn in their arms. In this case impunity is total. The truth is masked in the interest of peace. Many people continue to hold that this is too high a price to pay, even for peace – particularly since peace is still a long way off.

22. Beyond this common point of liberating memory, the truth commissions of different nations barely resemble one another. Some have an international character (El Salvador), others are mixed (Haiti), and others are entirely national (South Africa). Some have functioned in tandem with judicial tribunals (as in Argentina and Chile) while others are totally independent – in fact have specifically attempted to avoid setting the judicial process in motion. Some have been charged with launching general inquiries without naming names (Chile) while others have faced the task of hearing testimony and the admissions of those responsible (South Africa). Finally, some have had relative success while others have encountered only failure.

23. The experience of South Africa's Truth and Reconciliation Commission is of exemplary value. In that country the exploitation and violence had lasted for so long, and had been undertaken on such a vast scale, that to encompass all the responsibilities was quite infeasible on a purely jurisdictional level. The process in this case bore a strong resemblance to the act of repentance; it was perhaps no accident that it was a priest, Archbishop Desmond Tutu, who presided over the commission. The religious origins of repentance are clear enough. Peace constitutes the sacred in politics. The South African Commission was based on the following points:

- The institutionalization of the process in order to bring out the truth about thirty-three years of apartheid.
- The nonjurisdictional character and capacity of the institution.
- The voluntary recognition of the truth on the part of the guilty, and their acknowledgment of the deeds for which they were responsible (self-accusation).
- The openness of such recognition. (All sessions were public.)
- The suspension, through amnesty and immunity, of normal punishment for politically motivated crimes. More than 7,000 people petitioned for amnesty.
- The redressing of wrongs suffered by victims and their healing. More than 2,400 victims testified before the Commission, which in 1998 counted some 21,000 victims.

The goal of the process was to bring about appeasement. The bet made was that the truth about these many past sufferings, and about the tearing of the social fabric, would prepare the way for reconciliation – that is, for a possible future. In the light that these inquiries and reports have shed on South Africa's situation, however, we have seen that the process does not always really alleviate the suffering and frustration of the victims. Many close relatives of disappeared young people could be heard objecting that neither Nelson Mandela nor Archbishop Tutu had been forced to experience similar losses in their own families.

24. In fact, all truth and reconciliation commissions – because of their deep involvement with politics and its limitations – are founded on compromise. Short of destroying all of society, the parties involved realize that no one among them can benefit from a total victory. The oppressor realizes that he has lost the war and accepts repentance. The oppressed knows that total justice is dangerous and is prepared to grant pardon. Mandela said, "I was in chains, as you were in chains. I was set free, as you were set free. Therefore, if I can pardon my oppressors, so, too, can you."

25. Truth and Reconciliation commissions seem to bring the order of truth into harmony with the order of society. This result is both unexpected and astonishing, since the two spheres have such contradictory requirements.

We should nonetheless see very clearly that, in this case, neither repentance nor pardon has the real authenticity that it would have in the purely ethical realm. Political interest animates the entire process. Here, order and reconciliation become categorical imperatives. If good intentions and righteous conscience accompany the process of pacification, all the better. Machiavelli never wrote that politics and ethics were mutually exclusive. What counts, however, in these extremely complex operations of pacification through truth is not the rectitude of conscience but the final result: that society be appeased, and that peace be reinstated without recourse to violence, even legal or judicial violence. The infernal cycle of violence and counterviolence (however legitimate) must be stopped.

And so truth here becomes – paradoxically – the instrument of politics. The order of truth and the order of society join here to transform the negative character of the past, with its caravan of pain, injustice, and humiliation, into a possible and better future.

26. A purist might say that truth in the service of peace is not the real truth; that it is still a lie. To this we must respond that nothing in our humanity is thoroughly pure – nor is it thoroughly impure. The person who imagines that

humanity can be completely purged of lies, violence, and the capacity for destruction is naïve; just as the person who, convinced of humanity's incurability, would abandon it to its fate without making the slightest effort on its behalf is resigned and cowardly. Man is not permitted to hope. Religions have installed God and posited the immortality of the soul in order to help compensate for this deficit of hope. But this does not mean that giving up in any form is tolerable. To give up is tantamount to likening humankind to an animal or vegetable, lacking freedom, creativity, and grandeur. Moral action is the homage we pay to our intelligence. This is my definition of humanism.

Translated from the French by Miranda Robbins

A Finer Balance: An Essay on the Possibility of Reconciliation

Dilip Simeon

Introduction   I begin this address with a simple reflection on the key words in the title of this symposium: truth, justice, reconciliation. They mean a great deal to me intellectually and emotionally, and they are always accompanied by question marks: is there any such thing as truth, will there ever be a just society, may we dare hope for reconciliation? Like all great concepts, the words are too full of meaning to admit of any certitude. The title goes further, speaking of "experiments with truth," "transitional justice," and "processes of truth and reconciliation." These phrases in turn contain food for thought, especially for Indians. It was Mahatma Gandhi, after all, one of the greatest figures of the past century, who coined that germ of a Brahmasutra, "experiments with truth," as his unique contribution to ethical philosophy. In its own way the concept challenges the epistemological authoritarianism of market liberalism, Leninism, and the monoliths of identity, while also – in conjunction with the concept of *ahimsa* – suggesting an alternative to the nihilist ethics of postmodernity. The concept of transitional justice is also one to which Indian experience speaks in a special way. Our transitions are different from the stark changes in South Africa and Germany – yet they remain as painful. We are in perpetual states of temperamental, cultural, geopolitical, and economic transition. Our social space is suspended between tradition and modernity, we exist as a people made up of communities and also as a democratic nation-state of individual citizens, our economy lies poised between regulation and the lack of it, our cultural and religious psyche does not know what to preserve and what to forget. Our notions of justice veer between a hierarchical sensibility that calibrates punishment according to the status of wrongdoers and a jurisprudence that theoretically considers all citizens equal before the law. We know we are in transition. The only problem is that we don't know where the transition is headed.

The practice of reconciliation, too, is something we desperately need to learn. Vast areas of the subcontinent have remained under martial law for decades. The number of orphans in the Kashmir valley runs into the tens of thousands. Violence and terror have acquired a seamless trajectory. Communal and ethnic hatreds lurk beneath the surface of everyday life. The glorification of "masculine" virtue is a national pastime. Yet we Indians prefer to cling to our favorite symbolized grievances than to take the smallest steps toward comprehension and resolution.

The Threads of an Argument   The logic of my argument will base itself on the recognition that truth, justice, and reconciliation are sorely needed; that because they mean so many things to so many people, we must adopt certain rules of restraint and nonviolence while we live and discover what they are; that a society whose leaders do not adhere to such rules, or have an equivocal stance to political violence, is headed for self-destruction; that democracy and human equality are relatively youthful concepts in the Asian polity – and even globally; that the extension of these principles to the world economy is still not acceptable to those who occupy that economy's commanding heights; that destitution and oppression are still the common experience of millions of people, and that while this situation lasts, the preservation of democracy is crucial to the fulfillment of modest aspirations; that reconciliation is only possible between equals, and cannot even be attempted when various conflicting parties humiliate and stifle one another; that a properly functional judicial system is crucial to social stability; and that judges, like the rest of us, are mere mortals, and that the public sense of justice and fair play has therefore to be sustained by a social ethos and enlightened public opinion.

"Violence"   Systems of gross inequity are held together by and depend upon violence. This condition is true both within and outside India; the brutality of the age, and the volume of human energy and resources devoted to armaments, police, and paramilitaries, are indicators of its iniquitous character. The substitution of police methods for an institutional and social ethic in resolving conflict demonstrates the poverty of liberal theory. For example, the invention of a uniform, commercial "common sense of the market" is a manifestation of epistemic violence, one of those "universals" that postmodernism prefers to ignore.

The word "violence" itself has become tinged with euphemism, obscuring the reality of knives cutting through flesh, of warm blood on the pavement, of children screaming, of pain, fear, and agony.[1] Yes, violence is unfortunate, we say, but what of those horrific things that happen in the name of honor, glory,

---

1 I am indebted to Professor Namwar Singh for this insight.

and revenge? The language of vengeance and glory reminds me of the double peg of rum that soldiers and sailors of the colonial state would imbibe before going into battle – it deadened their nerves to prepare them for a journey into hell. The ruling elites of South Asia have long been accustomed to the use of incendiary language in the pursuit of power.

What are the psychic roots of the normalization of brutality? One of them, certainly, is the appeal of victimhood. One effect of identity politics is the conversion of all Jews, Muslims, Hindus, etc., into the permanent theoretical victims of their enemies. Victims become interchangeable with culprits – as Hans Magnus Enzensberger points out, the notion of the "innocent victim" is rendered meaningless in a situation such as that in the former Yugoslavia.[2] Women widowed by one atrocity picket the roads to prevent medical supplies from reaching the survivors of another atrocity. Young men take up arms to do unto others what others have done unto them. And how do we define the child soldiers who are filling the ranks of the paramilitaries from Sri Lanka to Liberia – are they victims or criminals? We have to accept the uncomfortable truth that the ubiquitous language of brutality has pushed victims and perpetrators together into a seamless whole. Not only are things of terror conceived in moments of beauty, but terror is the site to which its victims return as terrorists, having rendered, in their fervid imagination, vengeance itself into an aesthetic. We are confronted with incipient fascism, the doctrine of revenge elevated to ideological status. Do we not know its consequences? In daily life, despite a patina of civility and regulation, we occupy a space on the edge of barbarism. Every now and then we get a glimpse of the abyss: the schools of modern America, the killing fields of Yugoslavia, the wasteland on the West Bank, the prisons of Brazil, the streets of Soweto, the mind of the Taliban. And here in South Asia we keep victimhood as a talisman of identity, thus ensuring that we shall never be far from that edge.

Civil society is currently riven with the debate over state violations of human rights versus similar violations by the "militants" who supposedly represent oppressed people, minorities, etc. Parochial movements also cover a wide spectrum, having their own moderate and extremist fringes, which use each other with pragmatic cynicism. We invest much political energy in constructing cultural-ethnic identity as the quintessential historical Subject. Some of us even justify extreme forms of violence in the name of the oppressed. We transfer and preserve our most brutal impulses onto the boundary zone provided by identity. (That is why we are so addicted to boundaries.) Yet when we are faced with the

---

2 Hans Magnus Enzensberger, *Civil Wars: From L.A. to Bosnia* (New York: New Press, 1994), pp. 49–51.

consequences of our actions – which evoke further brutality – we claim protection under the banner of universal human rights. We employ exclusive language in the search for power and appeal to an inclusive category when we need breathing space. This ethical opportunism appears in the language of statehood as well as of resistance: remember that many of today's states are run by yesterday's rebels. The tactical and unreflective approach to violence in the language of resistance is symptomatic of the ideological reach of pragmatism. Indeed the similarity of the approaches to this question across the political spectrum demonstrates a hegemony of oppression without which patriarchy and exploitation would be impossible. Violence tends to blur political distinctions – note the contemporary ideological fuzziness and blurring of distinctions between right and left. It also leads inevitably toward depoliticization, as armed bodies emerge that specialize in killing and the brutal momentum of retribution.

Society's Need for Critical Theory   A dismissive attitude toward theoretical reasoning, its representation as the esoteric activity of elitist individuals, and its negative juxtaposition to so-called activism are popular with many social and political activists, including those in the burgeoning "NGO [nongovernmental organization] sector." This attitude generates cynicism, frustration, and fragmentation. Whether we like it or not, humans are fated to try to make sense of their environment. Faced with severe social crises, we have no option but to examine systems and causes. It is not enough to seek explanations that reduce everything to "human nature." We have to engage with the issue of structure.

Let us begin with the logic of democracy, an idea and practice linked to the concept of identity. The "rule of the people" presupposes that we know who "the people" are, even before we speak of their right to "self-determination." Democracy presupposes definitions of the "self," then, and of the ideologically defined boundaries of "the people." This issue is related to the birth of the nation state and to the notion of sovereignty. Identity is an ideological construction and therefore a matter of political power and class interest. The slogan that the Kashmiris have a right to "self-determination," for example, implies that their identity is self-evident. The moment the issue of the identity of Ladakhis or Dogras is brought into the argument, the latent authoritarianism of unilateral definitions becomes evident. We also need to distinguish between various streams of identity: religious, ethnic, linguistic, and so on.

The exploitation of labor has always been linked to identity, whether with African slaves on American cotton plantations, Tamil tea harvesters in Sri Lanka, the Irish builders of Britain's railroads, or the thousands of Indian indentured laborers, mostly of the so-called "low castes," who were sent all over the

British Empire to work on plantations. Identity has also played a crucial role in extraeconomic oppression, serving to intensify the exploitive process. Yet political mobilization around categories whose usage fluctuates between legal, ideological, and rhetorical definitions only creates confusion. The problem is whether these definitions are used in an inclusive or exclusive manner: discussions of identity combined with the experience of labor, or in opposition to systematic humiliation, can help build bridges between all oppressed people, but an exclusive usage can create division and bitterness instead. Identity is also subject to the logic of internal fragmentation, as more identities are generated within the confines of the community being constructed. We may also note that those who speak the language of "minority rights" often ignore the rights of minorities *within* the minorities, or for that matter the rights of individuals. In its exclusivist form, by attaching virtue and vice to entire communities, identity politics enables India's elite to erode the rights and status of the individual citizen and thereby subvert Indian democracy. When the legal system condones communal violence, for example, it becomes clear that not all of us enjoy equal protection under the law.

Take the issue of citizenship. Is this an abstraction that needs to be done away with, and replaced by a collection of identities? The institution of citizenship is constantly undermined by the "ragged edges of reality," but cannot be consigned to the dustbin – particularly when it is under attack from social forces that find democracy inconvenient. Economic and social injustice incessantly undermines the legal, political form of equality. Citizenship cannot remain unscathed by social stigma and economic servitude. Nevertheless, legal equality should not be seen as an abstract category imposed upon "traditional" communities, but as a toehold that the poor can use to actualize social democracy. Democratic constitutional rights are one of the platforms from which the working poor may defend themselves and improve their living and working conditions. Coalitions of exclusive identity cannot accomplish this goal, for they are oriented toward symbolic rather than substantive attainments. Insofar as they accentuate authoritarian tendencies in the polity, they might even undermine the rights of free speech, association, and peaceful agitation. No economy can function for a day without a working class, but if we judge from the language of today's politics, labor as a category has ceased to exist, except as a "factor of production." This is an indicator of the profoundly conservative ethos that was generated throughout the world during the last decade of the twentieth century. I have no doubt that it will change.

Critical social theory must engage with this question, and also with the possibility of a democratic division of labor at global and local levels – of an economy that is not left to the supposedly benevolent hidden hand of "market forces." What of the phenomena of informality and lack of regulation that are characteristic of the Indian economy? The dominant discourses of Indian economic nationalism have always boasted about the cheapness of Indian labor. Why is this a matter of pride? The control of mindless consumerism is one thing, but the cheapness of labor in India is achieved under the threat of destitution. Would not a more humane standard of life and work for the nation's nearly 400 million casual and agrarian workers and their families create a massive surge in patterns of demand and a boom for the capitalist economy? Why does this not happen, why does the regulation of labor conditions come so low on the list of priorities for Indian planners? I suggest that they are satisfied by the self-regulatory mechanisms that are already in place, and that go by the name of tradition, convention, and caste. From the standpoint of those who work, these phenomena offer nothing but a structure of physical intimidation, lubricated by the customary prejudices of caste society. Prejudices against the poor are now taken for granted, so that slums and pollution are dealt with not by improving salaries, working conditions, and housing but by throwing the poor out of the city precincts. Social Darwinism has taken the place of social theory.

Symptoms of degeneration are there for all to see. The lack of accountability has become pervasive, and is manifested as a decline of professionalism in many middle-class occupations. Elements of the medical fraternity appear to have completely forgotten the Hippocratic oath. There are lengthy lists of policemen who have been indicted by commissions of inquiry into communal riots only to end up being rewarded with promotions. It is no secret that the majority of civil service applicants these days select customs or revenue (income tax) as their first choice out of a possible twenty-four professions. With due respect to those of my former colleagues who have devoted themselves to maintaining academic standards, I must say that rampant absenteeism in the teaching profession has contributed greatly to the abysmal state of university education. Massive scandals periodically shake the world of banking and the stock markets. The political class has plumbed the depths of cynicism and criminality, but the common understanding of corruption reduces its causes to flaws in individual character and its scope to monetary matters alone.

There is much to be said on this matter. To start with, among the dictionary meanings of corruption, the one I find most relevant to this argument defines it as the "perversion from fidelity." However, I believe that the use of this word must also extend to the perversion of political and judicial institutions. Filling the atmosphere with communal hatred, inciting violence for political ends, suborning the loyalty of the police and military, pouring contempt upon the rule of law, treating some citizens as less worthy to live than others, remaining in public office while facing criminal proceedings – these phenomena, too, are symptoms of corruption. They are part of a systemic malaise, the locus of which is the subversion of democracy for the fulfillment of privileged interests. The common definition of corruption detracts from these broader issues, including, most importantly, the need to consider the lack of regulation as a systemic problem, not an individual one.[3]

There is another burning issue that could do with critical reflection. For many years, the Indian secular tradition tended to treat communalism (which I understand as the Indian version of fascism) as a collection of discrete, religiously oriented ideologies, some less dangerous than others. This was a massive analytic failure, one that strengthened the incipient fascist tendencies on the rampage in India today. Historically fascism based itself on a fabricated and exclusive ethnic identity. In India, however, the multifariousness of ethnic differentiation gave fascism a segmented character, which proved its greatest strength. Communalism was always *one phenomenon with different manifestations, rather than an arithmetic total of Hindu, Muslim, Sikh, and other communalisms.* Its self-sustaining tendency derived precisely from this discrete structure, with each reproducing the other. We need to remove ourselves from its compartmentlike appearance and concentrate on its generic uniformity. Indian fascism's ideological method defines democracy in arithmetic rather than institutional terms, despises democratic values, and favors hate-filled ethnic mobilization over the requirements of civic order and criminal justice. It uses so-called traditional values to express a fear of women and a hostility to gender equality; it also glorifies violence as a "masculine" virtue. Once we have comprehended the fundamental unity of all communalisms, we may understand that the Partition of India in 1947 was the achievement of Indian rather than Hindu or Muslim communalism. Vinayak Damaodar Savarkar was as much a believer in the Two Nation theory as Mohammad Ali Jinnah.

Finally, we urgently need an understanding of political conservatism. The conservative world view is not blindly opposed to things foreign, despite its sanctification of the domestic scene to the level of virtue; it is inconsistent in this regard. Technology is acceptable as long as it may be bent to the needs of state violence. Thus pragmatism shows itself a natural adjunct of conservatism. Nor is it opposed to violence, even of the extrajudicial variety. It is important to

---

3 This ideological beguilement in matters of intense public concern is not confined to India. It has been suggested that "the taking of bribes by government officials in [East European] countries can be viewed with equanimity to the extent that it at least indicates an understanding of how market forces operate in a liberal economic environment." *Transparency International Newsletter,* September 1996, quoted in Harry Shutt, *The Trouble with Capitalism: An Enquiry into the Causes of Global Economic Failure* (London and New York: Zed Books, 1998), p. 168.

stress that *today's Indian and South Asian elite is quite amenable to the pragmatic deployment of political violence*, just as long this violence is not directed at their economic privileges. Narratives of hurt religious sentiment, racial victimization, and thwarted imperialist destiny are the means by which the high and the mighty seek legitimation for extrajudicial violence.

The Perils of Absolute Truth   A major problem is the appeal of the notion of Absolute Truth. The idea that this or that "revealed truth" is the last word in perfection encourages a state of mind incompatible with intellectual growth and the democracy of the intellect, which to my mind are major markers of social progress. It is also conducive to authoritarianism and violence, emanating from both the state and its opponents. Among the many reasons for the eclipse of Soviet socialism was its paranoid stance toward ideas, its tendency to control and suppress the rich Russian intellectual heritage. Communist systems became akin to the structures of medieval Catholicism. Mixed with traditions of tsarist absolutism and caesaro-papism (the confluence of state power with religious authority), it became its own worst enemy. Hegel's "cunning of reason" stood the first Marxist state on its head. The sin of hubris – in this case of the left – brought nemesis on Russia, as it will on all those who claim that infallible knowledge gives them the right to commit irrevocable deeds. This includes the neoconservative currents that seek to hegemonize race, religion, sentiment, and identity in order to perform a demolition job on democracy. No, it is better to accept the tentative nature of truth, and to strengthen our search with restraint of body and spirit.

The latest avatar of epistemological absolutism in India is the elevated status of sentiment in popular and political discourse. (*Hamari bhavnaon ko thes pahunchi hai* – "our feelings have been hurt" – is our most popular Hindi phrase.) The practitioners of wounded sentiment have attained political power in recent years, and the country is agog with their success. Sundry politicians have busied themselves excavating things and matters to which to attach their outrage. The most significant consequence of this trend is the justification that self-appointed guardians of morality have obtained for violence and defiance of law, for cultural policing, book-burning, and the intimidation of artists and creative work in general. Film screenings have been disrupted, writers and painters threatened and beaten up, academic work and speculation subjected to the promise of dire consequences. These tendencies have their resonance in the realm of the mind. By valorizing particularity, fragmentation, and multiplicity in an imbalanced manner and at the cost of the quest for wholeness, the so-called postmodern sensibility has contributed to the erosion of moral values and the rise of ethical nihilism.

Truth is the whole, said Hegel, and this for me is another reminder of the need for balance. But the balance that is akin to truth is not merely the weighing of equal amounts, an artificial and abstract middle ground of vacuous neutrality. It is based rather on an acknowledgment of the multifarious nature of historical experience, the recognition of complexity, and a capacity to exercise judgment. But to judge one has to possess a standard of judgment, one that holds good in practical terms, even after the acceptance of difference. That practical standard can only be nonviolence. This truth engenders growth in human wisdom, and the transcendence rather than the negation of the past. This is what stares us in the face, but we are too cowardly to recognize it, for fear of losing face, losing innocence. Is it so difficult for left-wing intellectuals to acknowledge that horrible crimes were committed in the name of workers' liberation? For nationalists to see the evil that their nation is capable of? Revanchist forms of history-writing are asserting themselves the world over, from Germany to Japan, Russia to Britain. Justifications are produced for colonialism, imperial conquest, and even racism. Having overcome the paranoia of the Cold War, the Western world is inventing novel reasons for keeping the military-industrial complex in business. Today in India we have a government bent on replacing historical thought altogether, save for a litany of complaints about invaders invariably represented as Muslim. We are dangerously close to elevating communal prejudice to the level of state ideology. In Pakistan, on the other hand, history lessons begin with the arrival of Islam; the ideological foundation of the state is focused on an animus toward India and Hindus, and on the impossibility of coexistence. If the very structures of power are so dependent upon animosity, how may we hope for reconciliation?

Justice and the Judiciary   It is difficult to speak of the system of justice without a sense of despair. Indian justice does not have much to do with the truth these days. A notorious case of caste prejudice causing a miscarriage of justice is that of Bhanwari Bai, a village-level social worker or *sathin* in Rajasthan, who was employed under the Women's Development Program for implementing official policy on female empowerment. This included the prevention of child marriage and female infanticide, the protection of rape victims, and issues in health and education. On September 22, 1992, Bhanwari was gang-raped in the presence of her husband (who was severely beaten) by five upper-caste men incensed by her campaign against child marriage. The dilatory tactics of the police in response to her complaints were a personal ordeal, but the 1997 judgment of the court acquitting the rapists caused dismay among women's organizations. The judge averred that since no Indian rustic would stand by while his wife was raped, the complainant must have lied. He added that being "upper-caste" the alleged offenders could not have touched a "low-caste" woman, much less raped her. Cases of the molestation of "low-caste" women by "upper-caste" men are legion in India – yet this made no difference to the learned judge.

In November 1984 there took place one of the most shameful events in the history of independent India: thousands of law-abiding citizens who happened to be Sikhs were brutally murdered by mobs supposedly acting in spontaneous outrage at the assassination of Prime Minister Indira Gandhi by her Sikh bodyguards. Several leading Congress politicians were among those named by witnesses (mainly Sikh women). It took years for the first reports to be filed and years more for cases to be brought to trial. The procedure became subject to intrigue and manipulation, with several of the accused being let off on procedural grounds, such as the late filing of complaints – this although the judges were empowered to condone these delays in light of the trauma that these women had undergone. Twelve commissions of inquiry into various aspects of this pogrom (euphemistically named the "November riots") have had their say – the latest is still at work. The first of these, the Ranganath Mishra Commission, severely indicted the police for deliberately omitting the names of influential persons while filing complaints, dropping serious allegations, and pursuing investigations in a perfunctory manner. Needless to say, all of the senior politicians involved in these events have been acquitted. There have been a handful of convictions of less privileged individuals. Since there is no witness-protection program in India, the families of underprivileged victims of violence have no way of resisting intimidation. Some of these politicians have been readmitted into the Congress Party and will doubtless be campaigning in the next elections in the name of secularism and national unity. To date the Indian Parliament has not had the courage of conscience to pass a resolution condemning the mass murder of Indian citizens and condoling the surviving families. Our criminal justice system has enabled the guilty of 1984 to get away with mass murder.

On September 28, 1991, Shankar Guha Niyogi, beloved leader of the most influential autonomous workers' union in the country, was murdered in his sleep. His was a nonviolent movement, popular with many contract laborers and miners and irksome to the capitalists and liquor contractors of the area around the Bhilai steel plant. A dramatic trial resulted in the conviction of three prominent industrialists and their accomplices for murder – the first case of capitalists being jailed for killing a union activist. The Jabalpur High Court has since struck down the conviction. The case is in appeal before the Supreme Court.

In December 1992, the Babri Mosque in Ayodhya was destroyed in an act of mob frenzy, the culmination of a campaign for its "removal" by the leaders of the main party in the current ruling dispensation, the Bharatiya Janata Party (BJP). Hundreds of citizens perished in the (certainly foreseeable) riots that followed all over the country, including Bombay. Leaders of the various organizations that participated in the event have since then both claimed and disclaimed responsibility, depending on where and to whom they have spoken. The claims of logic and public morality have been subjected to verbal calisthenics bordering on art: the mosque was not really a mosque (although the whole point of the campaign was that Emperor Babar had erected a mosque upon the ruins of a demolished temple), it was a "disputed structure," and had really become a temple in 1949, when idols miraculously appeared inside it (in which case the accused actually demolished a temple); it was not demolished at all but blown up by a bomb; and so on. The criminal case against the forty-nine leaders of the BJP and its familial organizations has not yet been brought to trial, the framing of charges has been delayed for years, and the latest development is the suspension of charges against some of the (most distinguished) accused by the Lucknow High Court on account of a technicality. These persons include the Union Home Minister and the Union Human Resources Development Minister. The technicality is unlikely to be rectified as the state government is controlled by the BJP. Meanwhile the Hindu priest looking after the idols in the "disputed structure" was allegedly murdered, and nothing much is remembered of him except that he had opposed the entire campaign. On April 30, 2000, Subhash Bhushan Sadh, an official from Uttar Pradesh, the state where the demolition took place, boarded a train carrying documents vital to the Ayodhya case. He was to deliver these to the Liberhan Commission, which was inquiring into the events surrounding the demolition. As the train neared Delhi, the man was allegedly pushed out of the train, and told the police so in a dying declaration. He also revealed that his luggage contained important files – but the documents had mysteriously disappeared. I doubt that the truth of this episode will ever be known. I hope I am wrong, but I also doubt that the accused will ever face trial, let alone be punished.

In January 1996 a young female law student, Priyadarshini Mattoo, was raped and murdered in her flat. The accused was a fellow-student who had been stalking her for months. He also happened to be the son of an inspector-general of police. Written complaints had been filed against him, and Mattoo had been given police protection. The accused had been observed at the scene of the crime shortly before the murder. Despite overwhelming evidence – stalking, making telephone threats, shouting at Mattoo in public – he was acquitted on December 3, 1999, because of "lapses" by the prosecution. In fact the judge suspected that the prosecution had deliberately tried to weaken its own case. He faulted the Central Bureau of Investigation for not following procedure, for hiding evidence such as a fingerprint report, for fabricating evidence in favor of the accused. He speculated that "the CBI during trial knowingly acted in this manner to favor the accused." He recorded the attempt by the Delhi police "to assist the accused during investigation and also during trial. ... [Their doings] suggest that the rule of law is not meant for those who enforce the law nor for their near relatives." Nevertheless, the judge came to an astounding conclusion: "Though I know [the accused] is the man who committed the crime, I acquit him, giving him the benefit of the doubt."[4] What a record for the police! A young woman goes to them for help, is raped and killed while under their protection, the principal suspect is the son of a senior policeman, and he is acquitted. Another case of a young man killing a young woman in a fit of rage is in progress while I write – the Jessica Lal case. Those interested may observe the course of Indian justice: the young man and his associates have powerful connections, prosecution witnesses are turning hostile, and we may rest assured that some mystery will envelop the stark evidence. Who then killed Priyadarshini Mattoo? Did Jessica Lal drop dead of her own accord? Who knows? Who cares?

There are thousands of cases of miscarriages of justice in India. One may praise the honesty of the judge in the Mattoo case, but lay citizens might well ask him – if he was convinced of the suspect's guilt, why did he acquit him? Certainly there are magistrates and judges who perform their functions with commitment. However, in all good conscience I must ask my fellow citizens – are not judges part of society, and susceptible to human failings? Are they not accountable before the Constitution and provisions of law? May not the citizenry criticize the decisions of the courts when these are found wanting in truth? I believe the courts are an institution larger than and not reducible to the persons occupying them. Is it not possible, then, hypothetically, that a judge, too, is capable of contempt of court? And is it not true that dereliction of duty in law-enforcement agencies will contribute to public anger, frustration, and conflict? Is it really possible for the criminal justice system to effectively pursue a case wherein the Union Home Minister himself is a prime accused? The structural defects are glaring; the low status and lack of autonomy of the offices of public prosecution, the absence of witness protection, and the susceptibility of police investigations to political interference are high on the list.

India is undergoing massive economic transformations, and these changes are already causing disputes in matters of labor rights, protected tribal lands, and shady deals and contracts. The poorer classes of India will have absolutely

---

4 Judgment of the Additional Sessions Judge, Delhi, December 3, 1999, cited in the national press on December 4, 1999.

no recourse left if the courts fail them. If the system of justice does not improve drastically we shall move further from any chances at social stability and reconciliation.

The Conditions of Reconciliation   In a brilliant novel entitled *Der Vorleser* (The reader), published in Germany in 1995, Bernhard Schlink tells a story of a teenage boy who has a secret love affair with a woman in her thirties.[5] The woman mysteriously disappears, only to reappear when she is put on trial for being a guard in an SS slave-labor camp. Accused of the murder of Jewish prisoners, she is sentenced on the basis of a report that she herself claims to have written. The protagonist realizes, however, that she cannot have written the report, since he knows one of her secrets – that she is illiterate. But he keeps silent. During her long years in prison, he sends her books on tape, and over the years she learns to read. She makes a small bequest to a Jewish foundation in atonement for her role as a cog in the wheel of the Nazi system. In the end she commits suicide, the day before the protagonist is to bring her out into the normal world. *Der Vorleser* leaves us wondering about the meaning of guilt, remorse, punishment, and redemption.

Many of our favorite symbols and fables are attached to a grievance, either artificially or intrinsically. It would seem that the very act of self-definition conjures up injured innocence and righteous grief. How may we deal with this situation? The papacy may see fit to apologize to the ghost of Galileo five centuries after his incarceration, and to the Greek Orthodox Church eight centuries after the sack of Byzantium. But how far can we go along this road? Who will apologize to whom for the Inquisition, colonialism, fascism, and war? Ought we, on the other hand, to sit quiet when the current generation of Japanese children are taught that the Japanese occupation of East Asia in the 1930s was an act of altruism? That only Hindus suffered the loss and violence of Partition? That only Muslims did? What is the proper balance between remembering and forgetting?

Let me try and answer this. Reconciliation is neither the perpetual nurturing of grievance nor the cultivation of amnesia. It requires transcendence, which implies preservation as well as negation (as in rising above, leaving behind). It does not require us to be neurotic – rather, it is the cure for collective neuroses and emotional indigestion. Nor does it deny that humans are nostalgic beings attached to their history. Reconciliation is a decision based upon an acknowl-

5 Bernard Schlink, *Der Vorleser*, 1995, Eng. trans. as *The Reader*, trans. Carol Brown Janeway (New York: Pantheon, 1997).

edgment of the truth as far as we may know it. (The "final" truth of anything
will always remain elusive, but may we not commit ourselves to searching for,
experimenting with, the truth?) It is also the repudiation of collective guilt: the
descendants of racists are not responsible for racism. Reconciliation, however,
cannot be based upon a denial or manipulation of the facts. May we claim, for
example, that there was no such thing as the Holocaust, or that the fire-bomb-
ing of Dresden and the atom-bombing of Hiroshima were simple military
necessities? The last issue of *Time* magazine in 1999 summed up the history of
the twentieth century as a victory of "free minds and free markets over fascism
and communism." Along with William Clinton's essay in the same issue, it represented the Allied victory in World War II as an American one, completely
ignoring the role of the Red Army and the life sacrifice of 20 million Soviet citizens, compared to less than 300,000 Americans. Is this kind of megalomania
conducive to a reconciliation between peoples?

Can we say that Stalinist purges and terror were a pure invention of the
imperialists, that the Red Army committed no atrocities in Central Europe in
1944, that the United States committed no war crimes during the Vietnam War,
that the Pakistan Army never massacred civilians in Bangladesh, that the Indian
Army has committed no atrocities in the Northeast and Kashmir, that China
has an unblemished human rights record in Tibet (not to mention Tiananmen
Square), that the Rashtriya Swayamsevak Sangh (RSS) and its "family" had no
intention of destroying the Babri Mosque, that no temples were ever destroyed
by medieval Muslim rulers? Can we insist that the United Nations in 1948 gave
Israel the right to expand its borders forever, create settlements, and impede the
emergence of a Palestinian state, or that Hitler had the right idea about "purging
the country of the semitic races"? (This is the opinion of the ideological forefa-
thers of India's ruling party, the Bharatiya Janata Party. Israeli citizens may not
be aware that their closest admirers in India include people who believe in the
ideals and methods of Hitler.⁶) Can we claim all these things and still expect
sweetness and light all round? Individuals are free to adopt such views, but danger looms when they are incorporated into common sense. Historical knowledge must be pursued with respect, balance, and freedom from the fear of cul-

6 M.S. Golwalkar, *Sarsanghchaalak* or Supreme Leader of the RSS (the parent body and controlling
authority of the Bharatiya Janata Party) from 1940 to 1973, believed that "Germany shocked the
world by purging the country of the semitic races – the Jews. Race pride at its highest has been
manifested here. Germany has also shown how well-nigh impossible it is for Races [*sic*] and cultures, having differences going to the root, to be assimilated into one united whole, a good lesson
for us in Hindusthan to learn and profit by." Quoted in Christophe Jaffrelot, *The Hindu Nationalist Movement in India* (New Delhi: Viking-Penguin India, 1996), p. 55. In the Indian context
"semitic races" denoted Muslims, whom Golwalkar considered congenitally antinational, along
with Christians and Communists. Schools run by the RSS still teach the "positive side" of Nazism.

tural and intellectual policing of whatever variety. This can only be done by treating both its fortunate and its evil moments as part of a common heritage, by transcending the attachment to particularity that makes us deny the hateful things done by some of our ideological or ethnic ancestors

There can never be any peace and reconciliation without the adoption of nonviolence on the part of the resisters and the acceptance (without resort to state terror) of the loss of privilege on the part of the powerful. Reconciliation is only possible between equals – equals in spirit if not substance. The very act of reconciliation elevates the dignity of the parties concerned, and establishes their basic humanity. But has the spirit of democracy truly pervaded the political ethos of the world? The British prime minister of a few years back could scarcely conceal her sympathy for apartheid. Throughout the decades of the Cold War, the Western world treated racism as a kind of counterpoint to communism (our scoundrels versus theirs). The current U.S. Supreme Court recently decided that the right to vote and be counted was less important than the fulfillment of formal procedures. Hierarchy and caste prejudice still overshadow the implementation of justice in India. Until this fundamental illiberality is discarded by those who command power and substance in the modern world, there can be no reconciliation. *Is it not true that the very question of a truth and reconciliation commission only arose after the acceptance of adult suffrage by the rulers of South Africa?* It is only when we recognize the dignity of our interlocutors that we may begin the psychic task of healing. Such recognition must be founded upon truth, for truth liberates. The great among us are those whom every effort to humiliate leaves unscarred. Their dignity is unimpeachable – they are always equal in spirit, even when they are held in chains. Who can forget Nelson Mandela, who left behind twenty-seven years of incarceration without a trace of bitterness in his soul?

Truth and Solitude   We are fated to face some life crises solely as individuals. This is a commonplace. But there are some whose solitude in extremis will reverberate through the centuries. Jesus Christ, we are told, was one such. His life work is historically unverifiable, but it is a moving and passionate story. And the truth of it still eludes us. ("What is truth?" asked jesting Pilate, and would not wait for an answer.) Gandhi was another solitary seeker after truth; the man known as the Mahatma had a premonition of his assassination, and made a lonely decision to face it without state protection, in order to deliver his final message. What must have passed through his mind when he saw a young man shoot him at point-blank range? Generations will remember the loneliness of these singular individuals, as if to compensate them for not sharing their agony when they needed solace as mere mortals. This posthumous respect lightens the conscience of the living: to surround the sacrifice of a great soul with a crowd of memories becalms us somehow. Our collective remembrance enters the realm of public conscience, of the civic ethos, and acts as a lever of restraint – and of reconciliation. These were extraordinary human beings, whose lives were antidotes to the rampaging disease of injustice on a monumental scale.

Let us remember, too, the millions of ordinary heroes and heroines in the past century. I think of the soldiers of opposing armies who saved each other in the trenches of the Great War of 1914–18, a phenomenon then named fraternization. (With what gentle yet striking irony did nature mark the bloodshed by placing red poppies in the mud of the battlefields.) History also reminds me of Russian women in the late 1940s who rebuilt a devastated country and wept at the rare sight of young men; the victims and survivors of the Holocaust; the thousands of men and women in India during Partition who retained their humanity when everyone around them was conscious only of community allegiance.

What of those whose solitude is not leavened but exacerbated by time, whose pain is of no consequence because they were neither prophets nor leaders, because they left no footprints on the sands of history? When all is said and done and I look back upon the violent century just gone by, I am burdened with the memory of a man whom posterity has rewarded with erasure but whose sacrifice (when we remember him) challenges us with profound and disturbing reflections. I do not know what practical lesson to draw from it. All I can do is pay homage to the unknown artisan named Johann Georg Elser, whose monumental courage and love of humanity was and is enough to redeem the conscience of the German people, the honor of the German working class, and to contribute to the reconciliation of the German present with the German past. I shall tell his story in the appendix below.

In truth, Indians need justice and reconciliation to cross our bridges. How long shall we remain suspended in transition? When will Hindus and Muslims tire of stereotypical images of one another and perceive the ambivalent character of all human beings and cultures? When will our ritually "pure" elite recognize caste prejudice as a barrier to social growth and human development? When will we stop murdering little girls in the womb and in infancy because the stupid masculinity of our great culture obscures the oneness of the human race? Let us strive for the finer balance, the balance between the need for acknowledgment and the need to transcend what has been acknowledged, between the requirements of social order and the necessity of human dignity, between the continuity of institutions and the urgency of transformation, between the anger of resistance and the compassion without which resistance only generates further oppression. It is that balance alone that may strengthen a feasible version of transitional justice. Justice is too important to be left to the judges. It is nothing less than a matter of human survival.

Appendix: In Memory of the True Antagonist   On July 20, 1994, a syndicated article from Hamburg, entitled "Hitler Escaped Assassination by a Few Inches," was published in India.[7] It was written in memory of Colonel von Stauffenberg, who carried out the ill-fated bomb attack on Hitler at his eastern headquarters in 1944. This aristocratic officer was indeed a brave man, whose actions demonstrated the intense dismay that Hitler's regime had caused within the German army. But the statement that von Stauffenberg's attempt "was the closest anyone in Nazi Germany ever came to assassinating the fanatical dictator" is not true. Stauffenberg is justly remembered, but another German has been erased from the literature of resistance, although his plan came within minutes of saving the world from the horror of World War II. It was a more meaningful plan than that of the conservative opposition, which was activated only when faced with military annihilation.

That other German was Johann Georg Elser (1903–45), a man who had trained in carpentry and metalwork, become a cabinet-maker in 1922, and then worked in clock factories through the 1920s. In 1928 Elser joined a Communist-led trade union, as well as a front organization for it called the *Rotfrontkämpferbund* (RFK), but he had little interest in ideological matters, attending few meetings and spending more of his time flirting and playing music with a patriotic dance band. After Hitler became chancellor, in 1933, Elser's political contacts ceased altogether. In 1936 he took up employment in an armaments factory. In the fall of 1938, some months after the annexation of Austria and just before the Munich conference, this unknown man made the remarkable decision to assassinate Hitler. His resolve stiffened after the vivisection of Czechoslovakia: he knew that the Nazis were driving Europe toward war.

Working alone, Elser began stealing explosives from his factory. Learning that Hitler was due to address the Nazi old guard on November 8, the anniversary of the failed putsch of 1923, in the Munich beer hall called the Bürgerbräukeller, he attended the occasion and observed the Führer's movements. He then decided to plant a time bomb in a pillar near the speaker's rostrum. In March 1939, shortly after the Nazis annexed what remained of Czechoslovakia, Elser left his job and returned to Munich with his life savings of 400 marks. He

7 *The Pioneer,* New Delhi, July 20, 1994.

acquainted himself with the beer hall and took up residence at his parents' home in Königsbronn. Confiding only in his father, he worked briefly in a stone quarry, augmenting both his knowledge and his stock of explosives. Beginning in May 1939 he designed his device, and in August he rented cheap accommodations in Munich.

On August 5, 1939, Elser began implementing his plan. Each evening he would eat dinner at the Bürgerbräukeller, hide in a storeroom until the beer hall closed, then emerge to work into the night on the pillar inside which he would plant his bomb. He worked like this for more than thirty days, constructing a hollow space of eighty square centimeters with a small hinged door, neatly fitted to avoid detection. The space was lined with tin, to prevent accidental damage should a nail be driven into it, and with cork, to muffle the sound of the clocks that would detonate the bomb. Elser used two clocks, to make doubly sure the device would not fail. He carried the rubble out in his hands every night, and because he was working on his knees, they became septic. On Monday, November 6, 1939, he set the mechanism to explode at 9:20 P.M. on the coming Wednesday. Down to his last ten marks, he took thirty marks from his sister in Stuttgart, inspected the device on Tuesday, and then proceeded to Constance, on the Swiss border.

Hitler appeared on Wednesday, but cut his speech to less than an hour, ending it before 9:10 and leaving immediately thereafter. The bomb exploded at 9:20, killing a waitress and six members of the Nazi party and injuring about sixty people. A gap of less than ten minutes had saved Hitler and sealed the world's fate. Examined by customs officials at the Swiss frontier, Elser was found to be carrying a postcard of the Bürgerbräukeller, notes on munitions factories, and his old RFK membership card. This was his one mistake, motivated, perhaps, by sentiment. It was to cost him his life. He was detained on suspicion of being a spy and sent to Munich. Meanwhile the Gestapo had launched a manhunt for the unknown bomber. On November 13, after learning that the device had been planted at floor level, the head of the investigation asked to see Elser's knees. He confessed after fourteen hours of interrogation.

Hitler himself, and Himmler, the head of the Gestapo, refused to believe the confession. On November 9, two British secret agents had been arrested near the Dutch border. The Nazis were keen to use the bomb episode for anti-British war propaganda. Moreover, it was politically damaging for them to admit that a German worker had planned and executed such a coup. Elser was subjected to another prolonged interrogation in Berlin, by which time his family had been rounded up. Despite brutal torture, he refused to doctor the truth, which was that he had acted alone. He implicated no one else. To give credence to a "British plot" to be fabricated in a trial the Nazis planned to hold after their victory, he was kept alive for the duration of the war as Hitler's "special prisoner." When defeat stared them in the face, he was shot by guards on April 9, 1945.

In Elser's presence, reported the Gestapo, "one completely forgot that one was in the presence of a satanic monster."[8] Coming from such a source, the comment is testimony to the ordinariness of this man. In his book *The Führer and the People,* the Czech litterateur J. P. Stern writes that to find Hitler's true antagonist "we must look for a Nobody like himself, one who, sharing his social experience, yet lived and died on the other side of the moral fence."[9] (We must thank this professor for giving Elser his due place in the historical record.) Elser had the stubbornness to refuse to salute the swastika, and to leave rooms when Hitler's speeches were being broadcast, yet his motivations remained unintellectual. For him, doing something meant doing something with his hands.

Elser broke down under torture, saying that if his plan had not succeeded it was because it was not meant to succeed. May we blame a man in his desperate position for trying to survive? We also learn from the archive that he had begun attending church during the months before November 1939, making no distinction between Catholic and Protestant churches. He had prayed more in order to feel more composed, and had convinced himself that he would go to heaven "if I have had the chance to prove by my further life that I intended good. By my deed I wanted to prevent even worse bloodshed."[10] Stauffenberg had his comrades. Elser had no one. This inconspicuous man chose to act for decency, justice, and humanity, and into his deed he put the soul of the meticulous German artisan. As Stern says, the fact that he trusted no one is a discredit not to him but to the world he lived in. That few know of his existence today is a comment on our own times. Let us salute the memory of Johann Georg Elser, the little man with the great heart.

8 J. P. Stern, *Hitler: The Führer and the People* (London: Fontana Press, 1990), p. 126.
9 Ibid., p. 123.
10 Ibid., p. 131.

Trauma and Truth

Rory Bester

Introduction　Witnessing is always constituted in the shadow of muteness. The silent internalization of a firsthand experience can only be arrested if the witness decides (whether by choice or by coercion) to make that experience public. The conditions under which silent witnessing becomes public testimony are crucial to understanding the "history" constituted by memory. This history is not simply an inventory of what is remembered or forgotten; rather, it is the narrative tension between remembering and forgetting. Given the way that memories are on the one hand confirmed and protected and on the other hand abandoned, revised, and forgotten, we simply cannot begin to think of "remembering" without "forgetting."

Bodies such as South Africa's Truth and Reconciliation Commission (TRC) are important spaces where remembered history is negotiated in preparation for the archive. Here the tension between forgetting and remembering is the tension between witnessing and testimony. The imperatives of the truth commission are to control the circumstances under which a silent witnessing becomes a testimonial of everyday life – and that control must at least be vigilant and can sometimes involve coercion – and to be alive to the weight and magnitude of the circumstances under which the archive is forged out of memory.

These four processes – witnessing, testimony, memory, and archiving – offer important understandings of the narrative underpinnings of truth commissions, and of transitional justice more generally. The dominant focus of most truth commissions has been the exploration of human-rights violations: acts and experiences of violence and violation committed (and mostly denied) in the past are rearticulated in the present, creating an emotionally charged space where witnessing, testimony, memory, and archiving come together to grapple with a sense of the future. The ways in which witnessing is prevented from becoming testimony, the articulation of testimony in the absence of any firsthand account of a series of events, and the politically prompted transition from witnessing to testimony are some examples of the historical tensions that emerge in this situation. Tensions also appear between history as it is constituted in memory and the extent of that history's absence from and presence in the constitution of the archive. These issues are nowhere more acute than in the case of the TRC, where witnessing, testimony, memory, and archiving exist in a particular relationship to acts of detention, interrogation, and torture committed during the apartheid era.

The ways in which processes of witnessing and testimony were variously articulated and restricted under apartheid is very different from the ways in which these processes have been allowed to play themselves out in the TRC hearings. The TRC, through its use of public hearings and the formulation of a notion of amnesty, effectively allowed witnessing to become testimony and provided a space in which to broker an archive that traverses the divide between private and public memories of violence and violation. This divide is evident in the differences between Paul Stopforth's graphite drawings of scenes of interrogation and torture, from 1979–83, and the newspaper photographs and television footage of Jeffrey Benzien reenacting the "wet bag" method of interrogation and torture before a public audience in 1997.

While these two examples reflect the codes and conventions of utterly different visual discourses, they also represent two very different responses to the presentation of "truth" (or "fiction'"). It is the latter difference that this essay principally addresses. Stopforth's drawings are imagined responses to a witnessing that struggled to become meaningful public testimony. The artist's imagination compensates for a reality in which the continued use of interrogation and torture depended on an ability to frustrate the translation of witnessing into testimony. Benzien's demonstration of the wet-bag method breaks a crucial code of secrecy: it is "real" in so many ways that little is left to the imagination. It is important to note that it was the TRC that facilitated this representational shift from Stopforth's "imaginary" to Benzien's "real" space. This shift has a number of implications for the presentation of remembered history in a postapartheid archive that would mediate the future of a landscape marked by violence.

Apartheid's Spaces of Interrogation and Torture   In the three decades before the release of Nelson Mandela from prison, in 1990, and the unbanning of anti-apartheid organizations, the South African state neurotically refined and redefined legislation pertaining to classifications of detention without trial. Detention for interrogation, preventive detention, short-term detention, detention of state witnesses, and State of Emergency detention were provided for by specifically formulated sections of a number of acts of parliament.[1] The state used its legislative powers to construct the stage upon which individual members of the South African security forces could act with impunity. Such was the state's widespread use of detention without trial that 80,000 people are estimated to have been detained (for varying lengths of time) between 1960 and 1990.[2]

Detention, interrogation, and torture are central to what Allen Feldman calls the "performative construction of state power."[3] Sometimes acting within the chain of command, sometimes acting without "authority," security agents performed in ways that reiterated the power and authority of the apartheid state. Most notably, detention without trial created unchecked opportunities for the security police and other organs of the security forces to interrogate and torture detainees. Detention without trial, torture in detention, and death in detention (often as a result of injuries suffered during torture) are three narratives that went hand-in-hand with the maintenance of "law and order" in apartheid South Africa. They epitomize the power of the apartheid state not only to determine what activities were to be considered "antistate" but also to act with absolute impunity against individuals and groups involved in such activities (however remotely).

During interrogations by South Africa's security forces, detainees were submitted to unchecked beating, electric shock, suffocation, sexual violence, and mental abuse.[4] Ambiguity and disorientation are vital to the interrogator's practice, and to the continued existence of this practice beyond any given victim: within an interrogation room that is often located within the heart of the public domain (but is hidden from public view), the interrogator creates a narrative of abuse that is often without any sense of time and that fractures sensory experiences. The detainee can feel but not see, and never knows when the shouting in his or her ear may fall utterly silent. Space is disordered through forms of confinement that are both real and imaginary. Within this disoriented time and space, confession is offered as an "escape" from violation.

Each of these actions fits the definition of torture outlined by the United Nations Convention against Torture and Other Cruel, Inhumane, or Degrading Treatment or Punishment: "The intentional infliction of severe pain and suffering, whether physical or mental, on a person for the purposes of (1) obtaining from that or another person information or a confession, or (2) punishing him

---

1　These acts included the Internal Security Act (1950), the Suppression of Communism Act (1950), the Public Safety Act (1953), the General Laws Amendment acts (1963 and 1966), the Criminal Procedures Act (1965), the Terrorism Act (1967), the Internal Security Act (1982), and the infamous Proclamation R121 (1985), which initiated three successive states of emergency in the second half of the 1980s.

2　*Truth and Reconciliation Commission of South Africa Report* (Cape Town: Truth and Reconciliation Commission, 1998), 2:187.

3　Allen Feldman, *Formations of Violence: The Narrative of the Body and Political Terror in Northern Ireland* (Chicago: University of Chicago Press, 1991), p. 86.

4　Beating was always the most common form of torture used by the security forces, but the use of suffocation increased dramatically in the mid-1980s. See *Truth and Reconciliation Commission of South Africa Report*, 2:190.

for an act that he or a third person committed or is suspected of having committed, or (3) intimidating him or a third person, or (4) for any reason based on discrimination of any kind." This convention was used by both the TRC's Human Rights Violations Committee, in assessing submissions by survivors of human rights violations, and its Amnesty Committee, in examining applications for amnesty by perpetrators of human rights violations.[5]

But this definition of torture does not encompass the extent of the testimonial and archival silence that often surrounds both the actions of the torturers and the experiences of the tortured. Both are silent witnesses to the space and narrative of torture, but where the torturer's silence testifies to the impunity of the state, the victim's silence is a witness to disempowerment.[6] The interrogators define the act of looking. They command visibility but their actions do not. They control whoever is trapped by vision, and vigilantly ensure that their own vision never traps them.

It was within this politically charged landscape that Stopforth produced his graphite drawings of 1979–83. Stopforth's works grapple with the visibility and invisibility of practices of interrogation and torture in apartheid-era South Africa, and in this way mediate particular forms of witnessing, testimony, memory, and the archive. Interviewed in the *Rand Daily Mail* in 1978, Stopforth said, "I want to bring the facts home to those willing to look. My figures parallel something that we can't be witness to. We can't refuse to accept that these things happen."[7] Stopforth constituted his representations as proxy for something that most South Africans were unable to witness. His representations interrupted the carefully constructed archival silences that by and large prevented the witnessing and testimonial proof of interrogation and torture during the apartheid era. Refusing the silence that was so crucial to the history of apartheid memory, his art provides an important public testimony whose "evidence" exposes a particular politicization of the apartheid archive.

Imagined Space   The death of Black Consciousness leader Stephen Bantu Biko in police custody remains the most prominent of all deaths in detention during the apartheid era. After being arrested on August 18, 1977, Biko was detained

5 Ibid., p. 189.
6 The deep sense of humiliation and vulnerability experienced by victims of interrogation and torture often prevented them from speaking about their experiences. The cries and screams of emotional breakdown, the loss of bladder or bowel control during electric shock or suffocation, sexual violation, and the ultimate surrender of information all contributed to the victim's experience of shame in remembering his or her experiences. See ibid., pp. 188–89.
7 Paul Stopforth, quoted in Sue Williamson, *Resistance Art in South Africa* (Cape Town: David Phillip, 1989), p. 112.

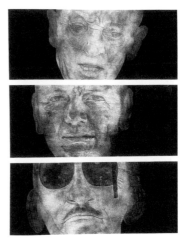

Paul Stopforth,
The Interrogators,
1979
Graphite and floor
wax on board
180 x 100 cm

and repeatedly interrogated and tortured at the Sanlam Building in Port Elizabeth, the regional headquarters of the security police. Although he showed overt signs of external and neurological injuries – in fact he had lapsed into a semiconscious state – a district surgeon signed a release permitting his transfer from Port Elizabeth to Pretoria, a long journey by road. He died from brain damage in a cell in Pretoria Central Prison on September 12.

The inquest into Biko's death relied on the testimonies of the three policemen involved in the interrogation, along with evidence from the two district surgeons who had "monitored" Biko's medical condition during his detention. The policemen testified that Biko had "become violent" during interrogation on September 7, and that in the police team's attempt to subdue him he had hit his head against the wall.[8] The presiding magistrate found no evidence of wrongdoing on the part of the security police. He did, however, refer the inquest findings to the South African Medical and Dental Council, on the grounds that there was evidence of professional misconduct on the part of the district surgeons.[9]

While the magistrate cleared the three security policemen of any wrongdoing, the inquest procedure – its need for testimony from these "surviving" witnesses – introduced their identities into the public domain. In addressing the

8 *Truth and Reconciliation Commission of South Africa Report,* 2:211–12, 4:112–13.
9 *Truth and Reconciliation Commission of South Africa Report,* 4:112–13. The South African Medical and Dental Council took more than two years to make a ruling, and ruled in favor of the doctors. Eight years after Biko's death, however, the Council reopened the case against Dr. Benjamin Tucker, who was found guilty on three counts of improper and disgraceful conduct and was struck off the role of medical practitioners.

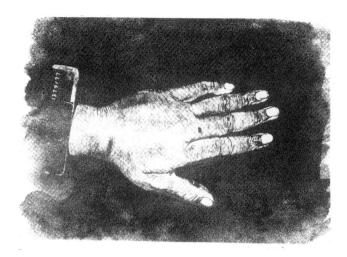

Paul Stopforth,
Untitled, 1980
Graphite and floor wax

interrogation and torture of Biko, Stopforth used these identities to "frame" a narrative. An exhibition of his work in February 1979, variously exploring themes of torture and death, included *The Interrogators* (1979), a vertical trip-tych of three close-up portraits of the security policemen who had beaten Biko in the weeks before his death. The substance of Stopforth's accusation, then, is based on the identities of these "witnesses" to the torture, rather than on the substance of their testimonies.

The cool gray graphite faces, almost translucent against the dark back-grounds, stare out at the viewer from within the frame, utterly confident in the knowledge that we will never be privy to the interiority of their space. It is only the single, barely visible chair, extending over the right side of all three portraits, that potently signals their secret practice: the ordinariness of the gov-ernment-issue chair, hardly noticeable in any other public space, takes on bru-tal connotations when placed in the dark, empty, and private interior of a police station interrogation room. Stopforth's stated intention with *The Inter-rogators* was not only "to show how terribly ordinary these men looked" but, in using the chair, to emphasize the extent to which even "the most mundane objects can take on frightening connotations in prisons and interrogation spaces."[10]

Stopforth continued his exploration of Biko's death in a series of twenty drawings from 1979–80, details of body sections, hands, legs, and feet drawn from photographs taken during Biko's autopsy. In their focus on body parts and

10 Stopforth, quoted in Williamson, *Resistance Art in South Africa,* p. 112.

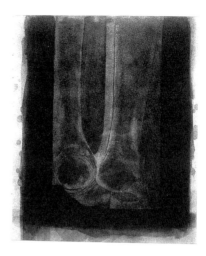

Paul Stopforth,
Biko II, 1980
Graphite and floor wax

their inversion of light and dark spaces, a reference to X rays, the images become fragments of medical knowledge. It is especially their translucent details – from the texture of skin to the clearly numbered wrist tag – that make them both vulnerable offerings of memorialization and clinical indictments of the medical testimony of the attending district surgeons.[11] They focus attention on the surgeons' complicity, not only in knowledge or medical witnessing of Biko's condition but in a testimony that fails to bear full witness, a testimony that is publicly silent, an archive that conserves little about the real responsibility for Biko's death.

Both *The Interrogators* and the Biko series evidence a particular kind of witnessing and testimony in relation to apartheid-era interrogation and torture, and to the death in detention to which these practices led. They speak brutally of not only the brutal effects of interrogation but the identities of the interrogators. But they are largely silent about the blind spaces of torture. The representation of such places involved a struggle to locate the details of a room or cell in the face of an archive that neither placed members of the security police in particular spaces nor implicated them in particular acts.

11 The TRC's special hearings on the health sector highlight the awkward relationship between medicine and political will in apartheid South Africa: "Of all the health professionals in South Africa, district surgeons working under the apartheid government probably had one of the most difficult jobs in terms of upholding medical standards and human rights. On the one hand, they were under a statutory obligation to provide medical care for prisoners and detainees, to record information on the mental and physical health of inmates and to ensure that proper health conditions existed in terms of basic sanitation, food and general health care. On the other hand, there was great pressure on them to support the police and prison authorities for 'national security' reasons." See *Truth and Reconciliation Commission of South Africa Report,* 4:111.

Paul Stopforth,
Interrogation Spaces II,
1983
Graphite on laminated
board
60 x 90 cm

While apartheid-era torture often took place in prisons, farms, detention camps, and private houses, it mostly happened behind the bland outer walls of the police stations of white South Africa. In the context of the continued concealment of human-rights violations from those years, Stopforth's *Interrogation Spaces* (1983) is crucial in attempting to bring the hidden spaces of apartheid into public view. The artist's imagination becomes a powerful substitute for the absence of an archive. While fairly abstract in its visualization of architectural containment, *Interrogation Spaces* is nonetheless a powerful rendition of the spatial isolation, dislocation, and disorientation that lie at the heart of the practices of interrogation and torture. As Stopforth suggests of this work, "The interiors are bleak and sinister, their original function no longer visible. They are now torture chambers – spaces thick with fear."[12]

The struggle to witness, and, more important, to bear meaningful witness, was one of the strategies that preoccupied antiapartheid activists. The state was struggling against witnessing, engaging in conscious repressions of memory that inevitably translated into absences in the archives. In the face of this overbearing opposition, the struggle to witness was often carried forward through the output of cultural workers using a range of different media. Stopforth's desire to create visual art dealing with a form of violence carefully hidden from vision reflects a desire and a determination to bear witness not unlike the desire that underpinned so much of the work of the TRC. But the aesthetics of truth that emerged out of the TRC's emphasis on witnessing and testimony pro-

12 Stopforth, quoted in Williamson, *Resistance Art in South Africa,* p. 114.

Paul Stopforth,
Interrogation Spaces IV,
1983
Graphite on laminated
board
60 x 90 cm

foundly rearticulated understandings of apartheid-era interrogation and torture. It is this shift that I would now like to explore through the example of
Benzien.

Witnessing Truth and Reconciliation   The TRC, established in terms of South
Africa's Promotion of National Unity and Reconciliation Act of 1995, is but one
of a number of examples of transitional justice in post-World War II global politics. The TRC was intended as restorative rather than retributive in nature. Its
staff traveled the country, soliciting oral testimonies from both perpetrators and
survivors of apartheid-era political injustice in order to generate archives that
would adequately reflect the nation's history after 1960. Running on the slogan
"Truth, the Road to Reconciliation," the commission tried to paint a "true" picture of the history of political trauma in South Africa, and thereby to contribute
to the reconciliation of a society polarized by racial prejudice. Promises of reparations to victims and of amnesty to agents of apartheid were the incentives for
giving evidence at the public hearings. The TRC solicited some 20,000 statements of human-rights violations and received a little over 7,000 applications
for amnesty.[13]

13 Only 10 percent of the statements of human-rights violations were heard at public hearings, but all
   of the applicants who applied for amnesty and met its requirements had to appear before the commission. Over half of the amnesty applications received by the TRC were refused, for one or more
   of the following reasons: the applicant denied any guilt; the action for which the applicant sought
   amnesty was not politically motivated; the action was outside the jurisdiction of the TRC; the
   action had been committed outside the amnesty's stipulated dates (March 1960–May 1994).

The TRC faced a number of social and political challenges when it began its proceedings in East London in April 1996, not least of them to ensure that the process became, as Sander Gilman suggests, "the memory of the past made real in the present."[14] The two outstanding features of the TRC process were the public nature of the hearings and the "individualizing" of the applications for amnesty, in other words, examining actions in relation to the individuals who had performed them rather than to the institutions or organizations to which those individuals belonged. These were the vehicles through which the TRC attempted to bring the past into the present: by individualizing applications for amnesty, it ensured a minimum accountability for the details of the past, details that it hoped would paint a more complete picture of apartheid-era human-rights violations; by holding hearings in public rather than in camera (as had been the practice of most of the truth commissions preceding South Africa's), it provided a public space in which witnesses could articulate their personal testi-monials of violence and violation. No previous truth commission had held pub-lic hearings on the scale conducted by the TRC, and this public space also allowed the testimonies to be accessed and witnessed by an audience in situ.

As a retelling and reenactment of narratives of apartheid-era violence, the TRC process was driven by the performances of individual witnesses. These testimonies, some defending apartheid and some decrying it, awkwardly tra-versed the lopsided space between victimization and vindication. The TRC's prioritization of these unique stories over and above institutional accountabil-ity was meant to encompass the circumstances of a history of the "everyday." Flawed as the TRC process may have been, it was an important mechanism that, in allowing individuals and communities a space in which to articulate experiences of oppression, attempted to ensure that the history of apartheid remain part of the consciousness (at least the archival consciousness) of the South African nation.

Making and maintaining the relationship between past, present, and future is one of the primary functions of the archive. Rather than recording the past neutrally, archives are structural forms that make ideological offerings of the past to fuel the fire of humanity's movement into the future. The TRC proceed-ings were inspired by the desire to remember. Its archive has been constructed at the expense of the ambivalence that drives forgetting. As Kenneth Foote writes, "Few events produce such strong ambivalent feelings as acts of violence, and as societies grapple with these feelings in public debate, the struggle comes to

14 Sander Gilman, "Truth Seeking, Memory and Art: Comments Following Four Weeks of Life in the New South Africa," in Allan Boyer and Candice Breitz, eds., *Africus Johannesburg Biennale*, exh. cat. (Johannesburg: Transitional Metropolitan Council, 1995), p. 36.

imprint itself on landscape."[15] But rather than letting this struggle imprint itself on the landscape of the archive, the TRC has reconstituted violence and violation in a manner that does not acknowledge or account for the slippages in meaning and value attached to violence. This is nowhere more clearly illustrated than in the formulation of amnesty.

Both amnesty and the archive are intimately linked to memory. But where the TRC's amnesty applications have often been characterized by appeal to the failure of memory, the mechanism of the archive is driven by a desire to sustain memory. The TRC granted amnesty to applicants whose actions fulfilled basic requirements. (The action had to be politically motivated, and committed between March 1960 and May 1994; there had to be a reasonable proportion between motive and method; the applicant had to make a full disclosure.) Indirectly, then, this amnesty legitimizes certain forms of violence, setting up hierarchies of violent acts that are alternately condoned and condemned within the same archive. As such, for example, the formulation of the amnesty archive is driven by questions of the criminal and the political. In distinguishing criminal from political acts, the code of the amnesty associates "criminal" acts with individual or personal motive and "political" acts with institutional or state sponsorship. With the amnesty hearings the TRC decided whether the criminal acts of agents of the state – acts that were criminal at a fundamental level, in the sense that apartheid can be characterized as a crime against humanity – should be decriminalized if they were politically motivated.[16]

Amnesty and the Archive   On July 14, 1997, after an adjournment for lunch, the TRC resumed its hearing into the amnesty application of Captain Jeffrey Benzien, a former investigator with the Terrorist Tracing Unit of the South African security police. In a community hall in Cape Town, Tony Yengeni, a victim of interrogation by Benzien in the late 1980s, continued his cross-examination of the applicant. Following a series of questions regarding the use of the "wet bag" method, Yengeni asked the commission to have Benzien demonstrate this particular form of interrogation and torture. After deliberation over the suddenness of the request, and uncertainty over the availability of a suitable bag,

---

15 Kenneth E. Foote, "To Remember and Forget: Archives, Memory, and Culture," *American Archivist* 53 (Summer 1990): 385.

16 The narratives of criminalization and decriminalization established by the TRC operate differently in the Human Rights Violations Hearings. One of the strengths of these hearings is that the apartheid victim's once-criminalized body undergoes a process of decriminalization through the performative reconstruction of violence and violation, a return of "citizenship" ("official" belonging) to the once-criminalized victim.

Left and opposite:
Jeffrey Benzien
demonstrating the
wet-bag method of
interrogation and
torture.
Photo: Leon Muller,
1997.

handcuffs, and a volunteer to play the victim role, the commission agreed, and
Benzien proceeded to reenact the wet-bag method to a frenzied audience and
media. Antjie Krog, a radio journalist for the South African Broadcasting Cor-
poration, later described Benzien's demonstration as "one of the most loaded
and disturbing images in the life of the Truth Commission."[17]

The bag used in wet-bag interrogation was a cloth bag normally used in
police stations to hold a prisoner's loose articles of property for the duration of
his or her arrest. In his amnesty application, Benzien describes his use of the
method as follows:

> I get the person to lie down on the ground on his stomach … with that person's hands
> handcuffed behind his back. Then I would take up a position in the small of the per-
> son's back, put my feet through between his arms to maintain my balance and then pull
> the bag over the person's head and twist it closed around the neck in that way, cutting
> off the air supply to the person. … On occasions people have, I presume, and I say
> presume, lost consciousness. They would go slack and every time that was done,
> I would release the bag.[18]

Benzien's demonstration of the wet-bag method catapulted his testimony into
the international media spotlight and subsequently became one of the best-
remembered contributions of any of the TRC's amnesty applicants. His performative reenactment of what had remained hidden within the words of so many

17 Antjie Krog, *Country of My Skull* (Johannesburg: Random House, 1998), p. 73.
18 *Truth and Reconciliation Commission of South Africa Report*, 2:192–93.

TRC submissions and testimonies suddenly brought to light a vision of the physical brutalities that had underpinned the hidden spaces of interrogation and torture in apartheid-era South Africa. Visual representations of Benzien's demonstration in the media (through press photographs and to a lesser extent television footage) have become archival moments and icons of the TRC process.

The space of interrogation, so intimate to the construction of power, suddenly shifted from a police station to a TRC hearing. If "the prisoner's confession is the interrogator's violence reaudited and redoubled as truth,"[19] as Feldman suggests, then Benzien's confession, in the context of an amnesty application before the TRC, is his own violence reaudited and redoubled as a narrative of remembering and forgetting, of conceding to the accusations of his victims without necessarily remembering particular acts of violence, of apologizing for what he remembers (as a "different" past) and of forgetting for the sake of a shared future. Benzien's performance thus visualizes history, with the perpetrator as the "knowing" performer, the narrator of the story. Benzien's demonstrative testimony invoked the double performance of violence, the original act and its reenactment in performance.[20]

At crucial moments in Benzien's confession his testimony enacted his own disempowerment. This was a narrative of inversion, a shift from the position of torturer to that of "tortured." Just as the torturer had marked the tortured in

19 Feldman, *Formations of Violence*, p. 136.
20 The volunteer who played the "victim" in Jeffrey Benzien's demonstration was Mncebisi Sikhwatsha, a leader in the African National Congress's Youth League.

apartheid space, so was the torturer "marked" by the tortured in this particular postapartheid setting.[21] Captured by the waiting photojournalists and television crews, the physical act of Benzien's confession to the use of the wet-bag method visually marked his body at the moment of material complicity. Benzien became "marked" by the "violence" of the photographic image: "The Photograph is violent: not because it shows violent things, but because on each occasion *it fills the sight by force*, and because in it nothing can be refused or transformed."[22] This visual image refuses the context of Benzien's amnesty application; so too does the space of spectacle.

Mediated Space   By making individuals account for a history and by allowing the public and the media to stand witness to that account of history, the TRC allowed itself to become a space of individual performance and public spectacle. Woven together, these cultural articulations of performance and spectacle often served to confound the TRC's narrative re-presentations of the memory of the past, and their meaningfulness as a sustainable archive. The TRC's archive is overwhelmingly a narrative of the body as the performative site of violence. In the South African context, it is the physically and emotionally marked body that narrates the history of apartheid-era violence. As Feldman writes, "The very act of violence invests the body with agency. The body, altered by violence, reenacts other altered bodies dispersed in time and space; it also reenacts political discourse and even the movement of history itself."[23] The marked body is not only a physical "site," a place, but also a visualized "sight," a space – a space of the discursive reenactment of violence – in that the photographic record of the performances before the TRC honed in on the body as a primary narrative agent. The photographic record of the TRC process became an archive of the body (as archive) and a visualization of the physical traces of the performative body as a site of trauma (both past and present).

Benzien's testimony on the wet-bag method was one of the most overt examples of the theatrical re-presentation of pain during the TRC amnesty hearings. The sight of Benzien demonstrating something that had until then been hidden from view became an iconic image of the TRC's work, and, as a consequence,

---

21 Throughout his amnesty application Benzien's sense of himself constantly shifts between "torturer" and "tortured." His obvious discomfort with the latter role probably accounts for his efforts to reestablish the former one, or at lease remind audiences of it. This rearticulation was most overt in his boast that the wet-bag method usually yielded results within thirty minutes, and in his declaration of its success when used on Tony Yengeni.

22 Roland Barthes, *Camera Lucida: Reflections on Photography*, 1980 (Eng. trans. New York: Hill and Wang, 1994), p. 91.

23 Feldman, *Formations of Violence*, p. 7.

invoked a space of spectacle. From Yengeni's desire to see what had been done to him to the TRC Commissioner Khampere's comment "We can't see Mr. Benzien" when the former investigator sat down on top of the volunteer (to which the chairperson responded, "We will just have to stand and have a look"), the politics of looking are fundamental to the narrative at hand. Further: they become an act of surveillance, of capturing Benzien in the act of his own complicity.

The photographic record of the TRC's performative body archive is primarily a media archive.[24] In addition to what the TRC has collected, ordered, and preserved in its own "official" archive, there is a vast archive of media images of its process; in fact press photographs, along with television coverage, constitute one of the dominant visual records of the commission's work. This record was made by careful watching of the performances of individual witnesses (whether as victims or perpetrators) to acts of violence. But the press's photographic archive was also instrumental in generating a public spectacle out of these performances. Public perceptions of amnesty applicants such as Benzien have been mediated by photographic and television images more than by any other testimony before the TRC. In Benzien's case this is mostly because of the uniqueness of his demonstration and visualization of the wet-bag torture method.[25]

This body of media-derived visual narratives is an archive that stands in the face of the TRC's own archive and five-volume report. In generating its own visual narratives around performance and spectacle, the media's archive has implications for the representational politics of the memory of violence. Fundamentally, the relationship between victim and perpetrator has been informed by the visual archive of this history as it has been constructed in the media. The generation of postapartheid identities in South Africa, and specifically the attempt to move beyond the edges of apartheid memory, is partly dependent on the construction and interpretation of these archival spaces.

Spectacles of Violence   Benzien's performative reenactment of the wet-bag method is evidence of a particular return to the spectacle of violence. The spectacle generated by visual representations of the performance established a tension between the image of Benzien framed in an admission of guilt and the

---

24 Most of the photographs produced in the context of the TRC were taken for publication in the news media. A number of photo-essays, however, stand out as editorial commentaries on the TRC's work. Most notable of these are the portrait essays by Jillian Edelstein and Geoff Grundlingh.

25 The most common image of amnesty applicants in media representation of the TRC process was that of the impassive, stone-faced individual listening to the accusations made against him.

image of Benzien being granted amnesty in February 1999.[26] The nature and
extent of this particular slippage – between his performative confession of guilt
and the archival decriminalization of his actions (through the amnesty granted
him by the TRC) – are crucial to the relationship between witnessing, testimony, memory, and the archive. Effected through the ideological space of the
TRC, this memorial inversion of the relationship between torturer and tortured
also raises issues regarding the role of photographic media in narrating testimony, engendering spectacle from performative acts, and archiving memories of
violence.

The slippage of expectations, between the refusal of amnesty and the granting of it, is irritated by the spectacle of the violated body. Activated by the
media's coverage of the process, this is a spectacle of the mediation of social relationships through images. Spectacle, as Guy Debord writes, "is not a collection
of images; rather, it is a social relationship between people that is mediated by
images. … All that was once directly lived has become mere representation."[27]
The memory that is the future of the archive is blunted by the mediation of disparate expectations by means of photographic images.

Within the performative space of the TRC process, which was often gripped
by a sense of theatricality and drama, the trauma of the private space of individual witnesses was transformed into the public spectacle of the violated body.
Effected, in part, through the role played by the print and electronic media,
spectacle runs the risk of reducing performative space to a cultural traffic in
body parts. The dismembered identities of trauma are traded as the currency of
different cultural psychoses. Benzien's demonstration of the wet-bag method, in
functioning as a narrative confirmation of the trauma of apartheid-era interrogation and torture, is one of the most overt examples of the threat that the spectacle of performance will dismember the body from its narrative. Castrated and
frozen by the frame of the camera, the body is made available for seditious judgments. But the media's representations mutilated Benzien's performance of violence, castrating the original narrative in a spectacle of mediated vision that
establishes the conditions for a slippage between the archived vision and the
amnesty verdict.

It is here that the photograph implicates itself in the TRC archive, not so
much as witness than as visual evidence and proof of guilt. Through an appeal
to a notion of politically motivated action, the TRC's reconstitution of the vio-

26 During and following his amnesty application Benzien continued to be an official in the South
   African Police Service. He is currently a captain in the Service's Air Wing in Cape Town.
27 Guy Debord, *The Society of the Spectacle*, 1967 (Eng. trans. New York: Zone Books, 1994),
   pp. 12, 14.

lated body (as archive) attempted to distinguish between overlapping narratives of criminalization and decriminalization. TRC photography, to some extent, is a re-presentation of this narrative reconstruction of criminalized and decriminalized violence. But like surveillance photography, this visual re-presentation is a vigilant observation that searches out and frames the moment of the incrimination of the performative body. Benzien's demonstration of the wet-bag method provided one such moment. In making the act of incrimination the focus of the re-presentation, TRC photography establishes a narrative of the expectation of decriminalization that stands in the face of the prospect of amnesty.

Conclusion   The TRC process has two important archival features. The first is the relationship between the ability to access the archive and the development of a culture of transparency; the second is the TRC's potential to generate a truly participatory archive. Writing about South African archival practice, Verne Harris and Christopher Merrett suggest that the right of access to official records is crucial to the development of a culture of transparency.[28] The TRC process is fundamentally about generating a culture of historical transparency that will ensure the public's right of access to a past that has until recently been not just unacknowledged but deliberately hidden from view. For Jacques Derrida, "Effective democratization can always be measured by this essential criterion: the participation in and access to the archive, its constitution, and its interpretation."[29] The second important archival feature of the TRC process is its potential as a participatory archive. The way in which the TRC was established has allowed everyone in South Africa the possibility of contributing to its archive. The statements and testimonies of victims and perpetrators of violence constitute an important oral archive of memories of apartheid-era history.

But the participation in the constitution of the archive is not sufficient for effective democratization of South Africa to take place. The interpretation of archival materials is as important as access to them. In providing access to its archive and offering interpretations of its archival material, the TRC has to think about mechanisms for reconciling the image of Benzien demonstrating the wet-bag method with the fact that he was granted amnesty. In TRC photography, the performative body becomes a vehicle for spectacle. In the construction of an archive of violence, where material so easily takes on the

---

28 Verne Harris and Christopher Merrett, "Towards a Culture of Transparency: Public Rights of Access to Official Records in South Africa," *American Archivist* 57 (Fall 1994): 680–92.

29 Jacques Derrida, *Archive Fever: A Freudian Impression*, trans. Eric Prenowitz (Chicago: University of Chicago Press, 1996), p. 4.

authority of "truth," will the Benzien narrative eternally remain spectacle? To what extent will the TRC archive produce and embody the performance of spectacle? What do the photographs of Benzien do to a sense of the visibility and invisibility of his amnesty narrative? What do this visibility and invisibility mark? What is absent in the violence represented in photographs like those of Benzien demonstrating the wet-bag method? These are just a few of the questions that need to be asked of the makers of the TRC archive. They are important questions, because, as Allan Sekula suggests, the archive not only authenticates the truth claims of the photograph but is embedded in the photograph itself.[30]

Between the disbelief and the grief, the TRC, as a mechanism of self-scrutiny, has not only to wrestle with heavy questions of forgiveness and responsibility but also to grapple with the extent to which reconciliation is dependent upon offering forgiveness and acknowledging responsibility. The emotional cost associated with acts and gestures of shame, humiliation, and betrayal, or else of benign lack of acknowledgment and open dismissal, have all made the TRC one of the most contested sites of postapartheid identity in South Africa. As the TRC phrase "Truth, the Road to Reconciliation" suggests, the generation of a narrative "truth" (in whatever form) is but the first step in a long journey toward reconciliation. What is going to take these testimonial performances beyond their "truth" toward a proper sense of healing is the construction of an archive that engages the problems and limitations of the "unofficial" archives in ways that negate the spectacle that has been so much a part of the TRC process. In the media's spectacular commodification of body and performance, meaning becomes overpowered by silence. The TRC has to guard against this silence in constructing its archive. This particular vigilance of archivability is crucial in ensuring that the road to reconciliation, to healing, remain unobstructed.

Like media images that position violence in a particular way, the archive plays an important role in positioning experiences of violence. Benzien's performative reenactment of the wet-bag interrogation method, and the representation of that performance by the media, have implications for the construction of an archival desire that is driven by amnesty. In that a postapartheid archive has to be constructed out of the narratives of amnesty applicants (who are prone to forgetting), there is a need for critical engagement with the practices and discourses of archives and archiving. This has to be done in a way that would account for the failure of memory, both on the part of applicants themselves

---

30 Allan Sekula, "The Body and the Archive," in Richard Bolton, ed., *The Contest of Meaning: Critical Histories of Photography* (Cambridge, Mass.: The MIT Press, 1989), p. 374.

and in the representations of the media. Fundamentally, what role, if any, will the TRC archive play in neutralizing the spectacle imagined in Benzien's demonstration of the wet-bag method?

There is also a need for vigilance against what the Benzien press photographs are bending toward. In the representation of violence, and the recuperation of memories of violence (whether overt or covert), there is a precarious relationship between history, memory, and representation. Slippages occur between the original act, its embodiment in performance, and its re-presentation in photographs. What do these slippages do to a sense of culpability, responsibility, and complicity? This essay is an attempt to understand the moments of public disaffection with the TRC through a discussion of visual images as representation and narrative. When Archbishop Desmond Tutu, the chairperson of the TRC, thanked "the electronic and print media for helping to tell ... the stories," little did he realize the narrative implications of his remark.[31] The complicity of media spectacle in the creation of a space of disaffection from the TRC process needs to be addressed in the construction of the TRC's archive. In the space between memory and amnesia, between the trauma of memory and the comfort of forgetting, how do we re-present the TRC without turning it into spectacle? It is imperative that the place of the past in contemporary social practice be examined, especially the extent to which the invocation of a contemporary is a negation of the past (or vice versa). Linked to this is a critical urgency to theorize the archive not only as an assumed space of uncontested memory but also as a site of retribution. And we must not forget, of course, who speaks in the name of archival recuperation.

31 Archbishop Desmond Tutu, Human Rights Violations Committee Hearing, East London, South Africa, April 8, 1996. See www.truth.org.za.

The Persistence of Memory:
The Search for Truth, Justice, and Reconciliation

Urvashi Butalia

On March 11, 1947, Sant Raja Singh of Thoa Khalsa village in the Rawalpindi district picked up his sword, said a short prayer to Guru Nanak, and then, with one swift stroke, brought it down on the neck of his young daughter, Maan Kaur. As the story is told, at first he didn't succeed: the blow wasn't strong enough. Then his daughter, aged sixteen, came once again and knelt before her father, removed her thick plait, and offered him her neck. This time his sword found its mark. Bir Bahadur Singh, his son of fourteen, stood by his side and watched. Years later Bir Bahadur told me the story: "I stood there, right next to him, clutching on to his *kurta* as children do. ... I was clinging to him, sobbing, and her head rolled off and fell ... there ... far away. It was such a frightening, such a fearful scene."

Shortly after this incident, Bir Bahadur's family fled Thoa Khalsa, heading toward the Indian border, where they hoped to find safety. India was being partitioned, and large-scale carnage, arson, rape, and looting among Muslims, Hindus, and Sikhs had become the order of the day. In many families, like Bir Bahadur's, the men decided to kill the women and children, fearing that they would otherwise be abducted, raped, converted, impregnated, polluted by men of the other religion – in this case Islam. They called these killings the "martyrdom of women."

It was only two years earlier, in 1945, that Bir Bahadur's family had moved to Thoa Khalsa. Talk of a possible partition was in the air and they were worried for their safety. Saintha, the village in which they had lived for many years, was a Muslim-majority village; in fact theirs was the only non-Muslim family there. It was this that had made Sant Raja Singh decide to move to Thoa Khalsa, where there were many more Sikhs than Muslims. Everywhere in India at the time, people were banding together with their own kind, believing that safety lay in numbers. Ironically, and tragically, it was in villages like Thoa Khalsa that the real violence took place. In retaliation for attacks by Hindus and Sikhs on Muslims elsewhere in India, villages in this part of Rawalpindi – inhabited mainly by Sikhs – came under concerted attack from Muslims for several days.

Shortly after Sant Raja Singh killed his daughter and several others, he asked a relative to take his life – perhaps the burden of the knowledge of what he had done was too heavy to bear. A single gunshot and he joined the ranks of the martyrs. Later, some ninety women of the village jumped into a well and drowned themselves to escape possible rape and conversion.

Forty years later Bir Bahadur told me these stories. I had met him while researching a book on oral histories of the Partition of India. In the lower-middle-class area of Delhi where he lived, Bir Bahadur was someone people looked up to – he came from a family of martyrs. Not only his sister but several other women had been killed that day. Bir Bahadur had been a boy at the time, but his memories were crystal clear and sharp. He remembered the fear and the violence, remembered too that when the attacks had begun to seem imminent, people from Saintha had come to Thoa in a delegation to offer his family protection in his "home" village. They were led by Sajawal Khan, the village headman. But his father had turned them away. They were Muslims, and although he had lived among them in safety and peace for many years, he no longer trusted them. Bir Bahadur has never forgotten this rejection.

Stories of such violence – and more – are routine when Muslims and Hindus speak of the Partition of the Indian subcontinent in 1947. The British decision to partition the country into two, India and Pakistan, led to the displacement of millions of people, a million deaths, and nearly a hundred thousand incidents of rape and abduction. Many other forms of violence became commonplace. Women were particularly vulnerable: not only was there mass rape and abduction but hundreds were killed by their own families, ostensibly as a form of "protection." Some had their breasts cut off, others had symbols of the "other" religion tattooed on their bodies. But while stories of violence are routine, what are less known are the stories of friendship that cut across the rigid borders drawn by the Indian and Pakistani states. In the year 2000, Bir Bahadur and I embarked on one such journey of friendship and reconciliation across what had until then seemed a somewhat intractable border.

It began with a phone call from Chihiro Tanaka, a Japanese television journalist. She was keen to make a program on an Indian taking the India-Pakistan bus to visit his or her relatives. She and a crew would travel along with this person, filming the journey and the "homecoming." She asked for suggestions; I offered Bir Bahadur. He had wanted to go back to his home village in Pakistan for years but had never had the opportunity, not because it was expensive but because visas between the two countries are almost impossible to get. Now the chance had presented itself.

Now in his seventies, Bir Bahadur Singh is a tall, statuesque Sikh with a flowing white beard. Always dressed in white, with a black turban and a saffron head-cloth showing through, he makes an arresting figure and stands out in a crowd. Bir Bahadur and his family were only a few among the millions of refugees who had fled from Pakistan to India. They carried nothing with them, and Bir Bahadur's key memories of the time are of hunger, fear, and cold. Once in India, he and his family had struggled to keep body and soul together. He tried his hand at different things, then, at eighteen, managed to put enough together to set up a small provisions store. Later his family arranged for him to marry a woman from a village close to his home in Rawalpindi, and together they brought up a large family. Bir Bahadur has never been rich, and has worked hard all his life for the sake of his children. A might-have-been politician (he stood for municipal elections on a Bharatiya Janata Party ticket some years ago and lost), he now leads a retired life, dividing his time between his farmhouse close to Delhi, his extended family of children and grandchildren, and his old (ninety-plus) mother, who lives nearby. He was beside himself with excitement at the news that he might get permission to travel to Pakistan and visit his home village.

With Japanese intervention, visas were swiftly arranged, and a few days later we left for Pakistan. Bir Bahadur arrived at my house with a small bag and a sackful of hard dry coconuts. These were to be his offerings to the people of his village. "There are no coconuts there," he explained, "and people love to have them." He had also written two letters, one to the people of his village, one to his schoolmate Sadq Khan, son of Sajawal Khan. "We were good friends in school," he said, "I am sure he will remember me." These he carried with him in the event that we did not make it to the village. He was convinced we would find someone, somewhere, who would carry his letters there, and that in response people from there would immediately arrive to see him. For days he had been like a child, excited and nervous. He had called me every day – sometimes two or three times in a day – to check on this or that detail. Would we be staying in a hotel? How much money should he bring? Would I be with them the whole time? Could we not persuade Chihiro to do a radio program instead of one for television (we did) – it would be much less obvious? Now that we were actually on our way, he could not believe his luck.

Heavy rain and bad monsoon weather delayed the flight. We spent a long and tiring night waiting at Lahore airport, uncomfortable in plastic seats. Occasionally Chihiro and I would doze off, out of sheer exhaustion. But not Bir Bahadur. Every time I opened my eyes, I found him wide awake, sitting on his haunches in one of the airport chairs, recounting his story to someone or other – now a family on their way to Karachi (also delayed), now two helpful employees of the airline (with whom he was quickly exchanging photographs and addresses), now the toyshop owner or the man selling tea. ... Hazy with sleep, I wondered wearily whether there was anyone at the airport he'd left out of this storytelling.

Islamabad is a city of wide boulevards and tree-lined roads. At night, speeding through the deserted streets, there was little to see. We arrived, exhausted, at our hotel at three in the morning after a twelve-hour delay in our flight. But this did not seem to have affected Bir Bahadur. Why did we want to wait till ten in the morning to set off, he asked plaintively, "I won't be able to sleep, let's go at six!" But this proposal was shot down firmly by our Japanese friend, and the time of our departure fixed for ten.

The morning rose clean and washed. Heavy rain had cooled things down and the sun seemed almost mild, the air clear of the oppressive humidity of the monsoon, the trees and plants a rich, freshly washed green. Armed with some water and our passports and visa papers, we set off for Thoa Khalsa. A wide, straight road led through fairly flat terrain to the outskirts of Islamabad. We'd been driving for an hour or so when we arrived at a turnoff, clearly a major junction. One side of the wide road was bordered at this point with small shops selling fruit, juices, cigarettes, food, snacks, and all the small knickknacks that travelers buy when they make stopovers. On the other side was a terminal for buses and tempos (three-wheeled taxis commonly used for local transport), with scooter and tempo drivers shouting out their locations, picking up point-to-point passengers, and quickly shuffling men into separate seats the moment they saw prospective women passengers. (One of the unwritten rules of tempo travel in Pakistan – and indeed often in India too – is that men and women do not occupy the same seat lest they inadvertently touch.)

We stopped here to ask directions, then turned off onto a narrower road to the left. A gate across the road proclaimed a level crossing, and a small signpost gave the name of the station. "This used to be our station," Bir Bahadur told me excitedly, "the train stopped here, and we'd have to take buses from our village to get here!" We stopped in the marketplace to get a better look. The car was immediately surrounded by a crowd of tall, hefty men in *shalvar kameezes*. They were everywhere: at the doors, in front of the car, virtually inside the driver's door. We couldn't move, and I began to panic a bit. In situations like this the rhetoric of hatred that India and Pakistan constantly rehearse comes back to haunt us, and although the situation is harmless enough, it suddenly acquires overtones of fear. But Bir Bahadur was unfazed: "Stop, stop the car," he told the driver unnecessarily, and wound his window down. He leaned out, trained his gaze on the tea stall across the road, and said, to no one in particular, "*Bhai sahib, bhai sahib,* excuse me, can you help?" A cyclist stopped to see what he wanted, and the crowd of men around the car suddenly transformed themselves from a threatening bunch to a group of curious and helpful onlookers peering at two strange women and an odd man, clearly from over the border for he wore a turban and there were no Sikhs in the area. "Welcome, welcome, *sardarji*," they said, "where have you come from? India? What are you looking for here? Can we help you find it?" (*Sardarji* is a term of respect used for Sikhs.) Bir Bahadur immediately launched into his story while Chihiro and I sat nervously, wondering if it was wise, in an unknown place in Pakistan, to recall stories of the violence of Partition.

"I'm from this area," he told them, "my father used to run a shop in Saintha, and I am looking for the road there. Do you know Sajawal Khan, from Saintha?" "Not Saintha," I whispered to him, "we need to know how to get to Thoa Khalsa." "Yes, yes," he said, turning to the man, "and we need to get to Thoa Khalsa as well. But first I want to find Saintha." It was at this point that it became clear to me that Bir Bahadur had decided on his own itinerary for this trip: no matter that Chihiro wanted to capture the drama of taking him back to the place where he had seen such a bloody history, he was determined to go to Saintha, his home village. I felt a curious mixture of relief (that we might not now have to confront what could have been an unpleasant situation), elation (that he had succeeded in doing exactly what he wanted), and concern (for Chihiro and her radio program, which, after all, had paid for us to be here). While these thoughts were turning around in my head and I was wondering how to break the news to Chihiro, I suddenly found that Bir Bahadur had invited one of the men outside into the car. Basheer, he told us, was a "son-in-law of Saintha" – his wife's family was from there – and had offered to ride there with us and help us find the place and the people Bir Bahadur was looking for. "Can you slide up a bit, *beta*?" he said to me, and I pushed myself into as small a corner as I could to make room for the rather large and hefty Basheer. We were breaking the unwritten code here: three of us in the backseat, one woman and two men. The available space was tight and it was up to me to ensure that our bodies remained at least an inch apart. Meanwhile everyone on the road offered us advice and suggestions, one person ran off and came back with six bananas, another asked if we'd like a cold drink, we must be tired, while a third offered us *mithai*. Finally, they waved us off with good wishes, extracting a promise from us that we would come back this way and stop for a cup of tea and some sweets.

And so we set off, down a long straight road, past large fields and scattered homes, the occasional tractor carrying bales of straw, and groups of women drawing water at village wells, their faces partially veiled. Slowly the landscape gave way to a gentle, hilly terrain. We could have been in India: everything looked exactly as it would on the other side of the border, in Punjab – the roadside shops, the villages with their mud houses, the scene at the well, the fields covered with stalks of wheat pushing their way out of the earth. "Son," said Bir

Bahadur to Basheer after a few minutes, "just keep telling me the names of the places we are passing along the way, just keep reminding me." Dutifully, Basheer did as he was told, and at one point, as we were passing a small rise on our left with stray houses scattered along its slopes, bordered by stubby bushes on the road, Basheer said, "That village is called Thamali."

"Stop, stop," Bir Bahadur said to Sain, our driver, "please stop. Thamali is where my wife used to live, it's her village." We swung over to the side of the narrow road and Bir Bahadur and Basheer leapt out of the car and began climbing. "I can't believe it," said Bir Bahadur excitedly, "we used to come here to play. There, there's the banyan tree we used to sit under, and over that hill was her grandfather's house, the water pump – please," he said, turning to me, "please can you take a picture of me by the tree, I'd like to take it back to my wife." As he stood there waiting to be photographed, the tree behind him, a small knot of people – husband, wife, perhaps a brother or brother-in-law and two children – came out of a nearby house. Bir Bahadur greeted the children, affectionately patting them on the head, and waited as the parents drew up. They came, faces open with welcome: "Where are you from, *sardarji*, how have you come here? Won't you come to our home and drink some sherbet with us?"

"No, no, my child," said Bir Bahadur to the young woman, "thank you for your welcome, my daughter. This village, Thamali, is where my wife comes from. I used to play here as a child fifty years ago, long before you were even born. See, see that tree over there? That was the tree we sat under. My wife's family home was over that hill, there was a pond and a water pump there. ... " The pond was still there, they told him, but of course the water pump had gone. The school, too – the building was there, but it was no longer used as a school. Thamali had been at the receiving end of the Muslim attack on Sikhs in March 1947, and many people had been killed. Looking at the small, peaceful village nestling in the July sun, it seemed hard to believe that such violence could have taken place here. I tried to picture the mobs that so many (not just Bir Bahadur) had told me about, the countryside resounding with the cries of murder and revenge, the thirst for blood. How would they have moved from village to village, I wondered inconsequentially, this thin ribbon of road probably wasn't here then. How must people have felt to see hundreds, thousands of attackers coming over these gentle, almost sleepy slopes? What protection did their houses offer? At which points did they negotiate? What do people do when violence breaks out in this way?

The people of Thamali, I remembered being told, had initially refused to believe that they could be attacked. Then someone from another village had persuaded them to climb atop one of the higher houses and look down at the area around them, and they'd done so, seen the mobs, and quickly started to evacuate the village. Some thirty to forty women and girls had been abducted from this village, among them two sisters of a family I had spoken to when I was working on my book. As with many Hindu and Sikh families from which women had been abducted and almost certainly raped, the family refused to acknowledge the existence of these sisters, for their history was a history of shame, best forgotten. And here we were, fifty years later, standing on that very spot, in the slanting, late-morning light, being welcomed by people from Thamali. "Please come," they insisted to Bir Bahadur Singh, "please come and bless our house." Bir Bahadur took a drink of water from the young woman, touched his hand to his brow, and blessed his hostess and her children. "We don't have time to stop, daughter," he said to her, "but I would like to give you something small as a token of my love for you who live in this village now." With this he called down to our driver and asked him to bring his bag out of the car. He pulled out two dried coconuts and held them out to the young couple, "This is a small offering, I know, but I would like you to have it. I have lived here, I know that it's not possible to get dried coconuts here. These are for you with my love, with love from your mother, my wife." Saying this he embraced these strangers he had met only a few minutes before, touched the bent head of the young woman of the house, and turned to us and said, "Come, let us move toward Saintha."

Twenty minutes later we rounded a bend in the road and Bir Bahadur suddenly let out a shout of recognition. "Look, look there," he said, "there's my old school. It looks just the same!" We looked. Atop a little ridge stood a small, low-slung building, with a narrow verandah running its length, and green-painted doors and windows. In the yard in front there was a solitary gnarled tree. It was under this tree, Bir Bahadur told us, that he and his friends had played during their school years, but, he asked, where was everybody? "It's a holiday today," we were told by one of the children who had by now attached himself to our little group. "But many of the students are in the village – you can come and meet them there."

As often happens in villages when outsiders come, by this time our party had acquired something of a following – a clutch of curious youngsters offering to help, a few scruffy-looking children, a stray dog or two. And as we made our way deeper into the village, this small crowd swelled with the addition of a few other young men. There were no girls, of course, nor any women. Within a few minutes we had arrived at a scene of considerable activity: a house was being built. Construction workers looking for all the world like the poor, bedraggled, and hungry construction workers one might see in India, their thin wiry bodies blackened by the sun, their only covering a scrap of tattered cloth, were busy carrying loads of cement from one place to another, while the owners, two burly, prosperous-looking men, stood and watched and supervised. The arrival of our little party caused some excitement. Work stopped. Everyone looked. "Welcome, welcome," said the two large men, instantly recognizing us for out-siders, while their welcome was echoed by the little knot of men – friends and neighbors – standing around. "You're from India, *sardarji*?" they asked, address-ing Bir Bahadur, to which he responded, "Yes, but first I am from here, this is my home." At this, information was exchanged and we were immediately invited into their home, an older building that stood nearby: "You can't go away like this – you are our guests, for us you are like God. Come, let us at least give you a cup of tea, a glass of sherbet." Bir Bahadur thanked them and said that he was anxious first to track down his friends before he settled down to spend any time, and asked their permission to carry on. "Only," they said, "if you promise to stop here on your way back. Are you going to stay the night? Stay with us."

We began walking. Some distance in front of us Basheer spotted three old people shuffling along, weighed down with heavy cloth bags full of provisions. Recognizing two of them as his parents-in-law, he rushed up to them and stopped them. We followed. Bir Bahadur introduced himself (Basheer had already given his parents-in-law the background to the story), giving his father's name first. The old man recognized the name, although he did not remember Bir Bahadur himself. The woman with them, who'd been standing silently, sud-denly opened her mouth in a wide toothless grin and poked Bir Bahadur in the chest. "Are you Biran?" she asked, using the nickname his friends had given him. "Yes, yes," said Bir Bahadur, somewhat surprised, "who are you?" But she wouldn't say. Instead she looked at him, mischief glinting in her eyes, and asked, "How is Santo? Is she still alive?" using the nickname for Bir Bahadur's mother, Basant Kaur, "and how is Maano?" – his dead sister. I slowly realized that the villagers in Saintha did not seem to know about Maan Kaur's death, or the hor-rible way in which she had died, or, if they did, they did not want to make any direct reference to it, and spoke instead as if she were still alive. "Santo is well," said Bir Bahadur, glossing over the second question, "she's in Delhi with all her grandchildren, but tell me who are you?" "I am," she said with a touch of drama, "Sadq Khan's wife." Bir Bahadur gave a great whoop of joy and instantly put his arms around her and lifted her off the ground. "My sister, my sister!" he cried, tears beginning to stream down his face. "Oh my sister, where is my brother? Where is Chacha Sajawal Khan? I heard he had died, is this true? Where is my sister Taj, with whom I used to play? I wrote a letter to you all some time ago. Did you get it?" Questions and more questions. The old woman answered some, avoided others. We later learned that her slight hesitation had been because she no longer had an "official" status as Sadq Khan's wife: he had taken another, younger woman as his wife. But right then all we knew was that the first contact had been made. Sadq Khan was alive and he was in the village.

Sadq Khan's father, Sajawal Khan, had been the headman of Saintha. Although Bir Bahadur's family had been the only Sikhs in a village of Muslims, as both moneylenders and shopkeepers they had been considered important. Sant Raja Singh had been respected and trusted in Saintha. This is how Bir Bahadur had described it to me earlier:

> The Mussalmans used to believe in us, trusted us so much ... that for example those who were workers ... those who used to serve ... if a money order came for someone, no one would go to their homes to deliver it. ... [The post office] was in Thoa Khalsa and the postman would not reach people's mail to them or get money orders to them. That was why, when Mussalmans went away to work from their homes, they would give our address as the place to receive their money orders. ... My father used to make entries in his register scrupulously ... this belongs to so and so, this belongs to so and so ... and then people used to come and buy their provisions out of this ... those people trusted us so much.

In return, however, the Sikhs did not extend the same kind of trust to the Muslims. They practiced the customary untouchability of Hindus toward Muslims, refusing to eat anything cooked or touched by them. In Bir Bahadur's words:

> If there was any function that we had, then we used to call Mussalmans to our homes, they would eat in our houses, but we would not eat in theirs and this is a bad thing, which I realize now. If they would come to our houses we would have two utensils in one corner of the house, and we would tell them, pick these up and eat in them; they would then wash them and keep them aside, and this was such a terrible thing. This was the reason Pakistan was created. If we went to their houses and took part in their weddings and ceremonies, they used to really respect and honor us. They would give us uncooked food, ghee, *atta, dal,* whatever *sabzis* they had, chicken and even mutton, all raw. And our dealings with them were so low that I am even ashamed to say it. A guest comes to our house and we say to him, Bring those utensils and wash them, and if my mother or sister have to give him food, they will more or less throw the *roti* from such a distance, fearing that they may touch the dish and become polluted. ... We don't have such low dealings with our lower castes as Hindus and Sikhs did with Mussalmans.

In 1945, when Sant Raja Singh had decided to move his family and business to Thoa Khalsa because he felt it would be safer there, the villagers of Saintha had tried to dissuade him. We'll keep you safe, they offered, we'll protect you from attacks. But Sant Raja Singh was afraid; he no longer trusted his Muslim friends. There were just too many stories of friends turning into enemies, of old, trusted relationships being betrayed. So he took no heed of their appeals. Once in Thoa, he felt, the family would be safer – should anything happen, the Sikhs could band together and fight. It wasn't like being a lone family amid people who could turn hostile at any moment. The tragedy of course was that in Thoa Khalsa the Sikhs were actually more vulnerable to attack, for the Sikh community there was a target, and the attacks lasted several days. And the tragedy was compounded when Sant Raja Singh rejected the offer of the villagers of Saintha. I quote from Bir Bahadur's description:

> When the trouble started the people came from there [Saintha]. You know that Ma Hasina, whom I mentioned to you, her son, Sajawal Khan, he came to us and said we could stay in his house if we wanted to. He came with his children. But we were doubtful, and today I feel that what he was saying, the expression on his face, his bearing – there was nothing there but sincerity and compassion, and we, we misunderstood him. We had all been through so much trouble and they came to give us support, to help us, and we refused.

In many ways Bir Bahadur's return to Saintha fifty years later was a journey of penance and reparation. For half a century he had carried within him the guilt of his family's refusal. He wanted in some way to appease this guilt, to lighten the load. "I just want to go to Saintha," he had said to me, "and take the soil of my village and touch it to my head. I need to ask their forgiveness." What if they will not forgive, I had asked, doubtful. "Of course they will," he said, confident. "After all, once you fight, what is there left but reconciliation, what is there left but forgiveness?"

Forgiveness, of course, is not so easily asked in something like this. All the time that Bir Bahadur spent in Saintha in the year 2000, neither he nor anyone else could bring themselves to refer to the violence that had taken place in Thoa Khalsa. I could not understand at the time, and I am still unable to do so, whether the villagers of Saintha knew what had happened to Bir Bahadur's family, and to his sister, Maan Kaur; whether they knew that so many women had jumped into a well and taken their own lives … and yet, I thought, surely they must have known. News, and particularly news of this kind, spreads easily between villages that lie close together, as these did. But whenever anyone asked Bir Bahadur about Maan Kaur – and a few did, but others did not, again making me wonder if they knew – he somehow evaded the question. Only once did he say to an old woman who asked: "She died." Maan Kaur's absence hung in the air in virtually every encounter we had, and yet, apart from the odd question or two, no one explicitly mentioned her.

We made our way farther into the village. A small house at the turn of the narrow strip of road we were following came into view. Bir Bahadur told us that this used to be a sweet shop run by someone he knew, and soon enough, almost as if on cue, a group of young women emerged, granddaughters and grand-daughters-in-law of the man in question. Yes, they confirmed, there used to be a shop there, but it closed after the old man died. The conversation was interrupted by the sudden arrival of a tall, emaciated, scruffy-looking old man in a brown *shalvar* and *kurta* and sporting a pencil-thin mustache and a short beard. He hesitated for a moment, listening. Then he fixed Bir Bahadur with a sharp direct stare and asked, "Are you Biran?" "Yes," said Bir Bahadur, "and who are you?" "You don't remember me?" said the man, "really, you don't remember me?" I couldn't tell whether he was angry or amused; there was a glint of something in his eyes. "No, I'm trying," said Bir Bahadur, "but I can't. Tell me your name." "You bastard," said the old man, "you nearly strangled me to death one day! You jumped on me and almost scratched my throat into ribbons," he said, gesturing wildly at his throat, and then leaping onto Bir Bahadur and making as if to scratch his throat. There was one of those moments of perfect stillness. Suddenly fear was palpable. I realized in a moment that even though the event was more than fifty years past, we had, after all, carried the history of that bitter division with us. I felt a stab of fear at our situation. And then we saw that the old man was chuckling quietly to himself. He had made a joke! "You crazy," said Bir Bahadur, once he'd been reminded of the story, "and I'll scratch your throat again!" and he leapt on him in mock attack, as the two tangled and laughed and cried at the same time and the old man, whose name was Aslam, recounted the story.

He and Bir Bahadur had been at school together, and one day Aslam had accepted a dare from his schoolmates to "pollute" Bir Bahadur's drinking water by putting the earthenware pot in which it was stored to his mouth. Hindus and Muslims did not drink from the same vessel, or keep their water in the same pot, for fear of pollution – the Hindus, that is, feared that the Muslims would pollute their water. It seemed incredible to me that Bir Bahadur's family, the only non-Muslim family in the village, could still keep to these taboos, but they did. The young Aslam had drunk from Bir Bahadur's pot and had then teased Bir Bahadur about it, at which the incensed young Sikh had attacked his friend and tried to scratch his throat. "You used to have such long nails then," shouted Aslam gleefully, "let me look at your nails now," and he grabbed one of Bir Bahadur's hands to examine it. The boys had fought, and had then been gently pried apart by the village elders, who had explained to Aslam that he should not have done what he did, that it was important to respect the customs of others – something, I thought, that we would do well to remember today.

Bir Bahadur had not remembered this particular incident, but water and food had played a major part in his journey home. "There are two things I want to do if we make it to Saintha," he had told me earlier, "to drink water from the village well and to eat in the home of a Mussalman." This was his private penance, his reparation, his way of asking forgiveness for the harshness and cruelty of Hindu "untouchability" and the purity and pollution taboos practiced by Hindus and Sikhs. Now he turned to Aslam and said to him, "Brother, can you take me to the village well. I want to drink the water from there." Wordlessly, almost as if he divined what it was that drove Bir Bahadur to make such a request – for between the first instance of playful pollution and today stood a long history of hate and violence – Aslam led us down the road to a half-covered well. Two young men from the village were dispatched to find a couple of tumblers, while others lowered the bucket into the well – which looked, at first glance, as if it might not be too healthy – and drew up a bucketful of clear cool water. Bir Bahadur took the tumbler from the young man who had filled it and held it out to him, and touched it to his forehead and drank deeply. He closed his eyes, and seemed to pray as he drank – I could not make out the words, but I thought he was asking forgiveness, not so much for himself but also on behalf of his people – and then he bent, took up a fistful of earth, touched that in turn to his forehead, and ran it over his turban. There was silence all around: all of us watching, somehow sharing in this most private of rituals and yet feeling a bit like intruders. I could feel my eyes prick with tears – how, I thought, how could we have done this to ourselves? How could we have allowed ourselves to be divided thus? And then the spell was broken as two old women, watching us from a balcony above the road, spoke up and asked Bir Bahadur if he was Biran. And he was off again. But not before he had turned to me and offered the remainder of the water to me: "Here child, you drink also," he said. After a moment of doubt about how clean or otherwise the water was – after all, the well was open to the sky, even though the water in the bucket looked clear – I decided that there were times when considerations of bacteria and health simply did not matter. I put the glass to my lips and drank.

News of Bir Bahadur's visit had spread in the village, and we had collected quite a large following. We moved on, Bir Bahadur and Aslam in the lead, talking about this field and that crop, this hillock and that house. We were heading, I guessed, toward Sadq Khan. Finding him, I realized, was not going to be hard – with the mysterious village grapevine at work, everywhere we went people came out to greet Bir Bahadur, their faces wreathed in smiles of welcome. As if in support of our little expedition, the day remained bright and clear, the heat and humidity miraculously restrained. Bir Bahadur meanwhile did not know whether to laugh or cry – as each new person came up and enfolded him in an embrace, his tears fell with a sort of abandon, drops of moisture glistening on his white beard. "These are tears of joy, *beta*, don't worry," he reassured me every time I looked at him. "I am so happy. Did I not tell you we would be welcomed?"

We crossed a small bridge over a nullah, skirted slushy wet mud still recovering from last night's heavy rain, and made our way through some low bushes up a green grassy slope. To the left and right just above us stood two houses, the one a makeshift sort of barn, the other an open, airy living space that held three or four old men and women. Between the houses ran a small lane leading to another house farther back. As we wound our way up, people came out of the house to greet Bir Bahadur and began to talk. I suddenly became aware that, for the first time since we had entered Saintha, Bir Bahadur's attention was distracted. He was not listening. Instead he was looking at the narrow lane that led to the house at the back. Through this, now, came a small, stocky man in a *shalvar* and *kurta*, a two- or three-day stubble on his face, shuffling along with difficulty. As he drew closer a sort of silence descended on our group, and we watched as he broke away from the clutch of old women and children outside the house and made his painful way down toward us. His face held a smile but his eyes shone with tears. I think both of them knew instantly who the other was, but for some moments it seemed as if we were all caught in a state of suspension. No one could move.

Then he came within a few steps of Bir Bahadur and said to him, in a whisper, "Biran, is it really you? After all these years?" And Bir Bahadur, laughing, crying at the same time, thanking God, begging forgiveness, opening his arms wide and saying, "Sadq, my friend Sadq ... the gods be praised ... Vahe Guru," he said, lifting his eyes heavenward, "Vahe Guru, my cup is full." With his arm around Bir Bahadur, Sadq Khan turned him gently toward the house and said, "Come, let me take you to your home." It was then that I realized that the house at the end of the lane, Sadq Khan's house, was the house that Bir Bahadur had grown up in.

As if on cue, the group of women and children broke into loud chatter. We entered a large courtyard, followed now by our entire entourage, and there was a great deal of good-natured banter: "So, Biran," they said to him, "have you come to take over your house? D'you want your property back? You'll have to tussle with us first you know." And Bir Bahadur laughed and said, "No, no, this is yours, not mine, it's yours." The house lay in a kind of protected hollow: a small field on one side, a courtyard bordered by two other houses on another side, a winding road running behind the house. At one end, young women cooked, their heads covered and faces hidden. We were shown around the house and I thought of the young Maan Kaur, playing with friends here, little knowing the terrible fate that awaited her.

But we were here to work. Suddenly, reminded that we should be paying attention to the radio program we had come to make, Chihiro thought that this might be a good moment to capture – the two friends meeting after all these years. So she tried to shoo everyone out of the room in which we now sat, a dark, cool room with only one window, much of the space taken up by two beds, a number of trunks, a couple of Rexene-covered sofas and a table. She turned the fan off: it was making too much noise, she said, and would disturb the recording. Someone immediately turned it back on, and its whirring, grinding noise resumed. Chihiro tried to get the children to leave and the two men to respond to her questions, without success. Eventually she gave up, and decided just to capture the background noises. She'd do her interview with Bir Bahadur later.

Outside, charpoys were now laid out in the shade of the old banyan tree and people had begun to congregate there. Years earlier Bir Bahadur had told me the story of Ma Hussaini, a neighbor, who had been like a grandmother to him:

> There was a Mussalman woman, Dadi, Dadi, we used to call her. Her name was Ma
> Hussaini and I would go and sit on one side of her lap and her granddaughter would sit
> on the other. I used to pull her plait and push her away and she would catch hold of my
> *jura,* my hair, and push me away. I would say, she is my Dadi, and she would say, she is
> *my* Dadi. … It was only after we came here [to India] after Pakistan was created that we
> realized that this woman we used to call Dadi, she was a Mussalmani. She used to have
> a garden of fig trees, and she had kept one tree for me and she would not even give the
> fruit of that tree to the *masjid,* she had reserved it for me.

Bir Bahadur's rival in Ma Hussaini's affection, her granddaughter Taj, had been married into a village nearby and had spent some time in the Middle East with her husband. This Bir Bahadur knew, for he and Taj had kept in touch while she was in the Middle East. But now down the slope behind the house came an old woman, hobbling along with the help of a stick – Taj's sister, come to meet her childhood friend. And soon quite a crowd had collected under the tree. "Did you ever receive the letters I wrote?" asked Bir Bahadur of no one in particular. Yes, he was told, two letters had arrived, one addressed to the village and one to some of the village elders who were now dead, so for a while they had lain around in the village postbox and no one had known what to do with them. Then they had decided to open them and the letters had been shared among all those in the village who were there at the time of Partition.

"I wrote you two more," said Bir Bahadur, "I was not sure I would be able to come here, so I thought I would send you the letters from Thoa." Where are they, he was asked, and he produced them from his pocket. So that everyone could know what was in them, Sadq Khan asked Bir Bahadur to read the letters aloud. Meanwhile he and another man with a black scarf tied turbanlike on his head went into the house and came out holding sitars. They strummed gently as Bir Bahadur read the first letter:

> I greet all my brothers and sisters of Saintha village and offer you my salutations. I am Bir Bahadur Singh, son of Sant Raja Singh, who used to run a *kirana* [general merchant] shop in Saintha. I have come to Pakistan from India to fulfill a long-cherished dream. All my life I have had but one dream – that is, to be able to come here and meet with all of you, and now I have come to realize this dream. I wanted to come back, to visit again the places where I played as a child, to meet with all of those people who gave me so much love; I knew that if I could do this, it would give me real happiness. I have forgotten the names of so many of you who were my childhood friends – it has been fifty-four years since I left Saintha village – but in my memory I have kept the names of some of the village elders I remember, and I am putting them down here: Chacha Mohammad Zaman, Masi Barkat, Masi Noor Jehan, Chacha Sajawal Khan, Chacha Sarwar Khan, Chacha Muran who was lame in one leg, my dear sister Taj, my elder sister Sultana who was given in marriage to Khodiwala village, Dari who became my friend at the time of his circumcision. So many of the children of our elders went to school with me. Chacha Sajawal Khan's mother, Ma Hussaini, or Dadi, in whose lap I used to play and under whose loving care I grew up. I have come to make your acquaintance, to renew my friendship with the families of our respected elders. I request you to come from Saintha to meet me [the letter was written when Bir Bahadur did not know whether he would make it to Saintha or not]. I will be ever grateful to you for this. If you can, I will be found at the address given below. My visa is valid for only four days and I will be waiting for you. I have full faith that you will surely come.
>
> My mother is still alive and it was also her desire that I come and meet with you once. When you think back on those old times, you will remember me. I have drunk the water of the Dhela Dulla stream and the village well, I still have the taste of Chacha Sarwar's guavas and the fruit from Khojiwala on my tongue. I remember my teachers, Sargat Ali and Saif Ali, from whom I learned so much. They lived in Sadda village. I studied in Skot school and was the only Sikh there. Those of our elders who are alive, please give my salutations to them, and those who have passed on, I ask you to pay my respects at their graves. For those of you who are alive, I hope you will accept once again the hand of true friendship that I extend to you. I am waiting for you. When you come, please bring me a handful of earth from our beloved Saintha and some water from the Dhulla stream where we played as children. Please also bring some photos and then we can sit and talk here.
>
> God be with you and may He protect you.

Then Bir Bahadur read the second letter:

> My brother Sadq Khan
>
> My beloved Sadq Khan, son of Sajawal Khanji, please accept my greetings. My brother,
> I am the son of Sant Raja Singh, who used to run a *kirana* store in Saintha. I have writ-
> ten you letters before this, and have also received replies, but for some time now I have
> not written. Please don't think that I have forgotten you and everyone else in Saintha.
> Every day in my dreams I taste the delicious figs of Dadi's gardens, and I swear to you
> on God's name that when the dream breaks, and I awaken, I can still taste the sweet-
> ness on my tongue. I remember *dadiji,* Chacha Sajawal Khan, and everyone from the
> village – your memories are still fresh in my mind. I remember Arif Bhai, who lost his
> life while trying to save me from snakebite – perhaps it was that God loved him too
> much and took him away. My sister Taj and I used to play in Dadi's lap, we used to
> fight over who had the right to sit there. I would say Dadi belongs to me and Taj would
> insist that she belonged to her and Dadi would take us both in her lap and give us
> abundantly of her love. I have memories of the *kharboozas* [melons] Masi Barkat fed us,
> the fruit Chacha Sarwar Khan gave us, and so many others. ... It is with these memo-
> ries in my heart that I have come from India to see you. I want to greet you and all my
> friends with whom I studied in Skot school. I have come to Thoa Khalsa and this
> evening I will return to Islamabad. My visa is only for four days. I beg you to come and
> meet me. I will do my best to come to Saintha but it may be that I will not be able to
> come. I am sending you this letter from Thoa Khalsa, please come here to see me.
> Your brother
> Bir Bahadur Singh (Biran)

The letters read, Bir Bahadur handed them over to Sadq Khan. As his voice
faded, the strumming grew louder, and soon a clear strong voice rose above the
noise of conversation, singing songs of loss and joy, welcoming long-lost friends
come from afar. Others joined in, and gradually a silence descended over the
gathering, each person thinking his or her private thoughts. The shadows began
to lengthen, the sun making its way to its resting place and quietly, tactfully, as
the singing continued, we were drawn aside and taken into the house to be fed.
As we began to move, we heard a voice say, almost as if in jest: "Our cup is so
full, we have even forgotten to eat! But the guests must be fed, for us this is
enough." Sadq Khan put down his sitar and followed us into the house, where
he ate with us. Then we said our goodbyes and set off. A long train of people
followed us through the village, some singing, some talking, some just holding
Bir Bahadur's hand.

We approached the small road we had taken into the village. Here the construction work had stopped, but the two men waited for us to make good our

promise to spend time with them on the way out. We were taken into the house, a long, shady room, set with sofas in deep red velvet. Small Formica-covered tables stood in front of the sofas, and on them were three plates of biscuits, three large bottles of Coca-Cola, and three glasses. We sat, the brothers sitting across from us and sundry other people from the village scattered all about. We could see the shadowy figures of the women of the household watching us from behind the *chilmans* – we must have been a strange sight. We had started off thinking this last stop on our journey was merely a formality. It turned out to be quite different. The owners of the house knew all about Bir Bahadur – for the daughter of Arif, the man who had died of snakebite while attempting to save Bir Bahadur from it, had married into their house. For Bir Bahadur there could have been no better way to end this journey of friendship and reconciliation.

But while one journey had ended, the other – to Thoa Khalsa – still remained incomplete. Should we go there or not? Bir Bahadur's clever sleight-of-hand that morning had initially sidelined the issue. And now it no longer seemed that urgent. Chihiro had her story – a happy one. In Saintha they had advised us against going – the people of Thoa Khalsa are not good, they said, they do not like strangers. They were being polite, of course – by strangers they meant Indians, or more precisely, Hindus and Sikhs. And who could blame them? Every such stranger must have been a reminder of that terrible and violent history of a half century ago. I myself wasn't sure about going, and wondered what kind of reception we would get: in 1947 the population of Thoa had been mostly Sikh, but now, there wasn't a single Sikh left there. They'd been replaced by Muslims, many of whom must have carried their own tales of violence at the hands of Hindus and Sikhs. Would they even want to see us?

And then there were other things. I have known Bir Bahadur for more than ten years now. I have interviewed him extensively for my research and we have kept in touch. In all that time, Maan Kaur's story has always remained at the edges of our conversation. Or perhaps that's not quite true: Bir Bahadur has never hesitated to speak of Maan Kaur, but he has always described her as heroic, a martyr to the cause of the religion, someone who embraced death willingly. I find this difficult to believe. She was sixteen years old. What could she have known or understood about the troubled politics of Partition? Of the hate and rage that suddenly seem to have consumed people who had lived until then as friends and neighbors? Could she really have believed that the cause of making a new nation would be best served by her death? Or indeed by the deaths, rapes, and abductions of countless other women?

For Bir Bahadur these were not the questions that troubled him. Maan Kaur had brought honor to his family, she had done them proud, and he admired her for that. Instead, it was his father toward whom he extended his understanding and compassion. He said as much to me once. "Imagine," he said, "imagine, a father who kills his daughter, how much of a victim, how helpless he must be."

We did not make it to Thoa Khalsa in the end. Not that we did not try; we did, in a half-hearted sort of way. But it turned out that Thoa Khalsa now fell inside Pakistan's "atomic ring," and was banned to foreigners. We returned to Delhi the next day, our journey done, the radio program made, a sort of forgiveness asked and given, Maan Kaur's story once again relegated to the realm of silence.

Crimes against Humanity:
Truth Commissions and the Pursuit of Justice

An Experiment in International Criminal Justice: The Philosophy, Methodology, and Working of the International Criminal Tribunal for the Former Yugoslavia

Gurjot Malhi

The subject of my talk today is the working of the International Criminal Tribunal for the former Yugoslavia (ICTY), based in The Hague, The Netherlands. In 1990, the first multiparty elections were held in the Federal Republic of Yugoslavia. The parties were basically organized on ethnic lines, which shortly led to conflict between different ethnic groups. Several Republics started to break away from the Yugoslav federal structure. It began in Slovenia, where there was a brief armed clash, with some allegations of war crimes. Slovenia and Croatia declared their independence from Yugoslavia in 1991. Later, fighting erupted in Bosnia and Herzegovina between ethnic Serbs, Muslims and Croats, amid allegations of large-scale crimes and atrocities.

The ICTY was established in May 1993 by United Nations Security Council Resolution 827, which gave us jurisdiction over crimes committed in the territory of the former Yugoslavia since 1991. The jurisdiction was to cover the period beginning on January 1, 1991; the Security Council set no end date for our mandate, which is ongoing until peace is established – a condition to be determined by the Security Council, which was to decide on the date when the mandate would end. Within the territory of the former Yugoslavia, no geographical restrictions were imposed on us – our territorial jurisdiction extends to the entire territory of the former Yugoslavia.

The Tribunal was set up under Chapter VII of the Charter of the United Nations, which states that the Security Council shall determine the existence of any threat to the peace, breach of the peace, or act of aggression, and shall take measures to maintain or restore international peace and security. Initially this meant either military intervention – the use of peace-keeping forces – or the imposition of sanctions. The establishment of the ICTY marks the first time in the history of the UN that the Security Council created an organization to take measures to maintain international peace by supplying criminal justice. The Security Council was very worried about the allegations of massive crimes committed during the conflict – mass rapes, mass murders, crimes of different kinds in the detention camps, mass deportations, and so on. The UN Secretary General, whom the Security Council had asked to come up with the Statute for the Tribunal, was both conservative and cautious in his approach, ensuring that only those crimes that were already unquestionably governed by customary international law were included in the Tribunal's Statute.

The Statute contains four articles that give us jurisdiction over different crimes:

> Article 2: Grave breaches of the Geneva Conventions of 1949, which include:
> • Willful killing
> • Torture or inhuman treatment
> • Extensive destruction of property, not justified by military necessity
> • And other measures regarding the treatment of prisoners of war and civilians

> Article 3: Violations of the laws or customs of war, which include:
> • Employment of poisonous weapons
> • Wanton destruction of cities, towns, or villages, or of undefended towns, villages, dwellings, or other buildings
> • Destruction of cultural monuments and plunder

> Article 4: Genocide, which includes various acts, for example murder or deliberately inflicting on a group conditions of life calculated to bring about its physical destruction, committed with the intent to destroy, in whole or in part, a national, ethnical, racial, or religious group as such.

> Article 5: Crimes against humanity. These are crimes committed in armed conflict, whether international or internal in character, and directed against any civilian population:
> • Murder
> • Extermination
> • Enslavement
> • Deportation
> • Imprisonment
> • Torture
> • Rape
> • Persecutions on political, racial and religious grounds
> • Other inhumane acts

Article 7.1 of the Tribunal's Statute gives us jurisdiction over individuals – the first time in human history that an international body has been given that authority. The Tribunal's jurisdiction extends to people who are responsible either as individuals or through a command responsibility that they may have had during the conflict.

The grave breaches of the Geneva Conventions mentioned in Article 2 include but are not limited to "willful killing; torture or inhuman treatment," and "extensive destruction ... of property not justified by military necessity" – for example, the shelling of a town full of civilians, over a number of days, in the absence of a clear military need. Other measures regarding the treatment of prisoners of war or civilians are detailed in the Statute.

Violations of the laws or customs of war include the "employment of poisonous weapons," the "wanton destruction of cities, towns, or villages," the "attack, or bombardment, by whatever means, of undefended towns, villages, dwellings, or buildings," the destruction of cultural monuments, the plunder or deliberate destruction of churches, mosques, and so on.

Genocide is a serious crime, and takes a lot of investigative and legal effort to prove. But it does have certain definable components: it includes various acts, such as murder or "deliberately inflicting on a group conditions of life calculated to bring about its physical destruction." These acts must be "committed with the intent" – this intent is very important, and legally very hard to prove – "to destroy, in whole or in part, a national, ethnical, racial, or religious group." You will note that this does not include a political group. To be categorized as genocide, the crime must be committed against a national, ethnical, racial, or religious group, and the intention has to be proved.

Before we can investigate violations of the Geneva Conventions and of the laws or customs of war, we have to prove the existence of an international armed conflict. Only then do these prohibitions come into effect. For crimes against humanity, on the other hand, the need to show that the conflict is international is removed – there still must be an armed conflict, but it need not be international in character. Crimes against humanity are those "committed in armed conflict, whether international or internal in character, and directed against any civilian population." They include "murder, extermination, enslavement, deportation, imprisonment, torture, rape, persecutions on political, racial and religious grounds," and "other inhumane acts" that are also defined in the Statute.

Isolated cases of murder or rape here and there do not fall under our jurisdiction; rather than crimes against humanity, those are criminal cases to be prosecuted under the laws of the country where they occur. Two components must be proven in order for us to prosecute crimes against humanity: first, the offenses must be widespread; second, they must be systematic. If rapes, for example, are committed in thousands, over a large area, over a number of months, that crime may be described as widespread and systematic. And only when crimes are widespread and systematic can we take them on.

As I said, Article 7.1 of the Statute authorizes us to prosecute individuals – any "person who planned, instigated, ordered, committed, or otherwise aided and abetted in the planning, preparation, or execution of a crime." We prosecute leaders, but it is rare to find a president or a general holding a gun and shooting someone. That kind of open-and-shut case is highly unlikely to fall in our lap. What we normally come across, investigate, and prove is that such a person was involved in a conspiracy to commit a crime, or failed to prevent one. In fact Article 7.2 of the Statute explicitly asserts, "The official position of any accused person, whether as Head of State or Government" – be it president, premier, minister – "or as a responsible Government official, shall not relieve such person of criminal responsibility nor mitigate punishment." Similarly, Statute 7.3 continues, "The fact that any of the acts referred to ... were committed by a subordinate does not relieve his superior of criminal responsibility."

These concepts of command responsibility are very important. As I said, you rarely have a smoking gun. It is through other actions, and the widespread, systematic nature of the crime, that we can prove someone's knowledge. The first requirement is to prove that the person in command was actually in command, whether *de jure* or *de facto*. In these kinds of conflicts we often find that a person is *de jure* the general, say, but is actually not in command at all; some relatively low-level person, perhaps a major in the intelligence service, may *de facto* have more power than the general does. So we have to investigate who actually had power during the conflict. We have to prove that a person had the power of command, that he was in a position to take action against his subordinates, that he had knowledge of crimes being committed. If crimes are committed over a long period and the person had access to daily information flowing up and down the chain of command, then he has an element of knowledge. Knowledge, command, and then the failure to prevent those crimes from occurring – or, if the crimes have already occurred, the failure to take action against subordinates – if all of these can be proved we can charge that person under Article 7.3, that is, command responsibility.

Not unlike the Westminster model of government, the Tribunal is a single unit with three components: the Chambers, the Registrar, and the Office of the Prosecutor. My own office is in the Office of the Prosecutor. The Chambers consist of fourteen judges, who are elected by the General Assembly of the United Nations from a list submitted by the Security Council. Recently, because of the large number of pending cases, a certain number of *ad litem* judges have also been approved and are set to join the Tribunal in the future.

The Registry services both the Chambers and the Office of the Prosecutor. The Registar is appointed by the UN Secretary General in consultation with the President of the ICTY. There is a Deputy Registrar, who is responsible for court work and for a detention facility at Scheveningen in The Hague. We have a Chief of Administration, who is responsible for personnel, budget, procurement, and financial matters.

The Office of the Prosecutor – the structure is presently under review – consists of the Prosecutor, currently Carla Del Ponte of Switzerland, and the Deputy Prosecutor, currently Graham Blewitt of Australia. There is a Chief of Investigations and a Chief of Prosecutions. Under the Chief of Investigations are four Investigation Commanders and various field offices. The Chief of Prosecutions heads the Prosecutions Division, which consists of a number of Senior Trial Attorneys, Legal Advisers, etc.

There are a number of investigation teams, each with a team leader. The investigators are generally police officers while the legal staff, of course, are lawyers, who act as legal advisers during investigations and as co-counsels when the cases go to court. Then there are analysts and language staff, because the work is done in English or French but the language of the region might be Serbian, Croatian, Bosnian, or Albanian. Each team also has administrative staff, secretarial staff, etc.

We also have analysts of different kinds – criminal analysts, military analysts, historians, research officers, etc. – who examine the role of people most responsible for the crimes; explore questions of command structure, orders of battle, excessive use of force, and so on; and go into historical issues, such as the constitution of the former Yugoslavia, government and army staffing, and other matters, some of which lead into questions of *de jure* and *de facto* power.

We begin an investigation by identifying a crime base. When I joined the Tribunal, in the beginning of 1995, it was still in its infancy, and we hadn't yet fully explored and understood the massive scale of the crimes we would be investigating, and which crime we should investigate and which we should not. One of our starting points in the beginning had been the report of the Commission of Experts on the Former Yugoslavia, which had been set up by the UN. Then there were reports from various agencies, like that of the UN High Commissioner for Refugees (UNHCR), the International Committee of the Red Cross (ICRC), and other groups, as well as from NGOs, newspapers, television, other media, and so on. Meanwhile some of our own investigations had also started. The conflict was still continuing; it wasn't easy to work in the former Yugoslavia just then. But the doors slowly opened. Our first witnesses were refugees in different parts of the world – Europe, America, Australia, Asia – and we went there to interview them and get their accounts. And so a base was established of individuals and groups involved in the crimes, people who had planned, organized, or implemented the conduct. We had to identify individuals on whom to focus the Tribunal's resources.

In our investigations as in any other large-scale investigation, there is a preliminary research phase, and then once the crime or crimes are fully identified
there is the investigation phase – interviewing witnesses, collecting evidence
relating to them, working with forensics and other sources. The indictment
process follows. At the end of the investigation, the evidence that has been collected is put before a group of lawyers from all over the world in the ICTY, who
spend days going over every aspect of the case to decide whether it meets the
rigorous international standards that would allow us to go ahead with the prosecution. Often they send the case back for more investigation – the evidence isn't
enough. This is a long process. Once the review committee is satisfied that we
have enough evidence for an indictment, we go ahead. It also happens that we
are told we don't have enough evidence, and we either drop the case or keep
investigating; but if we do have enough evidence, the case goes to the Prosecutor, who signs the indictment, and then it goes to a judge, who confirms the
indictment. The trial is held by a Trial Chamber of three judges. As I said, there
are fourteen permanent judges. They divide into three Trial Chambers of three
judges each, plus an Appeals Chamber of five judges. Right now *ad litem* judges
are also coming on board, making for many additional Chambers to dispose of
the pending cases.

Once people are indicted we trace them – this is the intelligence phase.
Sometimes the international military forces also get involved in arresting them.
Once arrested and brought to The Hague, in the pretrial phase, they are
detained in prison and make appearances in court. Case managers are
appointed, and then, during the trial itself, there is investigative support should
more work need to be done.

The Prosecutor's power to investigate derives from Article 18 of the Statute:
"The Prosecutor shall initiate investigations ex-officio or on the basis of information obtained from any source, particularly from Governments, United
Nations organs, intergovernmental organizations and non-governmental organizations." The Prosecutor "shall have the power to question suspects, victims
and witnesses, to collect evidence and to conduct on-site investigations" – with
"on-site investigations" meaning local interviews of witnesses, or forensic investigations of mass graves, of which, as you must know, there have been a number
in the former Yugoslavia. "In carrying out these tasks, the Prosecutor may, as
appropriate, seek the assistance of the State authorities concerned" – there is
mutual cooperation. In fact Article 29 of the Statute asserts that states are
obliged to cooperate with the Tribunal, and Rule 39 of the Rules of Procedure
and Evidence gives the Prosecutor power to seek their cooperation. Should the
state refuse to cooperate, the Prosecutor can ultimately report the matter to the
President, who reports it to the Security Council. This kind of refusal is of

course the extreme case. Then it is up to the Security Council to take any measure necessary.

We also cooperate a great deal with international organizations like UNHCR and ICRC, various NGOs, and the different UN military forces. These agencies have been closely involved in the former Yugoslavia, and often have access to documents and information that can be very valuable to us.

The military force supplied by the UN to help to stabilize Bosnia-Herzegovina is called the SFOR; in Kosovo it is KFOR. In Bosnia-Herzegovina we have cooperated a great deal with the SFOR. When, say, a Trial Chamber or a judge in The Hague has granted us a search warrant for a location somewhere in the field, a military establishment or a political office perhaps, the SFOR provides us the necessary security and support in searches and seizures. Exhumations are an important part of our work, and in areas where we are under threat, the SFOR provides security for us. It also renders assistance in other matters. We are definitely dependent on international military forces like the SFOR to affect arrests. We share intelligence with them, mostly on the indicted, as also in other matters of investigation. Many areas in the former Yugoslavia are mined, and must be demined before we start an exhumation or any other field operation. At this point we have our own contractors in place in Bosnia, who do the demining for us, but the KFOR gave us demining support in Kosovo last year.

We have field offices in different countries in the former Yugoslavia – in Sarajevo in Bosnia-Herzegovina, Belgrade in the Federal Republic of Yugoslavia, Zagreb in Croatia, Banja Luka in Republika Srpska, Skopje in Macedonia, Pristina in Kosovo. We also have a forensic facility, Helba Camp, at Visoko in Bosnia-Herzegovina.

In 1999, the forensic operations in Kosovo were done entirely through gratis assistance, that is assistance provided to us free of charge by different countries. About four hundred forensic specialists participated, from fourteen countries – Austria, Belgium, Canada, Denmark, France, Germany, Iceland, Luxembourg, The Netherlands, Spain, Sweden, Switzerland, the United Kingdom, and the United States. That year the need was sudden, and we did not have our own teams. In 2000, however, we established and set up our own forensic teams in Kosovo. Kosovo was entirely new territory for us, and our operations there had to be carefully planned, because forensic work on such a large scale had not been done at the international level before. The UN and other organizations had established some basic protocols on investigations, but we had to set up our own mortuary and field protocols. Extensive discussions were held with the UN administration in Kosovo and various international groups. Several organizations put together their combined brains and efforts in making our forensic operations in Kosovo a success. There was close cooperation and working protocols, on a daily basis, between us and the Victim Recovery and Identification Commission (VRIC); the Transcultural Psychosocial Organization (TPO); the Organization for Security and Cooperation in Europe (OSCE); the United Nations Interim Administration Mission in Kosovo (UNMIK); and the KFOR. All these organizations assisted us tremendously in our work. We also requested assistance from all 189 Member States of the UN; the Prosecutor sent out a letter, and many countries responded. We had to set up an infrastructure, to take care of this massive international deployment of experts, including the setting up of morgue facilities at Orahovac in Kosovo.

The mortuary staff is internationally constituted and includes forensic pathologists, scene-of-crime officers (police officers), photographers, anthropologists, radiographers, and evidence analysts. The field staff includes archaeologists, anthropologists, scene-of-crime officers, surveyors, soil experts, etc. We also have support staff – project managers for both Kosovo and Bosnia-Herzegovina, logistics officers, forensic engineers, plant operators, mechanics, storemen, computer people, and so on.

In 2000 we had 159 forensic experts in Kosovo and 105 in Bosnia-Herzegovina. They came from twenty-seven countries: the United Kingdom, France, Colombia, The Netherlands, Poland, Belgium, Denmark, Canada, Argentina, Egypt, South Africa, Ireland, Guatemala, the United States, Switzerland, Italy, New Zealand, Sri Lanka, Finland, Germany, Portugal, Spain, Norway, Peru, Barbados, Austria, and Australia. In addition to the staff I have mentioned, a number of countries provided teams – ten in all, from Austria, Belgium, Canada, Denmark, Finland, France, Sweden, Switzerland, the UK, and Germany – to work gratis, and these teams included 300 experts who also did forensic work on behalf of the ICTY.

As of March 15, 2001, we have publicly indicted ninety-eight individuals. In addition there are some sealed indictments. Thirty-six people are in custody at the detention unit in The Hague.

The people on trial include politicians, military generals, camp commanders, and sexual violators. Dario Kordic, who was sentenced recently, was a politician; General Radislav Krstic was a commander of the army of the Republic of Srpska. Miroslav Kvocka, Milojica Kos, Mladen Radic, and Zoran Zigic – all of them relate to the Omarska detention camp trial. And then there are sexual offenders – again, this is perhaps the first time in history that systematic, widespread sexual crimes have been investigated and prosecuted in the international arena. Radomir Kovac, Dragoljub Kunarac, and Zoran Vukovic are some examples of the sexual offenders we have prosecuted.

The convictions the Tribunal has produced include Dusan Tadic, the first person arrested – he had been a camp guard. The convicted persons belong to all ethnic categories – some are Serbs, some are Croats or Bosnian Croats, and some are Muslims. Indeed, crimes were committed by all ethnic groups. Different sentences have been awarded for different degrees of criminal responsibility. Tihomir Blaskic, for example, a Croatian general – he has had the heaviest sentence: forty-five years. And Dragoljub Kunarac, one of the sexual offenders in the Foca rape case, was sentenced to twenty-eight years. Goran Jelisic was sentenced to forty years. As I said, there is often no smoking gun, but sometimes one turns up: there is a photograph of Jelisic using a pistol to kill a civilian. Some of the convictions of persons in positions of authority resulted from charges involving the responsibility of command. A person may not have committed any murder or rape himself, but if he was in charge of people who committed such crimes, and had knowledge of the crimes being committed but failed to prevent them or to punish his subordinates, he has command responsibility, a very important concept, as I said before. The ICTY has also acquitted some people and they have gone back home. Zejnil Delalic and Dragan Papic are examples of this.

As of October 2000 the ICTY had 1,200 staff members from seventy-five countries. In 2001 we have a budget of $96,443,900. As of March 2001 our President is Judge Claude Jorda of France; our Vice-President is Judge Florence Ndepele Mwachande Mumba of Zambia; our Prosecutor is Carla Del Ponte; our Registrar is Hans Holthuis of the Netherlands; and we have judges from Australia, the United Kingdom, Portugal, Malaysia, Egypt, Guyana, Colombia, Morocco, Jamaica, the United States, Italy, and China.

Facts versus Truth: The Dilemmas of a Reluctant Member of a Truth and Reconciliation Commission

Vojin Dimitrijević

1. *The president of the Federal Republic of Yugoslavia established his Truth and Reconciliation Commission on March 29, 2001. I was listed as one of its members.*

The Commission's mandate is tentative and vaguely defined, and can remain moot here. More important is what Yugoslav society, my friends, and I myself think its purpose is. The issue is of course the conflict in the territory of the former Yugoslavia after 1990, a conflict that has dramatically affected all the constituent parts of that country, most of which have gained the status of sovereign states. The wording of the president's decision to establish the Commission suggests that its mandate takes it farther into the past than 1990; in fact the material for the first session – prepared by the president's staff – indicates that its authors imagined it as addressing the period since 1980, ten years before the armed conflicts began and eleven years before Yugoslavia dissolved (according to the earliest date ascribed to that event).[1]

The atrocities in the Yugoslav wars of secession, or of dissolution, more or less occurred after 1991. Should a body fashionably styled a "truth and reconciliation commission" be looking into the causes of savagery in armed conflict or into the causes of the conflict itself? In other words, which matters more – what happened during a war, or why the war happened? If I understand the causes of the war, will I better understand why it was so much more cruel and caused more suffering than many other international or civil wars?

As words, "truth" and "reconciliation" have their range of meanings, albeit ambiguous ones. But the syntagm "truth and reconciliation," linked to a body of people chosen to say or do something about these things, has acquired some specific meaning: it is colored for me by things I have read about Guatemala, El Salvador, Chile, Argentina, Rwanda, South Africa, and other countries. There

---

1 Some of the country's former constituent republics have officially proclaimed that Yugoslavia ceased to exist in 1991. Most foreign states recognized the new states in early 1992. The Federal Republic of Yugoslavia (FRY) was founded later in 1992, officially as the continuation of the old state. Until October 2000, the FRY government refused to acknowledge that the old state had passed away.

are people around me for whom the phrase has fewer associations; they think only of the most popular truth and reconciliation commission, the South African one. Most of my countrymen are exhausted by the national obsession with these wars, and with one of its major actors, the former President Slobodan Milosevic, until recently their leader. (The obsession was as mentally damaging when it opposed Milosevic as when it ran in his favor.) Those who know nothing of other nations' truth and reconciliation commissions obviously think this one will be a specifically Yugoslav or Serb affair, as unique as all of the miseries that have befallen the Serb "nation of martyrs" recently – or else, as nationalists would say, since time immemorial. Being an unhappy nation is like being in puberty: one's own depression and suffering are the only miseries around – until one meets another sufferer.

2. *I was trained as a lawyer.* I believe in my ability to deal with facts and their "qualification," a word that in legalese means subsuming an event or an action under a definition – for example, whether killing someone should be called murder, manslaughter, self-defense, or euthanasia. Qualification is partly done by judges, who use juries to establish facts; qualification demands training while establishing facts demands being an ordinary, everyday person (or this is what the major legal systems assume). The jury's decision is called the verdict, which means, etymologically, "saying truth." Judicial truth is recognized as a temporary truth; judges are under no illusions about the relativity of the truth in court – the trial must at some point end, and the law must be satisfied not with "truth" but with some approximation of it. In legal systems where verdict and sentence are pronounced at the same time and by the same body, appeal can be made even of the determination of truth. The truth of a higher court thus becomes a superior truth, but although the members of that court will probably have more experience in administering justice, they are by no means better experts in establishing the truth. In law, "truth" is an exaggeration.

I know something about law. Now, though, not only am I expected to say what happened on the level of fact, and to give it a name (genocide, ethnic cleansing, homicide, rape, torture, etc.), I and my colleagues on the Commission are also supposed to seek a "deeper" truth – to determine why this thing happened, how it was possible that it happened, what the causal links were, what the societal and moral environment of the whole conflict was. The material we received from the president even refers to crimes against peace. In legal terms this is aggression; in ordinary terms it means, Who started the war?

Do I fully understand the chain of events that led to war? Having taught international relations for a while, I remember that the Versailles Treaty, in placing the blame for World War I entirely on Germany, was not only historically inaccurate but made a huge mistake, very probably contributing to the rise of Hitler. Opinion on Germany's guilt is more uniform in the case of World War II, but the historian A. J. P. Taylor, whether seriously or for the heck of it, tried to demonstrate that other states and statesmen were as responsible as Hitler and his Third Reich. Even the Nuremberg Tribunal felt uneasy about judging war crimes; Rudolf Hess was sentenced not for war crimes but for crimes against peace. (He had been separated from the German government too early to be guilty of something else.)

As the preceding implies, I also feel I lack the professional skills to determine historical truths. Any historian, and there are some on the Commission, can come to me, show me something from the archives, and try to convince me that on a given day, so-and-so wrote to someone else, hinting that a Croat leader was scheming with his Macedonian counterpart to undermine the Yugoslav army's morale. This just reminds me of my experience with professional diplomats, who often tend to confuse information with wisdom, so that they think that they have an advantage over me because they have read the latest dispatches. Historical truths are provisional too; later generations of historians will interpret the same events differently as new documents come to light. Again, as a jurist, I fear the consequences of the Commission determining (by a majority vote!) that historical responsibility lies with this or that side in the conflict. And there is a frequent tendency in historiography to recognize self-appointed ethnic entrepreneurs as qualified national leaders.

Historians are certainly better equipped than I am to deal dispassionately with the distant past. In dealing with recent events, however, they are contemporaries and witnesses in the same way I am. Conversely, why should they trust me when I insist on the power to call witnesses? Am I not confusing historical truth with establishing facts "beyond a reasonable doubt"?

What if I determine that "Croats" started the war, or contributed decisively to its outbreak? Should I then repeat, mutatis mutandis, the imbecilic statement of the former president of the Croatian Supreme Court that no Croat could have committed a war crime, or a crime against humanity, because Croatia was defending itself against aggression? In group conflicts, is it only the unjust who commit crimes?

3. *I am afraid of Great Truths.* The spreading of truth has throughout history been a murderous exercise. How many wars have been inspired by the spreading of truth – truth about religion, truth about the past and its injustices, truth about races, truth about nations? At the most elementary level, truth is facts in context; it is the context that I am afraid of. Contexts can be exculpatory, replacing the brutal veracity of a crime with an abstract justification for it.

In the war we now have to deal with, the easiest way to detect a warmonger among the Serbs was his insistence on spreading truth. The Serbian state television invested a lot of money in programs which repeated ad nauseam that the Serb leader and his followers were right, and that they were entitled to combat any misinterpretation of their version of the truth, or any refusal to acknowledge it, by every means available. Back then, somewhere around 1990, an enterprising merchant opened a store in the Belgrade airport – it is probably still there – that had a sign above its doors in both Serbian and English: *SRPSKA ISTINA* – SERBIAN TRUTH. The store sold almost nothing but brandy (*rakija*) in a bottle containing a soaked wooden cross. Was this a bad joke, or the cynical essence of the Serbian version of the truth? I am reporting on this vulgar association for the first time. The poor storekeeper was neither bloodthirsty, nor an alcoholic, nor a religious zealot: he just wanted to please the powers that be. His denunciation of the baseness and manipulativeness of their "truth" was quite unwitting.

4. *I was a teacher* for more than thirty years, until I was removed from the university by a nuncio of the Serbian government. That government was predominantly composed of people who are now generally believed to have been thieves and embezzlers. Am I impartial when it comes to their role in Bosnia, Croatia, and Kosovo? Yet are thieves and corrupt politicians necessarily war criminals? Is their larceny perhaps too banal to be included among the truths we have to establish and report on to the public?

What is more important about my history as an educator is that my reputation rested at least in part on my ability to talk, to organize my words, to attract students and convince them that something was, if not true, at least supported by some authority. I was conveying the "scientific truth" – the result of the most recent research in political science, the learned opinions of the highest courts or of the most illustrious legal scholars. I had many students, most of them poor in quality. Ever since 1945, successive communist governments had insisted on enrolling as many young people as possible in the universities, to postpone the moment when they would face a limited future or even outright unemployment. After 1990 this situation only got worse. Most of the students were badly prepared, read no foreign languages, and came from secondary schools that had indoctrinated them with various sorts of collectivism and cheap egalitarianism, first of communist and later of nationalist provenance. To overcome their failures of attention, I and many of my colleagues had to resort to various kinds of theatrics, making them internalize some kind of truth by using tricks. Will I bring these tricks to the Commission? Will other members of the Commission use such tricks on me, and on the public? Someone has to write the report.

Other members can change a word or two, a sentence here and there, but essentially they can only vote for or against the draft. Being limited to written reports prevents the Commission from expressing its findings by other means.

5. In the last two decades *I have been a human-rights activist.* This makes me an individualist and a liberal, biased against most things collective – I am suspicious, for example, of both collective rights and collective responsibilities. Strangely enough, I have met many learned people, and read the writings of others, who choose to believe in one of these two things but not the other. Ethnic leaders clamor for the collective rights of their group, but are shocked by hints in the direction of collective responsibility or guilt. Why? Logically there is no right without responsibility; if there are collective rights, then there must be collective liability. Meanwhile most of those – especially in the Western media – who generalize about the collective responsibility of, say, Germans or Serbs, and who call for de-Nazification and for social catharsis, wouldn't dream of recognizing the collective rights of peoples, even as a metaphor for their grievances.

Shaped by my experience in national and international organizations advocating, promoting, monitoring, and protecting individual human rights, I inevitably tend to concentrate on individual cases and destinies. I would hold, for instance, that one murder can constitute an act of genocide given the proper motive. I believe that human rights have to be respected everywhere. I am disgusted by those who try to minimize the number of victims of the Holocaust, of the Jasenovac concentration camp in Croatia during World War II, or of the more recent massacre in Srebrenica, Bosnia. Will I be able to maintain a historian's sense of proportion? Am I not ready retroactively to condemn an entire political program because human rights have been violated in implementing it? This is a pertinent point in Yugoslavia: many people here pursued the attractive political ideas of liberty and equality announced by their leaders, yet still appear to have consented in the crimes those leaders ordered. Perhaps the pursuers are victims too?

6. In the last dozen years *I have been politically active* – very much so, in fact, between 1990 and 2000, a period coinciding with the wars I now have to review. The main thrust of my involvement was to help depose the regime in Serbia, which I considered retrograde, adventurous, tyrannical, and harmful to the very people it claimed to be leading to great things – liberty, dignity, a better future. My greatest complaint against the Serbian rulers, however, was their eagerness, indeed their thirst, to spark war. Their propaganda glorified war and their journalist mercenaries engaged in hate speech. I am not sure I can be

impartial in dealing with the friends of that regime outside present-day Serbia. Many Serb leaders in Croatia and Bosnia were close to Milosevic and his henchmen; many of these leaders now stand accused of ordering or committing war crimes or crimes against humanity. Am I less able to understand the situation in which they found themselves, their inspirations, and their political decisions because they were so close for so long to my principal political foes? Wouldn't I be more inclined to understand and sympathize with the people who opposed them, and who back then were in a weaker position, like the Bosnian Muslims? Victims are victims, not heroes – one does not necessarily become better by being a victim.

7. *I am a Serb, and was baptized a Serbian Orthodox Christian* – which amounts to the same thing in this part of the world, especially in Croatia and Bosnia and Herzegovina, where the war raged. Of course I didn't choose my ethnicity (or, for that matter, my nationality, my citizenship), but I cannot be indifferent to it either; just as I would expect the treatment I might receive from non-Serbs to reflect whatever prejudices – or affectation to have no prejudices – they maintained about Serbs and Orthodox Christians. For that matter, a circumcised male in an anti-Semitic environment can never stop being Jewish. Had an anti-Serb posse detected me, I would have been killed or tortured, even though the loudest Serb patriots considered me a weak and treacherous "mondialist," a *Nestbeschmutzer.* But those words are too strong – I do belong culturally to Serbia. Until the late 1980s, in fact, before the patriots got vulgar, nasty, and dangerous, I rather enjoyed being a Serb; I enjoyed telling foreigners our stories, describing our customs, our food. Believing the Serbian military tradition to be defensive, I even enjoyed being an officer in the army reserve.

On the Commission my ethnic belonging could work both ways: I might show a tendency to be soft on Serbs, but I might also be too hard on them. I cannot accept that all Serbs (or Muslims or Croats, for that matter) are criminals, but I am convinced that some of them are, and that criminal Serbs are my special concern and responsibility.

The complicating factor for this Commission in particular is that most of its members are Serbs, and the only two representatives of the clergy are Serb Orthodox. If I, both Serb and Orthodox, strengthen the Serb contingent by joining the Commission, will the Commission seem biased no matter what it does? On the other hand, if a body composed mainly of Serb patriots and Orthodox believers denounced only crimes committed by Serbs, its findings would gain additional authority, especially among the Serbs themselves. But this would again look artificial.

8. *Am I the best member for an ideal truth and reconciliation commission?* Is it the Commission's task to determine what actually took place in Serbia during the period of its collective nationalist obsession and (initially "democratic") dictatorship, or are we meant to find out what happened throughout the former Yugoslavia – a question involving what Serbs did to others, and others to Serbs? If prowar and antiwar Serbs reconcile with each other, how will Serbs reconcile with the nations around them?

If the Commission is not a court of law, it should not attribute guilt, it should establish truth. Yet what is the moral use of coolly determining what is true and false? That would go against the grain of my refusal, in recent decades, to accept the determinism of the political scientists who told me that the things I was rebelling against were bound to happen, that I was resisting the inevitable course of history, and that the outcome would be decided by others. How will truth contribute to reconciliation, except by creating a basis of fact that will not be disputed forever? Reconciliation will have to be tackled by others – but then the composition of the Commission seems irrelevant. Or is it not? If I believe that some of my colleagues on the Commission uncritically supported nationalist programs, that some of them were even close to being warmongers, and if some of them see me in the exact opposite terms but just as negatively, how can the Commission members expect to help bring reconciliation to people who have lost their children, their kin, and all their possessions? Should we refuse to sit at the same table with people of opposing political views, philosophies, and dubious pasts, or would that be intellectually dishonest?

9. *Epilogue.* What follows is the text of my letter of resignation to the president of Yugoslavia. Such letters belong to a genre, and must be composed in a certain way. The discussion above should make my letter easier to understand, but it still remains in many ways affected and unsatisfactory:

Belgrade, April 15, 2001

Dear Mr. President,

I ask to be relieved of membership in the Truth and Reconciliation Commission that you established on March 29, 2001.

I attended the preliminary meeting of the potential members of the Commission, on March 23, 2001, out of deep respect for you as the embodiment of democratic change in Serbia. But I had certain queries about the powers with which the future Commission would be vested, and about its method of work – issues that were not clearly specified in writing at the time. Before I received the draft promised for the next meeting, the Decision on the formation of the Truth and Reconciliation Commission was published in the official gazette of the FRY [Federal Republic of Yugoslavia].

Therefore it cannot be held that I was fully aware of the nature and functions of the body I was supposed to join, or that I gave my full consent to be its member. I will endeavor to explain why I could not agree to join the Commission.

Given the Decision, and the material prepared for the meeting scheduled for April 17, I conclude that the Commission is vested with very limited powers, of which the most important is the power to seek "understanding and support from state authorities, which would be under an obligation to allow the members of the Commission and its expert teams to examine their archives." These restricted powers – which do not include the right to call witnesses – blur the Commission's legal status. The fact that the Commission is entitled to adopt "an adequate document on its program and organization" does not help; the Commission cannot arrogate powers that the state has not delegated to it.

The work of the Commission is restricted by the section of the Decision that assigns to it the task of "organizing investigative activities aimed at uncovering documentation on social, ethnic, and political conflicts that led to war, thus casting light on the chain of events and its causes." In this context, as can be inferred from the material, the focal point of the investigation would be the period before the disintegration of the Socialist Federal Republic of Yugoslavia as a historical process. However, people who are not included in the present-day Federal Republic of Yugoslavia lived and worked in the former Yugoslavia. If the Commission is to pronounce judgment on a sequence of events that took place outside the present-day territory of the FRY, the public will not see it as unbiased and impartial if it is composed exclusively of citizens of the FRY (without even a single member from Montenegro).

The concept outlined in the Decision is further elaborated in the material prepared for the first meeting, which assigns to the Commission a vast field of work that no body of this nature could possibly master. For example, I quote the following tasks: confrontation with "horrifying aspects of the already established image of the Serbs and of Serbia itself"; reviewing "the demographic state of the nation"; and "linguistic studies." I am not convinced that the Commission can succeed in covering all of these issues, and am afraid that its failure might compromise the whole idea of truth and reconciliation in the region.

While the causes of war are diverse, the rules of humanitarian law, which both the aggressor and the victim of aggression must observe, are one and the same. As could easily have been assumed, the savageness of our wars is of paramount interest to me as a jurist. But the Commission seems to be expected to establish Great Truths. I am afraid of Great Truths, since brutal violence has been resorted to in their name and for the sake of their expansion. The process of reconciliation can be initiated by more modest means. The intentions don't matter here – neither who was right and who wrong, nor whose behavior can be accounted for and understood (and perhaps justified). What is important is who was human and who was inhuman.

Torture, Recovery, and Truth in Morocco

Susan Slyomovics

To describe the years since 1956, when they gained their independence, Moroccans use the Arabic words *zaman al-rasas* and *al-sanawat al-sawda* and the French phrases *les anneés de plomb*, *les années noires*, and *les années sombres*, "the years of lead," "the black years," "the dark years," phrases evoking an era of grayness and lead bullets. These were times of fear and repression, of forcible disappearances, farcical mass trials, and long prison sentences for many from a variety of political positions who, voicing opposition to the regime, became prisoners of conscience. In the urban areas, thousands from the student and intellectual communities of all political persuasions – Marxists, Islamists, nationalists, feminists, Amazigh/Berber nationalists – were arrested, held incommunicado at various sites (including Casablanca's infamous Derb Moulay Cherif detention center), tortured, and tried en masse in waves of political trials for the crime of "plotting against the state." Literature – their articles, books, magazines, broadsides, and cartoons – was the evidence of crime. Sentences ranged from a few months to the death penalty.[1]

During research trips in 1996, 1997, and 1999–2000,[2] I was introduced to the Moroccan community of human-rights activists, many of them students, poets, novelists, and artists who were or had been imprisoned together. From interviews with these men and women, an unusual discursive formation has emerged that links authors, writing, political detention, and torture: accusations of the guilt of political prisoners were based exclusively on their imaginative and political writings, and torture was applied to elicit written confessions. Nevertheless, a large body of writing was produced during decades of incarceration. Literary critic Elaine Scarry argues that one motive for inflicting physical pain is to destroy the voice that would express torture in language, thereby eliminating

---

1 The first part of this essay includes a revised and expanded section of my article "A Truth Commission for Morocco," *MERIP/Middle East Report*, no. 218 (2001): 18–21.
2 Funding was provided by grants from the American Institute of Maghribi Studies (1996 and 1997) and a Fulbright Award to Morocco (1999–2000).

Khalid Bakhti,
Islamist political
prisoner (1983–94),
making the victory
sign behind his cell
door, Ghbila prison,
Casablanca, 1986.
Clandestine
photograph, courtesy
Khalid Bakhti.

any representations by the victim.[3] By explicitly engaging questions of language and the difficulties of telling a story, Moroccan literature written in prison takes as its subject the overtly political insistence of witnessing.

Such works belong to an engaged literature of testament and commitment that has shaped literary themes throughout the Arabic-speaking world, in particular drawing explicitly on Palestinian *iltizam* or "commitment" literature.[4] More recent terms to characterize poetry emerging from political and social extremity occur in Carolyn Forché's anthology on the poetry of witness, where she proposes a third space for poems that do not belong purely to the realm of the political or the personal; instead, they are part of what she calls a "social" arena, which she defines as "a place of resistance and struggle, where books are published, poems read, and protest disseminated. It is the sphere in which claims against the political order are made in the name of justice."[5]

The political and Forché's sense of the "social" space are inseparable from precise questions of geographical location and historical time – where do you live, for whom do you write, when and under what circumstances did you write, which prison "published" your writing, and, even, what was the manner of your torture or death? The scope of the human-rights violations during the post-independence history of Morocco commands focus upon those events where

3 Elaine Scarry, *The Body in Pain: The Making and Unmaking of the World* (New York: Oxford University Press, 1985), pp. 3–11.
4 See my book *The Object of Memory: Arab and Jew Narrate the Palestinian Village* (Philadelphia: University of Pennsylvania Press, 1998), especially chapter 5.
5 Carolyn Forché, *Against Forgetting: Twentieth Century Poetry of Witness* (New York: W. W. Norton, 1993), p. 31.

Islamist political
prisoners group
photograph, Kenitra
Central Prison, 1992.
Clandestine
photograph, courtesy
Ahmed Haou.

history and memory, objective narration and witness testimony, overlap, intersect, and collide. A community of human-rights activists, many of them survivors of forcible disappearance, torture, political trials, and decades of incarceration, has long labored to reconstruct their country's history and to explain what actually happened, despite perpetrators' attempts to efface both material evidence and human witnesses. As with other projects in which a state appears to declare war on its own citizens, the attempt to present and analyze such a historical past of prison experience tests the limits of our ability to represent such topics.

"Where, after all, do universal human rights begin?" questions Eleanor Roosevelt during her last speech to the United Nations. She answers by pointing to "the small place," to local communities and everyday interactions: "In small places, close to home – so close and so small that they cannot be seen on any maps of the world. Yet they are the world of the individual person; the neighborhood he lives in; the school or college he attends; the factory, farm or office where he works."[6] In the Moroccan context a formative experience that served to forge a growing national will to consciousness of human rights was incarceration. Indeed Abderrahman Benameur, a lawyer and activist with al-Jam'iyya al-maghribiyya li-huquq al-insan (Moroccan Association of Human Rights), emphasizes that the Moroccan state has in effect criminalized all manifestations of political activity and thought – all political acts such as meetings, demonstra-

6 Eleanor Roosevelt, quoted in Mary Ann Glendon, *A World Made New: Eleanor Roosevelt and the Universal Declaration of Human Rights* (New York: Random House, 2001), pp. 239–40.

tions, and writing tracts that promote "nonofficial opinions."[7] Political imprisonment in Morocco is linked with nonauthorized views emerging from *any* political act. In what follows, the history and work of the Moroccan poet Salah El Ouadie, a prisoner of conscience from 1974 to 1984, is presented to exemplify the themes of writing during political incarceration at the time of Morocco's "years of lead," and the ways in which prison writing, as a critical and analytical weapon developed by dissidents against a regime, underpins current human-rights political activism.[8]

Prison Literature as Witness Literature: Salah El Ouadie   *Al-Aris* ("The Groom") is the misnomer nickname that El Ouadie's torturers assigned to him when they kidnapped him as he was leaving a wedding party. Dressed in tuxedo and bow tie, El Ouadie was forcibly "disappeared" into Derb Moulay Cherif. During the celebrated trial of leftists in Casablanca in 1977, he was condemned to twenty years imprisonment for undermining the security of the Moroccan state. He was subsequently amnestied and released from the Kenitra prison in 1984. Because El Ouadie had no pen or paper in Derb Moulay Cherif, his novel *Al-Aris* is written as a sequence of clandestine letters to his mother from memory. *Al-Aris* was published to great acclaim in 1998.

Dear Mother:

When they lifted the pole into the emptiness, as it happened, it, me, and all my weight carried by my handcuffs and my feet tied with a rope, and it was there, dear Mother, to speak truthfully, I understood I was being tortured. I said to myself, "Be a man," and I started to howl. You know how silent I am, how I hate noise, but the torture was intense. They interrogated me between one slap and another and strokes of the whip about names, concepts, and big words, So-and-so, Such-and-such, democracy, socialism, classes, citizens, countries, revolution. Then they brought an engine that hummed and maneuvered it near my skull and I in the situation could see nothing. I believed at first that this affair concerned an enormous fly. But the story of a fly took wing when they placed the apparatus on my skull, my neck, my limbs, and I felt a shock and jolt travel through my entire body. ... Here was electricity being installed in my body long before reaching the countryside and the villages, even though I made no request

---

7 Abderrahman Benameur, "Quelques remarques sur la détention politique," *Attadamoun* (Rabat), no. 2 (February 1982): 3–4, and "Man huwa al-mu'ataqil al-siyasi?" *Attadamoun,* no. 3 (February 1983): 8–9.

8 This thesis is developed in Barbara Harlow, *Barred: Women, Writing, and Political Detention* (Hanover: Wesleyan University Press, 1992).

to anyone. How can the government plead a lack of means – here they distribute electricity so generously without payment?[9]

As El Ouadie recounts his travails to his mother, his voice is one of Candide-like innocence. Caught in the terrible machinery of torture, the perplexed citizen comes to remonstrate with his torturers with gentle and humorous dignity, as if it were possible to converse with them as reasonable human beings:

> They asked me, while I was in the air, to tell the truth and I replied as soon as they stopped hitting me: "It is not required to beat me for me to tell the truth. Lower me and I'll tell you." So they became quiet and I understood they believed me because they lowered me. The strangest thing, Mother, is that when they released me I could no longer feel my body. For the first time in my life I felt that I was a mere thought, that is all, without a body, and all this was as a result of an excess of pain.

El Ouadie is momentarily tossed into a corner to be replaced by another political prisoner whose screams under torture pierce the dark cells and his consciousness. The author is forced to relive a torture session, this time, however, concentrating on what he has heard the police say as opposed to the pain he experienced, thereby permitting him to draw a series of parallels: the first one, equating the treatment of man to that of beasts, he rejects, while the second, between his individual plight and the degradation of the Moroccan population, he embraces:

> Here I understood what one of them said during my torture session: "Hit him in the head so as not to injure the skin." I thought they were speaking about sheep. I understood instantly that I was the sheep in question and I understood suddenly why they suspended me. Consider the confusion in their brains between a sheep and a human being. Perhaps they do not see why we should enjoy human rights because they take us for sheep. Ah, I get it. We must convince them that we are human beings, surely then they will stop beating and whipping us. … Silence served me well because I passed the night hearing groans from all sides around me. I understood I was not alone in this ordeal and other Moroccans were undergoing the same ignominy. This discovery encouraged me to patience and I found consolation in the age-old adage: collective

---

9 This and the following passages from Salah El Ouadie, *Al-Aris* (Casablanca: Dar al-Najah, 1998), come from a translation from the Arabic by the present author in Evelyn Early and Donna Lee Bowen, *Everyday Life in the Modern Muslim Middle East* (Indianapolis: Indiana University Press, 2001). I thank Latifa El-Morabitine, Ahmed Jebari, Ahmed Goughrabou, and Mustafa Kamal for their advice on the translation.

Salah El Ouadie, political prisoner (23 March Movement), rising to speak at the Casablanca conference to create the Moroccan Forum for Truth and Justice, November 27–29, 1999. Banner: "No to forgetting, no to revenge, truth and equity in order to truly turn the page." Photograph: Susan Slyomovics.

punishment is less painful. My imagination roved, I said to myself, "If this situation extended to all Moroccan citizens, the ordeal is minimized because there would be more people whipped than whippers, then the whip would become impossible, citizens could speak freely about politics and wages." The problem for me would be if the formerly whipped decide to become the whippers, whence their multiplication. As for me, I am, as you know, against the whip wherever its source.

At the novel's end, the reader is told that a fellow political prisoner mailed the twenty-six letters from Derb Moulay Cherif only after the author's death. The truth is that El Ouadie is very much alive. He continues to publish poems and articles. He is currently vice-president of Morocco's al-Muntada al-maghribiya min ajli al-haqiqa wa al-insaf (Moroccan Forum for Truth and Justice), a nongovernmental association established in 1999 by former victims of torture and repression seeking to establish a Moroccan commission for truth and reconciliation.

Islamist Political Prisoners and Human-Rights Campaigns   "The Power of the Powerless," the legendary 1978 essay by Vaclav Havel that was written and widely disseminated while Havel, currently the president of the Czech Republic, was still a political prisoner, raised an important question about dissident movements within the Soviet bloc that holds true for Moroccan political prisoners: "Why, in conditions where a widespread and arbitrary abuse of power is the rule, is there such a general and spontaneous acceptance of the principle of legality?" Although this "principle of legality," enshrined in various international covenants and instruments such as the Universal Declaration of Human Rights, is enunciated publicly and frequently, Havel notes, it remains an implicit, never discussed, universally agreed upon given.[10] The next section of this essay will discuss the principle of legality as it is found within the institutional structures of human-rights associations and from the perspective of a particular group, the Islamist political prisoners in Morocco. In doing so it will treat the universality of their prison experience while contributing to a study of the unities and dissimilarities that ground a religious movement's adherence to human-rights activism.

The first Moroccan Islamists arrested as nonviolent prisoners of conscience were called "Group 71," based on the number of those arrested and ultimately tried, on July 31, 1984. They were charged with plotting against the regime, the public display of illegal banners showing antimonarchy calligraphy, clandestine meetings to constitute groups deemed illegal, graffiti hostile to the state, the distribution of treasonous tracts, and the transmission overseas (notably to France) of tracts denouncing the monarchy. On June 20–21 of 1983, during the month of Ramadan, groups in Casablanca had put up posters and painted slogans on the beach, around the town center, and even on highway overpasses, so that the words could be read by passing motorists. These actions, timed to commemorate the second anniversary of the Casablanca "bread riots" of 1981, were defined by Islamists as part of the politics of *tahaddi* (defiance).

Many of the groups' slogans resembled earlier, Marxist graffiti of the 1970s, decrying the lack of democracy and justice, condemning the high cost of living, and calling for freedom of speech. Only when the banners were exhibited in court as part of their trial would specific Islamist slogans, incorporated into trial transcripts, see the light of day – for example, "If religion were installed in the country, there would be justice and human rights." Other banners called King Hassan II *al-taghut*, a Koranic term meaning "tyrant." The government also accused the Islamists, among others, of fomenting the second bread riots, in January 1984, although group members were already held incommunicado in detention by August 1983, six months before those uprisings.[11] The year 1984 alone would see more than eighty trials for "*délit d'opinion*" (crimes of opinion), with 1,600 persons tried. The arrests fell most heavily on two groups seemingly at opposite ends of the political spectrum: Islamist activists and the radical left, notably the Marxist-Leninists of the Ilal-Amam (*En avant*) movement.[12]

---

10 See Vaclav Havel, "The Power of the Powerless," *Open Letters: Selected Writings 1965–1990* (New York: Vintage, 1992), pp. 181–82.

11 See Ahmed Haou, "al-Mahkama" (The trial), *al-Jisr* (Rabat), no. 20 (July 1994): 13.

12 See Jean-Claude Santucci, "Chronique marocaine," *Annuaire de l'Afrique du Nord* (Valbonne: Ed. CNRS, 1985), pp. 650–52. Some of those charged had no political connections to either

Prison wedding of
Ahmed Haou, Islamist
political prisoner
(1983–98), and
Fatima Guarai,
Oukacha prison,
Casablanca, 1995.
Clandestine
photograph, courtesy
Ahmed Haou.

Taken to Derb Moulay Cherif, the Islamists, like so many political prisoners
before them, were forcibly "disappeared" and endured savage tortures while awaiting a trial that only took place some seven months later. Accounts of life in Derb
Moulay Cherif are increasingly being published in Morocco by victims of the
prison who come from all political persuasions.[13] The trajectories of interrogation
and torture for Moroccan political prisoners were in many respects similar, but
specific mistreatments were reserved for each group: while prison guards forced
Marxist-Leninists to recite the Muslim profession of faith, the *shahada*, Islamists
were forbidden from performing ritual ablutions and also from praying aloud,
which their torturers defined as a forbidden form of communication among
themselves. Ahmed Haou, the acknowledged leader of the Islamist political prisoners in Group 71, recalls his torturers telling him, "If we could put your God
through a session of *al-tayyara* [the so-called "airplane" torture, in which the victim is trussed and suspended to be beaten and electroshocked], we would do it."[14]

> movement, including Said Boudiaf, seventeen years old when he was arrested in Oujda, who spent
> five years in prison because of the political activities of his brother, Mohammed Boudiaf; Abdellah
> Fahd, who was sentenced to twenty years, and served thirteen, because he was unlucky enough to
> have slept over at the house of a friend who was arrested; Abderazzak Trigui, not even an Islamist,
> who was arrested while visiting a friend in the neighborhood and served fifteen years; and numer-
> ous individuals who were condemned to four years in prison for the crime of "nondenunciation" of
> already arrested family members.
>
> 13 See, for example, Abdelkader Chaoui, *Kana wa Akhaouatuha*, 1986 (first ed. seized, second ed.
>   Rabat: Al-Ghad, 1999); Abdellatif Laabi, *Le Chemin des ordalies* (Paris: Denoël, 1982, republished
>   in Morocco as *Le Fou de l'espoir* (Casablanca: Eddif, 2000); and "Rahal" (a pseudonym), *Dans les
>   entrailles de ma patrie* (Paris, c. 1982), republished under the author's own name, Abdelaziz
>   Mouride, as *On affame bien les rats* (Casablanca: Tarik Editions, 2000).
> 14 Ahmed Haou, interviews with the author, Rabat, 1999–2000.

Collectively and by consensus, Islamist prisoners organized a series of committees to negotiate with authorities, to produce communiqués to the Moroccan minister of justice and to the outside world, to demand improved conditions, to share food distribution, and to create, as the Marxist-Leninist political prisoners did, a rich cultural life in detention, including ceremonies, religious festivals, sports activities, cultural conferences, and the variety of celebrations that characterize closely knit human societies. They also produced clandestine prison newspapers: in the Ghbila prison in 1984 there was a newspaper called *Bidanciés*, Moroccan slang for "penitentiary," and in the Safi prison in 1985–86 there was *Madrasat Youssef* (Joseph's followers), named to honor the Joseph of the Koran, a potent symbol as an early political prisoner who had addressed a tyrant in these famous words: "Prison is preferable for me than doing what you demand." New models of organization and activism emerged from the space of prison. Only after 1990 did Amnesty International take up the cases of these prisoners abroad, after long written exchanges with the Islamists, who had to persuade the outside world that they were indeed nonviolent and had been arrested as prisoners of conscience.

Forms of Resistance   The status of "political prisoner" in Morocco is not defined by any laws; instead, it is acquired according to combined pressures exerted internationally and nationally, but principally it emerges as an identity definition from within groups of prisoners themselves, immediately upon their incarceration. The most extreme form of resistance universally available to prisoners to establish the claim to political-prisoner status has been the hunger strike, whether it be partial or, more dangerously, unlimited. The efficacy of the hunger strike depends on wide media coverage, that is, the passage of individual pain into the realm of public knowledge. It is the flip side to the fact of torture undergone by political prisoners. The hunger striker inflicts pain and deprivation on the body as part of collective willed decisions. The striker instigates his or her own physical destruction as an active participant who makes of the human body a weapon and a message projected outward to the world.

Extreme prison deprivations could call for extreme hunger strikes. In 1986, Islamists condemned to death began a hunger strike that lasted more than forty-five days, with some, like Haou, going into coma on the thirty-third day; force-feedings were initiated in the prison hospital on the thirty-seventh day. The strikers demanded and eventually received the right to information, medical care, direct and longer family visits, decent food, and the continuation of their studies. To gain and retain acquired rights, which were often subject to being rescinded by prison authorities, innumerable unlimited hunger strikes took place in the various prisons. When radio, television, newspapers, and books were initially forbidden for Islamist political prisoners in the Safi prison, hunger strikes of twenty-four or seventy-two hours were undertaken. In October 1985, in solidarity with another group, the Group 26 of Marxist-Leninists imprisoned in the same penitentiary, the Islamists joined leftist political prisoners in their hunger strike – one in which three Marxist prisoners, Moustapha Belhouari and the two Doureidi brothers, would die.[15]

Unlimited hunger strikes posed theological and spiritual problems for the Islamists. If one were to die as a hunger striker, would one be considered a *shahid* (martyr)? Does *Sharia* (Islamic law) authorize death by hunger strike? For many Islamist political prisoners, the inability to pursue a hunger strike to the point of death weakened its usefulness as a weapon, but there was no escaping its definition as an act of suicide, condemnable (*munkar*) and figuring among the greater sins (*kaba'ir*) leading to hell. Discussions led Islamists to conclude that they needed to find a pretext to stop before jeopardizing their health. Indeed Islamists originally housed together in Kenitra in 1985 were able to profit from the advice of earlier Kenitra hunger strikers: Driss Benzekri, of the Marxist-Leninist group Ilal Amam (imprisoned after trials in Casablanca in 1977), counseled them against hunger strikes except as a last resort, and to avoid unlimited ones but to come out mentally and physically intact. From 1987 on, Islamist political prisoners innovatively embarked on what they called *idrab tanawubi*, or rolling hunger strikes: a group of two to four hunger strikers would fast for twenty-four or forty-eight hours, then would be replaced by another group. The unlimited hunger strike persisted as a physical condition, but instead of being attached to the suffering body of a single prisoner, the state of being on hunger strike rotated among the collective bodies of the group.

If the prison hunger strike to the death prevented Islamists from being considered martyrs, the Moroccan state created martyrs when its courts liberally handed out death sentences, which were not always carried out but did lead to many years of residence on death row. Six of the members of Group 71, including Haou, were condemned to death. Prisoners embraced the martyrdom of being a political prisoner about to die, a status that resulted from specific political convictions and was validated by the state. When that status was removed – by the reduction of a death sentence to life imprisonment – its loss was keenly felt. Belkacem Hakimi, an Islamist political prisoner currently serving a life sentence in Oukacha prison, wrote in his diary on March 7, 1994,

---

15 See Hélène Jaffé, "Aux cotés des victimes de la répression," *Droits de l'Homme et violences au Maghreb et en Europe* (Paris: Publication Hourriya/Liberté, 1997), pp. 78–81.

Conference on human rights and Palestine organized by Islamist political prisoners within Kenitra Central Prison, 1992. Speakers, left to right: Belkacem Hakimi, Badr Idris Ouhlal, Hasan Elhasni Alaoui, Mohammed Hakiki, and Ahmed Haou. Hakimi remains imprisoned in Oukacha prison, Casablanca. Clandestine photograph.

They say our death sentence has been commuted and perhaps this is valid for me too. I really do not know from where this wave of sadness that invades me comes. I should be happy. But it is completely the opposite. I am sad and distressed. For me the death sentence was like a crown God placed on my head that mattered greatly. Everything was so clear to me: "You are dead, they are all dead." When I was condemned to death, I was free, very free, nothing mattered. Now, how will things unfold? Will fear finally inhabit my heart? Everyone knows they will die. But a death sentence is so concrete. I sensed death. I even touched it. More than that, I dared to befriend it. But now it confirms that it is always stronger. It escapes when I thought I had it. I truly fear it will vanquish me, make me submit to become like those "flocks of the silenced." People have a perverse logic, I would say even "reversed." Some came to congratulate me. Don't they know that this death sentence was God's promise to me that I have vanquished death forever, that I would "die" a martyr? Does this promise still hold? That's what I fear most.[16]

In effect the death sentence was enlisted as the supreme example, the sign of a proffered martyrdom in the world to come while remaining a fundamental attribute of, even a paradoxical metaphor for, day-to-day resistance against the prison world and the struggle to remain human and alive.

16 Belkacem Hakimi, prison diary, Monday, March 7, 1994/24 Ramadan. Translated from Arabic to French by Belkacem Hakimi, reproduced by permission of author. English translation from the French by Susan Slyomovics. See also Hakimi, "Bayni wa-bayn al-mawt," *al-Mishkat*, November–December 1988, pp. 108–9, and Hakimi, "Lettre à Aragon … d'un homme à mourir," *L'Infini*, no. 23 (1997): 62.

Postdetention Activism   By the late 1990s, all of the leftists and many Islamist political prisoners benefited from royal amnesties.[17] In the post-1999, post-Hassan II "new era" (*ahd jadid*), writings by El Ouadie and Haou, and their performances and political activism on behalf of the Moroccan Forum for Truth and Justice, seem to herald a different Morocco, willing to begin addressing the issue of a state's acknowledged crimes against its own citizens: decades of illegal detention, forcible disappearance, and torture.[18]

In 1998, in the last years of the reign of King Hassan II, a royally appointed and mandated Conseil Consultatif des Droits de l'Homme (Advisory council on human rights) began to hold meetings to discuss the "disappeared." The Conseil Consultatif and its president, Driss Dahak, issued a press release establishing a list of 112 people: 56 of these were declared dead with no accompanying information, the others were described as having disappeared in unknown situations, and to be presumed either dead or living abroad or in Morocco. While these figures are absurdly low, the memorandum implicitly confirmed the state's official recognition of the fact of forcible disappearance. On the ascension of King Mohammed VI to the throne, in 1999, the new king's first, televised speech from the throne confirmed his commitment to establish the rule of law, to safeguard human rights and individual and collective liberties, and to institute a constitutional monarchy, multipartyism, economic liberalism, and policies of regionalism and decentralization. On August 17, 1999, King Mohammed ordered the Conseil Consultatif to activate an independent indemnity commission with a mandate, to expire midnight on December 31 of that year, to indemnify former victims of forcible disappearance and arbitrary deten-

17 As of this writing, thirty-six Islamists claiming the status of political prisoner are still serving their sentences in Moroccan prisons, according to Lajnat al-Wafaa, founded on March 5, 2000, as an organization uniting former Islamist political prisoners. They belong to different organizations and were tried in a variety of political trials. For a complete list, see the Lajnat al-Wafaa communiqué *La'iha al-mu'ataqalin al-siyasiyyin al-islamiyyin* (March 5, 2000), published in *al-Sahifa* (Casablanca), March 25–31, 2000, p. 8.

18 By the 1990s, however, changes in the laws and in their application formally and legally recount the history of the treatment of political prisoners in Morocco. In a famous and much quoted speech delivered on July 8, 1994, King Hassan II promised "to turn the page definitively" and to "resolve the pressing issue of political prisoners." See Driss Basri, Michel Rousset, and Georges Vedel, *Le Maroc et les droits de l'Homme* (Paris: L'Harmattan, 1994), p. vii. Four years earlier, on March 8, 1990, the king had created a royal advisory council on human rights; in 1993, a new ministry of human rights had been formed; on June 21, 1993, Morocco had ratified the United Nations Convention against Torture (though this change was not in force until it was published, on December 16, 1996, in the *Bulletin Officiel*); in 1996, revisions to the Moroccan penal code had limited *garde-à-vue* – incommunicado detention, in the terms of Anglo-American law (Morocco has no *habeas corpus*) – to forty-eight hours, with one twenty-four-hour extension allowed at the prosecutor's discretion (although in cases of state security, the rubric under which political prisoners were tried, the *garde-à-vue* period remained ninety-six hours, with possible extensions by the prosecutor); and finally, in 1998, the ministry of justice and the prison administration had implemented a law that made autopsies routine for any death occurring in detention.

The speaker is Abdessamad Bouabid, Islamist political prisoner (1983–93), Oukacha prison, Casablanca, May 18, 1993. Banner: "Islamist political prisoners celebrate their liberation after ten years." Clandestine photograph, courtesy Abdessamad Bouabid.

tion. The council's bulletin describing the procedures, the mandate, and the membership of this indemnity commission was widely criticized by Morocco's community of victims and human-rights activists, two groups with overlapping memberships: the council had predetermined the number of "disappeared," and, most outrageously, had granted immunity to torturers and to all those responsible for a state apparatus of secret detention centers, illegal detention (*garde-à-vue*), unfair trials, and the systematic practice of torture in police stations and prisons. By the end of the year, on the December 31 deadline set by the council for filing claims against the state, only 5,819 dossiers demanding damages had been submitted to the indemnity commission.

Human-rights violations evoke several national responses: create a governmental organ intended to record the truth about past history; declare an amnesty, or prosecute those responsible, or do both; arrange indemnities for the victims and their dependents by means of official rehabilitation and material compensation. A Chilean national commission on truth and reconciliation formed in 1990 extensively documented violations but had no authority to judge those responsible. In Argentina, a national commission on disappeared persons, established in 1983, published its findings in *Nunca más* (Never again), listing almost 9,000 unsolved "disappearances" along with charts of secret detention centers; the results included over 1,000 cases in Argentine civilian courts. The South African Truth and Reconciliation Commission of 1996, chaired by Bishop Desmond Tutu, created several subgroups to promote national reconciliation: a Committee on Violations of Human Rights to identify victims and review compensation proposals, a Committee on Amnesty to grant amnesty or indemnities, and a Committee on Compensation and Rehabilitation to provide victims of human-rights violations with a public forum to narrate what befell them. South African victims of serious human-rights violations also have the right to file a request for compensation. It was South African policy to grant amnesty if information was fully disclosed about political acts, defined as acts committed by a political organization or a member of the security troops within the framework of obligations and authorities.[19]

The Moroccan indemnity commission, by contrast, began at the end, with indemnities, rather than at the beginning, with information seeking, where any genuine truth commission begins. Indemnity as conceived by the Moroccan Conseil Consultatif implicitly recognizes illegal state practices. Compensation suggests something compensatable. In Morocco, the problem of past human-rights violations is posed in material terms only, meaning that the only way for victims to be acknowledged is for them to file claims requesting indemnification. In Morocco, there are no public hearings and no attempts to provide the nation with an account of the past. Blanket amnesties were declared as part of the creation of the indemnity commission. An astounding example of a Moroccan official remaining in office despite much newspaper coverage of his misdeeds is Mahmoud Archane, former police officer and torturer at the Rabat Commissariat, and currently a member of parliament.[20] In Morocco, no one has been tried, crimes are considered to be unproven, and no Moroccan judge has proceeded to prosecution.

Even in situations in which truth and reconciliation processes are available, amnesty is hotly debated. In Moroccan practice, impunity is the rule for crimes that perpetrators have committed by order of governments or other authorities. Individuals often go unprosecuted because mitigating circumstances are offered, such as "following orders." Crimes are subject to a statute of limitations – in Morocco, twenty years. Meanwhile international instruments of human rights, though ratified, were not in force until recently in the country.

The response to the creation of a Moroccan indemnity commission in August 1999 was immediate. Groups of former political prisoners and human-rights activists formed the Moroccan Forum for Truth and Justice, electing a thirteen-member executive committee whose ten men and three women together represent a history of more than 200 mass political trials and tens of thousands of forcible disappearances. The Forum's executive committee

---

19 See John Borneman, *Settling Accounts: Violence, Justice and Accountability in Post-Socialist Europe* (Princeton, N.J.: Princeton University Press, 1997), and Martha Minow, *Between Vengeance and Forgiveness* (Boston: Beacon Press, 1998).

20 Articles about Ahmed Jaouhar, who names Archane as his torturer, are included in the January 4–10, 1999, issue of the Arabic-language weekly *al-Sahifa*. They are preceded by an interview and cover story in which Archane denies all such charges.

May 4, 2000, candlelight vigil and sit-in in front of Derb Moulay Cherif, principal torture center in Casablanca. Left: Hasan Elhasni Alaoui (Group 71 of Islamists) and his wife, Khadija Warab, a lawyer. Photo courtesy Elhasni Alaoui family.

includes not only leftists such as Benzekri (president) and El Ouadie (vice-president) but Islamists such as Haou (vice-treasurer).

The Forum's recommendations include public rehabilitation of victims, restitution of the remains of "disappeared" persons and the provision of death certificates for them so that they can be reburied, monetary benefits to victims and relatives, and medical care, education, and shelter for all those involved. According to the Forum, the state is obliged to recognize individual suffering by issuing extensive official reports with attention to individual cases. Getting to the truth about past abuses requires cooperation from state officials, various police forces, and ministries. So far, unfortunately, none of these has been prepared to participate or cooperate. Even the number of victims is unknown. By June 2000, the Forum had established a standard form to be sent to everyone who had suffered from arbitrary repression, or to those competent to write on behalf of the dead, the disappeared, or others unable to write themselves.

In relation to other national efforts, the Moroccan approach is so far the most underdeveloped and the least serious.[21] Both Chad and South Africa have changed regimes, a departure that allows for a clearer treatment of past violations. In Morocco the regime has not changed and is intent upon transforming itself from the inside, trying to become democratic while still retaining control – a process that parallels its approach to human rights. Difficulties initially arose when King Hassan II created the Conseil Consultatif as a nonindependent body with no clear mandate or procedures. The lack of change in Morocco under-

---

21 See Mohamed Moustaid, "L'Approche marocain est la moins réflechie," *Le Journal* (Casablanca), December 25–31, 1999.

scores a fundamental paradox: the country is paying indemnities, and paying off perpetrators, without acknowledging state crimes.

Reconciliation is a process. Even if the Moroccan authorities were to release information to help establish an official report on the past, the punishment of perpetrators might not be an outcome. Moroccan human-rights activists have demonstrated the will to move toward something resembling a truth commission for Morocco. The Conseil Consultatif's bulletin of early 1998 announcing a mere 112 "disappeared" in effect helped to launch the Moroccan Forum, and could still serve as a point of departure for a genuine truth commission. A working group of the Conseil Consultatif, the Commission de la Verification de l'Enquête (Commission of verification of the inquiry), was established in 1998. The original inquiry that identified only 112 "disappeared" could be redone, and the council's mandate and powers could be expanded. In this way a continuity with the previous regime of King Hassan II, who established the Conseil Consultatif and its working groups, could be maintained. King Mohammed VI has made no public criticism of his father (in fact Moroccan law prohibits any negative commentary on members of the royal family, present and past).

In April 2000, six months after the establishment of the Moroccan Forum for Truth and Justice, a group of Islamist former political prisoners created another human-rights organization, Tajammu' min ajli karamati al-insan (Assembly for human dignity), known by its acronym, "Tamkine," which means "strengthening," "consolidation," "enablement."[22] (The founders of Tamkine were members of the Forum, and remained so, maintaining its role as an umbrella human-rights group uniting all political prisoners.) Despite Moroccan laws requiring nongovernmental organizations to register with both the prefecture and the tribunal, Tamkine has been unable to obtain official authorization, and like many other associations must operate on the border between illegality and self-censorship.

The fact that people who have experienced torture, bogus trials, and long years of prison for their ideas have subsequently transformed this "gift" of pain and imprisonment into committed human-rights work is a somewhat astounding development that has been repeated country by country and in case after case. A similar intellectual trajectory has been followed by the Tunisian Islamists of the Mouvement de la tendance islamiste, or MTI, which in 1981–82 began to speak of human rights as part of its political platform. As documented by Mohamed Karem in his Ph.D. thesis, three main elements contribute to a recognition of the diversity of opinion and liberty of expression among certain

---

22 Communiqué, Tajammu' min ajli karamati al-insan (Tamkine), *Balagh min al-Jami'a al-huquqiyah al-wataniya* (Casablanca), May 12, 2000.

Tunisian Islamists: "The repression that fell on MTI activists, the support of the Tunisian League for Human Rights (LTDH) because they defended them and denounced this repression, and finally the internal debates within the movement on questions of referents, identity, strategy, and kinds of actions to adopt."[23] Beginning in the 1970s but more clearly in the 1980s, Morocco has seen the emergence of several human-rights organizations and in fact of a culture of human rights rooted in the struggles since independence to free the political prisoners who have peopled the kingdom's secret torture centers, commissariats, and tribunals.[24]

No matter where Islamist political prisoners locate themselves on the theoretical spectrum, from a movement to "Westernize" Islamists or to "Islamize" human-rights discourse, their responses are practical and organizational, given that thirty-six remain incarcerated. Tamkine is one of the latest initiatives. Islamist political prisoners can participate in several social, political, and religious movements: first, as activists in an international human-rights movement; second, as political prisoners belonging to an ancient cross-cultural collectivity of victims of abusive regimes; and third, as Islamists participating in an Arabo-Muslim Islamist movement. From the 1990s on, the Moroccan Islamist human-rights movement, born during particular historical circumstances and in response to gross human-rights violations, has faced a double struggle. First, members of Tamkine and the nonsectarian Moroccan Forum for Truth and Justice see their tasks as addressing and educating those within their own Islamist movements who may perceive human rights as an alien, Western, secular dogma imposed from outside to mask a rapacious economic imperialism. At the same time, the Moroccan Islamist human-rights movement confronts Moroccan human-rights activists who often may have emerged from the secular left, and some of whom may view Islamists as enemies of a universalist discourse of the rule of law promoting democracy and equal rights for women. In Morocco there is room for, if not a perceived need for, yet another human-rights association, one that continues to campaign in support of all Islamist political prisoners. Haou advances reason (*'aql*) and the possibili-

23 Mohammed Karem, "La Notion des droits de l'Homme au Maghreb," Ph.D. diss., Université d'Aix-Marseille, 1991, p. 231.

24 For excellent histories of the human-rights movement in Morocco, see Ann Elisabeth Mayer, *Islam and Human Rights: Tradition and Politics* (3rd ed., Boulder: Westview Press, 1999); Susan Waltz, "Making Waves: The Political Impact of Human Rights Groups in North Africa," *Journal of Modern African Studies* (Cambridge: Cambridge University Press), no. 20 (1991): 481–504, and *Human Rights and Reform: Changing the Face of North African Politics* (Berkeley: University of California Press, 1995); and Marguerite Missoffe-Rollinde, "De l'unanisme nationaliste au concept de citoyenneté. Le militant(e) marocain(e) des droits de l'Homme," Ph.D. diss., Université Paris VIII, 2000, 2 vols.

ties of reinterpreting existing sacred law (*ijtihad*) as modalities in which to work toward changing the idea that human rights are Western notions; Islam too, he observes, has its referents.

I have offered no analysis here of the large body of complex discourses on religion, politics, and human rights produced either by Muslim or Marxist thinkers, many of whom serve as sources and reference points for political prisoners.[25] Rather, what has been presented is the evolution of human rights in its lived context, mainly the interaction of the world of political prisoners and the Morocco they found once liberated from prison. Abdellah Lamrani, a member of Group 71 and a lawyer defending Islamist political prisoners, makes explicit the public connection between the fate of all political prisoners and the campaign for human rights: "Political prisoners are like wood. When they start to burn, the machinery of human rights turns."[26] Islamist political prisoners have produced a human-rights discourse that is modern in spirit. It is as inclusive as possible of diverse Moroccan political trends; to take Haou's approach, what is needed is a minimum platform around which Islamists and others can unite. In effect, since no single political party or bloc can achieve the rule of law, everyone is needed to solve Morocco's numerous, crushing problems. Moroccans interested in human rights have the will to move toward them and have identified several ways to produce change. Does the Moroccan state, on the other hand, have a desire for human rights, and an interest in finding a way toward them?

25 The bibliography is immense, including the Mayer, Waltz, and Missoffe-Rollinde works cited above; the large corpus of writings by Abdullah An-Na'im; Mohamed Moaquit, "Le Mouvement des droits de l'Homme au Maroc: Du Makhzen à l'état de droit," *Annuaire de l'Afrique de Nord* (Valbonne: Ed. CNRS, 1995), pp. 271–87; and articles in Basri, Rousset, and Vedel, *Le Maroc et les droits de l'Homme.*
26 Abdellah Lamrani, interview with the author, Casablanca, March 2000.

The Search for the Truth Before the Courts

María José Guembe

State Terrorism in Argentina   Between 1976 and 1983 Argentina experienced the most terrible military dictatorship of its history. On March 24, 1976, the military overthrew the constitutional president, María Estela Martínez de Perón, and formed a government junta that included the heads of the army, the air force, and the navy. The military had played a role in Argentina's history since the country's beginnings; it had always been a political player, and had been accepted in public opinion as the guardian of the nation's founding principles. Yet its crucial role on Argentina's political scene had led to permanent institutional instability: since 1930, the military had overthrown six constitutional governments.[1] The power of the armed forces had distorted their function.

The military had intruded repeatedly in government, but the 1976 coup was different. The program was not in this case limited to "reestablishing" social and economic order, as on previous occasions. Rather, the goals were radical changes in Argentine society. Beyond this, too, the salient characteristic of the new military dictatorship was the creation and implementation of a system of state terrorism. Since the early 1970s, Argentina had faced serious internal social conflict, with various armed political organizations practicing the use of direct force. Even before the coup, the constitutional government had responded through the secret use of military and para-police bodies to suppress political opposition. When the armed forces took power, one of their principal and immediate goals was to dismantle all means of political opposition and the economic, human, cultural, and social resources that supported it.

The junta dissolved the congress and assumed legislative functions, replacing nearly all of the judges and abolishing most of the individual rights established by the constitution. Although the military constructed a "legal" framework to allow them to suppress the population, they also established a system of secret

---

1 Those coups took place in 1930, 1943, 1955, 1962, 1966, and, most recently, in 1976.

plans and orders, circumventing judicial control. The clandestine, underground nature of the repression helped it both to evade international and Vatican diplomacy and to avoid conflict with the Argentine Catholic Church. It was also very effective, for even as it eluded control, it generated terror, paralyzing the defensive responses of the public.[2]

To carry out the repression, more than 600 clandestine holding centers were set up, the majority of them in offices of the military or police. Here people were detained after illegal arrest, that is, arrest without a court order. The kidnappings took place in homes, workplaces, on the street, in places of study. Many people were kidnapped along with young children or babies, and a large number of pregnant women were also arrested. The detainees were subject to extensive and repeated torture sessions in which the most aberrant methods were used to obtain information. Meanwhile the clandestine nature of the process made it possible to deny that prisoners were being held at all, and to avoid judicial investigation.

The whereabouts of most of the missing is still unknown. The only certainty is that the final decision as to their fate rested with the forces under whose orders they had been arrested. The most common way of disposing of them was to throw them, still living, into the sea. This method was favored because the military wanted to avoid opposition from the international community, and so opted against the responsibility of execution by firing squad or the carrying out of death sentences by some other means. Instead they were permanently "disappeared." At least 30,000 people were eliminated.

More than 500 children of the disappeared, some of them arrested with their parents, others born in prison, were illegally handed over to military families who registered them as their own. Even today, only seventy-four of these children have been recovered by their original families.

The system involved a systematic, widespread violation of basic human rights. The aim was to change the social, political, economic, and cultural structure of the country and to guarantee the uncontested power of the armed forces.[3] The clandestine, repressive doctrine of the dictatorship took on the character of state terrorism. For Hannah Arendt in *The Origins of Totalitarianism*, a terrorist state is one that, deliberately and as a political tool, clandestinely uses its power to threaten, kidnap, assassinate, torture, place bombs, wreak

---

2 See Carlos Acuña and Catalina Smulovitz, "Militares en la Transición Argentina: del gobierno a la subordinación constitucional," in Carlos Acuña et al., *Juicio, castigos y memoria. Derechos humanos y justicia en la política argentina* (Buenos Aires: Ed. Nueva Visión, 1995), p. 29.

3 This is the opinion of Emilio Mignone, founder of the Centro de Estudios Legales y Sociales. See Mignone, *Derechos humanos y sociedad* (Buenos Aires: Ediciones del Pensamiento Nacional, 1991), p. 54.

havoc, commit arson, and so on, with the complicity of official bodies and leaving its citizens completely defenseless.[4]

This was the situation in Argentina from 1976 until 1983.

Opposition and Accusations of Serious Human-Rights Violations   Indifference and confusion predominated in the response of the Argentine public. Individual relatives of the victims tried to report the disappearances through various channels, all in vain. Visits to civil or military authorities to request information, interviews with religious authorities, police and judicial reports – all were fruitless. More than 80,000 requests of habeas corpus were made during these years; most of them were rejected or filed away uninvestigated.

Human-rights organizations played an important role in recording the accusations and establishing systems for dealing with them – sponsoring legal action, receiving and compiling the testimonies of people who had been freed from the clandestine detention centers, documenting human-rights violations. The recognition that some groups achieved outside Argentina – the Mothers of the Plaza de Mayo, for example – was of major significance. These groups became symbols of the fight against authoritarian repression. International solidarity also played an important role. Missions from various international organizations were present in Argentina to put pressure on the Argentine military, to take reports from hundreds of people, and to let the world know what was happening. Outside help and Argentine use of international forums for the protection of human rights, such as the Organization of American States and the United Nations, supported opposition to the dictatorship.

The Recovery of Democracy   The military dictatorship did not fall because of public pressure, political opposition, or the activity of national or international human-rights organizations: its own mistakes were its downfall. The transition to democracy came through the crisis raging within the armed forces and the failed economic policy, problems aggravated by the war in the Falkland Islands.[5] These were what forced the military to hold elections and kept it from setting the conditions in the transition to democracy. It tried in vain to negotiate immunity for the crimes it had committed, and before stepping down it passed

---

4 Hannah Arendt, *The Origins of Totalitarianism* (New York: Harcourt, Brace, 1951).
5 Historically Argentina has claimed sovereignty over the Falkland Islands, in the South Atlantic, but they have long been ruled by Great Britain. In 1982, General Leopoldo Galtieri led an invasion of the islands to fight British rule. His resounding defeat was the beginning of the end for the regime.

what was called the "National Pacification" law,[6] which amnestied all the crimes "committed in the struggle against terrorism."

Democratic elections were held in Argentina on October 30, 1983, and Raúl Alfonsín, the Radical Civic Union candidate, was elected president. His campaign had featured a promise to put military personnel responsible for crimes against human dignity on trial. One of the first measures taken by the federal congress of the new government was an annulment of the amnesty law. Almost at the same time, the executive created the Comisión Nacional Sobre la Desaparición de Personas (CONADEP, the national commission for the "disappeared"). Designed to examine the cases of the many who had gone missing under the dictatorship, the commission was authorized to research the methods of state terrorism, process accusations and proof, and learn the whereabouts of the disappeared and of the children who had been taken from their parents.[7]

In less than a year, CONADEP received 8,960 reports of people who had gone missing, organized a database of 7,380 files documenting these cases, sent out more than 1,300 requests for police and legal records, located 340 clandestine detention centers, listed 1,300 persons who had been seen in these centers and were now missing, investigated cemeteries and mass graves where unidentified corpses were buried on military orders, and identified 80 cases to be investigated and tried. CONADEP also identified 1,351 people involved in the repression, although it was not authorized to release their names. Its greatest achievement was the report *Nunca más* (Never again), a strong condemnation of the repression.[8] The report confirmed the state's methods and terrorist practices: kidnapping, torture, clandestine arrest, the murder of defenseless prisoners. The example of CONADEP demonstrates the ability of democratic governments to investigate and shed light on what was intended to remain secret.

The push to put the members of the junta on trial was another strategy that the democratic government undertook by decree of the executive.[9] The government wanted to punish human-rights violations, but it also sought to guarantee the stability of the new democracy by incorporating the military into the democratic structure. As a result, the trials were initially to be the responsibility of the armed forces, with the civil justice system reviewing the sentences. The military courts postponed taking action, however, and civilian judges stepped in. On December 9, 1985, after a nine-month investigation, the justice system

6 Law 22.924, dated September 23, 1983.
7 Law 187/83, dated December 15, 1983.
8 *Nunca más* was presented to the president on September 20, 1984.
9 Decree 158/83, dated December 13, 1983, in which the nation's president ordered that the military courts conduct the hearing of a penal process against the military leaders.

announced that it had established the existence of a deliberate plan to carry out a clandestine policy of repression, and that this policy had been the main weapon of the dictatorship in its campaign to eliminate subversion. As a result, five senior officers of the junta were sentenced for crimes of homicide, illegal deprivation of freedom, torture, and other offenses. Four of the officers were to be excused from serving their sentences, because the judges found the evidence against them insufficient or inconclusive. Even so, the trial was a milestone in Argentina's recent history.

Meanwhile, around 2,000 cases were brought against lower-ranking personnel who were still on active duty. The trials caused great uneasiness in the military, which began to put pressure on the government, inducing it to pass a law preventing the prosecution of some of the accused by reducing the statute of limitations to sixty days. Anyone who had not been indicted within that period could be not be prosecuted in the future. This law, enacted at the very end of 1986, was known as the "Final Point" law.[10] Having passed it, the government expected that only a small number of military personnel would be brought to justice.

Yet the filing of reports only grew, and thanks to the work of certain judges, many military cases began to be processed. Accordingly, before long, the democratic government faced an open crisis in which the military demanded an amnesty. The result was the "Duty of Obedience" law,[11] which obliged prosecuting judges to presume that the military personnel on trial had been acting under orders. This presumption, which was to be applied regardless of any evidence to the contrary, led to members of the military being relieved from having to serve prison terms.

Both of these laws were applied by judges and recognized by the Supreme Court. The consequence was that the prosecution of crimes of state terrorism has been paralyzed for fifteen years. Impunity for serious violations of human rights during this period threatened to be restored in 1989 and 1990, when Alfonsín's successor as president, Carlos Menem, pardoned the very commanding officers who had been sentenced in 1985. Through these laws and decrees of impunity, the family members of victims of the repression have been denied access to justice. A number of international human-rights organizations have determined that the laws of impunity are incompatible with international treaties that Argentina has ratified.

The laws of impunity were in effect for more than ten years, and were finally abolished by the National Congress on March 24, 1998, twenty-two years after

10 Law 23.492, "Final Point," dated December 24, 1986.
11 Law 23.521, "Determination of the Extent of the Duty of Obedience," dated June 8, 1987.

the coup. The entire political leadership immediately pointed out that the repeal was merely symbolic since the laws had already been put into effect. Nevertheless, human-rights organizations interpreted that symbolic meaning as a step toward justice. Its effects will be analyzed later.

The Right to the Truth   An impasse in the social debate about the past developed after the rules of impunity were passed. Nearly ten years later, in 1995, a sailor named Adolfo Scilingo publicly confessed to his involvement in state terrorism: he said that he had thrown drugged, naked, but living prisoners from navy warplanes into the Rio de la Plata. This confession reopened the debate.

For the first time a member of the military itself had explained the methods it had used. Different social sectors reacted in different ways, but the state institutions, as usual, kept silent, acting only to silence the remorseful sailor. Scilingo's story, however, revived the public's need to know what happened. The CONADEP report had been unable to answer the requests of individuals for information about what had happened to their loved ones – what detention centers they had been held in, who had been responsible for their disappearance, their final fate, the location of their remains. The justice system, too, had been unable to satisfy the right to know. Now, in addition to these claims by families and individuals, a strong social desire began to be expressed addressing the need to build collective memory, to construct a sense of the past that, through critical reflection on what had happened under the junta, would move the society forward into the future.

The individual complaints had to be processed institutionally, and the system chosen for this was the judicial one. The judges had investigative power, and the system allowed the families the possibility of active participation in propelling the proceedings forward. The right to the truth was considered a collective right, and, as such, characteristic of democratic societies. Thus the "Right to the Truth Trials" were begun.

Although it was impossible to sentence all of the guilty, it was possible to gain detailed information on the methods that the military dictatorship had used. Exhaustive research was done. The legal action taken was based on international codes of human rights, on the right to the truth, and, as part of this right, on the right to proper mourning and to the cultural heritage that clandestine proceedings had denied. The Argentine state was asked to comply with international obligations based on the doctrines of the Inter-American Commission on Human Rights and the Inter-American Court of Human Rights. These official bodies recognize both the rights of relatives to know where the missing lie and the obligation of the state to investigate human-rights violations until the whole truth has been revealed.

In the particular case of abduction, the investigation required a redress that included the uncovering of the facts and their communication to the victims' relatives. Since abduction had been a state tool to disturb and confuse relatives and to deceive the public and the world, the truth of what had happened was indispensable. The state had to make all existing information available and to supply the means to reach the truth.

Attempts were made to get local courts to recognize this right to the truth, which had previously been the realm of international systems of justice. This involved a reconception of preexisting state duties and individual rights. The Argentine legal system had included the right to the truth among the rights born of the people's sovereignty and of the republican government specified in the Constitution. The argument was made, then, that the state could not pretend to be ignorant of its obligation to investigate. The right to the truth involved the right to answers from the state; everyone was entitled to ask the state to tell them what they had a right to know; the right to the truth was by extension an aspect of the right to justice. There was also a communal aspect to the right to the truth: the society had the right to know its past, as, among other things, a safeguard of its future. It had a right to know its institutions, its leaders, and events that had taken place within it if it was to find a way to solidify democracy through knowledge of its successes and failures.

As part of the right to the truth, the judicial petitions included the right to mourn. This right was seen as extending to cases of missing persons whose bodies had never been found. Recovery of the body, then, or at least information as to its fate, was part of the truth to be revealed.

The bases for claiming these rights derived from both internal, national law and international human-rights law. Internationally, the Inter-American Commission on Human Rights had been stressing the obligation to investigate Argentina's missing-persons cases since 1979, when its members visited the country and made the following recommendations:

> The Commission holds that the problem of the disappeared is one of the gravest faced by the Republic of Argentina in the field of human rights. Therefore the Commission recommends the following:
>
> a) That detailed reports be made concerning the circumstances of the the disappeared, by which shall be understood those apprehended in operations the circumstances and character of which imply the use of public force. ...
>
> c) That appropriate measures be taken to ensure that proceedings leading to the disappearance of persons do not continue. In this regard, it has come to the Commis-

sion's attention that there have been recent cases of this nature, which must be cleared up as soon as possible along with the others.[12]

In a report that the Commission released after the passing of the laws of impunity, it recommended "the adoption of the necessary measures to clear up the facts and identify those responsible for the human-rights violations that took place during the last military dictatorship."[13]

In the judicial realm, the Inter-American Court of Human Rights made a broad assertion of the state's duty to investigate in July 1988, in a case involving forcible disappearances in Honduras. The Court stated:

> The State is obligated to investigate every situation involving a violation of the rights protected by the Convention. If the State apparatus acts in such a way that the violation goes unpunished and the victim's full enjoyment of such rights is not restored as soon as possible, the State has failed to comply with its duty to ensure the free and full exercise of those rights to the persons within its jurisdiction. … The duty to investigate, like the duty to prevent, is not breached merely because the investigation does not produce a satisfactory result. Nevertheless, it must be undertaken in a serious manner and not as a mere formality preordained to be ineffective.[14]

In other words, the state must resort to whatever means it has at its disposal to investigate human-rights violations, and it must fulfill this duty on its own rather than depending on private initiative. The Court continued,

> The duty to investigate facts of this type continues as long as there is uncertainty about the fate of the person who has disappeared. Even in the hypothetical case that those individually responsible for crimes of this type cannot be legally punished under certain circumstances, the State is obligated to use the means at its disposal to inform the relatives of the fate of the victims and, if they have been killed, the location of their remains.[15]

These are the judicial bases on which the right to truth is based in the international order.

12 Inter-American Commission on Human Rights, report on the Argentine human rights situation adopted by the Commission at its 667th meeting, held on April 11, 1980, p. 7.
13 Report 28/92 Argentina, dated October 2, 1992. The same conclusion was arrived at in relation to Uruguay in Report 29/92, recommendation no. 3.
14 "Velásquez Rodríguez" case, sentence of July 29, 1988, Series C, no. 4, paragraphs 176–77, Inter-American Court of Human Rights.
15 Ibid., paragraph 181.

To put this right into practice in Argentina, the faculties of judicial power for gathering information were indispensable if the international commitment to investigate and make amends for the consequences of human-rights violations was to be fulfilled. Legal impunity was in any case to be construed as non-punishment, but was made even worse if the perpetrators could not be identified and the truth of what had happened was unknown. This is why judicial involvement had not come to an end; there were still rights to be protected.

Responses to Justice   On April 20, 1995, the judges passed a resolution stating that "public interest demands the determination of the truth in court (which is the way to achieve the highest values: truth and justice)," and that this demand should be safeguarded for its particular relevance in criminal prosecutions. The resolution acknowledged the rights to the truth and to mourning as integral parts of international human rights. The judges demonstrated their acceptance of this principle by quoting a sentence from the original petition: "Those who deny us the right to bury our dead are denying our humanity."[16] There is now case law in place that protects the right to the truth. Important measures have been taken toward that end, such as calling the main perpetrators of state terrorism back to the stand to testify. In an amicable resolution accord signed before the Inter-American Commission on Human Rights in 1999, the state has even committed itself to guaranteeing the rights of victims and their relatives to the truth.

The fight for the right to the truth does not exclude a struggle for justice, and in fact the "Duty of Obedience" and "Final Point" laws have now been repealed. On March 6, 2001, twenty-five years after the coup, a judge annulled the impunity laws as conflicting with the Argentine Constitution, the American Declaration of Rights and Duties of Man, the American Convention on Human Rights, the International Civil and Political Rights Pact, and the principles and objectives of the Convention Against Torture. This ruling, which seemed impossible just a few years ago, was the result of a charge made by the Centro de Estudios Legales y Sociales (CELS – the Center for legal and social studies), the organization to which I belong. The decision was confirmed by the Court of Appeals on November 9, 2001. It signifies an important move forward on the road to justice and also truth, since both go hand in hand. It is important to say that the Argentine state once again has the opportunity to guarantee justice, condemn crimes against humanity, and prevent their recurrence.

16 Federal Court of Appeals, April 20, 1995, case no. 761.

Conclusions   The Argentine experience demonstrates the use of nearly every tool we have in reckoning with the past: truth commissions, trials, amnesties, pardons, broad automatic amnesties, truth trials, trials abroad that bring universal jurisdiction to bear, economic compensation, and, twenty-five years after the fact, the reactivation of justice in the national courts through judicial nullification of amnesty. Since the adoption and implementation of each of these measures involved intense debate on the political scene, Argentina's traumatic past could not be resolved by automatically applying formulas based on theory. At the same time, however, theoretical plans were essential guides, for the state, for the victims and their relatives, and for civilian society.

The social and institutional process relating to this period is not over, nor can closure be one-sided. The lucid, active, imaginative, and obstinate participation of the human-rights movement, whose fight knew no territorial, legal, or temporal boundaries, has been essential. This movement and its particular characteristics are also the legacy of the dictatorship that inversely gave rise, for the first time in Argentina, to independent organizations with the staying power to contribute effectively to the consolidation of the institutional system, constituting a strong safeguard against a recurrence of these events. National appreciation of the progress in human-rights protection internationally proved an indispensable tool in the national human-rights movement's lawsuits. The knowledge that not only written law but inalienable social rights were at stake helped us to recover from our reversals and persevere.

There can be no mistake in the final conclusion: in Argentina, the progress we have made in this field in recent years we have made in spite of the state. The efforts of civilians who demanded maximum performance from the state in the reckoning process were a decisive factor. The outcome of the process is uncertain but the petition is undeniable.

Translated from the Spanish by Linda Phillips

Transitional Justice as Liberal Narrative

Ruti Teitel

Introduction   In recent decades, societies in much of the world – Latin America, Eastern Europe, the former Soviet Union, Africa – have been engaged in transition: postcolonial changes, and the overthrowing of military dictatorships and totalitarian regimes in favor of greater freedom and democracy. In these times of massive political movement away from illiberal rule, the burning question recurs: how should societies deal with their evil pasts? What, if any, is the relation between a state's response to its repressive past and its prospects for creating a liberal order?

The point of departure in the transitional-justice debate is the presumption that the move toward a more liberal, democratic political system implies a universal norm. Instead, my remarks here propose an alternative way of thinking about the law and political transformation. In exploring an array of experiences I will describe a distinctive conception of justice in the context of political transformation.

The problem of transitional justice arises within the distinctive context of a shift in political orders, or, more particularly, of change in a liberalizing direction. Understanding the problem of justice in this context requires entering into a discourse organized in terms of the profound dilemmas characteristic of these extraordinary periods. The threshold dilemma arises from the situation of justice in times of political transformation: law is caught between past and future, between backward-looking and forward-looking, between retrospective and prospective. Transitional justice is the justice associated with these circumstances. To the extent that transitions imply paradigm shifts in the conception of justice, the role of law at these moments appears deeply paradoxical. In ordinary times, law provides order and stability, but in extraordinary periods of political upheaval, law is called on to maintain order even as it enables transformation. Accordingly the ordinary intuitions and predicates about law simply do not apply in transitional situations. These dynamic periods of political flux generate a sui generis paradigm of transformative law.

The conception of justice that emerges is contextualized and partial: it is both constituted by and constitutive of the transition. What is "just" is contingent, and informed by prior injustice. As a state undergoes political change, legacies of injustice have a bearing on what is deemed transformative. Indeed, at some level it is the legal responses to these legacies that create the transition. In these situations the rule of law is historically and politically contingent, elaborated in response to past political repression that had often been condoned. While the rule of law ordinarily implies prospectivity, transitional law is both backward- and forward-looking, as it disclaims past illiberal values and reclaims liberal norms.

I. Punishment or Impunity   The core debate in the prevailing view of transitional justice is the so-called "punishment or impunity" debate, the debate over whether or not to punish the predecessor regime. Punishment dominates our understandings of transitional justice, which, in the public imagination, is generally linked with the trials of *anciens régimes*. The enduring symbols of the English and French revolutions, which effected transitions from monarchic to republican rule, are the trials of kings, Charles I and Louis XVI. A half century after the events, the leading monument to the defeat of the Nazis in World War II remains the Nuremberg trials. The contemporary wave of transitions away from military rule throughout Latin America and Africa, as well as from communist rule in Central Europe and the former Soviet bloc, has revived the debate over whether to punish. While trials are thought to be foundational, and to enable the drawing of a bright line demarcating the normative shift from illegitimate to legitimate rule, the exercise of the state's punishment power in circumstances of radical political change raises profound dilemmas. Transitional trials are emblematic of accountability and the rule of law, yet their representation far transcends their actual exercise; they are few and far between, particularly in the contemporary period, and their low incidence reveals the real dilemmas in dealing with systemic wrongdoing by way of criminal law. In transitional contexts, conventional understandings of individual responsibility are frequently inapplicable, and have spurred the emergence of new legal forms: partial sanctions that fall outside conventional legal categories.

The agonizing questions raised by successor-regime criminal justice include: whether to punish or to amnesty? Is punishment a backward-looking exercise in retribution or an expression of the restoration of the rule of law? Who properly bears responsibility for past repression – does it lie with the individual or perhaps with the collective, the regime, the entire society?

The Legacy of Nuremberg   Trials have long been used to express international legal norms regarding injustice in war, and to distinguish legal from illegal political violence. The foundational argument for successor trials has a rich historical pedigree going back to the trials of kings Charles I and Louis XVI to more recent trials including the Nuremberg trials, the Tokyo war-crimes trials, Greece's trial of its colonels, and Argentina's trial of its military commanders.

Since World War II, international justice has been dominated by the legacy, even the myth, of the Nuremberg trials. The significance of Nuremberg is best understood, in its full political context, by returning to the period after World War I, and to the policies set at Versailles and the failed national trials. The national prosecution policies were seen as hopelessly political, and their failures were said to explain the subsequent resurgence of German aggression. This view had repercussions for the rest of the century: the Nuremberg trials shifted the paradigm of justice from national to international processes. It is this shift that has framed both the successor-justice debate and the dominant scholarly understanding of transitional justice over the last half-century.

While there are many dilemmas associated with the application of criminal justice in the national arena, within the international legal system these dilemmas appear to fall away. In the abstract, the dilemmas of successor justice are seemingly best resolved by turning to an autonomous legal system. Within the national legal scheme, the question of justice may seem inextricably political, but international justice is thought by comparison to be neutral and apolitical.

A number of dilemmas recur in the deployment of law in political transition, most basically the question of how to conceptualize justice in the context of a massive political shift. But this problem is mitigated within international law, as the international legal system offers a degree of continuity. The postwar entrenchment of international legal norms affords a jurisdictional basis that goes beyond the limits of domestic criminal law. International law seemingly offers a way to circumvent problems endemic to transitional justice: international standards and forums appear to uphold the rule of law while satisfying core concerns of fairness and impartiality.

Another dilemma of transitional justice is how to ascribe criminal accountability for offenses that implicate the state in a policy of repression. Here, too, international law offers a standard, in the "Nuremberg Principles," a turning point in the conceptualization of responsibility for state crime. These principles for the first time attributed responsibility to individuals for atrocities under international law. In rejecting traditional defenses against such charges, Nuremberg dramatically expanded potential individual criminal liability under law. While, historically, heads of state enjoyed sovereign immunity, under the Nuremberg Principles public officials could no longer avail themselves of a "head of state" defense based on their official positions. Instead they could be held criminally responsible. Moreover, while, under the traditional military rule applicable in a command structure, "due obedience" to orders was a defense, under the Nuremberg Principles even persons acting under orders could be held responsible. By eliminating the "head of state" and "superior orders" defenses, the Nuremberg Principles pierced the veil of diffused responsibility characterizing the wrongdoing perpetrated under totalitarian regimes.

With the Nuremberg Principles, international humanitarian law came to offer a normative framework and language for thinking about successor justice. The wrongdoing of a political regime could now be conceptualized under the rubric of the law of war. Mediating the individual and the collective, the Nuremberg Principles – and World War II itself – left our understanding of individual responsibility permanently altered: they wrought a radical expansion of potential individual criminal liability, at both ends of the power hierarchy. The post-Nuremberg liability explosion has profound ramifications that have not yet been fully absorbed. The massive contemporary expansion in potential criminal liability raises real dilemmas for successor regimes deliberating over whom to bring to trial, and for what: the priority is to target those at the highest level of responsibility for the most egregious crimes. These dilemmas continue to appear in contemporary international criminal proceedings.

At The Hague, where war-crime trials are in process at this writing, developments are currently underway to expand on the postwar understandings of state persecution to include nonstate actors. This is seen in those developments in international humanitarian law in which understanding of the offense of wartime persecution extends beyond the international realm to actions within the state. It is also seen in the jurisdiction of the ad hoc international war-crimes tribunal addressing the former Yugoslavia, as well as in the jurisdiction of the proposed permanent International Criminal Court. In these contemporary instances a dynamic understanding of "crimes against humanity" moves beyond a predicated nexus of armed conflict to persecution, and becomes virtually synonymous with enforcement of equality of the law. Though the strength of international law may not be evident in the record of international trials, its profound normative force is evident in current international discourse, where it stands for what rule of law exists in global politics.

II. The Transitional Limited Criminal Sanction   Despite the call for criminal justice in the abstract, the history of the last half-century reveals recurring problems of justice within the norm shifts that characterize political transitions. Under such conditions, there are limits on the exercise of the power to punish, and justice is often compromised. These real rule-of-law dilemmas help explain why, despite dramatic expansions of criminal liability in the abstract, enforcement lags far behind. Indeed, transitional practices reveal a pattern of criminal investigations and prosecutions followed by little or no penalty. While punishment is ordinarily conceptualized as a unitary practice that includes both the establishment and the penalizing of wrongdoing, in transitional criminal law the elements of establishing and sanctioning have become somewhat detached from one another. It is this partial process, which I term the "limited criminal sanction," that distinguishes criminal justice in transition.

The limited criminal sanction constitutes compromised prosecution processes that do not necessarily culminate in full punishment. Depending on just how limited the process is, investigations may or may not lead to indictments, adjudication, and conviction. If conviction does ensue, it is often followed by little or no punishment. In situations of political transition, the criminal sanction may be limited to an investigation establishing wrongdoing.

The constraints on the limited criminal sanction are well illustrated historically, in, for example, the aftermaths to World Wars I and II, the postmilitary trials of Southern Europe, the contemporary successor criminal proceedings in Latin America and Africa, and the wave of political change in Central Europe following the collapse of the Soviet Union. Although the specific history is often repressed, post-World War II successor justice well illustrates the limited criminal sanction: even in the midst of trials mounted by Allied Control Council No. 10 after the war, the International Military Tribunal began a reversal of the Allied punishment policy, and between 1946 and 1958, a process of reviews and clemency culminated in the mass commutation of war criminals' sentences. A similar sequence unfolded in Germany's national trials, in which, out of more than 1,000 cases tried between 1955 and 1969, fewer than 100 of those convicted received life sentences, and fewer than 300 received limited terms. Years later a similar sequence unfolded in Southern Europe: Greece's trials of its military police culminated largely in suspended or commutable sentences. In the 1980s in Latin America, soon after the Argentine junta trials, limits on follow-up trials were imposed, and pardons were ultimately extended to everyone convicted of atrocities, even the junta leaders. In fact amnesties became the norm throughout much of the continent: Chile, Nicaragua, El Salvador.

The story has repeated itself since the communist collapse: ten years after the revolution, the story is the transitional limited criminal sanction. In unified Germany's border-guards trials, suspension of sentences is the norm. This was also true of the few prosecutions in the Czech Republic, Romania, Bulgaria, and Albania. History repeatedly reflects a limiting of the final phase of punishment policy. Sometimes the limiting of the criminal sanction is used strategically, as an incentive to achieve other political goals, such as cooperation in investigations or in other political projects; in Chile, a law exempting its military from prosecution was conditioned on officers' cooperation in criminal investigations relating to past wrongdoing under military rule. In postapartheid South Africa, penalties were dropped up front on condition of confession to wrongdoing, as crimes deemed "political" were amnestied on condition of participation in the Truth and Reconciliation Commission. This left a window open for investigations into past wrongs, a practice that could also be understood as a limited prosecutorial process.

Other contemporary legal responses, such as the ad hoc international tribunals established to adjudicate genocide and war crimes in Yugoslavia and Rwanda, reflect similar developments. The general absence of custody over the accused – currently only thirty-eight are in custody in the case of the former Yugoslavia – as well as the lack of control over the evidence and the many other constraints relating to war-crimes prosecutions, have left little choice but to investigate, indict, and go no farther. In Rwanda there has been resort to traditional criminal proceedings, which also reflect a form of limited criminal sanction.

The limited criminal sanction offers a pragmatic resolution of the core dilemma of transition: namely, that of attributing individual responsibility for systemic wrongs perpetrated under repressive rule. The basic transitional problem is whether there is any theory of individual responsibility that can span the move from a repressive to a more liberal regime. Indeed the emergence of the limited sanction suggests a more fluid way to think about what punishment does, in fact a rethinking of the theory of punishment: wrongdoing can be clarified and condemned without necessarily attributing individual blame and penalty. In effect, punishment is justified as inherent in the stages of the criminal process.

The transitional sanction, in other words, points to an alternative sense of the retributivist idea. Although the sanction is limited in character, it suggests that core retributive purposes of the recognition and condemnation of wrongdoing are vindicable by diminished – even symbolic – punishment. The recognition and condemnation of past wrongdoing themselves have transformative dimensions: the public establishment of wrongdoing liberates the collective. Mere exposure of wrongs, moreover, can stigmatize their agents, and can disqualify them from entire realms of the public sphere, relegating them to a predecessor regime. In the extraordinary circumstances of radical political change, some of the purposes ordinarily advanced by the full criminal process can be advanced instead by the sanction's more limited form.

The limited criminal sanction may well be the crucial mediating form of transitional periods. The absence of traditional plenary punishment during these shifts out of repressive rule suggests that they may allow more complex understandings of criminal responsibility to emerge through the application of criminal justice to the principle of individual responsibility in the distinct context of systemic crimes. Yet this perspective on punishment does not account well for its role in times of radical political flux, where the transitional criminal form is informed by values related to the project of political change. Ordinarily, criminal justice is theorized in starkly dichotomous terms, as animated by either a backward-looking concern with retribution or a forward-looking, utilitarian concern with deterrence. In transitions, however, punishment is informed by a mix of retrospective and prospective purposes: the decision whether to punish or to amnesty, to exercise or to restrain criminal justice, is rationalized in overtly political terms. Values such as mercy and reconciliation, commonly treated as external to criminal justice, are explicit parts of the transitional deliberation. The explicit politicization of criminal law in these periods challenges ideal understandings of justice, yet turns out to be a persistent feature of jurisprudence in the transitional context.

The limited criminal sanction is an extraordinary form of punishment, for it is directed less at penalizing perpetrators than at advancing the normative shift of a political transformation. It is well illustrated historically, not only in policy after World War II but also in the punishments following more recent cases of regime change. Performing important operative acts – formal public inquiries into and clarifications of the past, indictments of past wrongdoing – the sanction has advanced the normative shift that is central to the liberalizing transition. Even in its most limited form, it is a symbol of the rule of law, and as such has enabled the expression of a critical normative message.

This use to construct normative change is what distinguishes transitional criminal measures, even in their varying application from country to country. Where the prior regime was sustained by a persecutory policy rationalized within a legal system, transitional legal responses express the message that the policy was manmade and is therefore reformable. In that their procedures of inquiry and indictment act as rituals of collective knowledge, enabling the isolation and disavowal of past wrongdoings and individuating responsibility, they enable the potential of liberalizing change, freeing the successor regime from the weight of the earlier state's evil legacies. The ritualized legal processes of appropriation and misappropriation, avowal and disavowal, symbolic loss and gain allow perceptions of transformation, and the society begins to move in a liberalizing direction.

Transitional practices suggest that criminal justice is in some form a ritual of liberalizing states, providing them with a public method of constructing their new norms. These processes allow them to draw a line, liberate a past, and let the society move forward. While punishment is conventionally considered largely retributive in its aim, in transitional situations its purposes become corrective, going beyond the individual perpetrator to the broader society. This function is clear in the case of systemic political offenses, for example in the persistence of prosecutions of crimes against humanity – the archetypal offense addressed by transitional persecutory politics, which here use criminal law to mount a critical response to an earlier illiberal rule. Moreover, whereas punishment is ordinarily thought to divide society, the punishments exercised in transitional situations are so limited as to allow the possibility of a return to a liberal state. As such, criminal processes have affinities with other transitional responses.

III. The Paradigmatic Transitional Response   The operative effects advanced by the limited criminal sanction, such as establishing, recording, and condemning past wrongdoing, display affinities with other legal acts and processes constructive of transition. The massive and *systemic* wrongdoing characteristic of modern repression demands a recognition of the mix of individual and collective responsibility. There is an overlap of punitive and administrative institutions and processes; individualized processes of accountability give way to administrative investigations, commissions of inquiry, the compilation of public records, official pronouncements, and condemnations of past wrongs. These are often subsumed in state histories commissioned pursuant to a political mandate of reconciliation, as in South Africa. Whether or not bureaucratic forms of public inquiry and official truth-telling are desirable, and signify liberalization, is contingent on state legacies of repressive rule, but generalized uses of these independent historical inquiries can be seen in contemporary human-rights law.

The paradigmatic affinities discussed here bear on the recurrent question in transitional-justice debates: what is the right response to repressive rule, the response most appropriate to supporting a lasting democracy? The subtext of this question assumes a transitional ideal, and the notion that normative concerns somehow militate for a particular categorical response. But this is simply the wrong question: in dealing with a state's repressive past, there is no one right response. The question should be reframed. Among states, the approach taken to transitional justice is politically contingent, even at the same time that there appears to be a paradigmatic transitional response in the law. Transitional constitutionalism, criminal justice, and the rule of law share affinities in the contingent relation that these norms bear to prior rule, as well as in their work in the move to a more liberal political order.

Transitional Constructivism   How is transition constructed? What is the role of law in political passage? The paradigmatic form of the law that emerges in these times operates in an extraordinary fashion, and itself plays a constructive role in the transition. It both stabilizes and destabilizes, and in this respect its distinctive feature is its mediating function: it maintains a threshold level of formal continuity while engendering a transformative discontinuity. The extent to which formal continuity is maintained depends on the modality of the transformation, while the content of the normative shift is a function of history, culture, and political tradition, as well as of the society's receptiveness to innovation.

Just what do transitional legal practices have in common? Law constructs transitions through diverse processes, including legislation, adjudication, and administrative measures. Transitional operative acts include pronouncements of indictments and verdicts; the issuing of amnesties, reparations, and apologies; and the promulgation of constitutions and reports. These practices share features: namely, they are ways to publicly construct new collective political understandings. Transitional processes, whether prosecution, lustration, or inquiry, share this critical dimension. They are actions taken to manifest change by publicly sharing new political knowledge. Law works on the margin here, as it performs the work both of separation from the prior regime and of integration with the successor regime. It has a liminal quality: it is law between regimes. The peculiar efficacy of these salient legal practices is their ability to effect functions of both separation and integration – all within continuous processes.

Transitional law often implies procedures that do not seem fair or compelling: trials lacking in regular punishment, reparations based on politically driven and arbitrary baselines, constitutions that do not necessarily last. What characterizes the transitional legal response is its limited form, embodied in the provisional constitution and purge, the limited sanction and reparation, the discrete history and official narrative. Transitional law is above all symbolic – a secular ritual of political passage.

The legal process has become the leading transitional response because of its ability to convey, publicly and authoritatively, the political differences that constitute the normative shift from an illiberal to a liberal regime. In its symbolic form, transitional jurisprudence reconstructs these political differences through changes in status, membership, and community. While the differences are necessarily contingent, they are recognized as legitimate, in light of the legacies with which a given successor society has to deal. Moreover, the language of law imbues the new order with legitimacy and authority.

In modern political transformations, legal practices enable successor societies to advance liberalizing political change. By mediating the normative hiatus and shift characterizing transition, the turn to law comprises important functional, conceptual, operative, and symbolic dimensions. Law epitomizes the rationalist liberal response to mass suffering and catastrophe; it expresses the notion that there is, after all, something to be done. Rather than resigning itself to historical repetition, the liberal society sees the hope of change put in the air. Where successor societies engage in transitional-justice debates, they signal the rational imagining of a more liberal political order.

In periods of political upheaval, legal rituals offer the leading alternative to the violent responses of retribution and vengeance. The transitional legal response is deliberate, measured, restrained, and restraining, enabling gradual controlled change. As the questions of transitional justice are worked through, the society begins to perform the signs and rites of a functioning liberal order. Transitional law transcends the "merely" symbolic to become the leading ritual of modern political passage. It is a ritual act that makes the shift possible between the predecessor and the successor regimes. In contemporary transitions characterized by a peaceful nature and an occurrence within the law, it is legal processes that perform the critical "undoings," the inversions of the predicates justifying the preceding regime. It is these public processes that produce the collective knowledge constitutive of the normative shift, simultaneously disavowing aspects of the predecessor ideology and affirming the ideological changes that constitute liberalizing transformation.

New democracies respond to legacies of injustice in different ways, but patterns across their various legal forms constitute a paradigm of transitional jurisprudence rooted in prior political injustice. The role of law is constructivist: transitional jurisprudence emerges as a distinct, paradigmatic form of law responsive to and constructive of the extraordinary circumstances of periods of substantial political change. The conception of justice in transitional jurisprudence is partial, contextual, and situated between at least two legal and political orders. Legal norms are always multiple, the idea of justice a compromise. Transitional jurisprudence centers on the paradigmatic use of the law in the normative construction of the new political regime.

IV. The Construction of Liberal Narrative   The main contribution of transitional justice is to advance the construction of a collective liberalizing narrative. Its uses are to advance the transformative purpose of moving the international community, as well as individual states, toward liberalizing political change. Just how does transitional justice offer its narrative? What is the potential of law in constructing a story that lays the basis for political change? Let us begin with the trial.

The History of Law: The Uses of the Human Rights-Trial   A primary role of transitional criminal justice is historical. Trials have longed played a crucial role in transitional history-making; criminal justice in these situations creates public, formal shared processes that link the past to the future, the individual to the collective. Criminal trials are a historical, ceremonial form of shared memory-making in the collective, a way to work through controversy within a community. The purposes of even the ordinary criminal trial are not only to adjudicate individual responsibility but also to establish the truth about an event in controversy; this is even more true of the role of the trial in settling the historical controversies characteristic of periods of transition. Since transitions follow regime change, and periods of heightened political and historical conflict, a primary purpose of successor trials is to advance a measure of historical justice.

What sort of truths are established in such periods? I call them "transitional critical truths": namely, a shared political knowledge critical of the ideology of the predecessor regime. The collective historical record produced through the trial both delegitimizes the predecessor regime and legitimizes the successor. Repressive leadership may be brought down by military or political collapse, but unless it is also publicly discredited, its ideology often endures. An example is the trial of King Louis XVI, which served as a forum to deliberate over and to establish the evil of monarchic rule. Other leading historical trials, whether of the war criminals at Nuremberg or of Argentina's military junta, are now remembered not for their condemnation of individual wrongdoers but for their roles in creating lasting historical records of state tyranny.

Transitional criminal processes create authoritative accounts of evil legacies, allowing a collective history-making. The many representations that they involve – trial proceedings, written transcripts, public records, judgments – re-create and dramatize the repressive past. Radio and television reportage add to these possibilities (consider The Hague today). One might also add the Internet.

The contemporary, post-Cold War period has given rise to even more complicated and disaggregated understandings of responsibility and to a problematizing of public and private. Consider the growing focus on the role of the multinationals in World War II, and the monetary settlements that attempt to legitimate the transforming global private regime.

The connection between legal proceedings and history adverts to the broader role of law in constructing the narrative of transition. I turn to explore that structure in the next part of this essay.

Narratives of Transition   The narratives constructed in a transition, whether they develop out of trials, administrative proceedings, or historical commissions of inquiry, make a normative claim about the relationship of a state's past to its prospects for a more democratic future. As I will explain, the transitional narrative structure itself propounds the claim that particular knowledge is relevant to the possibility of personal and societal change. Narratives of transition offer an account of the relationship of political knowledge to the move away from dictatorship and toward a more liberal future.

Transitional narratives follow a distinct rhetorical form: beginning in tragedy, they end on a comic or romantic mode. In the classical understanding, tragedy implicates the catastrophic suffering of individuals, whose fate, due to their status, in turn implicates entire collectives. Some discovery or change away from ignorance ensues, but in tragedy, knowledge seems only to confirm a fate foretold. Contemporary stories of transitional justice similarly involve stories of affliction on a grand scale, but, while they begin in a tragic mode, in the transition they switch to a nontragic resolution. There is a turn to what might be characterized as a comic phase. Something happens in these accounts: the persons enmeshed in the story ultimately avert tragic fates, and somehow adjust and even thrive in a new reality. In the convention of the transitional narrative, unlike that of the tragedy, the revelation of knowledge actually makes a difference. The country's past suffering is somehow reversed, leading to a happy ending of peace and reconciliation.

The structure of the transitional narrative appears in both fictional and nonfictional accounts of periods of political transformation. National reports read as tragic accounts that end on a redemptive note. Suffering is somehow transformed into something good for the country, into a greater societal self-knowledge that is thought to enhance the prospect of an enduring democracy. After "Night and Fog" policies of "disappearance" throughout much of Latin America, for example, bureaucratic processes were deployed to set up investigatory commissions. Beginning with titles such as "Never Again," the truth reports produced by these commissions promise to deter future suffering. Thus the prologue to the report of the Argentine national commission on the disappeared declares that the military dictatorship "brought about the greatest and most savage tragedy" in the country's history, but history provides lessons: "Great catastrophes are always instructive." "The tragedy which began with the military dictatorship in March 1976, the most terrible our nation has ever suffered, will undoubtedly serve to help us understand that only democracy can save a people from horror on this scale."[1] Knowledge of

---

1 *Nunca más: The Report of the Argentine National Commission on the Disappeared* (New York: Farrar, Straus, Giroux, 1986), p. 6.

past suffering plays a crucial role in the state's ability to make a liberating transition.

Confrontation with the past is considered necessary to liberalizing transformation. The report of the Chilean national commission on truth and reconciliation asserts that knowledge and disclosure of past suffering are necessary to reestablishing the country's identity. The decree establishing the commission declares, "The truth had to be brought to light, for only on such a foundation … would it be possible to … create the necessary conditions for achieving true national reconciliation."[2] "Truth," then, is the necessary precondition for democracy. This is also the organizing thesis of the El Salvador truth commission, a story line seen in the title of its report, "From Madness to Hope." The report tells a story of violent civil war followed by "truth and reconciliation." According to its introduction, the "creative consequences" of truth can "settle political and social differences by means of agreement instead of violent action." "Peace [is] to be built on [the] transparency of … knowledge." The truth is a "bright light" that "search[es] for lessons that would contribute to reconciliation and to abolishing such patterns of behavior in the new society."[3]

Even where the reporting is unofficial, the claim is similar: that the revelation of knowledge – in and of itself – offers a means to political transformation. The preface to the unofficial Uruguayan report *Nunca más* (Never again) casts writing in and of itself as a social triumph, claiming that transitional truth-tellings will deter the possibility of future repression. It is the lack of "critical understanding which created a risk of having the disaster repeated … to rescue that history is to learn a lesson. … We should have the courage not to hide that experience in our collective subconscious but to recollect it. So that we do not fall again into the trap."[4]

In transitional history-making the story has to come out right. Yet these reports imply a number of poetic leaps. Was it the new truths that brought on liberalizing political change? Or was it the political change that enabled the restoration of democratic government, and then a reconsideration of the past? Or is it simply that, despite ongoing processes of political change, unless there is some kind of clarification of the concealments of the evil past, and some kind of ensuing self-understanding, the truth about that past will remain hidden, unavailable, external, foreign. In postcommunist transitions characterized by

2 *Chilean National Commission on Truth and Reconciliation Report*, trans. Phillip Berryman (Notre Dame, Ind.: Center for Civil and Human Rights, Notre Dame University, 1993).

3 *From Madness to Hope: The Twelve-Year War in El Salvador. Report of the Commission on the Truth for El Salvador* (United Nations Commission on the Truth for El Salvador, 1993), p. 11.

4 Servicio Paz y Justicia, *Uruguay Nunca más: Human Rights Violations, 1972–1985* (Philadelphia: Temple University Press, 1992), trans. Elizabeth Hampsten, pp. vii, x–xi.

struggles with past state archives, transitional accounts begin with stories of invasion and popular resistance; the foe is represented as the foreign outsider, before the story progresses to the ever more troubling discovery of collaboration closer to home and pervasive throughout the society. In the narratives of transition, whether out of a repressive totalitarian rule in the former Soviet bloc or out of authoritarian military rule in Latin America, transitional stories all involve a "revealing" of supposedly secreted knowledge. What is pronounced is the tragic discovery.

What counts as liberalizing knowledge? These productions are neither original nor foundational; they are, however, contingent on state legacies of repressive rule. The critical function of the successor regime responds to the repressive practices of the prior regime. After military rule in Latin America, for example, where truth was a casualty of disappearance policies, the critical response is the "official story." After communist rule, on the other hand, the search for the "truth" was a matter not of historical production as such, for the "official story" had previously been deployed as an instrument of repressive control; instead, it was a matter of critical response to repressive state histories, to the securing of private access to state archives, to privatization of official histories, and to the introduction of competing historical accounts.

The link between the exposure of knowledge and the possibility of change means that the possibility of change is introduced through human action. The very notion of a knowledge objectified and exposed suggests not only that there was somehow a "logic" to the madness but that now there is something to be done. The message propounded is the notion that, had the newly acquired knowledge been known earlier, events would have been different – and, conversely, that now that the truth is known, the course of future events will indeed be different. The liberal transition is distinguished by processes that illuminate the possibility of future choice. Transitional accounts hold the kernels of a liberal future foretold. The revelation of truth brings on the switch from the tragic past to the promise of a hopeful future. A catastrophe is somehow turned around, an awful fate averted. Transitional justice operates as this magical kind of switch: legal processes involve persons vested with transformative powers – judges, lawyers, commissioners, experts, witnesses with special access to privileged knowledge. Reckoning with the past enables the perception of a liberalizing shift.

Narratives of transition suggest that what is at stake in liberalizing transformation is at minimum a change of interpretation. The regimes of politics and of truth have a mutually constitutive role in this process: societies begin to change politically when their citizens' understanding of the ambient situation changes. As Václav Havel has written, the change is from "living within a lie to living within the truth."[5] So it is that much of the literature of these periods involves stories of precisely this move, from "living within a lie" to the revelation of newly gained knowledge and self-understanding, effecting a reconstitution of personal identity and of relationships. These tales of deceit and betrayal, often stories of longstanding affairs, appear to be allegories of the relation between citizen and state, shedding light on the structure and course of civic change.

What emerges clearly is that the pursuit of historical justice is not simply responsive to or representative of political change, but itself helps to construct the political transformation. Change in the political and legal regimes shapes and structures the historical regime. New truth regimes go hand-in-hand with new political regimes, indeed they support the change. As transitional accounts connect a society's past with its future, they construct a normative relation. In this sense narratives of transition are stories of progress, beginning with backward-looking reflection on the past but always viewing it in light of the future. If the constructive fiction is that earlier awareness of the knowledge now acquired might have averted the tragedy, a new society can be built on this claim. It is the change in political knowledge that allows the move from an evil past to a sense of national redemption.

Transitional narratives have a distinct structure. Their revelations of truth occur through switching mechanisms, critical junctures of individual and societal self-knowledge. There is a ritual disowning of previously secreted knowledge, a purging of the past, as well as an appropriation of a newly revealed truth, enabling a corrective return to the society's true nature. A new course is charted.

The practices of such periods suggest that the new histories are hardly foundational but explicitly transitional. To be sure, historical narrative is always present in the life of the state, but in periods of political flux the narrative's role is to construct perceptible transformation. Transitional histories are not "meta"-narratives but "mini"-narratives, always situated within the state's preexisting national story. They are not new beginnings but build upon preexisting political legacies. Indeed the relevant truths are always implicated in the past political legacies of the state in question. They are not universal, essential, or metatruths; a marginal truth is all that is needed to draw a line on the prior regime. Critical responses negotiate the historical conflict apparent in contested accounts; as political regimes change, transitional histories offer a displacement of one interpretive account or truth regime for another, so preserving the state's narrative thread.

The importance of establishing a shared collective truth regarding repressive legacies from the past has become something of a trope in the discourse of polit-

5 Václav Havel et. al., *The Power of the Powerless: Citizens against the State in Central-Eastern Europe*, ed. John Keane (Armonk, N.Y.: M. E. Sharpe: 1985).

ical transition. The meaning of "truth" is not universal, but rather is largely politically contingent. Accordingly, the paradigmatic transitional legal processes rely on discrete changes in the public's salient political knowledge for their operative transformative action. Legal processes construct changes in the public justifications underlying political decision-making and behavior, changes that simultaneously disavow aspects of the predecessor ideology and justify the ideological changes constituting the liberalizing transformation. Legal processes can make these changes in the public rationale for the political order because they are predicated on authoritative representations of public knowledge. In this way they contribute to the interpretive changes that create the perception of political and social transformation.

At the same time, transitional legal processes also vividly demonstrate the contingency in what knowledge will advance the construction of the normative shift. The normative force of these transitional constructions depends on their critical challenges to the policies, predicates, and rationalizations of the predecessor rule and ideology. Accordingly, what the relevant "truths" are is of disproportionate significance. In an example from this region, the Nanavaki commission accounts of the 1984 anti-Sikh riots, it is crucial whether a victim is identified as an "unarmed civilian" rather than as a "combatant." The critical truth turns on whether violence was "organized." Such findings of publicly shared political knowledge can topple a regime (at least on the normative level) by undermining a key ideological predicate of repressive national security policies. These reinterpretations displace the predicates legitimizing the prior regime, and offer newfound bases for the reinstatement of the rule of law.

Law offers a canonical language and the symbols and rituals of contemporary political passage. Through trials and other public hearings and processes, legal rituals enable transitionally produced histories, social constructions of a democratic nature with a broad reach. These rituals of collective history-making publicly construct the transition, dividing political time into a "before" and an "after." Transitional responses perform the critical undoings that respond to the prior repression – the releasing of justifications of the predecessor regime that is critical to political change. The practices of historical production associated with transition often publicly affirm what is already implicitly known in the society, but bring forward and enable a public letting go of the evil past.

Whether through trials or other practices, transitional narratives highlight the roles of knowledge, agency, and choice. Although the received wisdom on them is that their popularity in liberalizing states comes from their emphasis on structural causation, they are actually complex, densely layered accounts that weave together and mediate individual and collective responsibilities. By introducing the potential of individual choice, the accounts perform transitional history's liberalizing function. By revealing "truths" about the past, they become narratives of progress, and by suggesting that events might have been different had this knowledge been previously known, they invoke the potential of individual action. Their message is one of avertable tragedy. Their expression of hope in individual choice and human action goes to the core of liberalism and human-rights discourse.

Transitional narratives are also redemptive stories of return, of wholeness, of finding the way to political unity. They comprise a turn to the corrective and offer state and public an alternative, successor identity centered on political unity. Emphasizing the possibility of bounded choice, of the reconciliation of the potential for individual agency with set political circumstances, they also stress the possibility of societal self-understanding and of averting tragic repetition associated with liberation. The message is that, despite past bad legacies, the contemporary liberal state offers redemptive political possibilities.

Transitional justice offers a way to reconstitute the collective across racial, ethnic, and religious lines, to ground it in a contingent political identity responsive to its particular legacies of fear and injustice. So it is that transitional justice has become an enduring feature of political liberalization. As liberal narrative, though, it should not become a fixed identity; despite its appeal, its entrenchment as a story of unity could undermine its potential for a more revolutionary project. The entrenchment of policies of unity would stunt the development of party politics and a robust political culture. It would ultimately be illiberal. Transitional justice points instead to the significance of ongoing counternarratives and of nurturing transitional modality. These are the dynamic processes that characterize effective liberalization strategies and allow for ongoing political transformation.

The Immersive Spectacle:
Historical Testimony and the Limits of Representation

The Denial of Justice and the Loss of the Subject

Franz Kaltenbeck

Obstructed Representation On Thursday, April 5, 2001, Mr. Oumar Khanbiev, the Minister of Health of the Chechen government, tried to make a statement before the United Nations Commission set up to investigate human rights in his country. A nongovernmental organization, the Transnational Radical Party, had given him five minutes of its own speaking time. Leaving aside all questions of politics and sovereignty, Khanbiev testified only to his experience as a doctor during the Russian siege and bombardment of Grozny before the withdrawal of the Chechen resistance from that town. Arrested after working in a hospital to treat seventy-six people injured in a bombing at a place called Alkhan-Kala, he spent three weeks "in the hell of a filtration camp," of which he said, "It is difficult for me to speak about this. I will limit myself to only say that I have spent the most difficult hours of my life there." Khanbiev later went into hiding for eight months in a mountain village and subsequently fell sick because of the tortures he had endured. Speaking to the Commission, he estimated that over 20,000 people had disappeared in his country and that almost the same number was then imprisoned. He continued, "87,000 were killed, 200,000 injured, more than 30 percent of the population has been ousted from their homes, 90 percent of the hospitals have been destroyed. Nearly every type of weapon has been used in this war – fragmentation bombs and hidden mines included."[1]

Khanbiev could not make a more detailed statement: he was unable to use the full five minutes allotted to him. The Russian delegation interrupted him four times for procedural reasons and finally forced the session's chair to silence him. Khanbiev could neither describe the condition of his country's people nor present his proposal for a United Nations resolution on their behalf. It was probably for reasons of sovereignty that the chair retreated before the pressure from the Russians; a democratically installed commission denied the rights of a

---

1 Oumar Khanbiev, quoted in Jean-Claude Buhrer, "La Voix tschétchène étouffée à la commission des droits de l'homme de l'ONU," *Le Monde,* April 7, 2001, p. 2.

man trying to speak on behalf of his people, and who had cared for them – and even for Russian soldiers – as a doctor. The muzzling of an opposition politician may be everyday in authoritarian regimes, but is upsetting in an organization set up to establish peace.

The foreclosure of Khanbiev's speech shows that the distance between authoritarian regimes and institutions guaranteed by the "free world" is not as great as it seems. We have to admit to a certain continuity between brutal power politics and international arbitration. Perhaps the interesting paradigm of our time has to do not with concepts of the "rupture" and "cut" between political discourses but with those of "repetition" and "eternal return of the same."

Politics of the Subject   Does psychoanalysis have any political relevance today? In answering this question, psychoanalysts have two basic attitudes. There are those who say that psychoanalysis should lead politics – but this is wishful thinking. Others, more modest, discuss the many political metaphors associated with Freud's concept of the unconscious. Analysts fight against the repression of desire. They also remember a passage Freud found in Virgil's *Aeneid*, and made the motto for his book *The Interpretation of Dreams*: "If I cannot bend the higher powers, I will move the lower ones," says Juno, the wife of Jove. Authentic psychoanalysis is indeed closer to hell than to heaven.

Given all the misery in the world, some consider psychoanalysis a frivolous attempt to look after the neurotics and psychotics of the Western middle class. But psychoanalysis need not be defended against this reproach; its defense of the subject can be seen as acting politically, constituting an "answer to the real." The notion of the subject implies responsibility. "The subject is responsible," says Jacques Lacan.[2]

What does this mean? Let us say that the subject emerges where you don't expect it to. To illustrate this effect of surprise, let me recall a patient who dreamed that she had killed someone. Her family's search for the killer was paralyzing their lives, so she decided to admit that she was the murderess, announcing *"C'est moi la meurtrière"* (The murderess is me). Recounting the dream, the patient was astonished that she had used in her confession not the French noun *assassin* but *meurtrière*, which means not only a woman who kills someone but the loopholelike window from which the defenders of a fortress shoot without revealing themselves to their enemies. This association produced the subject of the signifier in question. But what is the real dimension of her production?

2 Jacques Lacan, "L'Etourdit," *Scilicet* (Paris) 4 (1973): 15.

The patient compared blind shooting from a loophole with her own speech: she uses speech to shoot the other. Also, on the one hand her speech is like the wall of a fortress, behind which she can hide herself and shoot. The other will not have time to shoot back. On the other hand she herself is the loophole, a hole in the wall of language: her speech is submitted to her oral drive, which is the real. The dream shows the articulation between the subject and her real self, the drive included in her symptom, her pathologically aggressive use of speech. The subject is produced by the contingent play of the signifier (the homonym *meurtrière*), but this contingency is linked to the real dimension of the subject's enjoyment (*jouissance*). Through her dream she became aware of her violent use of speech.

Many psychoanalytic patients may speak in their sessions of their unconscious feelings of guilt, as this young woman did, but every day we also see patients who are or have been mistreated by others. They suffer from real injustice. Let me mention the case of a woman, now fifty, who could never overcome what I would call her syndrome of powerless witness. Some forty years ago she had been unable to help her little sister, who suffered from a malformation of the heart that had led to a severe hypotrophy of the lungs. The problem could not be treated surgically at the time, and the two girls' brother had already succumbed to the same illness. When my patient was twelve years old, her father was killed in a car crash. A few months later her mother met another man, who was not tolerant of her sick little sister's crises of breath, and the girl, already terminally ill, was sent away, spending her last days living with foster parents. Having learned that her little sister was quite aware of being abandoned, my patient still feels very guilty about her own weakness. Having never found the courage to protest the brutal removal of her sick sister from her house, she feels paralyzed whenever she has to make a family decision. Surely in part as a result, her own son is a completely impractical young man, unable to separate from her.

Detectors and Attractors of Injustice   Injustice being one of the most important reasons for writing, we have a lot to learn from poets about the relationship between literature and injustice. Jean Genet wrote, "Writing is left to you when you are driven away from your given speech."[3] Melancholic poets are especially sharp detectors and attractors of injustice; their perceptions of the world being less veiled by illusion than neurotic perception is, they see what is wrong with

3 Jean Genet, quoted in Jean-Bernard Moraly, *Jean Genet: La Vie écrite. Biographie* (Paris: Éditions de la Différence, 1988), p. 39. The French phrase is "Écrire c'est ce qui vous reste quand on est chassé de la parole donnée."

the other. The beauty of language does not impress them. They pay a high price for their clairvoyance.

During the last two years before the death of the Romantic author Heinrich von Kleist (he engaged in a suicide pact with a lady friend), he wrote a series of works (drama, prose, essays) denouncing the abuse of power and deconstructing the devices of rhetoric. In *Prinz Friedrich von Homburg* (Prince Friedrich of Homburg), completed in 1811, a powerful elector (a prince of the Holy Roman Empire) has pronounced a death sentence against the play's eponymous hero. When the prince of Homburg requests a pardon, the elector gives him a choice: if he really believes that his condemnation is wrong, he will be pardoned. But this is the very proposal that he cannot accept. Why? Because he doesn't see how anyone can believe that he really had a good reason to find the death sentence unjust – everyone will say that he only wanted to save his own life.

Kleist was concerned by the bad object at the heart of the death drive, here incarnated by the elector. We find other incarnations of this object in his stories "Das Erdbeben in Chili" (The Earthquake in Chili) and "Der Findling" (The Foundling). In the latter, a father loses his son in an epidemic. As the man is leaving the town in which his son has died, another boy, threatened by the epidemic, asks to be taken with him in his coach. The father adopts this child, a substitute for his lost son. But the boy, grown up, becomes the cause of his and his family's ruin.

Kleist fought a merciless fight against the appearances of rhetoric and of language. In "Letter from a Poet to Another One"[4] he expresses the desire to get rid of such charming devices as iambuses, rhymes, and assonances; he wants to find a real form that would transmit his thought directly. His reflections on language may seem remote from our problems, but are not. Kleist destroys the old notion that clear ideas always find clear expression. This prejudice notoriously disadvantages those who have no rhetorical faculties, or who are intimidated when they have to speak in public, before a law court, say, or in an interrogation. "If an idea is expressed inarticulately you should not conclude that the idea had been thought of inarticulately; it would more likely be that the most confusedly expressed ideas are thought of most clearly," writes Kleist.[5] Shy people are often silent in conversation, and then, if they get excited about some issue at a certain point and do begin to speak, they may come out with something incomprehensible. Yet they must have had clear, pertinent thoughts. This argument is precious for everyone seeking the truth in the discourse of the other.

---

4 Heinrich von Kleist, "Brief eines Dichters an einen anderen," in *Sämtliche Werke und Briefe,* (Darmstadt: Wissenschaftliche Buchgesellschaft, 1983), 2:347–49.
5 Kleist, "Über die allmähliche Verfertigung der Gedanken beim Reden," in ibid., pp. 322–24.

Poetry is often considered esoteric, an expression of the inner self, disconnected from everyday life, let alone politics. The idea of "engaged poetry" derives from the prejudice that this supposedly esoteric quality of poetry excludes what is real. Recent history shows, however, that a poet can be a keener detector of political truth than many a social theoretician.

Durs Grünbein is one of the rare German poets who both comes from eastern Germany and never collaborated with the state security police (the Stasi) of the old German Democratic Republic. He owes this abstention more to his poetic consciousness than to lack of opportunity; although he was still in his twenties when the Berlin Wall fell – he was born in 1962 – there were East Germans who became police agents at the age of seventeen. Grünbein's first collection of poems, published in 1988, is a kind of "*tableau berlinois*" describing the condition of life in the East, a life weighed down by heavy bureaucratic machinery.[6] In trying to describe how people were dispossessed of their lives, how their bodies lost their contours, how they were deprived of their futures, he depicted the crepuscular moment of the Soviet system. His poems have been compared with the films of Charlie Chaplin, which show the comic condition of men at the height of the machine era. "Truth is naked to the bones" in Grünbein's poetry, writes the French critic Nicole Gabriel, who has explored the work's political dimensions.[7] Its language reveals what was really going on when the Berlin Wall fell, and with it the pompous rhetoric of the "workers' paradise."

What Grünbein teaches us is rather surprising. Instead of gratifying us with a hymn to the freedom attained with the dissolution of the Soviet empire, he describes an "eternal return of the same": an empire tumbled but people weren't set free. Instead they were recaptured by another empire, with its own violence and bureaucracy. The poet had understood his era: he had stood at the right place at the right time, at the frontier between two antagonistic political systems. Gabriel compares him to one of the dogs left behind by the border guards, their masters, when the wall fell. He was there when this terrible border was erased, awake enough to feel this truth himself: empires fall, and replace each other, without things really changing for the people. At these moments, in fact, the subject can know how lonely he or she is.

The poet Paul Celan lost his parents in the Holocaust. The Germans killed them both in 1942. His poetry is influenced by his loss, and by the destruction of the European Jews, but despite the tragedy to which it attests, his work was badly treated: written in a language that is hard to understand, it made many of

---

6 Durs Grünbein, *Grauzone, morgens* (Frankfurt am Main: Suhrkamp, 1988).

7 Nicole Gabriel, "Le Poète en 'jeune chien garde-frontière': Durs Grünbein et la 'Wende,'" *Études Germaniques* (Paris: Université Paris IV, 2000), pp. 73-95.

his critics aggressive. In a sense, Celan's poems provoked these critics to say what they really thought of him, his writings, and his origins.

To explain Celan's poetry, to decipher it, the French philologist Jean Bollack has analyzed scholarly critiques of it. Bollack shows how close Celan is to the historical events that affected him, and also how far off the mark many critics are in their interpretations of him.[8] Instead of recognizing the precision of Celan's references, they bury them under vague theories, understanding the poems as protests against the loneliness and isolation of the modern subject.[9] Other critics, writing under the influence of Martin Heidegger, explain the extermination of the Jews as an effect of the Germans' discomfort with the social dominance of technology. The concentration camps, these theoreticians say, were the ultimate expression of modern scientific civilization, which had lost some quality of *life*. (These critics forget that *life* was a master signifier of Nazi ideology.) Celan's poetry has in turn been read as the "objective reflection of a social dissolution . . . as the reproductive process of atrophy,"[10] his language showing the wounds inflicted by technology. Claiming that his language was not clear enough, critics have attributed Celan's hermetic writing to the world of machines, not to what happened between 1933 and 1945.

The most offensive thesis on Celan, discussed by Bollack in the fourth chapter of his book, emerged on the poet's suicide, which has been interpreted as the price he paid for the difficulty and incomprehensibility of his writings.[11] His work was not readable enough, not "in perfection," and this was what led him to jump into the River Seine. He was too ambitious, some of his critics say, he could not cope with his own narcissistic ambition, so he had to be punished for his hubris, his presumptuousness, and his daring. Don't old anti-Semitic notions about the arrogant, esoteric Jew echo in this criticism? The real pain Celan suffered was not enough for these critics. They had to add insult to injury.

The Joke as a Message of Desire   Let us now go back for a moment to the realm of psychoanalysis. In his book *Jokes and Their Relation to the Unconscious*, Freud developed the thesis that jokes produce pleasure by allowing us to satisfy tendencies otherwise prohibited by social conventions or reasonable thinking. Some people have a leaning to attack others verbally; jokes let them satisfy this

8 Jean Bollack, *Paul Celan: Poetik der Fremdheit*, trans. Werner Wögerbauer (Vienna: Zsolnay, 2000), pp. 69, 70.
9 Ibid., p. 135.
10 Ibid.
11 Ibid., pp. 144–50.

appetite without social proscription. The pleasure of harmless jokes often lies in homophonic plays with words; Freud discovered that the same language mechanisms structure a number of different symptoms. In that jokes defend pleasure against critical judgment from our conscious thoughts, the joke becomes a "factor of psychic power."[12]

For Lacan, the joke is a device we use to express our desire. Such devices are essential, for ordinary language does not permit adequate expression of desire; in ordinary language we can only demand, and the communication of our desire fails – we make more or less witty slips of the tongue. By making a joke, however, we render this failure acceptable for purposes of communication. Language recognizes and accepts the new signifiers created in the joke, even if the signifier is not part of its code. So, like a Trojan horse, the joke introduces desire into language, or into the Other, as Lacan would say.

So all seems well with the theory of the unconscious in the Freudian kingdom. Unconscious formations – dream, joke, lapse, symptom – show paths to the unconscious. The joke offers a remedy for the incommunicability of desire. The psychoanalyst need only imitate the joke to interpret the patient's verbal forms. But the joke also has a political dimension: it lets one tell an unpleasant truth to a strong and powerful other. For those who cannot directly say what they want, it really is a "factor of psychic power."

Unfortunately that success story had its limits. The joke recalls the generous offer that brought Khanbiev before the UN Commission. Situations exist in which the joke never works.

Bad News   Probably Franz Kafka had read Freud's book on the joke. On the night of September 22, 1912, he wrote a story called "The Judgment," all in one sitting.[13] In a letter to his beloved Felice Bauer a few months later, he says of this story, "it is a little wild and senseless and if it had not an inner truth (that which one can never establish, but which every reader has to admit or to deny) it would be nothing."[14] "A real birth covered with filth and slime" – this is how Kafka would refer to the writing of the story in his diaries.[15] In his love letter

---

12 Sigmund Freud, "Der Witz und seine Beziehung zum Unbewussten," in *Studienausgabe*, vol. 4 (Frankfurt am Main: Fischer, 1972), p. 125.

13 Franz Kafka, "The Judgment," in *Selected Short Stories of Franz Kafka*, trans. Willa and Edwin Muir, 1946 (reprint ed. New York: Modern Library, 1993), pp. 3–19.

14 Kafka, letter to Felice Bauer, December 4–5, 1912, in *Briefe an Felice und andere Korrespondenz aus der Verlobungszeit*, ed. Erich Heller and Jürgen Born (Frankfurt am Main: Fischer Taschenbuch Verlag, 1976), p. 156. Eng. trans. as *Letters to Felice*, trans. James Stern and Elisabeth Duckworth (New York: Schocken, 1973).

this becomes a "doubtful birth," but in the diaries he refers to the story's "doubtlessness."[16] What there is no doubt of is that he had Freud in mind during the writing – he says so in another diary entry, written the morning after that memorable night.

But why should we speak of it here? Why is it true? It is a story in which, because of a radical injustice, it is impossible for a subject to speak the truth. Kafka's writing, his way out, is his answer to this impossibility.

The story gives us bad news: some sixty years before Jacques Derrida, Kafka had understood that not every letter, however important it may be, always reaches its receiver. In the 1970s, in a paper on black holes, Stephen Hawking wrote a response to Einstein's famous aphorism, "God does not play with dice." "Not only does God play with dice," Hawking remarked, "he throws them where nobody would find them."

"The Judgment" is the strange story of a father who condemns his own son to death. There is an uncanny third person in the text, who precedes the father: it is a friend of the protagonist who lives far away, in St. Petersburg. Although Kafka's work is well-known, it may be useful to recount what happens in the story.

A Reading of "The Judgment"   On a Sunday morning in spring, the young businessman Georg Bendemann is sitting in his house, on the bank of a river, and writing a letter to an old friend who is now living abroad. This friend has left his country to work in St. Petersburg, but he has failed in life and now lives alone, an embittered bachelor. He is "a big child," Georg thinks. Should he encourage his friend to return home? It would be humiliating for him to come back a poor man.

The situation makes it impossible to send the real news from home, the things that have changed in Georg's own life: since his mother's death, his aging father has kept in the background of the family business, leaving it to Georg, who is doing quite well now – even better than when his father ran the business, which has grown unexpectedly. Georg would also prefer not to reveal his engagement, to a Fräulein Frieda Brandenfeld, a girl from a well-to-do family. But Frieda wants him to invite his friend to their wedding, so Georg has no choice: he announces his marriage and invites his friend.

This is the first time Georg hasn't filled up a letter to his friend with insignificant and indifferent social events to fill up space. The letter in his pocket, he

15 Kafka, *Tagebücher 1909–1923, Fassung der Handschrift,* ed. Hans-Gerd Koch, Michael Müller, and
    Malcolm Pasley (Frankfurt am Main: Fischer, 1997), p. 379.
16 Ibid., p. 357.

enters his father's room, when his troubles begin: seeing his father sitting in the dark, he thinks, "My father is still a giant of a man!" The remark corroborates Gilles Deleuze's and Félix Guattari's interpretation of the father in Kafka as a comic aggrandizement of the oedipal father.[17] Georg tells his father, "I really only wanted to tell you … that I am now sending the news of my engagement to St. Petersburg." He lifts the letter out of his pocket and lets it drop back. Let me dwell on the turmoil this letter creates. Before it, Georg has had no significant correspondence. But this letter announces that he wants to marry Fräulein Brandenfeld. Now, before sending the announcement to his friend, he also tells his father of his intention. This second announcement has a devastating effect, and the rest of the story is full of an angry dialogue between Georg and his father.[18] Suffice it to say here that the father has three contradictory positions regarding the friend in St. Petersburg.

In the beginning, he exhorts his son to tell him the truth: "I beg you Georg, don't deceive me. It's a trivial affair, it's hardly worth mentioning, so don't deceive me. Do you really have this friend in St. Petersburg?" Interpreting this *questioning* of his friend's existence as a sign of his father's advanced age and fatigue, Georg imagines domestic changes that would give him a better life. But now the father *denies* the friend's existence: "You have no friend in St. Petersburg. You have always been a leg-puller and you haven't even shrunk from pulling *my* leg. How could you have a friend out there! I can't believe it." Georg reminds the old man that he has already met the friend at their home. Guiding him to the bed, Georg lays a cover over him, which the father finds odd: there is a metonymic link between "to cover up" and to bury, but the father isn't ready to die. Now he comes up with a third statement, in which he claims to *know* Georg's friend: "Of course I know your friend. He would have been a son after my own heart. That's why you've been playing him false all these years. Why else? Do you think I haven't been sorry for him?"

From this point onward the old man becomes a "nightmare vision," a *Schreckbild*, and now we come to what Slavoj Žižek calls "the knowledge about the father's obscenity."[19] Watching this "image of horror," Georg yet has another vision: his friend in Russia "whom his father suddenly knew too well, touched his imagination as never before." He hallucinates seeing his friend: "Among the

17 Gilles Deleuze and Félix Guattari, *Kafka. Pour une littérature mineure* (Paris: Les Éditions de Minuit, 1975), p. 20.

18 I have analyzed this dialogue elsewhere. See Franz Kaltenbeck, "Quand Freud répond à Kafka," in *Dits et contre-faits: Séminaire sur la transmission de l'expérience psychanalytique* (Paris: Collège International de Philosophie, April 27, 2001). The papers of this conference are available at dire-subscribe@egroups.

19 Slavoj Žižek, *Did Somebody Say Totalitarianism: Five Interventions in the (Mis)Use of a Notion* (London and New York: Verso, 2001), p. 12.

wreckage of his showcases, the slashed remnants of his wares, the falling gas brackets, he was just standing up. Why did he have to go so far away!" Becoming more and more offensive, the father insults Georg's fiancée. He asserts that he is the representative of the friend "on the spot." This statement upsets Georg so terribly that he cries out, "You comedian!"

A subtle statement indeed! The father's inconsistency is indeed comical, but the cry of "You comedian!" also expresses Georg's wish: he wants his father to be only joking, rather than constituting the "nightmare vision" that he has actually seen. The exclamation is the first of four attempts at wordplay and jokes in which Georg tries to minimize his father's power, which has crossed all limits. But his rhetoric is poor. When the father explains that he is strong because he is not alone, for example – "All by myself I might have had to give way, but your mother has given me so much of her strength that I have established a fine connection with your friend and I have your customers here in my pocket!" – Georg says to himself, "He has pockets even in his shirt … and believed that with this remark he could make him an impossible figure before all the world. Only for a moment did he think so, for he kept on forgetting everything." After a last desperate attempt to make fun of his father, Georg comes to feel that "in his very mouth the words turned into deadly earnest." He has tried to use jokes to defend himself, but they have rebounded off the armor of the father's inconsistency, his link with Georg's dead mother, and the specter of Georg's friend. In the end the father condemns his son, and the death sentence is strangely linked with a judgment on the existence of his friend, almost as though Georg had denied it: "So now you know what else there was in the world besides yourself, till now you've known only about yourself. An innocent child, yes, but still more truly have you been a devilish human being! And therefore take note: I sentence you now to death by drowning!" Georg executes this sentence on himself, rushing out of his father's room and drowning in the river, all the while calling out softly, "Dear parents, I have always loved you."

It is worth mentioning that Kafka, in a letter to Max Brod, speaks of "these devilish powers" that are already there at the doorstep.[20] It is as if Georg had been driven to identify himself with these devils. The Lacanian father metaphor is a device for creation; "The Judgment" involves the opposite, the father as an agent of destruction. The story is what we might call an "antijoke," and also an "antimyth": Kafka has not told a tale of a hero overcoming his monstrous father through his wit, but has described in detail how the hero's jokes fail, and how he has to return to the water, from which, in myth, so many heroes have come.

---

20 Kafka, letter to Max Brod, October 25, 1923, quoted in Deleuze and Guattari, *Kafka. Pour une littérature mineure*, p. 22.

"The Judgment" is a kind of slapstick comedy about a son unable to make a good enough joke to halt the aggression of his almighty father. In difference to Deleuze and Guattari, I don't see the father in Kafka as just a comic exaggeration of Oedipus; the comic dimension in Kafka's writing is undeniable, but his texts are always layered. The comic does not exclude the serious. To understand this, let us return to Freud.

When Freud Answers Kafka   In 1915, when Freud wrote "Mourning and Melancholia,"[21] he had not read Kafka, but he seems to have understood part of Kafka's message in "The Judgment." At the heart of Freud's article is an attempt to answer this question: why do melancholics so often attempt suicide? His discussion relies on two concepts still new at the time: *narcissism* and *sadistic drive*, a dangerous mixture in combination. The problem of the melancholic's *passage à l'acte* confronts Freud with serious questions about identity. Are you really killing yourself when you commit suicide? Is the agent of suicide really the person who has been killed? Freud suspects that nothing is less certain than this coidentity between the agent and the victim. He is quite clear in his belief that the neurotic who threatens suicide, or announces the intention of suicide, actually wants to kill another person within. To solve the problem of the agent, Freud argues that melancholics have sadistic, aggressive emotions against other people, but turn these onto themselves.

On the other hand, there is a strange twist in narcissism that pushes melancholics into a deadly contradiction: they easily lose their love object, but remain identified with it. In this "narcissistic identification," as Freud called it, the object is introjected by the subject. The subject is the best place to lose and keep the object at the same time. When the shadow of the object has fallen on the subject, the subject cannot find it anymore, but even if the object is dead, it is not really lost – on the contrary, what really happens is a "loss of the subject" (*Ichverlust*). The object now occupies the place of the subject, and becomes very strong. Not only does it subjugate the subject, it also subjugates all of the subject's social relationships. In fact the object that has been incorporated by narcissistic identification will go on to crush the subject completely.

Reading Freud's paper carefully, one finds that he distinguishes between three "persons": the subject (*Ich*), the object (*der andere*), and the other (*die andere Person*). The subject has indeed become poor, for the object has subjugated his other, the person who constitutes his alterity. This new Freudian trian-

21 Sigmund Freud, "Trauer und Melancholie," *Studienausgabe*, vol. 3 (Frankfurt am Main: Fischer, 1970), pp. 193–212.

gle involves the same situation we find in "The Judgment," where Georg is the subject, his friend is his other, and the father is an object without limits. In this sense Freud has replied to Kafka without having read his story. He has supplied a clinical explanation for what the novelist imagined in Prague.

Because the father does not shrink from any contradiction, he mocks the real, which is, according to Lacan, the only category in which inconsistent events become possible. He owes his strength to others: to Georg's dead mother, and to the mysterious friend with whom he pretends to have established a "magnificent alliance." Commenting on the story in his diaries, Kafka remarks that the son is alone and "has nothing." As in Freud's explanation of melancholy, where the object crushes the subject, this father annihilates his son.

I do not claim here to be diagnosing Kafka himself, who was *not* a melancholic. His story is a kind of desublimating of the "factor of psychic power" that Freud called the joke. Kafka tells a story in which this factor fails, creating no social link: the son who incarnates the subject stays alone. Kafka is describing the process in which subjects lose all their symbolic supports. At the same time, though, the author transforms this failure into a comedy or a "grotesquerie." In Kafka's story, terror excludes wit but not humor.

The Attacked Subject   In the year 2000, Jean Hatzfeld, a reporter with the French newspaper *Libération*, published a series of narratives collected from survivors of the genocide of the Tutsis in Rwanda in 1994. Hatzfeld went to Rwanda several times, and was astonished by the public invisibility of the genocide's survivors. Their own muteness also stupefied him: "The silence and the isolation of the survivors in the hills are disturbing."[22] This silence reminded Hatzfeld of the long period after World War II before the survivors of the Nazi concentration camps could be heard or read. A great deal was written on the Holocaust during this period, of course, but the essential narratives of the survivors themselves took a while to emerge.

Despite the enigmatic silence of the Rwandan survivors, Hatzfeld was able to publish fourteen testimonies, most of them from Tutsis. The intensity of these narratives shows that they came from gifted people. At the same time, they reflect the traumas that the genocide had inflicted on these subjects. Jean-Baptiste Munyankore, a sixty-year-old teacher, suffers from nightmares: "During the night I'll go through an existence that is too crowded, crowded with people from my family, who speak with each other as people who are being killed, and

22 Jean Hatzfeld, *Dans le nu de la vie: Récits des marais rwandais* (Paris: Seuil, 2000), p. 172.

who ignore me and don't look at me anymore. During the day I suffer the pain of another loneliness."[23] Christine Nyiransabimana, a twenty-two-year-old planter, always has the same dream: she flees in the direction of the Congo but has to cross a field of cadavers that never ends.[24] Janvier Munyaneza, a fourteen-year-old shepherd, tells us that he could not see the faces of the killers who annihilated his family, for they passed him one behind the other, in lines, doing their "work" while he hid in the swamp. Nor does he know their names, but he does remember everything they did; he simply cannot either imagine or recognize their faces. It frightens him that he has no names or images of them. How can you hate an anonymous gang of killers? So Munyaneza's hatred remains an affect without representation.[25]

Édith Uwanyiligira, a thirty-four-year-old teacher who lost her parents and her husband, is in extreme distress because she doesn't know how her husband died or where he is buried. The couple had been in a refugee camp together, but one day *interahamwe* – the genocide's agents – came and took the men away. Uwanyiligira presents us with a strange paradox. On the one hand she says she has found some consolation in a new relationship with God. On the other she testifies to the isolation and loneliness of the survivors: "Everyone bears his pain in his own corner as if he were the only survivor, without being concerned by the fact that this pain is identical to all."[26] Uwanyiligira no longer feels the need to talk with other survivors about the genocide. She even says that she has pardoned the perpetrators: "If I don't pardon them it is I who will suffer." In the language of psychoanalysis we would say that Uwanyiligira's relation with God is a symptom she has created for herself in order to endure her loss. But this symptom carries a high price: she is even more isolated than the others are.

At the end of his long story, Innocent Rwililiza, a thirty-eight-year-old teacher, remarks, "The survivor has a tendency to disbelieve that he is really alive, which means that he is still who he was before, and in a certain way he lives a little from that."[27] These witnesses tell us that they were injured at the very foundation of their subjective lives.

Epilogue   Every kind of state terrorism is accompanied by a reinforcement of ideological conformity. In an appeal to citizens' egos, an imaginary unity is invoked through which they can be organized and integrated in a mass. Even

23 Ibid., p. 72.
24 Ibid.
25 Ibid., p. 58.
26 Ibid., p. 166.
27 Ibid., p. 113.

after a democratic regime is reestablished, this process forestalls justice and impedes the perception of truth. Even now, 65 percent of Serbs do not believe that non-Serbs were killed in their prison camps in Bosnia.

Such denials of justice and truth are in no way confined to the Serbs; they are very common. Justice and truth are problems that can only be handled when people are not completely identified with the reigning ideology, when they are not only egos but also subjects. Subjects are always divided between a part of them that can be represented through language (with the help of words, names, titles, ideals) and a part that stays outside such representations. This division is dangerous for conformist ideologies, because it means that there is a part of the subject that will never obey the terrorizing commands of power. Because of this resistance, the forces of terror attack their opponents not only in their bodies but also in their subjective life. Radical denials of justice always aim at a loss of the subject. There is a strong relationship between an oppressed minority and the silent part of the divided subject; both are smaller parts of a larger whole, but real acts of opposition against inhumanity always come from people who are terribly alone. And the effects of these acts are often so strong that they permit a whole society to liberate itself from subjugation.

There remains a more current reason to compare the political subject with the subject of psychoanalysis. The contemporary psychoanalytic clinic has to cope with the following difficulty: how is it possible to act with speech on the part of the subject that is not represented within the framework of language, to touch with words the unspeakable *jouissance* enclosed in the symptom? The politics of human rights are confronted with a complementary problem: today, nearly all important events are covered by the media. Very few places on earth stay out of their view. But this universal representation and imaging of the cruelest crimes, which now must be committed before the eyes of the whole world, are by no means followed up by the political decisions that would stop these crimes. Six years ago, 7,000 people were killed in Srebrenica, and 30,000 more were deported, within ten days, under the world's very nose. These people had been abandoned by a NATO army; the responsibility for this abandonment has still not been established. Meanwhile, after Yolanda Mukagasana lost her children during the Rwandan genocide she testified before a French parliamentary commission established to inquire into the role of France in that disaster. She says, "They accepted me as a witness, but behind closed doors, and my testimony does not figure in the final report."[28] Here the failure and symptom are on the side of those who see and know, not on the side of a secret place, hidden or concealed from the other.

---

28 Yolanda Mukagasana, quoted in Maria Malagardis, "L'Exorciste," *Libération*, May 23, 2001, p. 48.

In trials judging crimes of genocide and human-rights offenses, many of the accused deny their responsibility with the defense that they were acting under military or political command. They present themselves as ordinary men who were only following orders, instruments without their own will in a murderous chain. Yet it is this very argument that distinguishes the perpetrators of such crimes from subjects. Subjects are alienated, deported by language; they are nomads pushed around by signifiers, playthings of words. This is their *contingent* part. Subjects can be compared to immigrants who cannot choose the country of their destination. They simply have to go somewhere. But once they are on the road, they must use ruses to plot their journey, as Ulysses did. This is the subjects' *necessary* part. They have to recognize the demands of their drive and search for its satisfaction without getting overwhelmed by it. So they cannot trust only in the power of language – they have to get out of their alienation and separate themselves from the signifier that commanded them. In this respect the subject is the opposite of those perpetrators who flee their responsibility.

Archive Images: Truth or Memory?
The Case of Adolf Eichmann's Trial

Eyal Sivan

I come from Israel, a country where the political use, or "instrumentalization," of what we call memory is an integral element of the political culture. As early as the 1930s, David Ben-Gurion – later Israel's first prime minister – theorized "the transformation of Jewish suffering into Zionist redemption."[1] No other country in the world uses the memory of suffering as Israel does, to justify not just its policies but its existence. And obviously no other country dares to pretend to be preserving the legacy of the victims of one of the largest crimes in history.

Zionism (the Jewish nationalist movement) and its political expression (Israel) attained legitimacy through the genocide of the Jews during World War II. The United Nations' General Assembly Resolution 181, calling for the partition of Palestine between Jews and Arabs, was approved by a large majority in 1947 because the memory of the events of the war was still so fresh. Israel's political policies get their moral stature from the commonly accepted idea of that nation as the homeland of the survivors of genocide.

Beyond its relation to historical fact, the importance of this common belief is its place in the Western conscience. It gives Israel a privileged moral position: victims, we know, are generally seen as being on the side of good. Paradoxically, though, this "untouchable" position also weakens Israel, exposing it to a recurring criticism: how can a people that has suffered so much make others suffer? How can the victims' memory not prevent them from becoming criminals themselves? We hear and read such notions regularly.

To put the problem this way, however, is to ignore the political function of collective memory. "This screen-memory, which shows some of the horrors so as to hide others, is only the chosen weapon to defend all the lying strategies and murder propaganda," writes Rony Brauman.[2] As a political argument, memory

---

1 David Ben-Gurion, quoted in Idith Zertal, "Le procès d'Adolf Eichmann, ou la révélation de la Shoah," *L'Histoire*, no. 212 (July–August 1997).
2 Rony Brauman, "Mémoire, savoir, pensée," *Le Débat*, no. 96 (September–October 1997).

easily becomes an instrument that stimulates, encourages, and justifies different types of collective and political violence.

Did the genocide of Tutsis and moderate Hutus in Rwanda prevent the country's new regime from massacring Hutu refugees in Zaire in 1999, or from establishing a rule of terror at home? Did the memory of their persecution by the Nazis and earlier the Turks keep Serbs from killing Bosnians? Did the memory of Japanese war crimes keep China from building concentration camps and prosecuting Tibetans? Did the memory of the deportations of the Boers prevent their descendants from deporting black Africans in their turn? Did African-American soldiers' ancestry of slavery make them behave better than white soldiers in the Vietnam War? Did participation in the Resistance during the Nazi Occupation of France prevent some men from later becoming torturers in Algeria? The list is of course endless.

"What ethnic cleansing, what forced migration, what pulse of vengeance, has not found its inspiration in this linear memory and in the cult of the victim that is associated with it?" asks Brauman.[3] One reason for this, it can be argued, is that the linear vision of collective memory easily creates dichotomous and antagonistic categories. Nations rarely see themselves as criminal or cowardly; in the world of memory, they are either victims or heroes, sometimes both. Tzvetan Todorov writes, "The world of heroes, and maybe this is its weakness, is a one-dimensional world which includes only two opposed terms: we and them, friend and enemy, courage and cowardliness, heroes and traitors, black and white."[4] This is also the case in the representation of victimhood.

And of course this is also the case in Israel. Memorial vision was imposed on the country in the early 1960s through the trial of Adolf Eichmann, which opened in Jerusalem on April 11, 1961. As a senior officer in the Gestapo, Eichmann had been in charge of the mass deportation of European Jews, Poles, Slovenes, and Gypsies to the concentration and death camps. After his capture by the Israeli secret service, in Buenos Aires in 1960, he was tried in Jerusalem. The trial, in a brand-new theater auditorium called the Beth Ha´am (house of the people), was an international event – the first big public trial of a Nazi criminal since the Nuremberg trials at the end of World War II. More, it was the first trial dedicated entirely to the crime of the Holocaust.

To ensure that the event would "carry" – it was intended to be a lesson to both Israeli society and the world – the trial was conceived as a show. And what gave it its full spectacular dimension was the fact that millions of people around

---

3 Ibid.
4 Tzvetan Todorov, *Face à l'extrême* (Paris: Seuil, 1991), Eng. trans. as *Facing the Extreme: Moral Life in the Concentration Camps* (New York: Metropolitan Books, 1996).

the world could follow it on television. The U.S. election of John F. Kennedy the year before, with its election campaign fought out on TV, had demonstrated the impact of this new medium. Few realize that the first hearing in the Eichmann trial was held a month before the event's official public opening: on March 10, 1961, the court held a special session to discuss the request of the attorney general, Gideon Hausner, to permit videotape recording in the court "for the purpose of television broadcasts and cinema showings in Israel and abroad."[5]

This was an original request. The proceedings of no earlier court had been recorded in their entirety on video and broadcast on TV; "We know of no relevant statutory provision," the judges said.[6] Hausner's proposal was closely linked to the political purpose behind the Eichmann trial: for the young state of Israel, the exposure of the sufferings of the Jewish Holocaust victims was a political and didactic need. As an event, the trial was intended to become a monument in public memory. The guilt of the defendant and the revelation of the truth were secondary. In fact, as Hannah Arendt wrote, "it was the trial done by Zionism to Nazism."[7]

The staging and the filming of the trial were supposed to constitute a full representation of Jewish suffering during the war. Through the voice of the attorney general, they were to reflect Israel's position as the unique *owner* of these sufferings. Robert Servatius, Eichmann's defense counsel, strongly opposed the request for televisation, fearing the risk of "a distorted presentation of the proceedings," and "a desire [of the witnesses] to play-act before a worldwide audience."[8] Alternatively, he asked the court to make its consent conditional upon "an objective presentation of the proceedings."[9] Despite the general mediocrity of his defense of Eichmann, the remark is interesting: we might say that this idea about the objectivity of images is a function of the time, the 1960s, but even today we sometimes still hear "objective" visual documentation claimed.

After a short debate, the court concluded, this danger does "not outweigh the favorable aspects of the proposed recording."[10] The judges had mentioned

5 *The Trial of Adolf Eichmann: Record of Proceedings in the District Court of Jerusalem* (Jerusalem: Trust for the Publication of the Proceedings of the Eichmann Trial, in co-operation with the Israel State Archives and Yad Vashem, the Holocaust Martyrs' and Heroes' Remembrance Authority, 1992), vol. 1: March 10, 1961.

6 Ibid. Only about twelve hours of the proceedings of the Nuremberg trials after World War II were filmed.

7 Hannah Arendt, *Eichmann in Jerusalem: A Report on the Banality of Evil* (New York: Viking Press, 1963; rev. and enlarged ed. New York: Penguin Books, 1994).

8 *The Trial of Adolf Eichmann*, vol. 1: March 10, 1961.

9 Ibid.

these "favorable aspects" during the debate, quoting the philosopher Jeremy Bentham: "Where there is no publicity there is no justice. ... Publicity is the very soul of justice."[11] The decision, then, addressed the present moment, the time of the trial. Nothing was said of the future, or of the fact that the film would become a factual trace, an archive for future generations.

The Eichmann trial was of considerable importance from every point of view. The human and historical value of the evidence presented, and the extraordinary view that it provided of the Nazi death machine, gave it a dimension no earlier trial had attained. The Israeli state charged an American company, under the direction of the filmmaker Leo Hurwitz, with all of the video recording. In return the company commanded exclusive marketing rights to the trial images for a period of a year. About 500 hours of video were recorded for posterity. (A large part of these recordings, however, would eventually turn out to be unusable.) The Eichmann trial lasted over five months, and more than 100 victims and witnesses testified. It was the first time that victims of the Nazi persecutions had spoken publicly. The media attended for the testimony, and the world was fascinated and horrified by the stories that emerged.

Two months after the trial began, a unique witness took the stand. Before the court and the survivors, Eichmann responded to fifteen charges concerning the elimination of several million people. The prosecutor presented him as the incarnation of evil. In his defense he cited his obligation to obey orders from his superiors, but he meanwhile described in detail the functioning of a destructive engine of which he had been a chief engineer. Answering questions from the prosecutor, his own counsel, and the judge, he narrated exactly what he had done within the Nazi regime. Denying none of the facts, he gave the court a full view of the Nazi extermination machine.

What is striking, listening to Eichmann, is the fact that there is no contradiction between his own testimony and the victims'. But the perpetrator and his truth were of relatively little relevance to the purpose of the trial. In a filmed interview, Hurwitz would remember, "I was terribly excited that Eichmann was going to be tried because it had a possibility of exposing why these events happened. ... I felt sure that people in Israel would be interested in that ... but it seemed they were not interested in discovering the nature of fascism. They were only interested in dramatizing the terrible events that happened to Jews."[12]

10 Ibid.
11 Ibid.
12 Leo T. Hurwitz, interviewed by Susan Slyomovics, The Jewish Museum, New York, March 4, 1986.

Although Eichmann's trial was filmed, only a few images of the Holocaust victims, and a single image of the defendant declaring "Not guilty," became iconic representations of the trial. Of the hundred of hours of film, only a few canonical icons were left in memory. Eichmann was condemned to death on May 30, 1962. The following day he was hanged, and his ashes were dispersed in the Mediterranean. After the execution, the footage of the trial vanished, buried in an unknown archive. Memory replaced history.

In 1977, on the trial's thirty-fifth anniversary, the film was discovered, in the United States, and was returned to Israel. Shortly afterward the Steven Spielberg Jewish Film Archive was founded in Jerusalem, its mission the conservation of audiovisual material concerning contemporary Judaism. It was housed at the Hebrew University of Jerusalem.

In 1978–79, the Spielberg Archive decided to prepare a selection of seventy-two hours of the trial footage. The logic of the exercise was hard to understand: these seventy-two hours of images, recorded on poor-quality tape, were presented not as copies but as originals; the rest of the footage was declared inaccessible or nonexistent. Responding to criticisms of the archive in the 1990s, its director declared, "All the sensational moments of the trial are available. The essential is safe."[13] A few sequences were regularly sold, becoming standard illustrations of the trial. This trade in a few pieces of memory was obviously more profitable than the long and arduous task of archiving the complete material. The original tapes were stored haphazardly, and without adequate labels, in the only place the archive could find that was cool enough for purposes of conservation: an unused washroom. It was here that they were discovered, in 1991, by the production team of my film *The Specialist.*

A comparison between the catalogue of images and the trial transcript has shown that almost a third of the video archives, essentially evidence from camp survivors, seems to have been lost for good. This is a deep paradox for an archival institution dedicated to preservation. It shows to what extent, and how easily, the display of the *duty* of memory can replace the real *act* of memory.

If the videotapes of the Eichmann trial have turned out to be virtual archives, that is because the trial itself in fact fulfilled its purpose. The pleas of European Jewry, their torture, the memory of the catastrophe, found a home in Israel, where they became an indisputable source of national legitimacy, symbolized by the icon of Eichmann in the glass booth installed for him in the court. The staging of the trial, like the decision to film and record it, was intended to put the viewer in direct and immediate contact with the harsh testimony of the

13 *Ha'aretz Daily,* September 14, 1995.

survivors. The origins of this decision lay in the desire to reflect, in the optical sense of the word, the horror experienced both by those who had survived and by those who had died but would live again through the trial testimony's preservation of their trace. The viewers of the video footage were to be exposed to this horror alone; for this purpose, in the eyes of the Israeli state, the few minutes that we know from their many TV broadcasts were probably enough.

Hundreds of books and thousands of shorter studies have been written on the Eichmann case and trial, but not one scholar, scientist, or historian has discussed the video archive. Although it constitutes a full record of the trial, it seems to have been ignored as a historical document. Do scholars attach no truth to this material? Or is it only a question of time? One expert on the Eichmann case, Hans Safrian, of the National Holocaust Museum in Washington, D.C., has said he has no interest in seeing Eichmann or his trial.[14] In fact almost no scholar has wanted to hear the perpetrator speak. And what of the victims, the witnesses? The Eichmann trial video footage is one of the biggest filmed archives of their testimonies. It includes a full range of witnesses from all over Europe, from 1933 to 1945, from the rise of Nazism to the camps and the liberation. The women and men who testified in the trial did so just sixteen years after the event, when they were relatively young and their memory was still fresh. Yet the archives were forgotten. In 1982, Yale University recuperated the New Haven Holocaust Survivors Film Project, begun in the late 1970s, and transformed it into the Fortunoff Video Archive for Holocaust Testimonies. In 1994, Spielberg began the project of filming the survivors of the Shoah. But no one cared about preserving the images of the witnesses in the Eichmann trial.

What was this footage needed for if the images of neither the perpetrator nor the victims were to be used or even preserved, if historians haven't even looked at them as a document? There is no question of truth here; the beginning of an answer might be the question of the function of collective memory. The act of filming allows an emphasis on the spectacular function of the event: some images, mainly of victims, help to create icons of memory – what we used to call "monuments."

One of the most famous icons of the Eichmann trial is the fainting and the removal of a witness who collapsed under the burden of evoking the horror. Spectacular and moving, this tragic sequence became a symbol of the endless trial. Used in almost all of the films about the event, and in many others about World War II more generally, it clearly illustrates the issue of archive, truth, and memory.

14 Hans Safrian, at the conference "Il racconto della catastrofe," in Verona, Italy, in March 1998.

A deportation consists of several stages.

This and the following pages: Stills from *The Specialist,* Israel/France/Germany/Belgium/Austria, 1999, 128 min. Director: Eyal Sivan with Rony Brauman

The witness was Yehiel Di-Nur. Forty-five years old in 1962, a native of Poland, he had spent two years in Auschwitz, and was the only member of his family to survive. After the liberation he took the name "Ka-Zetnik," a play on the letters "KZ," for *Konzentrationslager* (concentration camp), and wrote one of the first books on Auschwitz published in Israel. Although he was famous in his country, he was known only by this pseudonym and had never appeared in public, even in photographs, before testifying in the Eichmann trial. There he spoke, in few sentences, about the "Planet of Auschwitz" and its inhabitants without names. "I see them, they are staring at me, I see them, I saw them standing in the queue,"[15] he said. Stopped by a question from the attorney general, Ka-Zetnik fainted and collapsed unconscious. In the deeply distressed courtroom, ambulance men ran to his rescue. Today, Ka-Zetnik himself does not recognize the description of Auschwitz he uttered on the stand as his own. Since the Eichmann trial he has taken back his real name and now situates Auschwitz in our own planet, as a specifically human construction rather than some unworldly and alien blight. If he is still afflicted by anxiety, it is now as a man facing the future: he is currently expressing himself as a citizen by struggling against the peril of nuclear weapons. In these circumstances since the trial, perhaps contemporary uses of the spectacular scene of Ka-Zetnik's fainting amount to a betrayal of Yehiel Di-Nur.

To make this kind of selection of a particular scene – in effect a form of film editing – involves a kind of censoring, since to choose is to eliminate. The truth

15 *The Trial of Adolf Eichmann*, vol. 3, p. 1237 (June 7, 1961).

of every film lies not in an unlimited absorption of reality but in a rebuilding of it, creating a structure and establishing criteria of choice. And strangely, although there is a great tradition of documenting, collecting, and archiving images and stories of victims, documentary cinema and archival work have rarely dealt with representations of perpetrators. This is true of both the Yale and the Spielberg projects; I might also mention recent projects in Rwanda, Bosnia, Argentina, and elsewhere.

It seems that images of victims fascinate, and their stories are recurrent subjects of study. This focus often seems to be defended as a *duty of memory*. How strange, though, that this claimed duty should fall on the victims rather than the perpetrators, who are far more commonly the subjects of fiction. And how strange also that in the case of the Holocaust, fiction films dealing with the perpetrators so often make use of aesthetic prototypes designed by the Nazis themselves, and more precisely by the Nazi filmmaker Leni Riefenstahl. Except for Ernst Lubitsch and Charlie Chaplin, directors dealing with this period tend to see the SS as they themselves wanted to be seen. Showing and hearing perpetrators like Eichmann would be a starting point for breaking the conventional clichés, if iconic ones, of their representation. Historians have certainly used documents of the Nazis to describe the process of destruction and to analyze the crime, but they haven't shown the criminals speaking for themselves.

When we discovered the audiovisual material relating to the Eichmann trial, we decided to follow the spirit of Primo Levi for our film *The Specialist*: in his preface to the memoirs of the Auschwitz commandant Rudolf Hoess, Levi invites the reader to discover a "human itinerary which is, in a way, exemplary" and describes this autobiography as "one of the more instructive books

ever published."[16] But writing is not an image; and the image may not be holy, but it has its own logic. So the film shows Eichmann onscreen. Here he is, animated in face and speech. He has a conscience, and speaks of his doubts in a man's voice. More, he is in a position of weakness in his glass booth, facing the judges who keep him under control. Here he is, frail, vulnerable, all in all: human.

Hidden behind fictionalized, quasi-mythic representations, perpetrators become inhuman – they become monsters, beasts, maniacs. The representation of victims, on the other hand, corresponds to the Jewish and Christian idea of redemption, so that their images work similarly to the crucifix on the church wall. It is true that to focus on the perpetrator is to risk making us identify with him; as he explains and justifies himself, tells us about his work, his joys, his sorrows, he looks like anyone else and we grant him our understanding. The technical problems he has had to resolve, his problems with his conscience, the "duty" that obliges him to follow orders – these are experiences that all of us can recognize. But it is precisely on this familiarity with him that we should count. It is in this small space, which involves identification, comprehension, and indulgence, that we can choose to evaluate him.

The use of dramatic recurring icons to represent crimes, the daily display of the sufferings of the victims, a thousand times seen, a thousand times commented on, turns them into clichés in the sense described by Roland Barthes: "Facing these images, we are deprived of our judgment. Somebody has trembled

---

16 Primo Levi, Introduction, in *Commandant of Auschwitz: The Autobiography of Rudolf Hoess*, trans. Constantine FitzGibbon (London: Phoenix Press, 2000).

for us, thought for us, judged for us. The photographer has left us nothing, just a simple intellectual acceptance."[17] When it comes to images of horror, I prefer to rely on the power of the imagination. I do not share the idea of their clarifying and denunciatory power. We hear that to show a crime against humanity is already to start to fight it. This kind of euphoric cliché eludes the question of political responsibility by substituting the show of horror for the thinking about horror. As Brauman and I have written, "When the political event is reduced to a pathetic current affair, pity paralyzes thinking and the aspiration to justice is reduced to a humanitarian consolation. Here you find the banalization of evil."[18]

After the Eichmann case it became part of the juridical show to film the trials of those who had perpetrated crimes against humanity. So it has been with Klaus Barbie's trial in 1985 and Maurice Papon's in 1996, both in France, and, of course, with the international criminal tribunals for the former Yugoslavia, in The Hague, and for Rwanda, in Arusha. The latter two courts are actually television studios. The trials are fully recorded; most of the images can be seen on the courts' websites. Ironically, the faces of the defendants are obscured, hidden. The court respects the dignity of the defendants and maybe even thought that what was really important was the testimonies of the victims. Here again we might ask, What will happen to these thousands of hours of images? How and to whom can we guarantee freedom of access to these materials, and the possibility of reconstructing narratives or making artwork out of them?

17 Roland Barthes, *Mythologies* (Paris: Seuil, 1957).
18 Rony Brauman and Eyal Sivan, *Eloge de la désobéissance* (Paris: Le Pommier, 1999).

"The Führer has ordered
the extermination...

As an integral part of the process of South Africa's Truth and Reconciliation Commission, it was decided to record and broadcast the full hearings on TV. (This was also done in Argentina.) At first the hearings were followed by large audiences all over the country. But they lasted a long time, and as the months passed, interest broke down. Few films were made during the hearings, but the question of the huge archive of moving images that the commission generated daily is an open one – as it is in The Hague and Arusha, and as it was at the Eichmann trial. In every case the purpose of the filming is the representation of the victims and the creation of a linear collective memory. Fortunately the images are not considered legal proof; unfortunately they are not considered part of construction of truth either.

An image is a representation of a segment of reality. The four black sides that construct or define the frame hide more than they show, and the truth as it is constructed through images can only be an accumulation of points of view of the same material. This construction depends on the ability to use archival materials not just to illustrate a single moment, speech, or memory, but to manipulate them freely so as to arrive at a new narrative.

Images can be objects of thought, but icons, as cult objects, cannot. The respect due to icons cannot be justified for images, which exist only through the work done on and with them. It is strange to remark that the use of images to testify to truth, and the creation of audiovisual or cinematic works pretending to be acts against oblivion, are on a growth curve. Memory has become a sort of audiovisual collective experience. Most of the compilations of images dealing with the Holocaust are convenient illustrations of commemorative discourses, and are characterized by the positive cliché "Never again." This memory, or rather this imposed mourning, is possible thanks to the constitution of a visual language. Where a living language is permanently evolving, and can be used for individual, subjective works or points of view, this visual language is constituted more as a code. Like road signs, its images can be read at a glance. Old-looking or deteriorated, they signify the past. Gray silhouettes running through trenches mean World War I. Railway trains with a musical background of violins mean the Holocaust. Snow and barbells mean the gulag. The codes are numerous. Together they make up a system of nontransparent images, an empty screen. Like the terms that are used to comment on them, they have become overused. The piles of corpses, the death factories of Auschwitz and Birkenau, the deportees behind the barbed-wire fences, the gray men running in the trenches of World War I – like the narratives of the victims, these have lost their *exemplarity*. In their one-dimensional narrative form, these historical images have lost their analogical power to stimulate a point of view and a reflection on the present.

But archival images can be used in a secular, contemporary way to create historical analogies. As Todorov writes, "Exemplary use of memory . . . allows the past to be used in view of the present. Memory can be used as a lesson about injustices acquired in the past and to help fight those taking place in the present, to help us to live our selves and to advance toward the other."[19] It is the utilization – or the manipulation – of the image that gives it its exemplary dimension. Through the use of all of the tools given to us by the contemporary arts, perhaps we can uproot images of the trials of men like Eichmann, and other perpetrators of crimes against humanity, from their memorial one-dimensional purpose. Bringing these images into our present, we can get a sense of our own environment. We can give these materials a "status of truth" that will allow us to renew the tradition of what can be called political art.

19 Tzvetan Todorov, *Les Abus de la mémoire* (Paris: Arléa, 1995), pp. 31–32.

It Is Difficult

Alfredo Jaar

Introduction   As a practicing artist I believe that the range of questions posed by this conference as a platform of Documenta11 offers a rare, much needed space of reflection on some of the most pressing issues of our time. This space of reflection is doubly necessary because it is put forth in the context of an art conference, and I emphasize the word "art," because we haven't heard that word in the last four days. The burden of the conference, then, is to shift the focus of contemporary art exhibitions from entertainment to serious discussion. There are few spaces left anywhere where these kinds of critical discussions can take place. Jean-Luc Godard has said of art that it "is not a reflection of reality, it is the reality of that reflection." This platform focuses on both reality and its reflection. As we have painfully witnessed in the last three days, reality is overwhelming. That is precisely why these spaces of reflection are fundamental, and I feel very privileged to have witnessed so many passionate and moving intellectual exchanges.

I have divided my presentations into four parts. First I will present an early work, from 1984, that relates to India. Second I will show some of the most relevant sections of my Rwanda Project, which lasted six years, from 1994 to 2000. Third I will show a few other projects to describe different strategies I have used in my work, and then I will conclude with a few remarks.

I   Bhopal, India, December 3, 1984, 12:45 A.M.: forty tons of toxic gas were accidentally released from a Union Carbide plant and spread throughout this city of a million people. The gas was methyl isocyanate (MIC), and the plant it leaked from was a pesticide factory in the city's north. Some 8,000 people were killed and more than 500,000 injured in the immediate aftermath of the tragedy, the largest industrial disaster of the last century. Today, nearly twenty years later, perhaps ten to fifteen people are still estimated to die each month from exposure-related complications, so that the total death toll is currently more than 16,000 people. The causes of the disaster are well-known: a cost-cut-

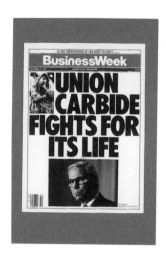

*Business Week
Magazine Cover,
December 24, 1984,*
1984

ting drive by the company reduced the number of key personnel and eliminated vital safety measures.

In January 1989 an agreement was signed between Union Carbide and the families of the victims, who were represented by the Indian government. There would be no trial; each family would receive some 15,000 rupees (430 U.S. dollars at the time). The *Wall Street Journal* had calculated that an American life was worth $500,000 and that consequently an Indian life was worth $8,500. For Union Carbide the settlement represented a loss of 43 cents per share in the stock market. Then, in 1991 a tribunal in Bhopal indicted the president of the company, Warren Anderson, and issued an international detention order for his arrest. Anderson is today a fugitive.

Three weeks after the accident, the headline on the cover of *Business Week* magazine for December 24, 1984, had this to say about it: "Union Carbide Fights for Its Life." I had started to research the tragedy and to accumulate images and information. I was shocked when I discovered this image. I displayed it in a blue frame with a red background. It is titled *Business Week Magazine Cover, December 24, 1984.* A second version of this work, which I showed in Documenta 8, in 1987, consists of a sequence of four black-and-white images.

I was shocked by the obscenity of this cover. I was shocked by the attitude of both Union Carbide and the American press – the indifference. But I felt a terrible inability as an artist to confront the tragedy and could go no further. In retrospect I realize that I had asked myself the question: "How do I make art when the world is in such a state?" and I had no answer. I would feel the same kind of inadequacy countless times in subsequent years as I approached different crises and tragedies around the world.

‖ Exactly ten years after Bhopal I went to Rwanda, to witness, document, and collect evidence about what would become the third genocide of the last century. Out of the material I collected there and in subsequent research I created the Rwanda Project, which I worked on for six years.

I will share with you some of these works. The first is a twelve-minute performance that I will reenact for you exactly as it was performed for the first time, in Chicago in 1995. Please take into account that this was directed to a specific audience at a specific time and place. *[In a darkened space, the artist showed slides which he accompanied with the following text. – Eds.]*

Untitled (Newsweek), 1994.

April 6, 1994: A plane carrying the presidents of Rwanda and Burundi is shot down above Kigali, the capital of Rwanda. Their deaths spark widespread massacres, targeting Hutu moderates and the minority Tutsi population, in Kigali and throughout Rwanda. The Rwandan Patriotic Front, which had been encamped along the northern border of Rwanda, starts a new offensive.

April 12, 1994: The interim Rwandan government flees Kigali for the town of Gitarama. Relief officials estimate that as many as 25,000 people have been killed in Kigali alone in the first five days of violence.

April 21, 1994: The United Nations Security Council Resolution 912 reduces the U.N. peacekeeping force in Rwanda from 2,500 to 270. 50,000 deaths.

April 30, 1994: At least 1.3 million Rwandans have fled their homes. More than 250,000 refugees cross the border into Tanzania, the largest mass exodus ever witnessed by the United Nations High Commissioner for Refugees. 100,000 deaths.

May 8, 1994: The Rwandan Patriotic Front gains control of most of northern Rwanda. As killings continue, hundreds of thousands of refugees flee to Zaire, Burundi, and Uganda. 200,000 deaths.

May 13, 1994: More than 30,000 bodies wash down the Kagera River, which marks Rwanda's border with Tanzania.

May 17, 1994: The United Nations Security Council passes Resolution 918, authorizing the deployment of 5,500 U.N. troops to Rwanda. The resolution says: "Acts of genocide may have been committed."

Newsweek cover,
June 13, 1994

Newsweek cover,
June 27, 1994

May 22, 1994: The Rwandan Patriotic Front gains full control of Kigali and the airport. 300,000 deaths.

May 26, 1994: Deployment of the mainly African U.N. force is delayed due to a dispute over who will provide equipment and cover the cost for the operation. 400,000 deaths.

June 5, 1994: The United States argues with the U.N. over the cost of providing heavy armored vehicles for the peacekeeping force. 500,000 deaths.

June 10, 1994: The killing of Tutsis and moderate Hutus continues, even in refugee camps. 600,000 deaths.

June 17, 1994: France announces its plan to send 2,500 troops to Rwanda as an interim peacekeeping force until the U.N. troops arrive. 700,000 deaths.

June 22, 1994: With still no sign of U.N. deployment, the United Nations Security Council authorizes the deployment of 2,500 French troops in southwest Rwanda. 800,000 deaths.

June 28, 1994: The U.N. Rights Commission's special envoy releases a report stating that the massacres were preplanned and formed part of a systematic campaign of genocide.

July 4, 1994: French troops establish a so-called "safe zone" in the southwest of Rwanda.

Newsweek cover,
July 23, 1994

July 8, 1994: As the Rwandan Patriotic Front advances westward, the influx of displaced persons into the so-called "safe zone" increases from 500,000 to 1 million within a few days. 900,000 deaths.

July 12, 1994: An estimated 1.5 million Rwandans flee toward Zaire. More than 15,000 refugees cross the border every hour and enter the town of Goma, which becomes the largest refugee camp in the world. A cholera epidemic sweeps through the camps in and around Goma, killing an estimated 50,000 people more.

July 21, 1994: The United Nations Security Council reaches a final agreement to send an international force to Rwanda. One million people have been killed. Two million have fled the country. Another two million are displaced within Rwanda.

August 1, 1994: *Newsweek* magazine dedicates its first cover to Rwanda.

[Sound, in darkness: Papa Wemba sings "Awa Y'okeyi."]

You have just heard Papa Wemba from Zaire, today called the Democratic Republic of Congo. At one point in Zaire you could find 1.5 million refugees, including those in Goma, the largest refugee camp in the world, which held 1 million people. In this song Papa Wemba is using a technique he learned from his mother, who was a *pleureuse,* a professional mourner, someone who sang and cried at funerals and in churches. He sings here in a minor key, which is very different from most contemporary singers who most of the time use a major key. Papa Wemba has said his mother's songs made his heart ache. *[The lights come up.]*

Signs of Life, 1994

The structure of this performance is very simple: I recited the events as a weekly chronology, beginning the moment the genocide started. I simply showed the barbaric indifference to the events on the part of one of the main newsweeklies (*Newsweek*) in the United States. In the last four minutes, when this song of love and loss is played, my intention was to offer the audience a space of mourning. My feeling then – in Chicago in 1995 – and sadly still today is that people had not mourned those million deaths.

Although I have begun with a graphic account of the Rwanda Project as it was first presented in Chicago, the first piece in the Rwanda Project took place before this performance and was done from Rwanda itself. One day we were walking around Kigali, the ruined capital of Rwanda, and found a half-destroyed post office. Some workers were cleaning up the floor and offered me a box of tourist postcards. From that moment on, I used the postcards to write down the names of the people I had started to meet on my trip, and sent them to friends around the world:

> Rubanda Tresifoli is still alive!
> Justine Numararungu is still alive!

This work refers directly to a classic work of 1960s conceptual art by On Kawara, who sent postcards to his friends announcing that he was alive. I wanted to make a parallel to that work, omitting the self-referential element by announcing that someone else, rather than the postcard's author, was alive. The piece is titled *Signs of Life*. Because there was no communication between Rwanda and the rest of the world, the postcards were sent from Uganda.

Rwanda, Rwanda,
1994

Joseline Mukayiranga is still alive!
Caritas Namazuru is still alive!
Jean de Dieu Hungulimana is still alive!

A few months after my return from Rwanda I was invited to create a public project in Malmö, a small town in Sweden. I was offered fifty outdoor advertising-display lightboxes dispersed around the city. I was not yet ready to show the most horrifying images I had taken in my life, so I simply put up a sign that said,

Rwanda, Rwanda, Rwanda…

I used a common font, Helvetica Bold, and repeated the word as many times as I could. It was a kind of cry that no one was hearing. Because the lightboxes had been offered to the institution sponsoring the art project, most of them were placed in marginal areas of the city. I actually liked that, the solitude of these cries lost in the city – it was a metaphor for the solitude of the Rwandan people during the killings.

The first major installation of the Rwanda Project was called *Real Pictures*. I see it as a group of monuments, memorials to the people of Rwanda. The works are black boxes. Inside each box is an image, but you can't see it; instead there is a text describing it printed on the box. I used these boxes as modules, bricks, to create monuments in a space of desolation and silence. I didn't feel that showing images of blood would make any difference. Instead I wanted a space of mourning.

Real Pictures, 1995

We are bombarded by so many thousands of images that we have lost our capacity to see and be affected by images. I wanted to try a reverse strategy. The logic here was that maybe if I didn't show the images you would see them better.

I was also asking the audience to start from zero – to forget for a second all the images they had seen, and maybe to try to understand the issues. Reading these very simple descriptions, maybe through the text they would understand better.

The next piece is called *Let There Be Light*. There are ten lightboxes on the left side and a special lightbox in the back. The small lightboxes on the left contain just one word, a word written in light – words like "Kigali," "Mibirizi," "Butare," "Amahoro," "Cyahinda," "Cyangugu," "Gikongoro," "Kibungo," "Rukara," and "Shangi," all totally meaningless for most of us. Yet these are the names of places where between 5,000 and 100,000 people were killed in less than 100 days. None of them has the connotation of a name like "Auschwitz" or "Guernica" – why? When we reach the end, we are confronted with a lightbox showing a changing sequence of four images. These are actually the first images I released from the 3,500 photographs I took in Rwanda. The images show a group of kids looking at a scene happening outside the frame.

The average time a spectator spends in front of an artwork in a museum is three seconds. If you stay long enough in front of this lightbox the image will change every fifteen seconds. This is the first image in the sequence. I am trying desperately here to slow down the viewing, I am asking for time, I am asking for at least one minute with the work. In this sequence we see these kids embracing, expressing pain, love, solidarity, all the things that we did not express as a world

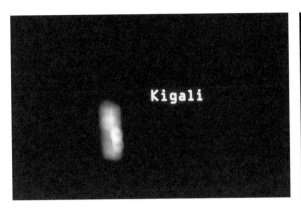

Let There Be Light, 1996

community, as becomes obvious when we walk in front of these meaningless names.

These children are looking at something that we will never see. Most of the media would have concentrated on what is outside the frame here, but I thought that maybe to show a very simple moment of humanity among these children would tell much more about the genocide.

This is another installation with two synchronized Quadvision boxes. The text says,

> Gutete Emerita, thirty years old, is standing in front of a church where 400 Tutsi men, women, and children were systematically slaughtered by a Hutu death squad during Sunday mass. She was attending mass with her family when the massacre began. Killed with machetes in front of her eyes were her husband Tito Kahinamura, forty, and her two sons, Muhoza, ten, and Matirigari, seven. Somehow, Gutete managed to escape with her daughter Marie Louise Unumararunga, twelve. They hid in a swamp for three weeks, coming out only at night for food.

This text stays on the screen for forty-five seconds. Those very few who are patient enough to stay that time will see the next sequence:

> Her eyes look lost and incredulous. Her face is the face of someone who has witnessed an unbelievable tragedy and now wears it. She has returned to this place in the woods because she has nowhere else to go. When she speaks about her lost family, she gestures to corpses on the ground, rotting in the African sun.

Her eyes look lost and incre-
dulous. Her face is the face of
someone who has witnessed an
unbelievable tragedy and now
wears it. She has returned to this

place in the woods because she
has nowhere else to go. When she
speaks about her lost family, she
gestures to corpses on the ground,
rotting in the African sun.

*The Eyes of Gutete
Emerita*, 1996
(Quadvision version)

This text lasts for thirty seconds. Third and final text:

> I remember her eyes. The eyes of Gutete Emerita.

Fifteen seconds. Up to now we have had forty-five, thirty, and fifteen seconds of text. For those who are still here, this is what happens now: for a fraction of a second we see the eyes of Gutete Emerita flashing onscreen. Then we go back to the first text.

In this work I am making a desperate attempt to balance information and visuals, information and spectacle. I am trying to suggest that this is the amount of information we must know in order for this image to make sense.

I met Gutete Emerita and spent an afternoon with her, we took her to the hospital with her daughter, she was visibly disturbed. Meeting Gutete Emerita was extremely moving, and very important for me and my project. I will never forget her.

I dedicated four works to Gutete Emerita. The next one is a space divided into two areas. Every wall is painted black. On the first wall we encounter an illuminated text some sixteen feet long. It is the story of Gutete Emerita. Walking along this text to enter the second space, the audience is invited to read it. But the font is very small; they have to get close to the text and walk slowly. The end of the text reads: "I remember her eyes. The eyes of Gutete Emerita."

Reaching the end of the corridor we turn left into a large space where we are confronted with a light table some six meters by six meters square. On its top

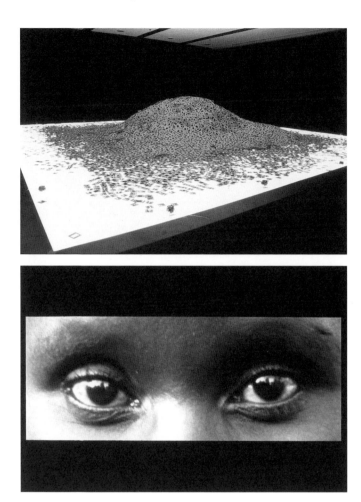

*The Eyes of Gutete
Emerita*, 1996
(light table version)

we find one million slides. We also find magnifiers, inviting the spectator to take them and look at the slides more closely. This is the moment I am waiting for – when someone takes a slide and puts their eyes one inch away from the image. It is the eyes of Gutete Emerita, the eyes that witnessed the genocide we did not want to see. As we look at the slides we realize that this same image is repeated one million times.

Here again I am trying both to create a powerful mise-en-scène and to supply enough information for that image not to be dismissed, for that image to make sense. I am desperately trying to go back to a certain kind of respect for images. All these works are exercises in representation, but they all fail, they are all condemned to fail. That's why I am always trying different strategies.

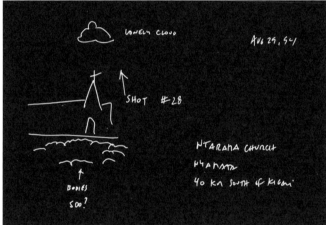

Field, Road, Cloud,
1997

This is another essay in representation, a very simple one. The audience is confronted with three landscape photographs: *Field, Road, Cloud.* Next to each photograph is a small frame that holds a sketch of the same landscape with annotations telling the viewer about the image. It is only when the viewer gets close, then, that he or she will understand what the images are about.

The sketch next to the first photograph shows that we are seeing Shot No. 15, we are looking at tea fields forty kilometers from Kigali, and we are going toward the Ntarama Church. The second one tells us that this is Shot No. 21, showing the road to Ntarama Church on the same date. The reason for these numbered sequences is to explain to the viewer that the images relate to a journey that took the photographer from here to there.

Emergencia, 1998

The last photograph is an image of a cloud. The sketch next to it identifies it as Shot No. 28 – a lonely cloud above the Ntarama Church. At the bottom left of the sketch is a text reading "Bodies, 500?" Only here does the viewer understand that in photographing the cloud in the sky the photographer is surrounded by some 500 bodies. Here again I was trying the possibilities of evoking without showing.

I next come to a retrospective of the Rwanda Project in 1998 in the Centre d'Art Santa Monica, located in an old convent in Barcelona. Here, along with the rest of the Rwanda Project, including the *Real Pictures* monuments, I presented another work, a sculptural piece titled *Emergencia*. The work is a metal pool, ten meters by ten meters. When the water is quiet and still, it reflects the space and the people there like a mirror. To reach the galleries where the other thirteen works in the exhibition were installed the audience had to walk through the central area holding *Emergencia*.

Every twelve minutes, the African continent, made out of fiberglass in a perfect 1.2 million:1 scale, emerged from the reflective pool. When it reached the surface, it stayed there for about a second and disappeared again. Spain is only fourteen kilometers from Africa at the narrowest point, you can actually see it from Cape Tarifa. It has the potential to be the door to Africa for Europeans and the door to Europe for Africans, but it has not played that role, because Spain is a racist country, as every country is racist. In this piece I wanted first to put Africa back on the map – it was after all right there, a few kilometers from us in Barcelona. I also wanted to create something else that I will explain in the next set of images.

The Gift, 1998

Emergencia is now installed in a closed courtyard in the Umeå Public Library, in Sweden. Now the pool reflects books – supposedly all our knowledge and information – and of course the architecture, and it also reflects the people who know about the functioning of the piece and wait. When the continent emerges, all the reflections are broken. It is as if the entirety of the knowledge in the world is put into question by what we know and do about the continent of Africa. The narcissistic impulse that this mirror invites is broken by the emergence of the continent.

A related project is a public intervention in Stockholm in 1998, when Stockholm was the Cultural Capital of Europe. This project is called *The Gift*. It is a box, printed in an edition of 15,000, and distributed free to people in the street by volunteers who asked, "May I offer you a gift?" We went to the most important public places in the city. The box is completely red on the outside and bears a simple inscription asking the recipient to open it from a specific side. Once it is opened, you can read a printed text on the inside of the box that says,

> What did you expect? We can only offer you a possibility. Please get out of yourself and give something to someone else. Please help Médecins Sans Frontières.

A text in small type at the bottom of the box asks you to open the box completely and refold it so the inside becomes the outside and the outside becomes the inside. A sequence of the photographs from *Let There Be Light* is now visible on the outside. The red box now becomes a money box, its top a wallet-size card with the account number of Médecins Sans Frontières. Besides giving informa-

Epilogue, 1998

tion about Médecins Sans Frontières, I wanted to give the organization visibility in 15,000 homes – and to raise funds for Rwanda.

I will now turn to a film project, *Epilogue* (1998). This is a three-minute floor-to-ceiling projection that begins with one minute of light, nothing but light. Here again is a work that demands time from the viewer – most people will enter the room, see the light, and just leave. But those patient enough will see a face emerging after that minute of light, the face of Caritas Namazuru, a Rwandan refugee who walked more than 400 kilometers to reach a refugee camp in Zaire. Her face emerges very slowly, one second at a time and one percent at a time. After thirty seconds, we reach a thirty percent definition of her face and we think we are finally going to see her, but then the image starts to fade again until we see another one minute of light. But those who have seen the image will experience an afterimage effect, so that the image of Caritas Namazuru will still be there onscreen, even after she is gone. The work is a piece about memory. How do we remember?

In the Koldo Mitxelena cultural space in San Sebastian, Spain, in 1998, I presented the same fourteen works from the Rwanda Project that I had in Barcelona, but I also created a new work for two courtyards. The courtyards were spaces of light, while all the other works in the hallways around were in relative darkness. People had to circulate around these courtyards to see the exhibition. Wanting to provide spaces for meditation, I offered a wall text and four cushions on the floor, where people could sit and think. The text was in Spanish. In English it reads as follows:

Meditation Space
(Tea), 1998

I am lured by faraway distances, the immense void I project upon the world. A feeling
of emptiness grows in me; it infiltrates my body like a light and impalpable fluid. In its
progress, like a dilation into infinity, I perceive the mysterious presence of the most
contradictory feelings ever to inhabit a human soul. I am simultaneously happy and
unhappy, exalted and depressed, overcome by both pleasure and despair in the most
contradictory harmonies. I am so cheerful and yet so sad that my tears reflect at once
both heaven and earth. If only for the joy of my sadness, I wish there were no death on
this earth.

This is a text by one of my favorite writers, E. M. Cioran, who died in 1995. So
the piece is also a kind of memorial to him.

Let's look now at this small device at the bottom right of the wall. I had
brought tea and coffee from Rwanda, and I asked a scent specialist to distill and
transform them into scents – the scents of Rwandan tea and coffee. The first
courtyard was filled by the scent of Rwandan tea, the second, where the text was
in Basque (one of two official languages in the Basque country), by the scent of
Rwandan coffee. The reason for this was that when I came back from Rwanda
my body smelled like death for months, and I could take showers and more
showers and I could still feel it. My psychiatrist insisted that it was in my mind,
not in my body. That is why I wanted to do a piece about healing and bring in a
different smell from Rwanda.

The last public project I made about Rwanda was in the city of Lyons, France,
in December 2000. Over three nights I projected these words on the façade of
the Hôtel de Ville: "Kigali," "Mibirizi," "Gikongoro," "Rukara," "Cyangugu."

Let There Be Light,
2000

As you know, Americans and Belgians have made a small effort to clarify their responsibility in the genocide. But France has been a little less forthcoming about it.

The last piece about Rwanda is called *Six Seconds*. It shows a girl whose image is out of focus; next to her is a small lightbox with the text "It is difficult." The girl is one of 100,000 Rwandan orphans whose parents were killed during the genocide. I met her for only six seconds – she was visibly disturbed and the image came out of focus. I wanted to use this image as a final image from Rwanda. Here I am trying to convey the pain and the sorrow through a beautiful image, through poetry. The text "It is difficult" is taken from a poem that I have used often in my work and is also the title of one of my books. The poem says:

> It is difficult
> to get the news from poems
> yet men die miserably every day
> for lack
> of what is found there.

The poem is by William Carlos Williams. How do we express the loss of life and still use poetry? I have been an artist for twenty years and I find it more and more difficult.

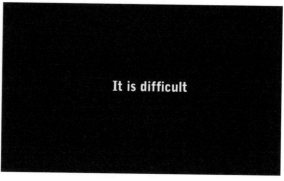

Six Seconds, 2000

III The strategies I employed in the Rwanda Project are specific to that project. Three other projects show different strategies of my work.

Over the last ten years, the three Scandinavian countries of Norway, Sweden, and Denmark have been generous in their assistance to the so-called developing world, and have welcomed one million refugees. Finland, by contrast, accepted only seventeen refugees during the year when I was invited to do a project there. In Helsinki in 1995 I did a piece about this called *One Million Finnish Passports*. At the request of the authorities, we had to put this huge pile of passports behind high security glass. Why one million? Because I calculated that in most European countries, approximately 20 percent of the population is either foreigners or people of foreign descent. Finland has five million inhabitants, so I am suggesting that they immediately welcome one million foreigners. The work was lit in such a way that people would see themselves reflected in the glass before seeing the passports. It was a sea of identity, ready to be filled by new faces, new colors, new sounds, new ideas. The most moving reaction to the work was that of a Finnish citizen who came back to the museum the next day after seeing it and brought his own passport and threw it on the pile as a sign of solidarity.

We have not spoken much about Chile during this conference. My friend José Zalaquett, a Chilean and former president of Amnesty International, was invited to attend but was ill. Isabel Allende, the daughter of Chile's former President Salvador Allende, was also invited but could not attend. So I wanted to include this piece because it relates to Chile.

I was commissioned to create a monument for Salvador Allende in

One Million Finnish Passports, 1995

Playground, 1999

Barcelona. In the monument, *Playground*, twelve easels are placed in a grid. Made of iron and metal and set in concrete bases, they cannot be moved. They stand in a little square facing a school called the Antonio Gaudí School, and kids from the school come to play in this playground at break and lunchtime. One of the easels has an inscription: "*La revolución no implica destruir si no construir*" (Revolution doesn't mean to destroy but to create). On the other side are the birth and death dates of President Allende.

Each easel has three colors – a dark color for the structure, a light color for the face, and a very light color for the frame. There is a sign explaining the work. It says, "Playground is an antimonument. It is a simple and useful gesture that transforms a square into a space where the children of Sant-Boi are invited

Lights in the City,
2000

to create new worlds. This work does not foster the cult of one person but creates a public service as an homage to an idea of society."

Playground represents a space of creation for anyone who wants it, but mostly for children: in the school office we set up piles of paper for anyone who requests them. And when they finish their drawings or their poems they can either leave the drawings as a public exhibition or they can take them home. As explained in the description panel, I wanted to create a space of creative and collective activity, a homage to an idea of society.

Playground is a permanent monument; *Lights in the City* was a temporary one, in Montreal, in 2000. The site – the part of the city called Old Montreal – is today an area of boutiques and stores, art galleries, bars, and restaurants. I was invited to intervene in a landmark building: the former seat of the Canadian Parliament. I learned in my research that this monument has burned several times in its history. On the two main floors are shops and galleries; the entire upper part, the cupola, is empty space.

Walking through the area on one of my research trips for the project, I discovered a rather banal building, with in front of it a sign saying "Accueil Bonneau." Going in, I discovered a shelter for the homeless. The shelter welcomes 3,000 people a month and gives them breakfast, lunch, and dinner at no charge. I was surprised to discover that Montreal, one of the richest cities in the world, has 15,000 homeless people. I learned that there was a second shelter 100 meters away, called Refuge des Jeunes, and a third shelter another 100 meters away called Maison du Père. I decided to do a project about homelessness and to transform this existing monument, the cupola.

Lime quarry, Robben
Island, South Africa

Inside the cupola I installed a 100,000-watt battery of red lights. Once they are triggered, the cupola becomes red. I connected the lights to each of the three shelters, where I also installed a sign explaining the project and a button: every time someone in the shelter pushed the button, the cupola would turn red. In this way everyone using the shelter could signal their presence to the city. I wanted to transform the building into a lighthouse sending out a distress signal, announcing the presence of people we don't see. This landmark monument became a shameful reminder of the unacceptable condition of the homeless in Montreal. The red cupola of course refers to the earlier fires in the building, but also to a fire threatening society itself.

Epilogue   This is the approach to Robben Island, a small island thirteen kilometers offshore from Cape Town, South Africa. As you probably know, this is where the apartheid regime held some of its top political prisoners, including Nelson Mandela, Govan Mbeki (the father of South Africa's current President Thabo Mbeki), Walter Sisulu, Mak Maharaj, and Ahmed Kathrada. On the island's grounds one sees different detention centers and facilities (if you can call them that). There is also a lime quarry, where thirty-two of the top political prisoners spent their days. Obviously this was forced labor – six to seven hours a day, five days a week, in the heat of summer or in the cold of winter, and with picks, chisels, and hammers, the most basic tools.

What was the lime used for? Simply to resurface or white out – yes, white out, pardon the irony – the roads of this infernal island. The brightness and glare of the stone blinded prisoners and guards alike, for both were forbidden to

Isivivana, Robben
Island, South Africa

wear sunglasses: the prisoners because the idea was to blind them, as simple as
that; the guards because it was not part of their uniform. Other effects included
extensive lung damage. It is said that Mandela did not cry on the day he left
prison because of the effect of the lime-quarry work on his eyes. He had lost his
capacity to cry.

This hellish activity was intended to kill the senses of the prisoners and to
break their bodies and spirits. Yet as you probably know, Mandela and the others transformed Robben Island into a place of learning, organizing study groups
that even included some of the guards.

In 1995, to commemorate the fifth anniversary of their liberation, the prisoners went back to the quarry. There Mandela and the others demonstrated for
the press what they had done there as prisoners. During the demonstration
Mandela stepped away from the crowd, picked up a stone, and walked a few
steps. He placed the stone on the ground, slightly off the middle of the road.
Seeing this, the other ex-prisoners did the same thing, piling their stones into a
cairn. In the Xhosa culture to which Mandela belongs, the construction they
made is called an *isivivana*; it is a sign for a safe place.

This very simple monument created by Mandela and the others is still there
– which is some kind of miracle, because the monument is very fragile and
stands almost in the middle of the road, where buses pass by every day. It is in
my view an extraordinary public monument of reconciliation. Its extreme
fragility is a good metaphor, I think, for the extreme precariousness of a long
and difficult process. And this is where I want to end – with this monument to
reconciliation created by men who cannot cry. *Shukria*.

The Logic of Reconciliation

Barbara Maria Stafford

I want to situate the current debates around personal, social, and political reconciliation within a larger (and, I hope, richer) domain, one entangling philosophy, theology, aesthetics, and ethics. This paper seeks to expose that wider expanse of analogy in which reconciliation appears as a special case. The historical concept I will be exploring – the perceptual judgment of sameness-in-difference – as well as its bridging practices are not unknown. But recently the concept has once again become allegorically inverted, either into the tautology of self-same identity or into the endless repetitiveness of "original" traditions. Post-Structuralism and Deconstruction relentlessly promoted the alienating strategies of radical difference. The unraveling of these isolating and anti-mimetic theories with the emergence of multidimensional electronic media, multiculturalism, and postcolonial and transnational studies offers new opportunities for trying to rejoin the fragments of an ancient suturing rhetoric with the contemporary search for connections. Moreover, in making individual sense impressions intelligible to others, boundary-crossing analogy redeems the mimetic power of images both from a reductive Cartesian technology of deception and from the inarticulateness of the Kantian nonrepresentational Sublime.

Analogy is the art of expressing kinds of relationship. Affinity and kinship provide a flexible framework for asking how any one thing might be provisionally yoked to any other thing in the vastness of the universe. As a dynamic method of inferencing, this cognitive and somatic conjunction assists in the discovery of homomorphic and homologous intermediaries among disjoint forms. Analogy is thus generative of fluid patterns of arrangement and possible narratives. It acknowledges the absence of purity in the repleteness and density of the experiential encounter.

Because my principal purpose is to bring back intersubjective analogy for serious consideration in light of the modern concern to reconcile, I need to sketch the simultaneously cosmological and epistemological order in which this transactional leap arose. I find it significant that, in the West, the problem of locating what we have in common – and the central role of images in that process – emerged as a response to the grim actualities of war in Iron Age Greece. If we look, however briefly, at the pre-Socratics and their genealogy of bifurcation, we observe the beginnings of dualistic reasoning. Getting beyond the limits of actual knowledge allowed one to seize a tantalizing, but foreign, reality. In Paul Grenet's words, the preclassical Greeks adopted an "analogical attitude" to cope with the challenge of how to depict the existence of what cannot be seen (such as a separate soul, or an elusive order), or to suggest the idea of an ephemeral substance without a body. Wind, smoke, shadow, dream, fire, and *image* were the phenomenological terms of comparison they borrowed to marry the suprasensible to the sensible realm.

But it was Heraclitus (536–470 B.C.) who turned analogy away from the kind of simple, vertical anthropomorphization found in Homer (who used personification to wed the quarrels happening atop Mount Olympus to battles raging below at Troy) and honed it into a general tool for scientific explanation. This "greatest of the Ionians" extended the core concept of a nature divided by war to law, ethics, and human conduct. Violent struggle, in his view, preceded any renovation of opposites, whether in the material, biological, or cultural spheres. This fact was not lost on Martin Heidegger and Michel Foucault. Yet, especially in the case of the latter, the reconciliatory potential dropped away.

Empedocles expanded the associative/dissociative binaries in Heraclitus's principle of change and further transformed them into dehumanized drives crisscrossing the universe. Love and Strife depersonalized celestial mechanics into rhythmic impulses imparting motion to the four elements. The implicit tension in this cosmology between the invisible springs of action and their visible effects was made explicit in the writings of Anaxagoras and Democritus. Their development of the physiognomic argument – asserting that behind all appearances lurks something more important that does not appear – was taken up most memorably by Plato (427–347 B.C.).

But it is not the philosopher of the Divided Line that I wish to recuperate here. Rather, I want to linger with the Plato who mollified the intractable dichotomies of the pre-Socratics by the addition of a mediator. To be sure, in the *Timaeus* and the *Symposium*, the Creator or Demiurge always stands *in between* thought and a more precious concealed reality. Yet this apparent valorization of the nonmimetic is tempered by another, forgotten aspect of Plato's dialectics of love. In the *Phaedo*, the *Parmenides*, and the *Politics*, he introduced *Logoi* – literally delicate resemblances floating in space in the middle of the universe – to embody the analogical notion of a third term. These ghostly representations, or fleeting *images*, enable us to make the transition from empirical things to otherwise unseizable intelligible Forms.

Plato uses a watery analogy to evoke the *Logoi*, comparing them to the mirroring waves in which astronomers observe eclipses. Importantly, this is a theory of "soft" (that is, approximating) mimesis, not of the hard facsimile or the empty but rigid simulacrum. The type of undulating motion implied in Plato's account is significant as well. The reconciliation of opposites in a subtly diversified unity comes about, not through drifting or vacillation, but by rocking between poles. Here we have the first glimmers of the mobile faculty of judgment at work, and along with it of *aesthetics* as perspicuousness, as a constantly adjudicating or balancing mode of sensory knowledge.

In this *participatory* theory of analogy (because extremes partake of and are thus modulated by a fluid medium), liquidity mediates the absolute opposition between incongruous orders – whether they be phenomena and noumena, or body and soul, or body and bodies. Louise Bourgeois's glassy installation art offers a protracted meditation on analogy-as-participation: instead of Plato's ebbing and eddying ripples, Bourgeois's evaporating moisture and sinuous flasks render irreconcilability approximate and distance near. In *Cell II* (1991), a host of Shalimar bottles are tightly grouped on a round mirror next to a pair of folded hands. This insistent parallelism of similar forms – varying only in scale and the amount of perfume remaining – contributes to their intrapermeability. It also obliges the viewer continually to estimate, and so adjust, her awareness of presence and absence, closeness and remoteness. *Le Défi* (1991) – the analogical counterpart to Damien Hirst's chilly pharmaceutical allegories and repelling medicinal chests – invokes the incantatory tradition of the Jesuit catoptric mirror-cabinet. This virtual *Wunderschrank*, or dramatic cupboard of shimmering transparent vessels, establishes a connective rhythm among the proportionally varied vases to cross the boundary and meet the viewer on the other side.

Felix Gonzalez-Torres's *Untitled (Perfect Lovers)* (1991) makes even more explicit this performative aspect inherent in the analogical jump to link. He explores the problem of creating equitable relationships by alluding to the difficulties of achieving synchronicity. Two identical wall clocks, displayed side by side, tick in harmony. Despite coming face-to-face with this incontrovertible evidence of a shared time, the beholder is simultaneously conscious of deprivation. The artist's very effort to establish a moment of mutuality evokes all those other vanished instants when minds and bodies were not conjoined.

There is a vital distinction to be drawn, then, between being antithetical and being inimical. I cannot lay out here (as I do in my book *Visual Analogy*) how, already beginning with the theurgical Neoplatonists of the later fourth and fifth centuries, analogy became converted and inverted into the negative dialectics of allegory.[1] Not unlike the situation in Iron Age Greece, this, too, was a warring period, but one of immensely greater complexity. This divisive epoch witnessed the agonizing dissolution of the Roman Empire, mass diaspora, and the heresy struggles waged by an orthodox Christian monasticism against the hydra of syncretic heterodoxy sprouting in the East.

Allegory, I argue, involved a twin gnostic gesture that hardened over time. Its formal strategy established either a bureaucracy of truth or coteries of nihilism. Either no unfilled space was to be left within the minutely segmented universe (thus obstructing any reconciling leap to resemblance) or all matter was to be cleared out, leaving an untraversable chasm (producing, most recently, the unmoored spin of the signifier). Analogy, as a method for mediating, that is, maintaining a balanced or proportional relation between the world of experience and the noetic realm, disappeared into a clutter of clogging avatars or into a vacuum. Paradoxically, the dichotomizing result was the same: only the identically minded get closer together.

I have recounted this hermeneutical tale of fundamentalist sedimentation and romantic estrangement elsewhere. Here I can only complicate the foundational story of analogy by introducing Aristotle's *predicative* version into the mix. For Aristotle (470–384 B.C.), analogy is both poetic and mathematical-philosophical. As a trope (from *tropein*, to turn) it belongs to the larger domain of metaphor, which is in turn a component of logic. "Translation" best describes its rhetorical function, since metaphor transports words from one order of reality to another. Similarly, speech and conversation conduct meaning through a network of connections going both ways.

Contrary to Plato's participatory dialectic – modeled on the wavy rocking of water – Aristotle develops a judiciary logic rooted in the visual vocabulary of geometry. Significantly, perspicacity continues to play a central, if altered, role. Specifically in the *Topics* and the *Prior Analytics*, analogy is discussed in terms of conformity and congruence, equity and inequity, as Kant will later do when examining the operations of judgment. As a type of incomplete induction enabling us to reason from the particular to the general, this comparative procedure constituted an art of discovery, not a rigorous method. For Aristotle, invention – whether in poetics or in logic – hinges on the creation of an *equivocal* middle term, one that literally stands in between the singular instance and the general rule. Note that its lack of fixity also implies mobility, an alternating between poles.

1 For the background to the present essay see my *Visual Analogy: Consciousness as the Art of Connecting* (Cambridge, Mass., and London: The MIT Press, 1999). Also see "The Demon of Analogy," a section in my introductory essay, "Revealing Technologies/Magical Domains," in *Devices of Wonder: From the World in a Box to Images on a Screen,* exh. cat. (Los Angeles: Getty Museum of Art, 2001).

Similarity, in this system, is the result of a provisional unity, one that rises above each of the individual cases to span items in different or distant categories. Because there are so many variables in bringing disparate properties together under a common rubric, resemblance is partial (i.e., equivocal, not univocal, shifting between the recognition of congruence and incongruence). If the image-in-the-middle, according to Plato, always floats, the middle term in an Aristotelian syllogism always remains ambivalent. In sum, both Plato and Aristotle – despite their important differences – suggest that the reconciliation of contraries comes about through motion. It is through continuous kinetic adjustments that far-apart agents gain proximity or that ordinate things can be fairly coordinated. Moreover, both philosophers emphasize the arcing role of vision in the struggle to overcome alienation. Whether we speak of the imagination's leaps of insight or the jumps of the eye, it takes perceptiveness to recognize and produce junctures.

A constant theme of metaphysics from the later Neoplatonists to Augustine, Descartes, Kant, and Karl Barth was the need to overcome resemblance. In one way or another, mimetic or analogical theories posited mirroring as a central and positive aspect of their operations, while allegory refused to reflect. Discussions of similarity became hopelessly entangled in the growing polemics surrounding the perils of vision. Pursuing the branchings of resemblance, it was feared, might lead us astray or seduce us into seeing erroneous connections.

Thus for Nietzsche it was only by an aphoristic refusal of plenitude that creation could take place. For Heidegger, Being came into its own through painstaking differentiation from beings. For Walter Benjamin, the decline of aura belonged to a downward spiral shaped by the melancholic interplay of nostalgia and loss. Paraphrasing Ruti Teitel, I want to ask why the most negative form of representation – i.e., nonmimetic allegory – has become emblematic of advanced artistic and social theory. This predictable set of outcomes, I believe, is the lopsided result of following an immature and one-sided cultural pattern.

In order to insert the unrealized analogical project into modern times, I want to recuperate a generally underrated philosopher. Leibniz (1646–1716) deserves to be recognized as the heir of the Plato of the *Logoi*. His multifaceted work is deeply relevant: first, because he proposes a participatory theory of reconciliation that functions within a postcoordinate world; second, because a positive view of optical technology drives his entire system; and third, because, at a fundamental level, his metaphysics, epistemology, and ethics are an *aesthetics*. That is, images are not used as mere illustrations but as the embodiments of his philosophy. Without them there would be no understanding.

This great German polymath is our contemporary precisely because – unlike Plato – he can no longer credibly invoke the natural world as a support for images. For him, the connective medium that will engender a community of agents acting upon a diversity of interests at particular points of time and space must be an optical device. The encyclopedism of the late *Monadology* (1714) – a kind of cosmic pointillism – took up the Scholastic challenge to connect God with man. Leibniz, however, transformed this medieval quest into a spatiotemporal game, a gigantic jigsaw puzzle binding the infinite atomic diversity of the universe into compossible concordance. We will see that a very special sort of mirror performed the acrobatics of coordination.

An encyclopedist, mathematician, philosopher, linguist, and simultaneously a utopian and pragmatic political theorist, Leibniz pictured the cosmos not as it appeared when reflected – static and flat – within a conventional looking glass. Instead he deployed a magically illusionistic realm of repeatable objects visible from myriad vantages. In this ontologized theory of perception, the substance of every living thing acted as the unique point-of-view of its soul. The body behaved as if it were wearing one of those multifaceted spectacles that the Jesuit Athanasius Kircher describes in his *Ars Magna Lucis et Umbrae* (1678). Peering through these curious lenses results in the environment slivering in a distinctly personal way. But reciprocity rules Leibniz's system, and the world also looks back at us. Subjects and objects are momentarily reconciled, just as happens when we gaze into the bulging convexities of a *sorcière* mirror. In this undulating silvery surface – the technological analogue of the watery *Logoi* – apparitional objects project their particular shapes outward to intersect with the look of the viewer. Each distinct locus of matter peeps out from its own angled vantage and re-presents to itself the aspect it witnesses.

The doctrine of preestablished harmony is the ultimate logic of the link. Like a digital computer, this connective system is both automatic and interactive. Monads are caught up endlessly in feedback loops. For Leibniz the world is an infinity of converging series, capable of being extended into each other around unique points. Significantly, a sophisticated theory of analogy undergirds the entire system: "Now this connection, or this adaptation of all created things to each and of each to all, brings it about that each simple substance has relations which express all the others, and that, consequently, it is a perpetual living mirror of the universe."[2] As I have been arguing, this "living mirror" is not flat but curved – like the *sorcière* mirror or the metamorphosing spectacles. It animates forms by visually rocking them across a swelling surface.

Leibniz instantiates this scheme of obtaining as great a variety as possible while maintaining the greatest order by invoking one of those glazed cosmolog-

2 Gottfried Wilhelm Leibniz, *Monadology,* 1714, § 56.

ical cabinets or catoptric coffers constructed by the Jesuits. These microcosmic chests are themselves the virtual counterpart to the material *Wunderschrank*. If cabinets of curiosities housed encyclopedic collections of disparate objects that had to be hyperlinked through the viewer's insightful "jumps," the mirrored cabinets of the Jesuits boxed the dynamics of an intersecting and reverberating network of light. As Kircher recounts, the faceted walls, floors, and wings of these crystalline theaters of the world multiplied and modified enshrined tiny bits of cork, vegetation, coins, medals, stones, miniature figures, and diminutive buildings to infinity. Leibniz spells out the implications of this new kind of digital communication: "And as the same city looked at from different sides appears entirely different, and is as if multiplied perspectively; so also it happens that, as a result of the infinite multitude of simple substances, there are as it were so many different universes, which are nevertheless only the perspectives of a single one, according to the different points of view of each monad."[3] Although all monads experience the same world in its totality, they only clearly experience their part of the world.

Here we are given a foretaste of Leibniz's theory of blur. Today we would call it "noise." There is an important difference to be drawn between Descartes's allegorizing notion of the deceiving senses and Leibniz's existential awareness of the limits of human knowledge. Clear and distinct panoramic vision is God's alone. For, at every moment, emotionally charged minute perceptions well up within us, but without rising to consciousness by being focused through reflection. "It is they [the *petites perceptions*] which form I know not what, these tastes, these images of the sensible qualities, clear in the mass but confused in the parts, these impressions which surrounding bodies make upon us, which embrace the infinite, this connection which each being has with all the rest of the universe." Leibniz puts such half-formed inklings and inferences in the middle to cloud linear vision. These filmy intermediaries allow us to extend ourselves multidimensionally, revealing vistas where all things may yet conspire.

By reopening the case for analogy, I have tried to get historical constructs to join our present. Reconciliation is a convergent process somewhere between clemency and condemnation. Separating from an old regime or a prior position entails both a gap and a motion toward something new with which we hope to become partially integrated. I have argued that this limited passage, or unfinished work of transition, needs to be situated within a larger philosophical and aesthetic imaginary, one in which visual media assist in the work of redemption.

3 Ibid., § 57.

Artworks as analogues of transitory realities have long established a space for reflection where the subtleties of individual, social, and cultural repetition get played out for all to see.

African Literature and the Rwandan Expedition

Manthia Diawara

In 1998, poet Nocky Djedanoum organized a trip for several African writers and one filmmaker to go to Rwanda. They were to produce books and a film on the genocide of Tutsis and moderate Hutus, which took place four years earlier. The aim of Mr. Djedanoum, a Chadian who resides in Lille, France, where he is the director of an annual book fair called Fest'Africa, was to break the silence of African artists and intellectuals on human-rights violations in Africa. Djedanoum and his fellow travelers presented their project as "the duty of the African writer to remember"; they believed that art, by preserving the memory of the 1994 genocide, had the capacity to heal people, to prevent ethnic violence, and to contribute to the reconciliation of different groups. Djedanoum's colleagues on the trip included Tierno Monenembo (Guinea), Boubacar Boris Diop (Senegal), Véronique Tadjo (Côte d'Ivoire), Abdourahman Waberi (Djibouti), Monique Ilboudo (Burkina Faso), Koulsy Lamko (Chad), François Woukoache (Congo), and Jean-Marie Rurangwa (Rwanda).

The Rwandan African Writers' Expedition raises several important issues for African artists and intellectuals living in Africa and abroad today. First there is the question of political commitment as a moral duty for the artist, at a time of gross human-rights violations not only in Rwanda but also in Sierra Leone, Sudan, Nigeria, the Democratic Republic of Congo, and Côte d'Ivoire. What is the poet or the public intellectual to do under the threat of repressive regimes in the isolated nations of Africa that the rest of the world has turned its back on? Finally, if the artist is committed, whom does he or she write for? I have raised these questions about the status of the artist and the public intellectual in Africa, and the reception and legitimacy of such artists and intellectuals in the public sphere, that I believe are addressed by the Rwandan Expedition.

The issue of commitment has always existed with regard to African literature and art. The Negritude poets first declared their *engagement* when Aimé Césaire, in *Notebook of a Return to My Native Land* (*Cahier d'un retour au pays natal,* 1939) stated his identification with the Congo against Belgian colonialism and celebrated the dignity and heroism of "those who never did invent anything" against the inventors of weapons of mass destruction and those who committed pogroms and other crimes against humanity in the name of progress. The Negritude poets put their reputations on the line for the freedom of Africa; their poetry drew its artistic resources from the movement of decolonization and the struggle against racism. It enhanced the legitimacy of Césaire and the Negritude poets in France – where their main audience lived – that they had the support of Jean-Paul Sartre, André Breton, and other artists and public intellectuals at the time.

After the Negritude movement, Frantz Fanon's *The Wretched of the Earth* (1961) became the most celebrated writing about commitment in the letters of Africa and the diaspora. With that book Fanon went beyond the text to put his body and life on the line in Africa, blurring, thereby, the lines between the writer and the guerrilla fighter. In fact *The Wretched of the Earth* inaugurated a new form of writing and commitment based on the experience of the author as a revolutionary in the battlefield. It is still today the most enduring document on decolonization and human-rights violations in Africa. Ironically, also, Fanon's call for the violence of the oppressed against the violence of the oppressor has equally been influential beyond Africa. Instead of bringing the warring sides to reason and reconciliation – as Fanon had intended when he theorized the peace of mind that was to be had at the conclusion of the violence of the oppressed – it might have exacerbated it; it might have increased violence from Algeria to Rwanda, Palestine, and Afghanistan. Fanon's committed ideas may also have fallen into the hands of people who are against decolonization, progress, and human rights. I will come back to the unforeseen excesses in Fanon's theory of violence in the section below where I discuss the Rwandan Expedition and the writers' total identification with the Tutsi-led government.

But there is little doubt that Fanon had redefined the Sartrean notion of *engagement* by taking the writer out of Paris's cafés, where he was safe and free to express himself, and transporting him to the frontlines in Algeria. Many poets and writers have since followed Fanon's example in Africa. Mongo Béti even went as far as to criticize a fellow writer, Camara Laye, for writing *The African Child* (*L'Enfant noir*, 1953), a romantic novel, when the writer's place was in the decolonization and independence movement. There are other famous examples, such as in South Africa, during the struggle against the apartheid regime. Breyten Breytenbach was imprisoned (joining Nelson Mandela on Robben Island) for both his views and his activities with the African National Congress. Poet Dennis Brutus was also shot in the leg for his involvement in the fight against apartheid.

In postcolonial Africa, writers have continued to put their lives on the line in the defense of human rights, democracy, and peace. In the 1960s, Nobel laure-

ate Wole Soyinka went to jail for defending the Igbos' right to self-determination during the Biafran War. While in prison, the defiant Soyinka wrote a novel,
The Man Died, about his experiences. The case of Kenyan writer Ngugi wa
Thiong'o, who challenged corruption and neocolonialism in his country, also
provides a good illustration of the Fanonian commitment. Wa Thiong'o, too,
was thrown in jail and later sent into exile.

After Ngugi wa Thiong'o's exile in the 1970s, however, fewer and fewer
writers were able to follow Fanon's example. Dictatorial regimes in Africa
clamped down on all forms of dissent, including the artistic ones. The burgeoning public sphere that was emerging in countries like Nigeria, Ghana, and
Uganda was soon destroyed by presidents-for-life. The center of African literature in English moved to London, while the locus of Francophone literature
returned to Paris. Even though the writers continued their critique of the
African regimes, they were removed from the situation, and wrote mostly for a
Western readership. Writing in exile, African authors had to rethink the form
and content of their works. They had to become more reflexive and individualist, and less Fanonian and existentialist.

One exception, however, was Ken Saro-Wiwa, who lived in Nigeria and
wrote protest literature against the oil companies and the corrupt Nigerian government. When Saro-Wiwa, like Fanon, realized that writing was not enough to
expose and stop either the environmental crimes of Shell Oil Company in Ogo-
niland or the racism directed against ethnic minorities in the Niger Delta
region, he formed a resistance movement, MOSOP (Movement for the Survival
of the Ogoni People), to organize peaceful protests against Shell and the military dictatorship. Saro-Wiwa also created links between his organization and
international human-rights and environmental groups such as Amnesty International, Greenpeace, Human Rights/Africa, The Body Shop, Friends of the
Earth, and PEN. In the words of Rob Nixon, Saro-Wiwa was "the first African
writer to articulate the literature of commitment in expressly environmental
terms."[1]

Saro-Wiwa and his MOSOP gained momentum in Nigeria and abroad, and
became an embarrassment for Shell Oil Company, which urged Sani Abacha's
military junta to silence them. First, during a peaceful protest of MOSOP, the
Nigerian army killed 2,000, destroyed villages, and displaced 80,000 persons.[2]
Then Saro-Wiwa was arrested with eight other Ogoni leaders. They were tried
on trumped-up charges and hung without anybody being able to stop Abacha.

1 Rob Nixon, "Pipe Dreams: Ken Saro-Wiwa, Environmental Justice, and Micro-Minority Rights,"
 Black Renaissance / Renaissance Noire 1, no. 1 (Fall 1996), p. 43.
2 Ibid.

Thus, with Fanon, Soyinka, wa Thiong'o, and Saro-Wiwa, we have illustrations of courageous commitment on the part of African writers. We see intellectuals turned guerrilla leaders; writers who put their pens and their lives at the service of a revolution; and literature that identifies with the rights of one group that considers itself oppressed by another. Such a commitment requires the artist to occupy an ethical position and exert a high moral authority that reduces the function of art to propaganda, and makes everything else secondary to the larger aim of defeating what is deemed to be evil. In addition to rendering literature more eloquent to sing the praises of the revolution, commitment also encourages the author to make ideology his or her main source of inspiration. Influenced by the Negritude movement, the anti-apartheid struggle in South Africa, and the liberation of Angola and Guinea-Bissau, poets and novelists have demonstrated that being at the front line is the best source of and inspiration for African literature; that the best literature is resistance and propagandistic literature. They have gone from writers to social and political commentators, to even taking up arms to defend what they consider to be right. It is in this sense that one understands Saro-Wiwa's worldwide reputation as a martyr and a champion of ethnic minority rights and environmental justice.

The Rwandan Expedition, therefore, reminds one of the paucity of courageous intellectual commitment as well as the lack of a public sphere in Africa today. That the genocide in Rwanda took place without the world hearing from African intellectuals and their struggle to prevent it is an indication of the death of the public intellectual on the continent and the triumph of Afro-pessimism. That there are human-rights violations everywhere – the mutilation of innocent civilians in Sierra Leone, slavery in Sudan, violence and murder against women in the Sharia-ruled Northern Nigeria, and the atrocities committed by Rwandan and Ugandan-backed rebels in the Democratic Republic of Congo – without African intellectuals in other nation-states expressing outrage and concern constitutes a betrayal of the legacy of Fanon and Saro-Wiwa who had died for the revolution. One only reads of and hears the protest against such crimes in Western media.

Could it be that the advent of the nation-state in Africa, by isolating intellectuals from one another and anchoring their symbolic capital in nationalism, contributed to the diminution of the intellectual public sphere in Africa? It is also clear that the decline of the public intellectual in Africa, as in most emerging nations, is due to Western monopoly of media outlets. Africa lacks newspapers, television networks, and book publishers that have an influence beyond an individual nation-state. Moreover, the Western press and intellectuals speaking from the West – New York, Paris, and London – have more legitimacy than their local counterparts in Africa.

In addition to exposing the crisis of commitment on the part of African writers, the Rwandan Expedition raises concerns about the need for an African public sphere and the legitimacy of African intellectuals in that public sphere. I have already mentioned the difficulties posed by nation-states which, more than in colonial times, isolate writers from one another or silence them. African writers from different nations feel closer to each other in Paris, London, and New York than in Bamako, Freetown, Kinshasa, and Kigali. Most Africans learned about the Rwandan genocide from the Western media, which covered it with the usual stereotypes of Afro-pessimism, exoticism, and tribalism. Reading about it in the *New York Times*, *Le Monde*, and the *Guardian*, one never gets the sense that the Tutsis and the Hutus are similar to the Israelis and the Palestinians, the Serbs and the Bosnians, and the Hindus and the Muslims in India and Pakistan. Territorial, nationalist, and ideological struggles in Africa are seen as tribal warfare, while similar struggles elsewhere are less dismissively or pejoratively described.

One year after the genocide in Rwanda, when the books started to come out, Wole Soyinka's was the only African voice. Predictably, it received less attention than books that were written from the Western point of view, like Philip Gourevitch's *We Wish to Inform You That Tomorrow We Will Be Killed with Our Families: Stories from Rwanda*.[3] Ironically, a review by Soyinka in the *New York Times* lent the legitimacy of an endorsement by an African intellectual to the book. It leaves one to wonder if, were there a vibrant public sphere in Africa, Soyinka's *Open Sore of a Continent*[4] would have remained in the shadow of European and American writers on Rwanda. One is also left with the feeling that Africans cannot rely on the press and the writers in Europe and America to address adequately its human-rights issues; and that, without a Pan-African public sphere, human-rights abuses will go unchecked at the national level.

During colonial times, human-rights issues were limited to land occupation by the colonizers and their oppression of the natives. Poets and writers could denounce such violations from liberal circles in Paris and London, where their voices mattered the most. Today, however, with Africans killing each other in autonomous nation-states, their suffering seems remote from European capitals, and from one African capital to another. It is therefore urgent to build an alternative public sphere, which is Pan-African and capable of undermining the autonomy of nation-states and the hegemony of Europeans and Americans in the media, in order to highlight human-rights issues in Africa.

---

3 Philip Gourevitch, *We Wish to Inform You That Tomorrow We Will Be Killed with Our Families: Stories from Rwanda* (New York: Farrar, Straus & Giroux, 1998).
4 Wole Soyinka, *The Open Sore of a Continent: A Personal Narrative of the Nigerian Crisis* (New York: Oxford University Press, 1996).

Clearly, my point here is not to deny the significance of the criticism of human-rights violations in Africa coming out of Europe and America. On the contrary, as I have shown here, Saro-Wiwa's protest movement against Shell Oil Company and the Nigerian dictatorship was successful because of its links with human-rights organizations in the West. Saro-Wiwa's ability to mobilize such organizations on behalf of the Ogoni people forced the Western media to pay attention to them, and to put pressure on Shell and Nigeria. Indeed, the Rwandan Expedition, under discussion here, came from Europe, even though the writers and intellectuals are of African origins. The expedition received funding from the Fondation de France and the French Ministry of Foreign Affairs, and that support legitimated the writers' mission to the Rwandan government. (Had the African writers been funded by another African country, the Rwandan government would have been less receptive.) French institutions also made it possible for the writers to publish their works and thus provided an important space for African voices on the genocide in Rwanda.

Finally, when we look at the current tragedy of Safiya Hussaini in Northern Nigeria, we find the only movement in her defense is coming from Europe and America. The Sharia court in Sokoto state in Nigeria has condemned Hussaini to death by stoning because it has found her guilty of committing adultery and having a child out of wedlock. The federal government in Nigeria has refused to intervene and save Hussaini's life against this primitive application of the Sharia. There is no credible space in Africa – on television or in newspapers – from which to organize a protest by African writers, intellectuals, and artists against the violation of Hussaini's human rights, and the cowardly manner in which the federal government in Nigeria has turned its back on her. Clearly, therefore, if the world does not come to her aid, she will be killed by an archaic law put in place by religious fanatics. The Western media – the BBC and Radio France Internationale in particular – have done a good job of keeping Hussaini's story in the news. Some Internet links, such as Afrik.com, have also developed discussion forums to inform and mobilize people to her cause.

My argument in favor of an African public sphere is, however, to prevent cases such as Hussaini's from falling between the cracks when they are not covered by the media in the West. The point of view of African intellectuals in Africa is important in undermining the autonomy of the West's representation of the continent as the heart of darkness, tribalism, and infectious diseases. African writers' commitment to respect for human rights in Africa will also constitute the best form of self-determination, the best prospect for the defeat of Afro-pessimism, and the best protection of the citizens of the continent against ethnic violence and abuse by dictators and religious fundamentalists.

The Rwandan Expedition teaches us this much: that Africans must break their silence on human-rights violations. As Djedanoum puts it, to be silent is to treat all crimes the same way, as normal and natural. African writers must break their silence to take their place in the world. Certainly writing collectively about an issue, as the authors of the Rwandan Expedition did, is one way to bring attention to it. A public sphere can also be constituted through the media, such as a Pan-African television network that competes in Africa with CNN (USA), TV5 (France), and the BBC (UK). The communication of the issues of human rights would also be facilitated by the creation of Pan-African newspapers with regular editorial contributions by African public intellectuals. Finally, as we have seen with the Rwandan Expedition, African writers and artists should organize meetings on human-rights issues in different African cities in order to make their presence felt.

Let us return now to the Rwandan Expedition proper, in order to analyze some of the difficulties inherent in such a project. First, as I have pointed out, the expedition arrived in Rwanda in 1998, four years after the genocide took place. As one young woman said in the documentary that Woukoache made on the writers' trip, *Nous ne sommes plus morts* (We Are No Longer Dead), "When the genocide was being prepared, why did you and other writers not write about it? I would have liked you to have the sign of solidarity before the genocide took place."[5]

Having arrived on the scene late, the writers could only adopt a style of writing that was reflexive, that is, self-conscious of its own removal and distance from the historical event that was the subject of the writing. They had no existent connection to the events except through the trauma of memory. Theirs is a sense of guilt that they had to negotiate through their writings. In *Murambi, le livre des ossements* (Murambi, the Book of Bones), the novel written by Boubacar Boris Diop, Cornelius, the main character, returns home four years after the genocide to find that his own father had plotted the massacre of Tutsis in a school where they were supposed to be protected from the Hutu extremists. To add to Cornelius's pain, he learned that his father has betrayed his own wife and son, Cornelius's mother and brother, with the other unsuspecting Tutsis. Cornelius's guilt is therefore double: his Hutu father is a perpetrator of genocide and his Tutsi mother is a helpless victim, whose death, like that of more than 800,000 other Rwandans, he could not prevent on those fateful days of April 7 through 15, 1994. As another character tells Cornelius, "Some people feel guilty for surviving the genocide. They are asking themselves what sins have they committed in order to be still alive."[6]

5 *Nous ne sommes plus morts* (We Are No Longer Dead), documentary film (Rwanda/France/Belgium) by François Woukoache, 2000.

The writers in the Rwandan Expedition are, in a way, like Cornelius; they are embarrassed by their delayed action, and they face the task of making amends both to the dead and to the survivors. In the preface to his book, *Moisson de crânes* (Harvest of Skulls), Abdourahman A. Waberi apologizes for writing about the genocide because words are inadequate for describing what he has seen during his short visit to Rwanda. He has only let go of the book in the hope that the words will serve a reminder of those who are dead: "What else can [the writer] do but to invoke, but for a moment, the souls and the presence of the people departed, to touch and caress them with timid words and silences, and to fly by them, like a bird, because one can no longer share their fate."[7] For Véronique Tadjo, too, in *L'Ombre d'Imana: voyages jusqu'au bout du Rwanda* (Imana's Shadow: Journey to the End of Rwanda), the most difficult thing for a person visiting Rwanda after the genocide is how to live with the presence of death everywhere: "The particles of the massacre are floating in the air. The dead accuse the living of using them still. The dead want to be buried. They are rebelling. They want to disappear in the ground."[8]

The purpose of writing for Rwanda is therefore to ask for forgiveness from the dead, and to help the survivors to heal and to prepare for reconciliation. There is a mourning scene in the documentary film by Woukoache, where people gather at a cemetery for an annual ritual in memory of the dead. The women are dressed in white and they sing the words of a long poem that underscores the feeling of grief and trauma of the survivors of the Rwandan genocide. As the camera pans slowly from one end of the mass grave to the other, following the rhythm of the song, the spectator becomes a participant in the funeral ritual, and begins to feel the pain of the Rwandans. The poem opens as follows: "I recall you. / It is the second time that we will be burying our own / Who died without us being able to help them, / Who were buried in places unknown."

The identification with the dead and the living in this scene reveals in fact the most effective way of representing the genocide in Rwanda. It contrasts with other scenes in the film, and the novels written for the expedition, that depict piles of human bones massed together at schools and churches where the massacre took place. If there is an artistic lesson to be learned from the Rwandan Expedition, it concerns how to present this horrific crime and help the survivors overcome their trauma. To me, most of the realistic representations of human

---

6 Boubacar Boris Diop, *Murambi, le livre des ossements* (Paris: Stock, 2000), p. 182.

7 Abdourahman A. Waberi, *Moisson de crânes. Textes pour le Rwanda* (Paris: Le Serpent à plumes, 2000), p. 14.

8 Véronique Tadjo, *L'Ombre d'Imana: voyages jusqu'au bout du Rwanda* (Arles-Méjean: Actes Sud, 2000), p. 27.

skulls and other evidence of the genocide dull the imagination or paralyze the viewer under the power of evil.

The mourning scene in *We Are No Longer Dead*, on the contrary, draws its aesthetic resources from traditional rituals of mourning that speak directly to the dead, and from the symbolic use of one mass grave to represent others. The scene is also effective because of the respect that it shows the dead by not exposing their nakedness in public places.

Tadjo, too, makes recourse to traditional myth and magical realism in her novel, *L'Ombre d'Imana*, to render the genocide alive for the reader. In a compelling scene, she describes the anger of a dead man who returns to punish the living. This man, who was beheaded during the genocide, was cross at the survivors for failing to bury him properly. His punishment was a torrential rain that did not stop for days and nights. The living called a diviner to see if he could stop the rain. The diviner spoke with respect to the dead, asked for forgiveness for all the pain that the dead had suffered before dying, and promised to let him rest in peace with a proper burial. The rain stopped as the diviner turned to the living and said, "You must bury the dead according to our rituals; bury the dried-up bodies; the bones that are aging in the open air. You should only keep the highest memory of them."[9]

The diviner here is also the African writer, whom Tadjo describes elsewhere in the novel as one who "pushes people to lend an ear and exorcizes [their] repressed memories. The writer has the power to heal the wound and write about everything that can bring a little hope."[10] Tadjo is critical here of the Rwandan government for exposing so many bodies in the open air in order to prove that the genocide took place. For Tadjo, not burying the dead is a lack of respect for human dignity, and an invitation for further genocide: "The Hutus are afraid of the Tutsis because they are the seat of power. The Tutsis are afraid of the Hutus because they can take over power. Fear remains in the hills."[11]

Many of the writers of the Rwandan Expedition, in fact, posit their artistic and social *engagement* at the service of the reconciliation between the Tutsis and the Hutus. For this reason, the main characters of the novels are often hybrid, with Hutu and Tutsi parents. In *L'Aîné des orphelins* (The Eldest of Orphans), by Tierno Monenembo, Faustin is a fifteen-year-old boy with a Tutsi mother and a Hutu father. In the beginning of the novel, his parents are killed by Hutu extremists and he is taken to a concentration camp at gunpoint by a Tutsi child

9 Ibid., p. 56.
10 Ibid., p. 38.
11 Ibid.

soldier who accuses him of being a "genocideur."[12] The rest of the novel (though the plot is not linear) depicts Faustin's ordeals as a gang member in Kigali, in juvenile detention camps, and finally awaiting execution in prison on a murder charge. The novel describes present-day Rwanda as still trapped in determining who is a Tutsi and who is a Hutu; in the meantime, it is a hell for children like Faustin. It, too, is an indictment of the present government's unwillingness to move beyond the genocide.

For other writers in the Rwandan Expedition, writing is to identify with the Tutsi point of view because they are overwhelmingly the victims. Every Hutu is also seen from their perspective as a potential agent of genocide. The writer's role becomes, therefore, to help the Tutsis to reconstruct the memory of the genocide; to engrave it as evidence against revisionists and negationists; and to document it as a singular event for future generations to remember. I will return now to what I called the unforeseen excess in Fanon's theory of violence to discuss what I consider here as the writers' total identification with the Tutsis as victims. One of the biggest problems facing the African states, as they move into democratic regimes today, concerns the human rights of ethnic minorities. We have seen that in Nigeria, the Ogoni people and other small ethnic groups are invisible in the struggle for power that opposes the "Muslim North" and the "Christian South," Hausa, Yoruba, and Igbo. In Zimbabwe and South Africa, white minority rights are inextricably tied to land distribution issues and democracy. How the writer identifies with the victimhood of a minority group is therefore never a straightforward issue – not even in the case of Tutsis in Rwanda.

I was surprised therefore to find that some writers in the Rwandan Expedition relied on the Israeli model to describe the Tutsi experience in Rwanda. For the genocide, they used expressions like "the Holocaust," "the Tutsi Shoah," "the Final Solution," "Never again," "Tutsi Diaspora," "negationist and revisionist." The writers were also influenced by Jewish writers on the Holocaust, such as Primo Levi and Elie Wiesel. Finally, they allowed their writing to justify the view that the Tutsis are permanent victims even though a Tutsi-led government is occupying the seat of power. This logic of permanent Tutsi victimhood mobilizes the whole country against one enemy only – the Hutu extremists in Rwanda and the Democratic Republic of Congo – to the detriment of nation-building, peace, and reconciliation. The text that succumbs to this total identification with the ideology of the ruling party in Rwanda is *Le génocide des Tutsis expliqué à un étranger* (The Genocide of the Tutsis Explained to a Foreigner) by Jean-Marie Rurangwa.[13] In this book, the author reminds us that it was first in

12 Tierno Monenembo, *L'Aîné des orphelins* (Paris: Ed. du Seuil, 2000).

1959 that the Hutus attempted genocide against the Tutsis. That led to the exile of Tutsis in Uganda, Tanzania, and Congo. The Hutus have since demonized the Tutsis as outsiders, bloodsuckers, and snakes that the country must rid itself of. The massacres of 1994 were therefore the "Final Solution," that is, an attempt to kill all of the Tutsis in Rwanda. For all of these reasons, Rurangwa argues that we must keep in mind the memory of the "Tutsi Shoah."

As I have indicated with regard to Fanon's theory of violence by the oppressed, this type of total identification with the Tutsis, as the only side deserving justice, blinds us from critical judgment when human-rights violations are committed by them. An unproblematized adoption of the Israeli model by the Tutsis is also what prevents writers who take their side from criticizing the Rwandan Popular Front (RPF) for invading the Democratic Republic of Congo and committing the human atrocities that are well-documented today. For the RPF, the Rwandan soldiers are going inside Congo after the Interhamwe, the Hutu extremists who committed the 1994 genocide. But the fact is that they have killed several hundred thousand innocent people, and displaced countless others in the process. Seven years of devastating war in the Congo, since 1994, and there is no end in sight.

The Israeli model posits, in fact, a form of ethnic absolutism that is incapable of the kind of reconciliation seen in South Africa. As the Tutsis claim the genocide in order to be beyond reproach in their conflict with Hutus Interhamwe, they remove the possibility of reconciliation and peaceful coexistence with any Hutu who rejects the ideology of the RPF. What Rwandans are rejecting, in fact, is democracy, because their country will remain locked in conflict as long as the ethnic groups will not let go of their claim to a special status. Meanwhile, the war between the Hutus and the Tutsis in Rwanda and Congo has destroyed the economy of the two countries, and the future of the children.

In *Murambi*, one of the most complex texts of the Rwanda Expedition, Boris Diop has one of his characters saying, "It would not be easy for those who have suffered so much to sort out things, to put behind the worst in order to remember only the best."[14] For this character, only the capture and trial of people who perpetrated the genocide would cure Rwandans of the trauma that they are now suffering. But history must go on and a new Rwanda must be born. That's why another of Diop's characters, Cornelius, says that, as horrible as it is, "there is life after the genocide; it is time to move on to something else."[15]

13 Jean-Marie Vianney Rurangwa, *Le génocide des Tutsis expliqué à un étranger* (Lille: Le Figuier, Bamako, and Fest'Africa Editions, 2000).
14 Diop, *Murambi*, p. 143.
15 Ibid., p. 224.

With the Rwandan Expedition, one dares to dream of a renewed life and space for African literature. After slavery and colonialism, disease and human-rights violations are some of the most important crises facing Africa today. The intellectuals' role in the public sphere is crucial to denouncing such violations and arguing for democracy and tolerance.

**The Politics of Witnessing:
Trauma, Memory, and the Narration of Truth**

The Democratization of Memory

Lolle Nauta

Multiple Pasts?   No nation can avoid the task of creating an account of the past, and traditionally the past belongs to the victors. It is those in power now who determine who was right back then. In the apartheid era in South Africa, the Museum of Cultural History in Kaapstad contained almost nothing on slavery – an institution generally recognized to be an integral part of the country's history. Similarly, during the rule of Hastings Kamuzu Banda in Malawi, one could discover every detail of the dictator's biography in the nation's historical museum but hardly anything about his allies in the independence struggle against the British. The closer Banda came to seizing absolute power, the more of these former allies of the regime landed in jail, and the emptier the museum became.[1] It may be hard to seize power, but appropriating the past is also no easy task.

Why are nations in need of a past? Because they need a "we" – a designation of what their citizens have in common. Even if this identity is to some extent fictive (as Benedict Anderson has demonstrated so well[2]), that doesn't make it less real. A common past is helpful; it shows what the "people" have always had in common, what they have shared for a long time. How else can it be decided who belongs and who doesn't? A common past can also serve the nation's need to legitimize its geographical boundaries. It provides the bricks and even the cement for the self-awareness of a national community and its political class.

Every year in my own country, The Netherlands, we commemorate the victims of the German occupation of 1940–45, and also those who fell fighting the Japanese in what was then called Dutch East India and is now Indonesia. The government's declaration of a national holiday on May 4 and 5 states that on these days "the liberation of the kingdom from German and Japanese occu-

---

1 Hastings Kamuzu Banda was the president of Malawi from 1966 to 1994 and "President for Life" from 1971 to 1993.
2 See Benedict Anderson, *Imagined Communities: Reflections on the Origin and Spread of Nationalism* (London: Verso, 1983).

pation should be commemorated and celebrated." This official formulation, in which the nation creates a concept of its past, equates the Japanese occupation of Holland's former colonies with the German occupation of the Netherlands. Having suggested that these two occupations can be compared to one another, the formulation ignores the fact, for example, that the Dutch were themselves an occupying power in the colonies, and fought to suppress the independence movement, which was backed by the Japanese. In this version of the past, literally official because produced by the state, the Dutch people are portrayed as the victims of powerful aggressors whom they bravely resisted both at home and abroad.

In recent decades, Dutch authors, artists, scholars, and journalists have confronted the less happy sides of the nation's colonial past. There have been many cases of "coming out," in which former army men, both soldiers and officers, have admitted to having participated in atrocities. These facts have even been discussed fairly openly in the Dutch parliament. Nevertheless, on the national level, the official image of the past persists in relatively unblemished form. The need for a common past is tenacious, and in the drama of this past it seems as if people can only play one of two roles: hero or victim. In past years, The Netherlands has demanded an apology from German and Japanese politicians for their nations' actions during World War II. Yet the government did not allow the Dutch queen to apologize in the name of her country on a visit to Indonesia in 1995. She had to limit herself to the neutral statement, "It fills us with sorrow that so many people were killed in this fight or were marked by it for their entire lives."

The past in The Netherlands is Janus-faced – there seem to be two fundamentally different attitudes toward it. On one side is the official attitude that recurs like a repetition compulsion every year on May 4. Politicians, the military, and representatives of many organizations parade past the National Monument in solemn observance to lay wreaths and give speeches. Here a consensus reigns as to what should be commemorated and celebrated, and the relationship to the past is ritualized. On the other side is the unofficial attitude, no less a part of public consciousness for being expressed in novels, works of art, scholarly writing, and media debates. Here there can be no talk of a consensus; instead the past itself is contested. Writers like Rudy Kousbroek and Graa Boomsma have convincingly contested the equation of the German and the Japanese occupations. Veteran organizations have criticized and threatened them for it.

The function and source of the ritual attitude are clear: as argued above, it is a question of the constitution of a national identity – an identity backed by a state that considers itself the representative of the people. But what is the source of the second face of the Janus head? Why argue over the past? What does that achieve? Isn't it all relative and subjective anyway? How has it happened that in recent decades, in many nations of the world, so many controversies have arisen around coming to terms with the past? What are the means they employ, what interests do they express, and what groups do they represent?

Democratization of Memory   The term "truth commission" has not existed for long:[3] in a dictionary I have from 1999, the Dutch equivalent, "*waarheidscommissie,*" does not yet appear. Expressions like "monument against slavery" and "Holocaust memorial" are neologisms too. Language, it goes without saying, responds to social developments – and what kind of development are we dealing with here? How has it happened that, as Timothy Garton Ash writes, "The relationship of societies to a difficult past is one of the most important problems of this era"?[4]

The question has a quick answer and a less quick one. The quick answer: the issue arises out of specific social upheavals. Without the end of apartheid there would be no South African Truth and Reconciliation Commission. Without the fall of the Berlin Wall there would be no Enquete-Kommission Aufarbeitung von Geschichte und Folgen der SED-Diktatur in Deutschland (Inquest commission on the history and consequences of the SED [Sozialistische Einheitspartei Deutschlands] dictatorship in Germany). Without the end of the Salvadoran civil war there would be no Comisión de la Verdad para El Salvador (Truth commission for El Salvador). The phrase "social upheaval" here, however, is clearly vague; further elucidation is needed of the quick, unsurprising answer, and it runs: for the relatively new phenomenon of truth commissions and the like, we can thank those who have fought for freedom and democracy. When it becomes clear what freedom and democracy have to do with problems of justice and truth, our quick, trivial answer can be replaced by a more complicated one.

As mentioned, the ritual attitude to the past is ultimately based on a form of victor's justice. We commemorate victims, but our commemoration takes place in the context of a retrospective view of the elimination of an enemy. The freedoms we enjoy today, it is said again and again, could not have been achieved without painful sacrifices. But isn't the second, more analytic kind of approach to the past – clearly the kind involving truth commissions, etc. – just as much a

---

3 See Priscilla B. Hayner, *Unspeakable Truths: Confronting State Terror and Atrocity* (New York and London: Routledge, 2001).
4 Timothy Garton Ash, "The Truth about Dictatorship," *New York Review of Books,* February 19, 1998, p. 35. See also Ian Buruma, *The Wages of Guilt: Memories of War in Germany and Japan* (New York: Farrar, Straus, Giroux, 1994).

victor's affair? Those who benefited from the apartheid system have ultimately lost; and one can say the same of those who held power in the former GDR, some of whom were even sent to jail by German courts. Surely this, too, looks like victor's justice.

But that is not the case. One cannot say that this is victor's justice, because the process of "transitional justice" sets fundamentally different attitudes to the past in conflict with one another. It is an open question whether those who benefited from apartheid have suffered actual damages as a result of the work of South Africa's Truth Commission. As Mahmood Mamdani has shown, little has so far changed in their economic position.[5] The commission's task, however, did not include the discussion of these problems. Political compromises made at the time of apartheid's fall meant that its political representatives would not be criminally charged. As for the punishment of former SED officials in Germany, that, too, was contested – especially in the progressive press.

Processes of transitional justice are characterized by competing attitudes to the past. Who have justice on their side? "The truth" is not yet codified under the new, more peaceful circumstances; it will have to be dragged into the light, and to a certain extent reinvented, since it has toiled so long in the service of the former regime. Who will control it now?[6] Given questions like these, transitional justice clearly involves not the secure perspective of the victors but a nonritual approach to the past and to the uncertainties of the democratic process.

In nonritual approaches to the past, new groups or classes of society lay claim to their own history – they sue for it, so to speak. Until now they have literally lacked a recognized history; it has not existed, or at best has existed underground, passed along by word of mouth. It was not contained within the earlier society's official self-image, which was constantly retouched by propaganda. Do you speak of oppression? Terrorists were justly punished. Do you speak of murder? The man jumped out of the window, he wasn't pushed. Do you speak of the wrongfulness of slavery? Blacks were children, and the constitution only applied to those with civil rights. These types of justification, which retrospectively deprive the so-called "freed" of their past, are tenacious, and are not automatically refuted by social change. Shifts toward democracy take paths determined by the specific social situation; in the beginning there is the political fight, and only later, sometimes even decades later, comes the reappraisal of everything that has happened. Processes of emancipation typically advance only

---

5 Mahmood Mamdani, "The Truth according to the TRC," in Ifi Amadiume and Abdullahi An-Na'im, eds., *The Politics of Memory: Truth, Healing, and Social Justice* (London and New York: Zed Books, 2000), pp. 176–83.
6 See Antjie Krog, *Country of My Skull* (Johannesburg: Random House, 1998).

with great difficulty and have a long-drawn-out history. If the social group in question is unsuccessful in bringing its past to light, it will lose its path toward freedom and democracy.

It is precisely here that we encounter the nontrivial significance of contested concepts like freedom and democracy. In victor's justice there is always a continuum between the past and the present: the Ministry of Propaganda tinkers with history until the prevailing situation seems its logical development. As narrated by the Ministry, history becomes the red carpet on which those in power march into the present, propelled by their self-created repetition compulsion. In the nonritualized approach to the past, however, such a continuum cannot exist. Things happened in the past that today are barely comprehensible. Individuals and groups who participated in these events may now lead quiet lives, and may not want to hear about what they once did; yet countless people still suffer from the dark events that marked the lives of their parents and ancestors. What is needed is not a retouching of history but, often, a writing of it for the first time.

With a truth commission the relationship to the past shifts paradigmatically. Where victors colonize memory, the truth commission democratizes it. Neither winners nor losers, neither perpetrators nor victims, have the final word. The democratization of memory seeks to avoid a future repetition of the horrors of the past.

The relation between memory and democracy is not a theoretical construction: processes of memory require a real, existing democratic context, a space in which competing claims can unfold. In Germany, for example, the debate over the Nazi past did not begin until the 1960s. An important catalyst for this debate was the student movement for a democratization of German society, which was not yet completely de-Nazified.[7] In the United States, similarly, the debate on the history of slavery really only began after African-Americans successfully fought for civil rights, in the 1950s and '60s.[8] It was only then, for the first time, that there was a call for monuments, that museums were founded, books were written, and scholarly debates were conducted on the many aspects of slavery. The new citizens refused to live with an amputated past. The right to know about the conditions of life in the past is among the civil rights of a democracy. The process of democratizing memory, with all its detours and wrong turns, is part of the confusing situation of a pluralistic society that must come to terms with conflicting internal interests.

7 See Gesine Schwan, *Politics and Guilt: The Destructive Power of Silence,* trans. Thomas Dunlap (Lincoln: University of Nebraska Press, 2001).

8 See Gert Oostindie, ed., *Het verleden onder ogen, Herdenking van de slavernij* (The Hague: Arena/Prins Claus Fonds, n.d. [1999]).

The Effort of Memory   Four different aspects of the effort of memory will be discussed here. Before doing so, however, it may be useful to state that societies face their problematic histories with varying degrees of adequacy. As I have said, nations living under dictatorships have no interest at all in dealing with history well; for them, the red carpet suffices. It does not follow, however, that nations that are democratic always resist the seduction of the red carpet. Slavery, for example, was abolished in the Netherlands in the nineteenth century, by which time it must already have been clear that this peculiar institution contradicted the fundamental equality of all individuals. Yet for decades after its abolition, no mention of it was to be found in Dutch history books. The national history of the seventeenth and eighteenth centuries remained as glorious as ever. Only in recent years have lively discussions of problems of slavery been heard, and only now, in 2001, has it been decided that a national monument on the history of slavery will be built. England, one of the first nations to abolish slavery, was also ahead of other countries in founding a museum of its history, in Liverpool.

In Holland, the public debate on slavery, with the ensuing discussion of a memorial, comes thanks to pressure from immigrant groups from the former colonies, especially those in the Caribbean. It is a case of their history being brought to light, and of their democratic right to their own past. A liberal democratic society that refuses to recognize its problematic past discriminates against the social groups that carry this unrecognized past around with them.

What does this have to do with those who did not commit any atrocity, and who probably never would have? What do they have to do with this history? To what should they confess? They never sold slaves or put Jews and Gypsies in concentration camps. Why should anyone even deal with memory work in their own society?

This point concerns the first aspect of the effort of memory: it is appropriate when the truth of one's own way of life is under debate. In a democratic society, citizens have the right to perform the work of memory. Those who want to inform themselves about their own society run up against these problems whether they like it or not. Teachers, spiritual leaders, journalists, historians, and others who pass on knowledge of their society should not overlook this.[9] They have a responsibility to the truth. They are concerned with contexts in which recognizing the past as a part of the existing way of life is absolutely necessary – even if, as individuals, they had nothing to do with it.

The truth is not relative. It can compel one to recognize the past as a part of one's own political self-understanding. This is what Jürgen Habermas is aiming

9 See Frank Martinus Arion, "Een 'beau geste,'" in ibid., pp. 19–23.

at when he writes about the Holocaust Memorial in Berlin: "As citizens of this country we take an interest in the darkest chapter of our history – in the criminal activity of the perpetrator and the problematic behavior of the generations of perpetrators – especially when we are interested in reconstructing our own political identity."[10]

The effort of memory, however, is not only a matter of disclosing the truth; there is also the political question of how much disclosure a society can stand without disintegrating. I have already mentioned Mamdani's entirely legitimate critique of the way the Truth Commission spared the beneficiaries of apartheid. The commission's work, however, under the direction of Bishop Desmond Tutu, would not have been possible without such a concession. In this respect the truth can indeed become relative. Not only questions of truth but inevitable problems of power assert themselves in the effort of memory. Tutu's modesty in delivering the commission's report to President Nelson Mandela was no accident; to sum up what had been achieved, he remarked, "There has been some truth, some reconciliation. Now there is a face, there is a name for the cry of anguish."[11]

The issue of a truth commission's authority, and general questions as to whether a truth commission or even a tribunal should be set in place during the establishment of democracy, are much to the point. As studies of the roles of truth commissions show, no broad answers are possible. Much depends on the political context. Even when it is quite clear that the deposed regime committed crimes, legal action cannot always be taken in cases where punishment is merited on moral or legal grounds. And this brings me to perhaps the most difficult point, and to the third aspect of the effort of memory: the necessity of justice. Justice does not depend on truth findings and pragmatic policy questions alone. The democratization of memory affects not only the past but the future as well.

In which ways can victims be offered restitution? Moral recognition and revelation of the truth are not enough; material support is also essential, as was provided in postwar Germany, for example, to the survivors of the Holocaust. The material compensation that was paid to the relatives of the disappeared and murdered in Chile and Argentina can also be mentioned here.[12]

Financial reparations to the descendants of slaves are controversial. How are the damages that their ancestors doubtless suffered, and that they themselves continue to suffer, to be assessed, and translated into concrete sums of money?

10 Jürgen Habermas, "Der Zeigefinger: Die Deutschen und ihr Denkmal," *Die Zeit* (Hamburg), March 31, 1999, pp. 42–43.
11 See Peter Hawthorne's article on the Truth Commission's report in *Time,* November 9, 1998.
12 See Hayner, *Unspeakable Truths,* p. 314.

Which persons and groups should be considered for such payments? In my opinion general sociopolitical measures are more in order here: support must be supplied to groups that lack economic, social, and cultural opportunities, just as their ancestors did. The fact of being economically deprived or underprivileged can easily be transmitted from generation to generation; imaginative and promising social projects are needed, and a fair amount of money will have to be spent on them. Though financial reparations cannot reverse history, they offer prospects for the future. Social and material agencies provide public recognition that people have been done injustice, that in the past they have been victims of political crimes. If they have been frozen in a bad situation, as some of them have, this may help them to move out of it. Paradoxical though it may sound, just the acknowledgment that cruelty and abuses of power were suffered can serve to ease the "victim status" of the people affected.

It sometimes happens that suffering in the past is instrumentalized instead of palliated. Groups and even whole peoples can be politically seduced into insisting on their victim status. Their former suffering becomes their most valuable asset, and everything that happens is evaluated in its light. In this way the suffering is kept alive instead of overcome. Genocide can be justified, for example, in the name of a genocide suffered. Similarly, while compensation can be a first step toward justice, a repetition compulsion in dealing with traumatic memories can be the occasion for new injustices. The state of Israel is an example; Israeli Arabs and Palestinians are deprived of their legitimate civil rights. I am not one of those who believe that Israel has no legitimate rights in Palestine – a view, incidentally, that a majority of Israeli Arabs and Palestinians no longer hold. But it remains true that uncompromising groups in Israel commit injustices that they justify by appealing to the oppression of their own people in the past. In this way they instrumentalize their previous suffering. The ties with the past are not loosened. This kind of memory effort makes history something permanent, an immovable obstacle in the future.

Memory efforts that are not publicly visible do not exist. Here we touch the fourth aspect of the process under consideration. When people in new democratic circumstances confront the past, such a confrontation must find cultural expression. Recognition in a purely formal sense – through apologies, for example – is not enough. The same is true of monetary compensation. Memory efforts have a surplus value in relation to the facts, to power, to morality, and to money, and this surplus value can find expression in art. Our everyday languages are practical instruments formed by all kinds of experiences. Works of art create new languages and open up worlds that were previously unknown.

As signs of efforts of memory, works of art can only be unconventional, surprising, even provocative. To bring individuals and groups to the point of asking themselves what actually took place back then, traditional means are insufficient. People just pass them by. Instead of monuments one needs countermonuments, obstacles to conventional memory such as those made by the Austrian sculptor Hrdlicka, or, in the past, by painters like Goya and George Grosz. These works of art don't bow to the heroes of the past but instead make it possible to discuss the terrors of repression and war. They force the spectator into the work of memory, like it or not.

Such countermonuments raise questions about the traditional monuments one comes across in every great city. What should happen to them? Must they be maintained as symbols of the ritual attitude to the past, something every nation seems to need? Or should they, as an organization in Germany once suggested, be technically outfitted so as to slowly sink – a couple of centimeters a year – into the ground?

In my opinion, they must remain where they are. Nations, after all, haven't disappeared from the earth as yet. The democratization of memory is not a process of harmonization. It is contradictory, bringing to light unknown and unpopular chapters of history. It should not marginalize other attitudes to the past but put them in question. The controversies it starts can be carried out publicly and peacefully, and can include debate on the symbols through which individuals and groups are trying to come to terms with their past.

Translated from the German by Diana Reese

Constructing Memorials

Susana Torre

The international mobilization of shame over state violence has inspired the creation of numerous new artworks and monuments. These memorials are not merely reminders of pain and loss; they are also part of the worldwide opening of cultural memory to previously unacknowledged violations of human rights.[1] However, like monuments to conquest – whose aim is nearly the opposite[2] – they may be doomed eventually to fall into oblivion, their original purpose forgotten and their intended message ignored. Thus the challenge before their organizers, designers, and builders is to find ways to keep alive the memory of victims of crimes against humanity in the hope of preventing future generations from ever allowing such suffering again.[3] It is essential, then, to ask, What are the processes and circumstances that give memorials an enduring visibility? What are the factors that give a mute structure the power to construct or evoke a story about a past and to impart lessons for the future?

Ultimately, I believe, a building alone cannot summon the persistent reinscription of memories without commemorative ceremonies specifically connected to its program.[4] However, there are certain conditions that make a structure more or less effective at provoking or inviting such reinscription. Although one of these conditions may be more important than the others in any given memorial, they always achieve their effects in combination. To understand how they interact, we shall need to consider each separately. I call them *site*, *purpose*, and *representation*.

1 I am using the concept of "cultural memory" as it is developed by Jan Assman in "Collective Memory and Cultural Identity," *New German Critique* 65 (1995), to signify collective memory inscribed in rituals, texts, images, and monuments recalling momentous historical events. See also the pioneering work of the French sociologist Maurice Halbwachs, *La Mémoire collective* (Paris: Les Presses Universitaires de France, 1950).

2 Current literature makes a distinction between "monuments," built to commemorate victories, and "memorials," dedicated to grief and loss. See Marita Sturken, "The Wall, the Screen and the Image: The Vietnam Veterans Memorial," *Representations*, no. 35 (Summer 1991): 118–42.

3 Throughout this essay I use terms such as "victim," "atrocity," and "crime against humanity" in their legal sense, as it has evolved since the Nuremberg trials after World War II.

4 On the concept of memory as it is embodied in rituals, see Paul Connerton, "Commemorative Ceremonies," *How Societies Remember* (Cambridge: Cambridge University Press, 1989), pp. 41–71.

Krzysztof Wodiczko,
Projekcja Publiczna
(Town Hall Tower
Projection), video
projection on the
tower of the town hall
of Krakow, Poland,
1996

Site   On a night in 1996, Krakow's most shameful intimacies lit up its proudest
public space, as artist Krzysztof Wodiczko projected images evoking domestic
violence against women onto the fourteenth-century tower of the town hall.
Only the women's hands were visible – one holding a candle, another peeling
potatoes with the same knife that had threatened her life – as each woman's
voice was heard telling her story. As in his many other public art projects, Wodiczko was projecting the testimony of victims and witnesses of violence onto a
major public landmark.[5] The resulting overlapping of personal and collective
memory was designed to enlarge the cultural meaning of a place through an
event – itself memorable – that announced a discomfiting fact: the state's failure
to protect women and children from violence, sometimes fatal, in contrast to its
success in persecuting undesirables, often by violent means. Wodiczko's projects
take monuments and other sites whose iconic meaning has been forgotten and
appropriate them for the construction of a new memory. Against the passivity of
stone, mortar, and metal, his projections stimulate active remembrance in the
audience, witnesses who become responsible for the memory's preservation as
the images fade from sight.

Wodiczko's installations allow him greater latitude of expression than
would more permanent memorials to probe difficult truths. Public monuments, by contrast, are meant to embody official memory, which often
involves a compromise between competing stories. Another difference is that
after Wodiczko's projections the sites he has used revert to their customary

5 See Ken Shulman, "A Monument to Mothers and Lost Children," *New York Times*, September 20,
1998, Arts and Leisure Section, pp. 40–41.

Women in Military
Service for America
Memorial, Arlington
National Cemetery,
Washington, D.C.,
dedicated 1997

invisibility, except as they may be charged with new meaning in the audience's personal memories.

As Wodiczko's work recognizes, site is critical in the construction of cultural memory. By *site* I don't mean only a specific plot of land, but its position in the palimpsest of cultural memory that is the city. Whether ambitious structures or simple tablets with commemorative inscriptions, monuments reveal a hierarchy of memory in public space. When a memorial is placed at the actual location of the event it commemorates, the connection between site and meaning is direct, and the site itself is the real memorial. When a memorial is remote from the site of the event, it becomes more dependent on its relationship to the city's symbolic *lieux de mémoire*.[6] Brigadier General Wilma Vaught understood this when she chose a site hidden behind the existing ceremonial entry wall of Arlington National Cemetery for the Women in Military Service Memorial, in preference to more visible sites offered by the state.[7] She evidently thought that embedment in one of the most hallowed places of the U.S. military, no matter how tenuous, would enhance the memorial's power.

The Washington Mall is the United States's most sacred framework for memory. This is why the promoters of the Vietnam Veterans Memorial insisted on that setting, as due reparation for the years of national indifference

6 The term is Pierre Nora's. See his essay "Between Memory and History: *Les Lieux de mémoire*," *Representations,* no. 26 (Spring 1989), for a discussion of this concept.

7 Marion Weiss, codesigner of the memorial, discussed this decision in her presentation at the conference "Inherited Ideologies," at the University of Pennsylvania in March 1995. See also Weiss, "The Politics of Underestimation," in Diana Agrest, Patricia Conway, and Leslie Weisman, eds., *The Sex of Architecture* (New York: Harry N. Abrams, 1996), pp. 251–62.

The display of the entire NAMES Project AIDS Memorial Quilt on the Mall, Washington, D.C., October 9–11, 1992

and hostility to the soldiers of that war.[8] But the Mall also evokes memories of protests as well as mourning. Thus the display of the NAMES Quilt, whose every piece represents a person who has died of AIDS, elicited eerie associations as it covered the entire mall, much the way the living had in rallies demanding the government's attention to human rights. Recently, demands that cultural memory be made more inclusive have led to the construction, on the Mall's margins, of new memorials to Martin Luther King, Jr., and to black patriots who fought in the Revolutionary War. Similarly, it is the location of the planned World War II memorial on the Mall, rather than its contested neo-classical style, that gives the project its special significance. By its placement between the Washington Monument, a celebration of the nation's independence, and the Lincoln Memorial, commemorating the end of the Civil War, it seems to imply that the saga of national unity has been finally achieved through a "definitive" war, a war that signaled the beginning of the hegemonic presence of the United States as a world power. After the planned World War II memorial, however, a permanent moratorium on memorials on the Mall has been decreed, threatening to turn what was an open framework into a kind of straitjacket for memory.[9]

8 Senator Charles McC. Mathias, Jr., an early supporter of the memorial organizers, identified the site. Because the selection did not follow established procedure, it required the approval of Congress. The story of how this was obtained is well described in Joel L. Swerdow, "To Heal a Nation," *National Geographic*, May 1985, pp. 555–73.

9 See Elaine Sciolino, "Fighting for Space in Memorial Heaven," *New York Times*, June 26, 2001, p. A24, and "Agencies Limit New Memorials on Coveted Washington Mall," *New York Times*, September 7, 2001, p. A14.

The long-hallowed memories attached to a particular site can also be used in more subversive ways, that is, to undermine the place's preexisting associations. Such is the effect of building a recent Holocaust memorial on Vienna's Juden-platz, a square where an old plaque celebrates the medieval burning of a syna-gogue as the praiseworthy punishment of "the terrible crimes of the Hebrew dogs."[10] The siting of Berlin's Holocaust memorial on the former site of the Berlin Wall, adjacent to the Brandenburg Gate, makes a less ironic but no less powerful statement: its location implies that the city's partition and the wall that reified it were somehow connected to the monstrous crime commemorated there. The implication is that recognition of that crime is necessary for the city's reunification.

Promoters of other memorials may have given too little attention to the importance of site. In Buenos Aires, Argentina, for example, human-rights groups mobilizing to build a "Monument to the Disappeared, Detained and Assassinated by State Terrorism" – a monument to be located in a newly desig-nated "Parque de la Memoria" (Park of memory), far from the city center – seem to have been more concerned about the use of public funds than about fighting for a more compelling, accessible site in which to inscribe the memory of the military state's political intolerance.

Purpose By *purpose* I denote the underlying agenda, usually manifested in the selection of the site, the type of its inscription (museum, archive, or memorial), and the formulation of the ideas and values to be represented, whether that for-mulation occurs with or without broad consultation. Memorials to the victims of atrocities cannot satisfy demands for truth and justice; these are issues better addressed by truth commissions, courts, and human-rights groups. Memorials, rather, serve the aims of creating a place for grieving, publicly recognizing suf-fering, and acting as a permanent reminder of a crime so that it may not be repeated. In these ways they can help survivors transform their present trauma into a past – into memory.[11]

How such aims are to be achieved is articulated in the memorial's program. In their different ways, archives, museums, and memorials filter and frame how and for what purpose memory will be preserved. Archives and museums, in their retelling of a story, become sites of perpetual reinscription – unless the process of inscription has been so hindered by the politics of assigning blame

---

10 See James E. Young, *At Memory's Edge* (New Haven and London: Yale University Press, 2000), p. 109.
11 I am grateful to Dr. Marta Aizenman for her insight on this matter, and for her recommendation of Judith Herman's *Trauma and Recovery* (New York: Basic Books, 1992), especially chapter 9, "Remembrance and Mourning," pp. 175–95.

that silence replaces narrative. This is the case, for example, with Tuol Sleng, in Phnom Penh, Cambodia.[12] Some types have evolved to contain multiple forms of inscription, as in the National Holocaust Museum in Washington, D.C., which includes galleries for historical narration, extensive archives for scholars, and major symbolic spaces.

Memorials are usually built as sites for grieving, symbolic graves. This function is especially important when there is no actual known burial place, as in the case of people whom the authorities or terror forces have caused to "disappear."[13] Memorials then become surrogate sites for mourning, a ritualized performance that is necessary to continue reinscribing the memory. Without such rituals these sites tend to become "invisible," or at least unnoticed, unless they are attached to a larger site of memory.

Unlike an archive or museum that presents a multiplicity of viewpoints, including that of the victims, a memorial tells one story, which tends to become identified as official memory – at least when the memorial is built in a public space and with the resources or the implicit or explicit approval of the state. There are of course many unofficial memorials (New York City's ubiquitous murals depicting police brutality, for example, which may appear on public streets but occupy private walls, as posters do), and these neither demand nor imply official consensus; an artist with a contrary view may simply paint another mural on the same or an adjoining wall. But official memorialization, in officially controlled public space, does not easily tolerate dispute. When people want to challenge official memory, they almost always feel obliged to topple or remove the old monuments. This happened not long ago in Jedwabne, Poland, when it was revealed that a massacre of Jews attributed to the Nazis had in fact been carried out by the Jews' own Polish neighbors. Local officials were not content to try to "correct" the message of an existing memorial to the massacre, or to build a new one beside it – an approach that would have documented the memorial's own history, including the attempted shift of blame.[14] Instead, at least partly out of embarrassment, they felt it necessary to erase the previous official history and replace it with a new one.

12 Unlike didactic exhibits at some of the former concentration camps in Germany, which feature exhaustive research aimed at creating an understanding of the historical framework, those at Tuol Sleng consist of photographs and documents presented as bare evidence of atrocities, but without a narrative structure.

13 A moving testimony on this situation can be found in Gustavo Bruzzone's interview with Tati Almeyda of the Mothers of Plaza de Mayo, Buenos Aires, "Quiero tocar el nombre de mi hijo … " (I want to touch my son's name …), in *Ramona* (Buenos Aires) 9–10 (2000): 10–12.

14 See Adam Michnik, "Poles and Jews: How Deep the Guilt," *New York Times*, March 17, 2001, p. B7.

The purpose of some memorials is to attempt a form of retribution, a symbolic settlement of accounts that facilitates reconciliation without forgiveness.[15] This is the underlying text of many prominent recent memorials, including Berlin's Holocaust memorial; as described above, the siting of this memorial on the former line of the Berlin Wall, adjacent to the Brandenburg Gate, is an appeal for acknowledgment of the connection between the state's complicity in crime and the subsequent partition of the city and indeed of the entire nation. This is a clear example of how *site* can be used to express a memorial's *purpose*.

In the United States, the organization promoting the Vietnam Veterans Memorial specifically stated its purpose as encouraging national reconciliation, which the memorial was to do by focusing on the names of dead and missing soldiers and on the grief shared by both those who had supported the war and those who had opposed it. Reconciliation was further aided by the participation of celebrities, intellectuals, and politicians on both the right and the left, who helped raise funds from a wide spectrum of the U.S. population. The project of reconciliation within the United States, however, required an amnesia about the devastation of Vietnam, and the incomparably larger loss of life there. This has prompted other veterans to return to Vietnam to establish a very different type of memorial, explicitly directed more toward the future than the past: the founding and supporting of schools, as a gesture of goodwill initiated by individual Americans.

Some artists have attempted to counteract the traditional redemptive and consolatory purposes of the memorial. One such "countermonument" is the German artist Jochen Gerz's conceptual memorial *2146 Steine – Mahnmal gegen Rassismus* (2146 stones – monument against racism), in Saarbrücken, Germany (1993).[16] The work consisted of replacing seventy cobblestones in a major square in that town, in front of an old palace that had once served as a local headquarters of the Gestapo. The cobblestone replacements, identical with the originals, were inscribed with the names of obliterated Jewish cemeteries in Germany – of which there were over 2,000 – but then were placed with the carved side down and the unwritten-on face up, so that the information would be invisible. The square was officially renamed "Place of the invisible memorial." Gerz believes that visitors provoked by the name will want to "repair and fill in

---

15 Avishai Margalit, a professor of philosophy at the Hebrew University in Jerusalem, states that "reconciliation, unlike repentance, is a symmetrical relation." See the report of the working conference "Truth and Reconciliation," organized by the Prince Claus Fund for Culture and Development and Documenta11 at The Hague, July 6, 2000 [see p. 63 in this volume]. In my disagreement with his assertion I draw from Jacques Derrida's speculative argument in "On Forgiveness," *On Cosmopolitanism and Forgiveness* (London and New York: Routledge, 2001).

16 See Young, *At Memory's Edge*, pp. 140–44.

Jochen Gerz, *2146
Steine – Mahnmal
gegen Rassismus Saar-
brücken* (2146 Stones
– Monument Against
Racism Saarbrücken),
Saarbrücken,
Germany, 1990–93

the now absent event with their knowledge of it,"[17] although the ability to remember over 2,000 cemeteries would be beyond most people's expectations.

Gerz's memorial returns us to the question of an artist's latitude of expression, for his work was created without the knowledge of the local inhabitants or authorities. Confronted with the memorial as a fait accompli, the Saarbrücken parliament's Christian Democratic Union contingent walked out on the vote to rename the square after a memorial whose existence could be doubted. The countermonument, originating in a "subversive" art practice, was in the end legitimized ex post facto as official memory through cultural, not political, discourse.

Gerz's work had the virtue of opening the discourse of memory construction to criticism from within, a much needed debate over half a century after the war, a period in which hundreds of Holocaust memorials had been built all over the world. But each tragedy is unique, and must unfold in its own time before it can reach the stage at which such a work is appropriate. Valuable as countermonuments are as cultural critique, we cannot expect them to replace redemptory memorials when the time is proper for grieving.

Political activists have also given us countermonuments in the form of ritualized ceremonies. The Mothers of Plaza de Mayo's iconic circular procession around the central monument in the Plaza de Mayo, Buenos Aires, Argentina's most important public space, still continues today, eighteen years after the reinstatement of democratic government ended the period of disappearances and

17 Jochen Gerz, quoted in ibid., p. 144.

Mothers of Plaza de
Mayo's circular proces-
sion, Plaza de Mayo,
Buenos Aires

assassinations under the military regime of 1976–83.[18] The purpose of these
demonstrations is to prevent national closure on the episode; with this march,
in which any woman wearing the emblematic white scarf can stand for a
Mother, the activists continue to press for a revocation of the amnesty granted
to the kidnappers and killers, and for the return of their spouses and children –
"alive." Even in the face of evidence that bodies were dumped from military
planes into the Rio de la Plata, making them irretrievable, the Mothers fear that
accepting their relatives' death, and the compensation offered by the state,
would preclude the punishment of the guilty. In their literal embodiment of
lived memory, they continue to oppose, symbolically and politically, the very
idea of memorialization.

Unlike Gerz's countermonument, constructed by the individual memory of
historical events, the Mothers' presence on the square is a perpetual reminder of
unfinished justice, challenging observers to join in the construction of a present-day collective memory. The Mothers' own memorial to their disappeared, a
counterinstitution that expands the range and types of memory inscription, is a
nomadic popular university, whose courses – ranging from political analysis to
street performance art – seek to keep alive the utopian political ideals now
homogeneously attributed by the Mothers to all the victims of state repression.[19]

18 I discuss the formal structure of the Mothers' ritualized march in my essay "Claiming the Public
   Space: The Mothers of Plaza de Mayo," in Diana Agrest, Patricia Conway, and Leslie Weisman,
   eds., *The Sex of Architecture* (New York: Harry N. Abrams, 1996), pp. 241–50.
19 The curriculum of the Universidad Popular Madres de Plaza de Mayo can be found at
   www.madres.org/universidad/escuelas/arte/programa.htm.

Sir Edwin Lutyens,
Memorial to
the Missing of the
Battle of the
Somme, Thiepval,
France, 1932,
and India Gate,
New Delhi, 1921

Representation   *Representation* refers to the designs and visual languages employed to communicate the ideas that are the main purpose of the memorial. What should memorials to victims of atrocities represent? Trauma? Loss? The brutality of the perpetrators? The grief of the survivors? The continuity of life? The suppressed ideals of the victims? The question of representation is bound in with the memorial's purpose and program; even if these have not been made explicit, representation must always presuppose them. And as we have seen in the discussion of the siting and purpose of the Holocaust memorial in Berlin, representation is also bound in with the site and the context, which will often inspire the design.

In general, memorials created by architects gravitate toward the tropes of official memory, whereas those created by artists have sometimes successfully undermined those tropes. But representation is in either case bound in with the history and structure of the preexisting practices and discourses of architecture and art. In earlier times, the continuity provided by architectural styles contributed to the intelligibility of all civic buildings, including memorials, even when they bore the burden of representing historical trauma, such as the extraordinary loss of life in World War I. Some scholars have interpreted Sir Edwin Lutyens's Memorial to the Missing of the Somme at Thiepval, France, as an "antimonument," because he challenged the traditional monumentality of the arch by inscribing its otherwise unornamented surfaces with the names of the 73,357 dead and missing soldiers, and by multiplying or inverting some architectural features.[20] Nonetheless, its intelligibility as a monument relies upon the conventions of the trope, as does Lutyens's other war memorial in New Delhi. India Gate is similarly inscribed with the names of colonial soldiers

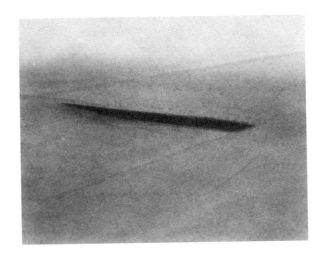

Maya Lin, competition sketch for Vietnam Veterans Memorial, Washington, D.C., dedicated 1982

– though in this case the structure is more conventionally used as a monumental entrance to a precinct of colonial government buildings and open spaces. In any case, the time for such gestures is past. The old unified language of memorials has been shattered; when the subject is rupture, absence, and loss, classical arches and columns – the enduring tropes of victorious monuments – have become unbearable.

In the search for a new language of memorials, the two paradigmatic projects of recent years are Maya Lin's Vietnam Veterans Memorial, in Washington, D.C., and Daniel Libeskind's Jewish Museum, in Berlin (not to be confused with the Berlin Holocaust memorial discussed elsewhere in this essay). These works share a language of abstract minimalist forms that stand in opposition to their immediate contexts – the neoclassical structures in the Washington Mall, and the baroque building housing the neighboring Berlin Museum. Both achieve their exemplary quality through powerful convergences of the narratives of site, purpose, and representation. The ways in which they represent loss, however, are very different, each work being anchored in the specific history of that which is mourned.

As discussed above, the choice of a site in the Washington Mall for the Vietnam Veterans Memorial was understood as a kind of compensation for past public indifference to the veterans' losses, and the memorial's stated purpose was to provide a place for national reconciliation. The representation of loss is most

20 See Hélène Lipstadt, "Thiepval in the Age of the Anti-Monument," *Harvard Design Magazine*, Fall 1999, pp. 65–70. In her thoughtful and detailed analysis of Sir Edwin Lutyens's monument, Lipstadt also discusses the views of other scholars and designers, including Vincent Scully and Maya Lin.

Jewish Museum,
Berlin, designed by
Daniel Libeskind,
1998–2001

obvious in the names of the dead soldiers carved into the monument's stone, and the design itself is a symbolic grave, cut into the earth and barely defined by the stone's polished black surface, in which visitors see their own faces. The inescapable association of oneself with the collective loss is deeply emotional, giving the memorial an enormous power of catharsis. Lin's minimalist forms, eloquent as they were, did not represent the heroism of the soldiers in a way recognizable to many veterans, who passionately demanded to have it publicly acknowledged. Thus a conventionally figurative statue of soldiers was added nearby to record the contested official narrative of the memorial.

In the case of the "extension of the Berlin Museum with the Jewish Museum department," as Libeskind's building is officially called, the design was chosen through an architectural competition in which the representation of loss was a requirement. In that the brief challenged the designers "to acknowledge the terrible void [in the city's history and culture] that made this museum necessary," it specifically prevented the form from suggesting "reconciliation and continuity" – quite the opposite of what was required for the Vietnam Memorial.[21] The structure, which is physically separate from the Berlin Museum but connected to it by an underground corridor, derives its lightning-bolt-like plan from the designer's distortion and fragmentation of the Star of David, as he sought to create a "metaphysical map" of the city by joining the addresses of Berlin's cultural figures with that shape. But the spatial continuity of the structure, instead of allowing an uninterrupted display of historical exhibits, is purposely broken up

---

21 See Young, *At Memory's Edge*, p. 159.

by several multistoried voids, marking the loss of narrative stability. The voids intersect the plan along a line conceived as the structure's conceptual backbone, the opposite of a conventional axis with spaces to either side, leading and building up to a major ceremonial space. The function of Libeskind's axis, however, is to void space, to make it inaccessible, and to enforce spatial fragmentation. Permanent loss, like that caused by the Holocaust, involves that which can never be attained or recovered.[22]

Both memorials are conceived within the possibilities of an expanded architectural discourse, and both are immediately intelligible. For this reason they have influenced the designs of scores of other memorials. Unfortunately, what many subsequent designers have emulated is not Lin's and Libeskind's method of finding the form in the specific historical facts in each case, but rather the memorials' surface characteristics. Thus countless state and municipal Vietnam memorials merely reproduce a version of a V-shaped black shiny wall inscribed with names.[23] There is even a traveling version, a folding "wall" half the size of the original, which can be displayed in places where there is no permanent memorial as a backdrop for local commemorative ceremonies. What these popular memorials represent is no longer the loss. Rather, they are representations of a representation, rooted in neither context, site, nor purpose but deriving all their authority and civic intelligibility from their model. Through postmodern artistic and design practices such as reproduction and collage, elements of such paradigmatic memorials have reappeared in such dissimilar places as Argentina, Rwanda, Bosnia, and South Africa, regardless of the particular nature of the human-rights violations committed in each place. They have become inscribed in what Andreas Huyssen has called the "transnational discourse of memory,"[24] referring to all suffering in general and no suffering in particular.

The Monumento a las Víctimas del Terrorismo de Estado (Monument to the victims of state terrorism) being built in Buenos Aires is an example of the representational possibilities and limitations of these transnational art practices. The memorial consists of three parts: a large mound cut through by a passage lined with stone panels, on which, on alternating sides, are inscribed

22 This fragmented space has proven an intractable challenge for curators, as the space frustrates the succesful display of objects. Daniel Libeskind may have intended this space more as a symbolic memorial to loss and absence than as a place to recover the loss through the presence of cultural artifacts.

23 Web links to the sites of most U.S. Vietnam veterans' memorials can be accessed through http://grunt.space.swri.edu.

24 See Andreas Huyssen's essays "El Parque de la Memoria. Una glosa desde lejos," *Punto de Vista* (Buenos Aires), December 2000, pp. 25–28, and "El Parque de la Memoria: The Art and Politics of Memory," Harvard University DRCLAS Winter 2001 Newsletter, available at www.harvard.edu followed by a search for "Huyssen."

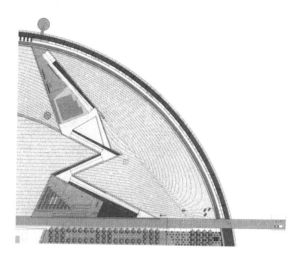

Parque de la Memoria
(Park of Memory),
Buenos Aires, design
by Baudizzone,
Lestard, Varas Studio
and associated archi-
tects Claudio Ferrari
and Daniel Becker

the names of the victims of state violence; a space inside the mound, to be used
for exhibitions and lectures on issues related to the losses memorialized here;
and a grouping of eighteen sculptures, twelve of which were selected through
an international competition.[25] The site is a stretch of newly planned water-
front parkland that will also hold a number of other memorials. It is far from
the city center and from the Plaza de Mayo. It is close to military institutions,
however – including the infamous Escuela Superior Militar Argentina
(ESMA)[26] – and to the incomplete Ciudad Universitaria, created by the military government in the early 1970s to enclose and control faculties with a history of political activism.

What is being represented here? At first glance the design is a hybrid of the
Vietnam Veterans Memorial, including the ancillary sculptures, and the Jewish
Museum in Berlin. But despite the names inscribed in it, the uninterrupted
jagged gash is not a symbolic grave. Rather, it is a passageway to a real grave, the
river in which many of the victims were dumped while still alive. The memorial
has been described as a "deep wound" in a "breast" (the mound), in whose
depth private grieving is to be hidden.

An alternative proposal by the architect Clorindo Testa would have extended
the memorial's meanings to include specific historical context and references to

25 For the names and works of the artists participating in the competition, see www.parquede-
   lamemoria.org.ar. The designers of the monument are Baudizzone, Lestard, Varas, and Becker &
   Ferrari.
26 Torture chambers were maintained at the Escuela Superior Militar Argentina under the military
   government of 1976–83.

Clorindo Testa,
proposal for Parque
de la Memoria (Park
of Memory), Buenos
Aires, 1999

the class origin of most of the victims.[27] In his proposal, a similar passage inscribed with names would have been covered with a metal trellis and a Santa Rita (bougainvillea) vine, evoking at once the residential patios in working-class neighborhoods – where many of the victims lived – and a blooming suture over the "wound." The carving of the names on the panels would have been supplemented with engravings of contemporary newspaper pages, instructing visitors about the victims. In the context of the official story of the repression, these men and women were homogenized in death; with the information Testa proposed supplying, it would have been clear that they were a diverse group, with a range of political beliefs, including proponents of armed struggle, people accused of no more than owning subversive literature, and innocent friends and relatives who may not have been politically active at all. This would have made the modus operandi of the state terrorists, and the arbitrariness of the terror, more apparent.

Whereas in the case of the Vietnam Veterans Memorial the statue of soldiers was added in response to political demands, the sculptures in Buenos Aires represent the artists' personal responses, for which no agreed-upon set of issues was collectively developed. Their primary form of inscription will be as artworks in a sculpture garden, a framework that will reinforce their self-referential condition and the ahistorical abstraction of the ideas they represent: utopia, absence, convulsion, silence.

27 Clorindo Testa's proposal received a Fourth Mention in the international competition, which received 665 submissions, but it will not be executed.

Constructing Memory: Themed Enclosures and Transnational Discourses   The sites of memorials may have many-layered meanings, a collective struggle may take place to clarify their purposes, values, ideas, and emotions, and the clarity of their representations may be compelling, yet none of this is necessarily enough to make specific memories endure. Unless reinscribed generation after generation, cultural memory fades, and its markers may be assigned new and contradictory meanings. We therefore need to understand how the reinscription of memory may be affected by two recent trends: the defining of enclosures of memory in the city, and the emergence of a "transnational discourse of memory."

In response to a worldwide demand for memorials to victims of atrocities or to a suppressed historical past, planners have moved to restrict building in sites deemed overcrowded by monuments, or have proposed extending existing sites. In Washington, D.C., for example, land behind the U.S. Capitol building, which closes one end of the now protected Mall, has been made available for recent and future memorials, including the National Memorial to Japanese-Americans, which commemorates them both as World War II heroes and as victims of internment.

Urban planners have also seen new memorials as elements of urban development, creating spaces specifically for that purpose. The south end of New York's Battery Park City, where a new memorial to the great famines in nineteenth-century Ireland is to be located,[28] is one example (although all plans for that area must be in abeyance after the attacks of September 11, 2001); Buenos Aires's new Parque de la Memoria is another. Both show the influence of postmodern urbanism and one of its favored devices, the theme park. Will themed precincts like these develop their own framework for the inscription of memory? Or will they be marginalized repositories from their inception? To claim attention in these new memory parks, will each memorial have to be made spectacular, and will this quality work against their meditative and reflective functions?

Older memorials invoked painful social conflicts through the semblance of people identified with them, such as Martin Luther King, for civil rights, or Abraham Lincoln, for the abolition of slavery. The new memorials instead attempt to represent the issues themselves, and the concepts and emotions associated with them. We need to be alert to the danger that the transnational discourse of memory that inscribes and is inscribed by these memorials may become so general, so generic, that the memory of each specific violation is severed from the historical conditions that produced it.

---

28 See David W. Dunlap, "Memorial to the Hunger, Complete with Old Sod," *New York Times*, March 15, 2001, p. E1.

September 23, 2001. Postscript As I was readying this essay for its editors, I watched from my rooftop as the towers of the World Trade Center were destroyed in less than an hour and a half by a suicidal terrorist attack. At this writing, it is thought that the toll of the missing and presumed dead could exceed 6,000 – people of all economic classes, ethnic groups, and nationalities. Since September 11, 2001, the people of New York have been congregating in public squares in spontaneous memorials and vigils, to mourn and to reassure ourselves of our solidarity with other living people. To most cosmopolitan New Yorkers, the towers were not symbols of the United States's financial power, as they were intended to be a quarter of a century ago; that power is by now physically dispersed, and better symbolized by the flickering of stock indexes on computer screens. In the premodern frame of reference of the attackers, however, the World Trade Center and the Pentagon must have been sexually charged symbols of their enemy's financial and military might, and the destruction of the towers the emasculation of the enemy. Did they expect Westerners to look at this destruction as a kind of countermonument, a vengeful memorial to the Iraqi or Palestinian victims of American bombs? And how are the victims of the attack on the World Trade Center to be memorialized themselves? Does one memorial deny the other?

The rubble is not yet cleared, and there have already been calls to rebuild the towers in the manner of the Soviet reconstruction of buildings and entire urban districts razed in World War II, trying to replicate what was there before. Others want the site to remain open, a space of silence and commemoration, in the manner of the memorial to the victims of Timothy McVeigh's attack on the federal office building in Oklahoma City. Two artists whose workspace was on the 91st floor of the north tower have already proposed an ephemeral memorial in the form of powerful beams of light rising from a reflecting pool, reflecting a view of the towers as "ghost limbs we can feel even though they are not there anymore."[29]

But capitalist logic will demand the rebuilding of a valuable Manhattan property, and nationalist sentiment will likely demand the restoration of the skyline as the most visible sign of the country's unbreakable strength, even if large financial-service companies may never return to occupy the site of their catastrophic loss. To build a new World Trade Center on the ruins of the old would be to pretend that what happened never did; to focus the discussion on how the site should be rebuilt – instead of on what should be built, and why – would be to confuse purpose with appearance. A rebuilding of the site capable

---

29 See "Filling the Void: A Memorial by Paul Myoda and Julian LaVerdiere," *The New York Times Magazine*, September 23, 2001, p. 80.

of matching the imagination of those who plotted its demise will require an understanding of the extent to which New York is a "world center" for so many different communities, cultural and scientific as well as financial. New York is a cultural artifact that now belongs to the world because it embodies the potentialities of the urban global community. That is the reason it should be made whole again. And any rebuilding of the site will be entwined with the issue of what is to be memorialized and how it is to be represented.

Between Truth and Reconciliation:
Experiments in Theater and Public Culture

Rustom Bharucha

Traversing a series of fragments – stories, anecdotes, memories, and testimonials – this essay will reflect on the instabilities of truth and reconciliation within the relatively marginal sites of theater and public culture. I would stress these instabilities not just because truth and reconciliation mean different things to different people in different cultures at different points in time, particularly at moments of crisis; more critically, I would emphasize that the relationship between truth and reconciliation is essentially volatile. This would not appear to be the case when we see these terms coupled together, as it were, bound by a seeming causality – at a normative level, an exposition of truth would seem to result in the possibility of reconciliation. In actuality, however, this is not always the case. My strategy in this essay, therefore, will be to infiltrate the seemingly innocent conjunction "and," in order to open up its troubled dynamics. Indeed, "and" could prove to be more explosive than either "truth" or "reconciliation."[1]

It is perhaps inevitable that the performative mode of analysis adopted in this essay should draw on my own background in theater. Indeed I have consciously opted for a certain play in the narrative, an informality of tone, and a nonlinear structure to expose some of the sacred cows of the truth and reconciliation discourse.[2] Not that this discourse is my immediate subject here, but arguably no reflection on truth and reconciliation today, in whatever context,

---

1 By problematizing what lies *between* "truth" and "reconciliation," rather than "truth" itself as "the road to reconciliation," I take a somewhat different strategy from the philosopher Avishai Margalit, who also questions "the putative causal relation" between truth and reconciliation. For a pithy critique of this causality, read his essay "Is Truth the Road to Reconciliation?," presented at a seminar on Truth and Reconciliation, organized by the Prince Claus Fund for Culture and Development and Documenat11, The Hague, July 6, 2000 [see pp. 61–64 in this volume].

2 This discourse has grown in several languages and spans several continents where truth commissions have functioned in societies confronting the vicissitudes of "transitional justice." Between 1974 and 1994 there were at least nineteen such commissions, in Bolivia, Chile, Argentina, El Salvador, Uganda, Chad, and Ethiopia. In recent years, however, it is the commission in South Africa that has dominated the truth and reconciliation discourse through the sheer depth and range with which it has been discussed, not least in the global media. The South African Truth and Reconciliation Commission (TRC) officially started its work on February 1, 1996, following its

Rustom Bharucha

can afford to ignore its spectral omnipresence. Now hegemonized as a model for truth commissions elsewhere, the postapartheid Truth and Reconciliation Commission of South Africa, or the TRC as it is more widely known, serves as both inspiration and provocation for my own problematization of truth and reconciliation in this essay. Even as I do not confront its historical moment directly, it interrupts my narrative, asserting its presence when I least expect it. At times it strategically disappears, only to haunt my own unanswered questions. Unavoidably, I deal with the TRC experiment obliquely, or through erasure. What is *not* said about it is perhaps more significant than what gets written in this essay.

Genocide, torture, massacres, institutionalized racism: these axiomatic horrors underlying the quest for transitional justice are not the primary reference points in this narrative, even as I focus on communal violence in the Indian subcontinent. But here again the references are oblique, and when they appear more directly, they are mediated through representations of different kinds. Likewise, even as I shift the grounds of this essay from theater practice to public culture, the legacies of Dachau and Hiroshima are mediated through spectatorial speculations within the imaginary recesses of memorial museums, located within the interstitial tensions of the civil and the political. I make these qualifications at the outset of my essay to prepare the reader for the indeterminacies of what is perceived to be marginal. What is marginal need not be valorized, but it has the potential to offer another perspective on dominant narratives, and even to deflect their hegemonic assumptions. My intervention in the truth and reconciliation discourse is one such experiment in telling a different story.

The "Truth" of Storytelling   There can be few illusions about truth in the practice of theater, where truth is neither an absolute nor a given. Indeed there is no one truth but many possible truths – mutable, fluid, and above all deviant – that have to be constantly produced from the guts, bodies, and voices of actors. Given the transitory nature of theater, truths are constantly breaking down; given its repetitions, truths have to be reconstructed, relived. The paradox of truth-making in theater increases when one acknowledges that theater can be

formal sanction in the South African parliament in July 1995, through the Act on the Promotion of National Unity and Reconciliation. In December 1996, President Nelson Mandela appointed seventeen commissioners of the TRC, who, along with eleven co-opted members, formed three committees: the Human Rights Violations Committee, the Amnesty Committee, and the Reparation and Rehabilitation Committee. The proceedings of the TRC ended on July 31, 1998, and its final report was handed to President Mandela on October 29 of the same year. Its repercussions in postapartheid South Africa have spawned a growing discourse on truth and reconciliation, in both the civil and the political sectors of society.

one of the most illusory places in the world, where it is legitimate to lie know-ingly.[3] And yet truth matters.

I will be focusing here not so much on the gradations of lying in relation to truth as on three motifs that run through my discourse: evidence, memory, and storytelling. Stories matter in any exposition of truth, not only because they enable us to illuminate elusive realities but because they help us to deal with the aporias of pain. The writer Isak Dinesen once said, "All sorrows can be borne if you put them into a story or tell a story about them."[4] The word "borne" is equivocal: in the context of Dinesen's statement, it means "endured," but it also hints that pain is actually "born" – created, stimulated, embodied – through the telling of the story itself. Endorsing Dinesen's statement, though not my equiv-ocal reading, Hannah Arendt extends it in her reflections *Between Past and Future*: "To the extent that the teller of factual truth is also a storyteller, he brings about that 'reconciliation with reality' which Hegel ... understood as the ultimate goal of all philosophical thought."[5] Perhaps this is a magisterial assumption on Arendt's part, even though it is generous in its qualification ("*To the extent* that the teller of factual truth is also a storyteller"). There is no such qualification in the Report of 1998 that emerged out of the Truth and Reconcil-iation Commission of South Africa, where it becomes only too clear that the teller of factual truth is not a storyteller, or, more emphatically, that the story-teller is no teller of facts.

In fact the Report differentiates sharply between "factual or forensic truth" and "personal and narrative truth," among other truths. Predictably, "factual truth" is defined as a form of scientifically "corroborated evidence," drawn on "accurate information through reliable (impartial, objective) procedures," framed within a social-science methodology of research.[6] This truth is unequiv-

---

3 This is somewhat different from the political realm, where lying can be regarded as the uncon-scious prerogative of politicians, their second nature. Certainly Hannah Arendt has no illusions in this regard: she designates lies as "necessary and justifiable tools not only of the politician's or the demagogue's but also of the statesman's trade." While the professional truth-teller is out of place in the world of politics, the liar is "already in the midst of it." An "actor by nature," he refuses "to say what is" (the truth-teller's responsibility); rather, he "says what is not so because he wants things to be different from what they are." In short, he is a "man of action," which the truth-teller is not. Arendt, "Truth and Politics," in *Between Past and Future: Eight Exercises in Political Thought* (Harmondsworth: Penguin Books, 1993). The question is: how do we view the actor in theater, who is neither a professional truth-teller nor a habitual liar? It would seem that the actor's position is more liminal, as he or she is committed to conveying the truth of "what is" while recognizing the illusion of "what is not."
4 Isak Dinesen [Tania Blixen], quoted in Arendt, *Between Past and Future*, p. 262.
5 Ibid.
6 Truth and Reconciliation Commission, *Truth and Reconciliation Commission of South Africa Report*, quoted by Mark Sanders, "Truth, Telling, Questioning: The Truth and Reconciliation Commission, Antjie Krog's *Country of My Skull*, and Literature after Apartheid," *Transformation* 42 (2000): 74.

ocally prioritized in the Report. "Personal and narrative truth" conveyed through the medium of storytelling, in contrast, is granted at best some kind of "healing potential" for the victims in particular.[7] Yet it would be disingenuous to deny that these stories provided the primary evidence of the TRC – indeed, the most terrible truths of the violence of apartheid were voiced through personal stories. But to what end? Ultimately it would seem that the "truth" of storytelling was too "subjective" to hold up as accurate evidence. Within the rigors of the written word, as opposed to the volatility of the spoken word, the "veracity" of stories was called into question, even if "they provided unique insights into the pain of South Africa's past."[8] Given this patronizing attitude, it is hard to imagine that apartheid's storytellers could be reconciled with reality, still less with their fractured selves – although this lapse would be emphatically denied by the TRC's advocates.

Having acknowledged this lapse, I would also emphasize that there is a privilege in telling a story, even a sense of empowerment. Some stories become epics in their own right, so much so that it is possible, in retrospect, to view the entire TRC proceedings as one master narrative, out of which have emerged best-selling documentary metafictions like Antjie Krog's *Country of My Skull* (1998). This masterpiece of reportage, compiling the testimonies of both the victims and perpetrators of apartheid, has all the ingredients of a Hollywood blockbuster in the Steven Spielberg tradition. Sadly, many hundreds of truths that were never submitted to the TRC are unlikely to be part of this blockbuster. It should be remembered that out of the literally millions of South Africans who were persecuted, humiliated, tortured, and evicted from their homes during the apartheid regime, only 21,400 submitted statements in around 140 public TRC hearings countrywide. This is a record in its own right, but it also falls terribly short of exposing "the entire truth." We need to acknowledge, then, that not every history of pain finds itself articulated in a story: this truism has yet to be fully acknowledged in the globalizing of human tragedies and world crises.

In India as well, we are seeing how the narrative of the Partition is being centralized as the master narrative on the basis of which the trauma of the subcontinent can be assessed. I would not deny the importance or the pain of articulating this narrative; the problem is that it threatens to become *The* Partition, marginalizing other partitions that have yet to be narrativized. What happens to these unacknowledged partitions, these undisclosed truths? Their stories, I suspect, remain submerged in the unarticulated narratives of pain, and it is these

---

7 Truth and Reconciliation Commission, *Truth and Reconciliation Commission of South Africa Report*,
   5 vols. (Cape Town: Truth and Reconciliation Commission, 1998), 1:112.
8 Ibid.

narratives – these minor stories and small instances of pain – to which I would like to call attention in this essay. I draw inspiration in this regard from Walter Benjamin's finely inflected refusal to distinguish between major and minor events: "A chronicler who recites events without distinguishing between major and minor ones acts in accordance with the following truth: nothing that has ever happened should be regarded as lost for history."[9]

Questioning Ancestry   With this truth in mind I present my first fragment of evidence. It is drawn from a meeting with an Australian aboriginal storyteller, a grandmother figure who greeted me at a conference in Brisbane with the words, "You are walking on the land of our ancestors." I remember responding tentatively: "Yes?" A question rather than an affirmation, because her statement left me with doubt, unrest, and yet a need to believe in its truth.

1) At one level I doubted the statement because there was no visual evidence to support it – the storyteller's words signified one thing but the site of our conversation (the anonymous lobby of a modern hotel) seemed far removed from the land of anyone's ancestors. I could not relate what I was hearing to what I was seeing.

2) I also felt uneasy because I couldn't help picking up a fundamentalist echo in the words "land of our ancestors." This echo comes from the politics of my own location in post-Ayodhya India, where invocations of ancestry by the Hindu Right invariably affirm an exclusionary, territorial, atavistic "truth." This "truth" gets verified through quasi-fascist uses of traditional categories like *pitribhumi* (fatherland) and *punyabhumi* (holy land),[10] which have assumed specific antiminoritarian connotations in India's contemporary political culture, apart from legitimizing claims on land and "disputed sites" on a communal basis.

Of course I am aware that these are different contexts of ancestry. In the context of Hindutva, ancestry is claimed by sections of the majority community in power, who are inexplicably threatened by "minorities" who remain "foreigners," "barbarians," if not "traitors" at a civilizational level, and who refuse to be

---

9 Walter Benjamin, "Theses on the Philosophy of History," in *Illuminations: Essays and Reflections* (New York: Schocken Books, 1968), p. 62.

10 The history of these terms goes back to the rhetorical foundations of Hindutva, whose ideologue V. D. Savarkar defined "The Hindu" in 1923 as "a person who regards the land of Bharatvarsha from Indus to the Seas as his Fatherland [*pitribhumi*], as well as his Holy Land [*punyabhumi*] – that is the cradle land of his religion." Quoted in Tapan Basu, Pradip Datta, Sumita Sarkar, et al., *Khaki Shorts, Saffron Flags* (New Delhi: Orient Longman, 1993), p. 8. Since this particular authentication of ancestry is unavailable for other religious communities, notably Muslims, this logic inevitably brands them as foreigners, if not as *mlecchas* (barbarians).

accommodated within the presumably "tolerant" norms of brahminical Hinduism. In contrast, the First Peoples of Australia claim land rights and the restoration of dignity on ancestral grounds even as they have been ruthlessly minoritized over the years, and inadequately represented in government. Obviously different political constituencies are shaping contexts of ancestry in different ways in these cases. Even so, the fundamentalist echo remains, and I am disturbed by it.

3) A third dimension needs to be acknowledged: not every truth registers at a general, ideological level. When the aboriginal storyteller tells me, "You are walking on the land of our ancestors," it is a direct statement, made personally to me, with full eye-contact (the much fetishized sign of "authentic" communication in theater language). For all my reservations, I am compelled to recognize its "emotional truth." Indeed I can't deny that I am in the land of *her* ancestors, but these ancestors are not necessarily *ours*. Indeed I have no particular desire to connect to the land of *my* ancestors, because it would be irrelevant to my sense of truth.

The relativity of truth, then, depends not merely on different locations and contexts, but on different needs, privileges, and deprivations. For whom is it absolutely necessary, at an existential or political level, to assert a truth relating to ancestry? And for whom is it an irrelevance, even an embarrassment? How does one justify critiquing the valorization of one truth at the expense of ignoring another? And conversely, how can one not critique a particular truth if it offends one's "moral sense," to appropriate a phrase of Gandhi's?

Memory and Evidence   In any invocation of the past there is an activation of memory, which may be one of the most volatile agencies in determining the evidence in any context of truth and reconciliation. I recently conducted a workshop, "Land and Memory," with a group of indigenous people called the Siddi from the Indian state of Karnataka. Of negroid descent, the Siddi migrated to India some two centuries ago from the eastern states of Africa, some as slaves, others as traders. Today they live in scattered settlements in different states of South India and in Gujarat in western India, speaking different languages, practicing different faiths, almost oblivious of each other's existence. Not only do they fail to constitute an identifiable "community" within the nomenclature of the state, they are so marginal that they don't seem to matter at all. This is the fate of those minorities in India who fail to constitute a viable vote-bank. As the unacknowledged blacks of the subcontinent, the Siddi of Karnataka live for the most part an extremely marginalized existence on forest land, which is technically illegal.

Unlike the aboriginal peoples of Australia, the Siddi would seem to have no primordial link between land and memory. From my interaction with the people of Manchikeri, who work as agricultural laborers, it became clear that they do not – indeed cannot – claim land on ancestral grounds. This would be counterproductive for them, given that their origins in Africa (marked by the color of their skin) continue to highlight their "foreignness" in India. The more salient point is that the Siddi have no articulated "memory of Africa" as such, nor are they particularly traumatized by this absence of knowledge relating to their racial origins; indeed they are not even curious about it. But if they have no memory of Africa, this does not mean they have no memory of the land on which they may have lived for twenty to thirty years. Memory, it should be remembered, is an elastic phenomenon; one can go back thousands of years, or one can call attention to the moment that has just passed but that is already a memory.

From the Siddi I learned that memory is not "a storehouse of the past"; it is more like a processing agency that is constantly transforming "the present" into a historical record. Significantly, the primary source of mnemonic transformation for the Siddi is song, through a musical tradition called *damami* (which literally refers to a drum), and the richest evidence of their history is also song. *Damami* is both a means of recording the present and an inventory of the past. Unlike truth commissions, which see a definite rift between what is remembered through stories and what gets accepted as evidence in written historiography, the Siddi make no separation between what is remembered and what counts as evidence.

A problem inevitably arises when this evidence is not acceptable or intelligible within the language of the state. In their struggle for political identity, for example, the Siddi seek to be categorized within the official nomenclature of the state as Scheduled Castes (SCs) or Scheduled Tribes (STs), categories that come with specific benefits and privileges relating to housing loans and educational facilities for children. The difficulty concerns the negotiation of this language of the state with the oral tradition in which Siddi history is documented and lived. During my "Land and Memory" workshop I confronted precisely this schism of conflicting languages, not least when we encountered the minister of social welfare for Karnataka, who disrupted our workshop with a thoroughly meaningless visit. After enduring the paternalistic non sequiturs he directed at a bunch of "lazy natives," I realized it was time for an experiment.

"Why don't we improvise the minister?" I suggested to the Siddi after the minister left. In the reenactment that followed, the actor-minister, appropriately masked, sitting regally on a red plastic chair, demanded to see the documents of the Siddi: "You're liars. You don't have any rights on this land. Where are your documents?" To which one of the Siddi women pointed out some trees: "See those trees? We planted them with our own hands some twenty years ago. Those trees are our documents." This, I realized, was a subaltern truth that countered the official truth of documentation, reversing its logic and asserting a different criterion of evidence, based on ecology rather than bureaucratic certification.

This is not the place to elaborate on how the process of generating awareness through theater can be activated in real life. What I would emphasize is that my work with the Siddi could only begin after I had confronted their seeming "reconciliation with reality" through song. Only by rupturing this tradition of song through improvisations and exercises was it possible to arrive at some critical confrontation of political truth. I had to move from reconciliation to truth, thereby reversing the dominant assumption that reconciliation is only possible through an exposition of truth. Let me now focus on this causality to demonstrate how it can be ruptured through a reflexive intervention in yet another theater experiment.

The Fiction of Reconciliation   For this I will have to tell you a story – or, more precisely, a story within a story. I have told this story elsewhere, in contexts relating to secularism and intercultural exchange.[11] If I narrate the story again, it is because it has not yet been exhausted; indeed, from its fictional interstices it yields new insights into the possibilities of reconciliation. Underlying the story is the problematic reality of caste in India as at once a politicizing agency for social change and one of the most enduring forms of dehumanization. Caste is a particularly tricky reality to tackle in theater, not least because it tends to get "invisibilized" within the seemingly secular structure of modern theater. I remember a company of actors who once reassured me, "We don't have any caste in our theater. We're all outcastes anyway." I thought this was a joke until I actually started to cast the production I was directing for them: only then did I realize how casting could catalyze a caste war in the group.

Some years ago I conducted a workshop in the rural area of Heggodu, Karnataka, where I have conducted most of my theatrical experiments. Before the workshop started I had seen a photograph of a low-caste *dalit*, a landless laborer. The photograph had been taken not far from Heggodu; it showed the laborer

11 Rustom Bharucha, *The Politics of Cultural Practice: Thinking Through Theatre in an Age of Globalization* (London: The Athlone Press, Hanover: The University of New England Press/Wesleyan, and New Delhi: Oxford University Press, 2000), pp. 121–22, and Bharucha, "Negotiating the 'River': Intercultural Interactions and Interventions," *The Drama Review* 41, no. 3 (Fall 1997): 34–35.

tied to a stake, stripped almost entirely naked, with a shit-smeared *chappal* (slipper) rammed into his mouth (as the caption to the photograph indicated). This instance of "documentary truth" detailing an atrocity on a particular *dalit* testifies to the widespread phenomenon of caste violence, particularly in rural India.

I cannot say that the photograph catalyzed my interaction with the actors, but it was there somewhere in the back of my mind. In my theater work I have found that the moment I articulate the intention underlying my intervention in a workshop, the process of finding truth has already been instrumentalized. The reality is that when you posit truth, you are unlikely to find it, because it has already been assumed or predetermined. To discover truth in theater you have to accept that it is inadvertent; it hits you when you least expect it, through an unfolding of the political unconscious.

Another truism of theater: you have to work with what is available. In this particular workshop I found myself in a large empty room with fifteen young actors from different parts of Karnataka. The only object in the room was a water container with a stainless-steel cup from which we all drank unconsciously. I began an exercise with this cup in which it was transformed into different objects. At one point it became a bomb. I took the bomb from the actor who had transformed it and placed it in the center room. "Can you believe that this is a *saligrama*?" I asked.

What is a *saligrama*? A small, fossillike sacred stone that can fit in the palm of the hand, it embodies the godhead. I had not seen a *saligrama* at the time, but I had imagined it through the fiction of the writer U. R. Anantha Murthy, of Karnataka. In an episode in his novel *Bharathipura*, a young Brahmin socialist returns from England to his ancestral home, which adjoins a temple-town in Karnataka. Fired with socialist truth, he embarks on a mission to free the untouchables in his village by making them enter the temple, which they are prohibited to do. Being something of a performer, he is not content merely to facilitate the action; he is compelled to *perform* it, in a ritual of de-casteing himself (and others). Taking a *saligrama* from outside the prayer room of his ancestral home into the public space of the outer courtyard, where the low-caste laborers have assembled, he shows it to them and asks them to touch it. They instinctively retreat in fear – after all, it is taboo for them even to see it. The more our socialist hero tries to reassure them that "it's only a stone," the more its sacred aura is enhanced. Finally he commands them to touch it – he may be a socialist but he is also a feudal lord. And they have no option but to do so. Then they flee in terror, leaving him examining the *saligrama* alone. Finally he throws the stone into the darkness.

"Can you believe that this cup is a *saligrama*?" How this question surfaced from my own political unconscious I cannot say, but I do know that even as I was uttering the question, the coercive possibilities of my directorial intervention were not lost on me. Such is the trust implicit in the imaginary explorations of the theater, however, that I found the actors exposing their individual caste truths through specific gestures in relation to the "*saligrama*." While some of the upper-caste actors had no difficulty in caressing, anointing, and prostrating themselves before the object, the low-caste actors either retreated from the "*saligrama*" altogether or tried to touch it only with great diffidence. This was a moving and painful revelation of the differentiations of caste, which were surfacing for the first time in our group. Needless to say, our secular solidarity was completely shattered.

It was at this point that I felt the need to intervene with another fiction, but one of my own making. When truth is exposed in theater at very personal levels, you can't retreat from it. You can't stop the process right there because it would be too painful. You have the responsibility to transform that moment of pain into something else, or you risk disrupting the possibility of reconciliation. Entering the narrative of the actors as an actor in my own right, I thought aloud: "This was a cup which we took entirely for granted. At some point it became a bomb. Then it became a *saligrama*, in which some of you believed and others didn't. But now, when I look at the *saligrama*, I realize that it's only a cup of water, from which we can all drink in a ritual of our own making." We passed the cup around, and when it returned, I asked, "Does the cup feel different from the time when you first started the exercise?" And from the smiles and intimate solidarity of the group, I could feel that it was very different, because *we* were different. Something had happened to us as a group. We had traveled from a rather painful exposition of individual truths to a reconciliation as to how we could relate to each through an acknowledgment of difference.

On a less euphoric note, I would acknowledge that even within the protected confines of theater, no reconciliation is absolute. Indeed most reconciliations are fragile, partial, and in constant need of renewal. While one group of individuals could reconcile with each other's differences, this very reconciliation could be the source of tension with another group. Such was the insight I received all too harshly following the *communitas* of the "*saligrama*" experience. In a room adjoining the theater workshop, another "experiment" was at work, conducted by the Rashtriya Swayamsevak Sangh (RSS), who were indoctrinating the young boys of the village with familiar invocations of militant Hinduism, reinforced through allusions to "our" Vedic ancestry. Needless to say, there is no place for minorities in this ancestry.

The questions that I am now compelled to ask in the aftermath of the workshop necessarily complicate the imagined comfort and endurance of reconciliation. If caste differences can be resolved within a theatrical framework, is it possible to extend these lessons to antisecularist forums? What are the limits of conflict resolution through imaginary processes? Can the imaginary be translated into the political? More concretely, is it possible to reconcile differences across religious and political communities? Or do we accept that, at the best of times, in the most democratic of circumstances, reconciliation is only possible between and across individuals? Reconciliation across entire communities is a harder proposition.[12]

Limits of Truth Commissions   With these questions we have obviously entered the political domain, a domain in relation to which the experiments in theater that I have described so far are linked yet separated. Now I would like to complicate the agencies of truth and reconciliation further as I confront the emotional dynamics of truth commissions. Obviously there can be no direct transference between the process of truth and reconciliation facilitated through an intimate workshop and the more formal proceedings of a truth commission. The workshop, it could be argued, is far too private, even hermetic, in its process of exploring truth through fiction and symbol. It can prepare the ground, as the "*saligrama*" workshop did, for a more inflected secular bonding and interactivity with cultural difference, but it would be a mistake to read in this preparation any guarantee of political enlightenment. The workshop was nothing more, though nothing less, than a performance.

It could likewise be argued that the South African TRC functioned as a performance in its own right – a grand performance, in fact, represented live in the actual forums of the hearings and also disseminated through daily radio and television programs. On these multiple sites, the "extravagant drama" of the TRC, as Albie Sachs describes it, was played out in a wide range of registers, at levels of pain and trauma that would be hard to imagine. Witnesses periodically broke down, and unlike judges in court, Archbishop Desmond Tutu, the commission's chairperson, was seen weeping openly during the sessions, as well as praying,

---

12 The paradigmatic example of reconciliation across communities is the much cited aftermath of the Great Calcutta Killing of August 16, 1946, in which 4,000 people were killed. In a historic intervention, Gandhi became a one-man truth commission to whom perpetrators and victims on both sides of the communal divide presented their testimonials, and peace gradually prevailed with the acceptance of collective responsibility and the advice of the Mahatma to "turn the searchlight inwards." While this event is a landmark in the history of conflict resolution, it begs the question of whether the reconciliation across communities could have been initiated and sustained without Gandhi's messianic and personalized intervention. To whom were "Muslims" and "Hindus" reconciling – to each other? To Gandhi? Or to each other via Gandhi? For a sound analysis of this event in a larger cross-cultural perspective on truth commissions, see Rajeev Bhargava, "Between Revenge and Reconciliation: The Significance of Truth Commissions," unpublished ms., 2000.

lighting candles, and bursting into song. Tellingly, this "extravagant drama" was at once authenticated as the primary site of "truth" and discredited for its emotional "excess." Instead of accepting the tears, cries, and sobs of the victims as nonverbal signs of the destruction of language through pain, they became the very grounds on which the exposition of truth was distrusted. Archbishop Tutu was taken to task for reducing the hearings to "tearful occasions," thereby undermining his own impartiality. As Claudia Braude has written, the commission's impartiality was undermined by "truth that is *felt*." Tears "raise[d] questions about the TRC's legitimacy." Indeed, "truth and tears counter[ed] each other."[13]

Only a few independent interlocutors of the TRC process were able to deal with the phenomenological complexity of emotional breakdowns in illuminating the truth underlying the witnesses' testimonials. Here is one such analysis, which focuses on a particular eruption of crying that interrupted the testimonial offered by Nomonde Calata:

> For me, the crying is the beginning of the Truth Commission – the signature tune, the definitive moment, the ultimate sound of what the process is about. She was wearing this vivid orange-red dress, and she threw herself backwards and that sound ... that sound ... it will haunt me for ever and ever ...
>
> ... [T]o witness that cry was to witness the destruction of language ... was to realize that to remember the past of this country is to be thrown back into a time before language. And to get that memory, to fix it in words, to capture it with the precise image, is to be present at the birth of language itself.
>
> But more practically, this particular memory, at last captured in words, can no longer haunt you, push you around, bewilder you, because you have taken control of it – you can move it wherever you want to. So maybe that is what the Commission is all about – finding words for that cry of Nomonde Calata.[14]

Deeply sensitive as this analysis is to history and sound, the reality is that it constitutes a minority view. It would be more accurate to say: "What the Truth Commission is all about – *not* finding words for that cry of Nomonde Calata."

13 Claudia Braude, "The Archbishop, the Private Detective and the Angel of History: The Production of South African Public Memory and the Truth and Reconciliation Commission," *Current Writing* 8, no. 2 (1996): 61.
14 This fragment from the dense analysis of Nomonde Calata's cry is made by one of Antjie Krog's numerous interlocutors in *Country of My Skull* (Johannesburg: Random House, 1998), pp. 55–66. The interlocutor is identified as "Professor Kondlo, the Xhosa intellectual from Grahamstown," who makes his comments while listening to extracts from Nomonde's testimonial on tape. Krog is both a listener and the recorder of the entire event, including both the voices of Nomonde (on tape) and Kondlo (live).

Apart from the incapacity to deal with the nonverbal dimensions of truth-telling, a fundamental discrepancy was built into the very structure of the hearings. If the radical though unconventional premise of the TRC was to facilitate the voicing of truth in a public forum, where the perpetrators of the crimes had the assurance of receiving amnesty for their actions (so long as they could be related to "political objectives"), then the possibility of reconciliation for the victims via the negotiation of reparations needed to be followed through within the nonjudicial structure of the hearings. To posit a nonjudicial structure for the exposition of truth, and at the same time to accept a judicially "rigorous" mode of verifying the truth through an independent committee, is to risk abdicating truth after facilitating its utterance. While amnesty for the perpetrators of political violence was the *condition* on the basis of which the TRC was allowed to be set up in the first place, the legal and moral right of the victims to obtain reparation was *postponed* until after the hearings could be adequately assessed and discriminated. Clearly there is a disruption in the time-continuum of this truth and reconciliation process, which demands a critical rethinking of the political implications of telling stories in public.

The irony is staggering: even as the victims continue to wait for their meager reparations, the perpetrators of violence have assumed their new roles as the beneficiaries of the South African global economy. Instead of using this irony to initiate a new process of truth, the majority of the TRC's supporters continue to uphold the reconciliatory power of sharing "the pain of South Africa's past" through stories. "What is important," as the TRC Report implies, is "not so much *what* is told (which has to be verified, and is thus suspect), but rather *that* telling occurs."[15] Likewise, skeptical as he is that "truth" can be regarded as "a road to reconciliation," the philosopher Avishai Margalit is sanguine because, even if retributive justice for the victims is unavailable (this "can be too costly or a political impossibility"), the positive outcome of the TRC was that the suffering of apartheid's victims was duly "recognized."[16]

One could quote many other instances in which the perceived emotional catharsis of telling stories has been interpreted as a contribution to the culture of reconciliation. Here is a diary extract from one of the Commissioners of the TRC, Piet Meiring, who approaches an old Xhosa woman shortly after she has narrated the brutal torture and subsequent killing of her fourteen-year-old son:

15 Sanders, "Truth, Telling, Questioning," p. 75.
16 Margalit, "Is Truth the Road to Reconciliation?" p. 64 in this volume.

"Please, tell me: was it worth it?"

The tear marks were still on her cheeks. But when she raised her head and smiled, it was like the dawn breaking:

"Oh yes, sir, absolutely! It was difficult to talk about these things. But tonight for the first time in sixteen years, I think I will be able to sleep through the night."[17]

One wonders if this is still the case, or whether the old woman has been summarily forgotten after her heartbreaking evidence. It would be useful to know, for instance, if she received any medical or material help while waiting to hear from the Reparation and Rehabilitation Committee, if indeed she qualified for any compensation in the first place. Reconciliation without reparation, it would seem, is at best a wish-fulfillment for the TRC's historians, at worst a perpetuation of injustice for apartheid's victims. First the victim tells her story, she is ostensibly "healed" through the process, she "touches the hearts" of her listeners, the TRC is duly "enriched" through the process, but ultimately she is subject to the rhetoric of a reconciliatory discourse over which she has no control. It is assumed that she endorses the official point of view being articulated in her name, but in actuality the possibility of her dissent or sense of betrayal or frustration with the TRC process is not even acknowledged.

As the TRC has formally come to an end, the utopian hope built into the voicing of victims' stories becomes increasingly more difficult to sustain, both at human and ideological levels. It would be better to acknowledge the limits of the South African "experiment," whose premises, however idealistic and quirky, were not intrinsically flawed; the problem is that the experiment didn't go far enough on its own terms. It allowed itself to be hijacked by other bureaucratic, judicial, and political protocols and strictures that not only compromised the moral authority of the commission but may even have perpetuated the trauma of the victims themselves.

Between the exposition of truth and the possibility of reconciliation there needs to be a modulation of energies whereby the listeners and interlocutors of truth, including the perpetrators, assume a collective responsibility in caring for the future of the victims. The keyword here is "care," which, more often than not, is circumvented within the nonjudicial processes of truth commissions, despite tokenistic gestures for providing remedial and psychological facilities for the victims and their families. In the absence of any sustained follow-up in consolidating new modalities for "caring," it could be charged that the TRC in

17 Piet Meiring, "Truth before Justice and Reconciliation: The South African Experience," address at the Centre for Dialogue and Reconciliation, New Delhi, December 2, 2000, pp. 5–6.

South Africa merely imitated formal judicial procedures in which the very idea of "caring" is obliterated within the mechanisms of justice.

In this regard I would call attention to an astonishingly "transgressive" truth acknowledged by the Indian legal scholar Upendra Baxi in relation to the absence of the "spheres of caring" within "the governing rhetoric of rights and justice."[18] I emphasize "transgressive" because Baxi's prioritization of "care" works totally against the grain of judicial omniscience and nonnegotiability, which is the source of much activist disillusionment in India today. As he puts it, "Constitutional decision or policy-makers present themselves as being just, even when not caring. ... it is notorious that constitutional cultures remain rights-bound, not care-bound."[19] Baxi attributes this indifference to "the poverty of social theory imagination," where justice is actually separated from fraternity (or sisterhood) – fraternity, "in its most minimal sense, of concern for fellow-citizens." In any case it becomes necessary to uphold other agencies of caring that can supplement the amnesia of the law. "Just" verdicts "beyond all reasonable doubt" can and frequently do result in the traumatization or displacement of ordinary people with no adequate rehabilitation or reparation, still less reconciliation to their fractured lives. This is a fact that demands a different reading of truth in relation to the abdication of justice.

The Performativity of Suffering   Moving farther outside the theater into the public sphere, I will now elaborate on other ways of giving testimonials, ways that are not catalyzed by directors or writers or truth commissions but are performed by ordinary people in states of crisis. I consciously use the word "performed" because there is a strong gestural, somatic, and visual dimension to the ways in which victims choose on occasion to present themselves, not to highlight their victimhood but to protest the crimes inflicted on them. In this regard I would like to focus now on the sociologist Veena Das's research on the anti-Sikh riots in New Delhi in 1984 following the assassination of Indira Gandhi by two Sikh security guards, leading to a carnage of communal violence that activated memories of Partition. In one fragment of her research, Das describes a group of Sikh women whose men have been slaughtered in the riots:

> As long as their suffering was not acknowledged and addressed, [the women] insisted on sitting outside their ruined houses, refusing to comb their hair, clean their bodies, or

18 Upendra Baxi, "Saint Granville's Gospel: Reflections," *Economic and Political Weekly*, March 17, 2001, p. 928.
19 Ibid.

return to other signs of normality. Here the somatic practice drew deeply from the
Hindu tradition of mourning and death pollution … I am not claiming that this discourse was explicit – it functioned rather as an unconscious grammar, but fragments of
it were evoked when the women insisted that the deaths of their men should not go
unavenged. I remember one instance in which there were rumors that Mother Teresa
would visit the colony. X [a politician from the Congress Party] … implored the
women to go back to their houses, to clean up the dirt and to return to some normality.
They simply refused, saying he could himself sweep the remains of the disaster if that
offended him.[20]

Anger and revenge, so emphatically silenced in the proceedings of the South
African TRC, are the two motifs that surface in this fragment. What matters to
these women is not reconciliation but the recognition of the truth of violence on
their own terms, which assumes a performative dimension. On the one hand
there is the collective display of bodies in a state of "pollution," which, as Das
reminds us, recalls at a mythic level the violated figure of Draupadi from the
Mahabharata. Shared by the five Pandava brothers, lost in a game of dice, and
subsequently humiliated and raped, Draupadi refuses to remove the "signs of
pollution from her body" – notably her disheveled hair, which is invariably used
as a sign of her anger. In Kathakali performance the actor playing Draupadi
always tugs "her" hair as a reminder of what has been done to her. In their Drau-
padi-like mythic personae, the women described by Das are not grieving widows
and victims; they are not doing what we expect them to do, as demonstrated in
documentary reportage and the television news, which capitalize on the grief of
others. Instead they are witnesses, even sentinels, of their own suffering.

Along with this witnessing there is a decision-making process at work here
relating specifically to how the women wish to be seen in the eyes of the law,
which in turn would prefer *not* to see them in that state. In this process Das
emphasizes that the "passive display of pollution" is so "terrible" that "it could
not even be gazed at." However, this very difficulty (if not assault on the eyes)
converts the "female body into a political subject that forcibly [gives] birth to a
counter-truth of the official truth about the riots."[21] The body, then, is not just
a source of pollution; it becomes a site of political evidence.

There are many such instances in the contemporary history of activism in
India, where women activists have been assaulted and even gang-raped. Instead

20 Veena Das, "The Spatialization of Violence: Case Study of a 'Communal Riot,'" in Kaushik Basu
and Sanjay Subrahmanyam, eds., *Unravelling the Nation: Sectarian Conflict and India's Secular
Identity* (New Delhi: Penguin Books, 1996), p. 201.
21 Ibid.

of covering up their scars, they have vigilantly "guarded" the signs of violence on their bodies *as evidence* in order to obtain adequate testimonies, through medical examination, of the crimes inflicted on them. While these testimonies have not always resulted in justice, they invariably assume a symbolic significance, becoming "stories" that feed the imaginaries of resistance and provoke renewed struggle in the absence of reconciliation.[22]

Representing Victimhood   Once again we return to stories and to what happens to the truth of evidence in the process of telling them. It is one thing for a woman to tell her own story, quite another when it is told for her. While one cannot assume that the first narration is necessarily more "true" than the other, the exploitative potential of another telling the story of her life cannot be ruled out. It all depends on *how* the story is told, to *whom* it is being shared in the first place, and *why*.

At one point in the multilayered narrative of *Country of My Skull*, which is as much an experiment in storytelling as it is an agonized reflection on telling the truth of the TRC in South Africa, Krog recalls a conversation with Ariel Dorfman. Known for his stories dealing with the truth commission in Chile, which unlike the South African TRC was held behind closed doors, closed off from public scrutiny, Dorfman acknowledges that his writing is a hybrid of "what he's heard" and of "what he makes up."[23] Krog questions him: "Isn't that a sacrilege – to use someone else's story, a story that has cost him his life?" To which Dorfman responds candidly, "Do you want the awful truth? How else would it get out? How else would the story be told?"[24]

This stark revelation is made "fictional" in an extraordinary stroke of reflexivity as Krog incorporates this conversation into another, more intimate conver-

---

22 The case of Bhanwari Devi is symptomatic here. A *sathin* or social worker based in the most feudal constituencies of Rajasthan, she was the target of a gang rape by a group of upper-caste men who reacted violently to her activist interventions in the propagation of child marriage. While her exemplary courage in testifying to the violence inflicted on her is widely recognized, the rapists were acquitted of all charges in November 1995 by the district sessions judge in Rajasthan, who claimed, "Since the offenders were 'upper' caste men and included a Brahmin, the rape could not have taken place because she [Bhanwari Devi] was from a 'lower' caste." Quoted in Teesta Setalvad, "Thrice Oppressed," *Communalism Combat*, May 2001, p. 13. This is the kind of judgment that legitimizes *dalit* women's slogans like "We are untouchable by day and touchable by night." Ibid., p. 9.

More recently Bhanwari Devi has been subjected to yet another form of violence through a sensationalized version of her life story in a commercial film, raising many of the same issues precipitated by Shekhar Kapur's representation of the life of Phoolan Devi in *Bandit Queen*. While I do not deal with these specific controversies in this essay, I have them in mind as I question the politics of representation in the next section.

23 Ariel Dorfman, quoted in Krog, *Country of My Skull*, p. 361.

24 Ibid.

sation that she is having with an unnamed male companion.[25] While she ago-
nizes about the idea that writers in South Africa should "shut up for a while"
since they have no right to "appropriate a story paid for with a lifetime of pain
and destruction," her companion remonstrates with her "*over*-respectfulness" to
the victims' suffering through allusions to the history of Germany.[26] More
specifically he recalls the taboos relating to the representation of Auschwitz,
which almost assumed a "holy character" that could not be "trivialized" through
fictional narration. Encapsulating the antirepresentational argument, Krog's
companion says,

> It's all well and good to listen to victims in court cases … but artists should keep their
> grubby hands off the stories. German artists could not find a form in which to deal
> with Auschwitz. They refused to take possession of their own history. So the inevitable
> happened. Hollywood took it away from them. A soap opera laid claim to the statistic,
> the metaphor, the abstraction that was Auschwitz.[27]

From this intervention it is possible to reiterate the endless debate on the ethics
and necessity of representing the unspeakable horrors of ethnic cleansing, genocide, and mass slaughter, even while acknowledging the difficult, even exploitive
dimension of the enterprise. For the purpose of this essay, however, I would like
to steer the discussion back to the modalities of reconciliation. Taking
Auschwitz as a cue, I will focus now on memorial museums, in which the
dialectics of solitude and trauma are played out in increasingly more complex
and controversial ways in public culture. If the earlier sections of this essay have
dealt with different modes of performing (or dissimulating) truth, I would now
like to focus on the aporias of spectatorship. Moving away from my participatory interaction as a director with the truths unfolding in theater workshops, I
would now like to enter the more anonymous yet troubling intimacy of museums as dream-sites.

   As a prelude to this closing section of my essay, and as a bridge with the earlier sections, I would like to raise a few questions: What happens when you are
not a victim yourself, but you become a spectator of someone else's pain? How

25 The intimacy of the conversation is framed, and distanced, by Krog's prefatory note that she is
   drawing on at least four texts: *Het Loon van de Schuld*, by Ian Buruma; *Guilt and Shame*, ed. Herbert Morris; *Imagination, Fiction, Myth*, by Johan Dagenaar; and *After the Catastrophe*, by Carl
   Jung (Krog, *Country of My Skull*, p. 359). These citations contribute to the metacritical dimensions
   of Krog's conversation, which can also be read as an unacknowledged love story. For a Derridean
   reading of how Krog invents the figure of the beloved to complicate her mode of storytelling, see
   Sanders, "Truth, Telling, Questioning," pp. 80–83.
26 Krog, *Country of My Skull*, p. 360.
27 Ibid., p. 361.

do you deal with it? How do you resist the obvious possibilities of voyeurism, or the mere consumption of other peoples' suffering? How do you sensitize yourself politically to the histories of others that might not have touched on your own? Memorial museums enable us to address these questions. Since they constitute a vast area of research, I will extrapolate my analysis around two moments of spectatorship through which I will further question received assumptions of truth and reconciliation.

In Dachau, the journey through the concentration camp, at once simulated and real, ends in a statement that underlies the raison d'être of every memorial museum: *What happened must never happen again.* This reads like an affirmation of world citizenship and humanitarian solidarity, which one is compelled to endorse dutifully. However, as one exits the protected civil space of the museum, where one passes as a tourist, and enters the public sphere, where one is marked as a foreigner, one realizes that the statement may be something of an illusion. Back in the desolate anonymity of one's Munich hotel, one suffers with the memory of Dachau, and it is this post-Holocaust museumized suffering to which I would like to call your attention now.

Is not this suffering essentially narcissistic, masochistic, parasitic, unproductive, even factitious? How can one accept the condition of becoming an imaginary surrogate victim of a reality to which one is not connected at a historical level? Ian Buruma has written ironically of the "joys and perils of victimhood," which he contextualizes specifically within the second generation of Holocaust survivors, who fabricate identities for themselves. He makes the strong point that the survivors of Auschwitz themselves did not mark themselves as victims; they wanted to get on with their lives and integrate with society as far as possible. It was their sons and daughters who developed a "vicarious virtue" by marking themselves as minorities through a "sentimental solidarity of remembered victimhood."[28] In an even more scathing critique, Buruma dwells on the effects of the Holocaust industry – its celebration of "kitsch and death," its "pseudo-religion," and even its stimulation of an "Olympics of suffering." These are epithets used by a growing number of the Holocaust's critics, some of whom would regard the Jewish tragedy as overrepresented at the expense of acknowledging other tragedies faced by other communities.

Buruma's critique is legitimate, but it is also insufficiently reflexive, if not unconsciously derisive of the suffering of others. There are at least three problems with his position:

---

28 Ian Buruma, "The Joys and Perils of Victimhood," *The New York Review of Books*, April 8, 1999, p. 4.

1) In focusing on the second generation of victims and survivors in predominantly Western societies, particularly in the United States, and in assuming all too readily that they have been atomized by a homogenized, metropolitan, global culture, Buruma uses his critique of fictitious victimhood to undermine the legitimate search of minorities in diasporic cultures to assert new identities for themselves. Not every assertion of a minority identity is necessarily a product of victimhood, imagined or real, but this seems to be the underlying assumption of Buruma's critique. In essence this position cannot be separated from a larger agenda of multicultural-bashing from a liberal secular-humanist perspective.[29] It is one thing to expose the limitations or even racist implications of multicultural statism, quite another to play into the antiminoritarian rhetoric that reduces advocates of identitarian politics to opportunistic "victims."

2) While there is evidence that "historical truth" is being replaced in academia by theories of "social construction" and "subjectivity," Buruma overstates his fears by claiming that "when all truth is subjective, only feelings are authentic, and only the subject can know whether his or her feelings are true or false."[30] Feelings for Buruma can only be "expressed, not discussed or argued about."[31] This is precisely the unstated animus that underlies the reticence on the part of the TRC Report to acknowledge the veracity of "personal or narrative truth," as conveyed through stories and testimonials. Buruma is articulating the same prejudice, but with considerably more eloquence and precision.

Other echoes of the antiperformative prejudice examined earlier in the essay can be traced in Buruma's refusal to accept any ritualization of suffering or healing – he even has problems with the lighting of candles in the precincts of Auschwitz. Without undermining the possible excesses of relating such rituals to larger instances of historical trauma, it is necessary to point out that these seemingly ahistorical signs of subjectivity and emotion have a place in the writing of history. They do not necessarily *replace* facts; they *complicate* them. And

29 It comes as no surprise that Buruma should endorse Kwame Anthony Appiah's urbane yet condescending dismissal of the search for new identities by middle-class "hyphenated Americans" who seem to "fear that unless the *rest of us* acknowledge the importance of *their* difference, there soon won't be anything worth acknowledging" (my italics). Appiah, "The Multicultural Misunderstanding," *The New York Review of Books*, October 9, 1997. It would be interesting to question how Appiah positions himself in relation to "the rest of us" – as a nonhyphenated American, or as a hyphenated American-Ghanaian, upper class and cosmopolitan, who doesn't need "the rich, old kitchen comforts of ethnicity"? There are far too many putdowns in this disparagement of the less cosmopolitan seekers of multicultural identity, and it needs to be countered or at least counterpointed by the more sympathetic reading of "new ethnicities" offered by Stuart Hall in "New Ethnicities," in Bill Ashcroft, Gareth Griffiths, and Helen Tiffin, eds., *The Post-Colonial Studies Reader* (London and New York: Routledge, 1995).
30 Buruma "The Joys and Perils of Victimhood," p. 7.
31 Ibid., p. 8.

that is what Buruma fails to acknowledge – that while the history that replaces "historical truth" with "subjectivity" is flawed, the omniscient, objective, fact-bound history that seems to "write itself," in Roland Barthes's words, is also flawed in its own right.

3) Finally there is an unacknowledged cosmopolitan insularity in Buruma's position. As he puts it somewhat too breezily, "It is perhaps time for those of us who have lost religious, linguistic, or cultural ties with our ancestors to admit to that and let go."[32] Perhaps it would be prudent to qualify that assertion with the suggestion that there are millions of people in the world for whom such ancestral ties cannot be so easily severed. We may have problems with these ties – and I have indicated their "fundamentalist echoes" in my encounter with the aboriginal storyteller earlier in the essay – but we cannot dismiss them as irrelevant, as indeed I did in my first response to the subject. The surest way of playing into fundamentalist prejudice is to dismiss claims of ancestry instead of subjecting them to critical scrutiny.

Problematizing Memorial Museums   Having acknowledged these problems, I would also admit that the cult of victimhood has been uncritically celebrated in the context of memorial museums, where there has been a tendency to spectacularize suffering and to market it within the logic of global capitalism. Curatorial practices have also reified the remnants of destruction and genocide without sufficiently historicizing them. The hermetic confines of the museums themselves have enhanced the self-absorption of specific communal histories. In this regard it would be almost blasphemous to imagine that a Jewish museum could contain even a fleeting reference to the predicament of the Palestinian peoples. Memorial museums do not deal with the process of history as such, including peace processes, however flawed. Essentially they are embodiments of time warps, where it is assumed that "what happened" should "never happen again," even if there has been no confrontation with "what has happened" in the intervening years. The memorial museum memorializes itself.

The way out of this impasse could be to seek a dialogic space within the museum whereby the seemingly heuristic divisions of the civil and the political can be brought into crisis. To activate this dialogic space one may have no other option but to invite controversy rather than to pretend that it doesn't exist. Perhaps memorial museums are not meant for reconciliation alone, but for reconciliation ruptured with disturbing truths. The reality is, however, that the rheto-

32 Ibid.

ric of reconciliation more often than not camouflages truth, as in the declara-
tions of peace that have accumulated since Hiroshima was destroyed, eliding
any real confrontation with Japanese imperialism and colonial aggression during
World War II. The nationalist historiography around that war has yet to be
destabilized.

Within this impasse, the Peace Memorial Museum of Hiroshima can be
regarded as a particularly strong propagandist agency of reconciliation – reconciliation cast in the symbol of "peace," not least because this propaganda is
implicit and rendered through some undeniably heart-wrenching evidence. To
submit my own spectatorship to critical scrutiny, I would call attention to one
particular image in the museum dealing with the reconstruction of Hiroshima,
which, inexplicably, had a more harrowing effect on me than the meticulous
documentation of the bombing itself. It is well known that every living being in
the human, animal, and plant world in the immediate periphery of the atom
bomb blast was reduced to nuclear dust. Miraculously, however, beyond the
planned agenda of the reconstruction process itself, a sign of ecological renewal
manifested itself a few years later. This renewal was represented through a photograph of a particular bamboo plant, if I remember correctly, that started to
grow out of the devastated Hiroshima soil.

Today I continue to be profoundly moved by this image, but I am also troubled by what it compels me to forget: namely, the ruthless policy perpetrated by
the Japanese government of leveling entire forests in poorer Asian countries in
order to protect its own environment. The most excruciating lesson – I am
tempted to say blessing – of ecology, embodied in the photograph of the bamboo plant, needs to be juxtaposed in my view with the ongoing ecocide legitimized by the Japanese government within the priorities of industrial capital
and national environmental protectionism. Ecology cannot be used to justify
ecocide.

However, there is another symbol of the Peace Memorial Museum that I
would uphold precisely because it incorporates its own contradiction: the flame
of peace that flickers outside the museum precincts is meant to burn "forever" –
so long as there are nuclear weapons in this world. This is a troubling symbol,
because fire is sacred and is meant to last infinitely, without any conditions
imposed on its longevity. Symbolically the extinction of fire signifies the end of
the world. Here I cannot "unmark" my Zoroastrian background, where fire has
a specific religio-cultural significance that I do not question, for all my secular
priorities. Perhaps, the *atash* (the Holy Fire) is the only sign in my life that
approximates the condition of an absolute. And yet, in confronting the flame of
peace in Hiroshima, I realize that almost nothing could be a greater source of
celebration – indeed, the beginnings of a nuclear-free utopia – than if this flame

could be extinguished forever. I am caught in an aporia between wanting to accept the reconciliation provided by the sacredness and eternity of fire and recognizing the truth of its extinction. This in-between space, I believe, is not just liminal but troubling. If memorial museums can create trouble, then they are worth supporting.

Rethinking Silence   One other reason for the significance of the flame of peace could be linked to the intercivilizational, interreligious, and intercultural resonances that are tapped, perhaps inadvertently, through the cultural memories of the museum's international spectators, of which I am one. Memorial museums need to work across the borders of the imagination in order to destabilize the nationalist holds of specific governments in territorializing the tragedies of the past. Perhaps we need to hyphenate museums – Jewish-Palestinian, Japanese-Korean, Indo-Pakistani – or, better still, we need to get rid of these national and communal categories and imagine an altogether different nomenclature for museums on a conceptual and symbolic basis.

It could be argued, however, that some cultures could resist the very idea of memorial museums as an aberration, a deviation from their own civilizational norms. In India, for instance, we do not have memorial museums commemorating the Partition, among other communal atrocities. A pragmatic explanation could be that while we have many museums in India, we don't have a museum culture – unlike Germany, for instance, where going to the museum is part of everyday cultural life, at least for a large section of the population. Within this culture the Jewish Museum in Berlin is merely a postmodern extension (and partial subversion) of a museological ethos and grammatology that have been nurtured over the years.

At a more political level, one could argue that memorial museums in the Indian subcontinent at this point in time could only intensify the xenophobic hold of nationalists in claiming cross-border tragedies on an exclusionary basis. At a more philosophical level, one could question whether "the past" can be meaningfully museumized in a country like India, where the past is alive in so many ways, hybridizing, mutating, and intersecting with conflicting "presents."[33] At a moral level, however, it is questionable whether "suffering" and "trauma" need to be memorialized at all.

Here it becomes necessary to question the cultural valences and resonances of silence, which more often than not are equated in monolithic terms with

33 See Bharucha, "Beyond the Box: Problematizing the 'New Asian Museum,'" *Third Text*, no. 52 (Autumn 2000): 15–18.

repression, cowardice, or fear. Indeed, if there is any element in the discourse of truth and reconciliation that is consistently rejected, it is silence. Silence is unacceptable in dealing with any tragedy or atrocity, even if the absence of justice is tolerated. You have to speak out. That is the underlying imperative of almost any exposure of violence, whether it concerns apartheid or the genocide in Rwanda or the Partition in India. While it is ethically and morally questionable to endorse silence when the truth of a particular crime has yet to be acknowledged, however, it could also be argued that the breaking of silence should not be made into a dictum. Silence can be a political or cultural choice. As "the other side of silence"[34] gets articulated with significant effect, we should not forget the worlds within silence for which it is much harder to find an adequate language in words. Perhaps we should acknowledge that silence can be, in certain cases, for particular individuals, the only means of "reconciling with reality."

Time and Reconciliation   Along with silence we need to open the dimension of time, which underlies whatever I have addressed in this essay, as I have traced the instabilities of evidence, memory, and storytelling through experiments in theater and public culture. It is commonly assumed that time heals, and that with the passing of time, the scars are supposed to fade away. Certainly we know that this is not the case when there is a time-frame on the processes of truth and reconciliation, as in South Africa, where there were specific schedules for hearings, consultations, meetings, and submissions of reports. This bureaucratic pressure of time seems almost ludicrous when one confronts the truism that centuries of oppression cannot be removed overnight. And yet, as the veteran of the Chilean truth commission José Zalaquett has affirmed, "The process [of Truth and Reconciliation] must stop! Just as a patient undergoing a critical operation should not stay in the theater too long, a truth commission should know when to call it a day."[35] Hopefully one assumes that the unacknowledged doctor in Zalaquett's metaphor will not prematurely stitch up the patient before attending fully to his or her problem, or worse still, after dismissing the patient as a "hopeless case." Whether or not the operation is "successful," the point is that while the process of reconciliation may begin with the deliberations of a truth commission, it certainly doesn't end there.

We should not presume to imagine that new societies can be born in the aftermath of even the most time-conscious and efficient of commissions. This

34 See Urvashi Butalia, *The Other Side of Silence: Voices from the Partition of India* (New Delhi: Penguin Books, 1998).
35 José Zalaquett, quoted in Meiring, "Truth before Justice and Reconciliation," p. 9.

kind of hubris would place an act of social engineering over and above the capacities of human beings to understand and live together through the violence that continues to divide them at civic and political levels. In her epilogue to *Country of My Skull,* Krog acknowledges that few people believe that the TRC process achieved reconciliation; indeed surveys indicate that "people are further apart than before."[36] This does not mean that the process of reconciliation is not going on, but to realize its outcome we need a larger envisioning of time. As Krog sees it, "Reconciliation is not a process. It is a cycle that will be repeated many times."[37] The unspoken assumption here is that if reconciliation is destined to repeat itself, so will the memories of violence that refuse to die.

Rejecting any attempt to read reconciliation as "a mysterious Judaeo-Christian process," Krog implicitly works against the ethos of forgiveness that animated Tutu's almost evangelical faith in the redemptive powers of the TRC. The point is not, as some dissenters have argued, that forgiveness is a specifically Christian virtue that is psychologically unacceptable or unintelligible in indigenous African contexts, even though, in Xhosa, "reconciliation" is rendered as "*uxolelwano,*" which is much closer in meaning to "forgiveness."[38] Forgiveness, it could be argued, is an important element of many other faiths, and indeed it may be necessary to forgive in order to survive the trials of the past.[39] The problem does not concern the cross-cultural epistemological valences of "forgiveness" as such; the problem is whether forgiveness can be activated across individuals and communities for the restoration of a new society. Sadly, the realities on the ground in South Africa reveal that forgiveness, insofar as it has been activated, individually or collectively, has not produced the kind of reconciliation that was anticipated by the TRC.

Confronting this reality, Krog opts for more secular solutions to human coexistence, for which she draws on evidence that is more likely to be associated with a social scientist than with a poet. Pragmatically, and in a tone totally at odds with the questioning nature of her book, Krog falls back in the closing paragraphs of her epilogue on the most banal truism of conflict resolution. She reduces reconciliation to "one of the most basic skills applied in order to survive conflict"; its "essence" is "survival," its "key" the art of "negotiation" – less negotiation than an almost biological need to get on with life.[40]

---

36 Krog, *Country of My Skull,* p. 448.
37 Ibid., p. 449.
38 Ibid., p. 243.
39 See the concluding section of Bhargava, "Between Revenge and Reconciliation," for a broader perspective on "forgiveness" that counters Mahmoud Mamdani's more provocative position that forgiveness is an "invitation to reconcile with rather than conquer evil." See Mamdani, "Reconciliation without Justice," *South African Review of Books* CIV (1996).
40 Krog, *Country of My Skull,* p. 448.

This resilience is determined less by civility or good faith than by "our genetic make-up," as Krog puts it all too emphatically, in a vocabulary that is clearly not her own.

An equally unconvincing source of evidence comes from the postapartheid refashioning of identities, which Krog views as a "fundamental step" toward reconciliation.[41] It is hard to share this optimism, particularly as she views "blacks" redefining themselves within the "African renaissance." One is compelled to ask: Which sections of the blacks are in the process of "redefining" themselves in this mode? Can this so-called "renaissance" (replicating the "Asian renaissance" of East Asian global capitalism) not be seen as another form of neoimperialism in the new South Africa? Even as the beneficiaries of global capital among the black elite are ready to assert a new, cosmopolitan, neoliberal, "renaissance" identity for themselves, they are not prepared to share the economic benefits of this "renaissance" with their less privileged brothers and sisters. Nonetheless, they hold on to the racial category of "black" in its most literal and essentializing sense. This privileged position of "wanting to have it both ways" – race and capital – can certainly fuel the propagation of new identities, but are these likely to produce a culture of reconciliation, as Krog seems to imply? Or is not a new culture of emergent disparities and divisions in the making?

I have problematized just one "identity" here to point out that the politics of identity can catalyze, metabolize, and disrupt the hierarchies of any given society, but there is no guarantee that in this process new hierarchies are unlikely to emerge, or that reconciliation across older divides is likely to be stabilized. To seek reconciliation beyond the constraints of specific identity constructions, we need to do more than posit the multiple or hybrid identities that have become postmodern tropes. Perhaps we need to counter the very concept of "identity" with the enigmas of the "self," just as we have to complicate the exigencies of "time-frames" for the implementation of truth commissions with the "cycles of time" in which reconciliation is destined to play itself out.

For this we need another vocabulary and perspective, for which I would like to turn, unexpectedly perhaps, at the conclusion of this essay, to the philosophy offered by the one of greatest seers of time in the contemporary world, Jiddu Krishnamurti. Unlike the architects of truth commissions, Krishnamurti questions the very assumption that there can be a positive outcome in negotiating a path from truth to reconciliation or from violence to nonviolence. In his barely veiled critique of Gandhi, for instance, he emphasizes that the evolution from violence to nonviolence implies that you need time to become nonvio-

---

41 Ibid.

lent. In working toward this "ideal," which Krishnamurti equates with an "escaping process," all that emerges is a "division" in the mind, which can only perpetuate "conflict."[42] Indeed "the very resistance to conflict is itself a form of conflict."[43]

If this is not a language that one associates with activism of any kind, I should qualify that Krishnamurti is addressing not political time but what he describes as "psychological time," which is determined by the interval, the division, the gap, between "this" and "that," between "one action and another," between "one understanding and another," between "seeing something, thinking about it, and acting."[44] This very *movement* embodied in time, carrying the conceptual baggage of our thoughts, memories, desires, and motives, which are the very cause of our suffering, compels Krishnamurti to posit "a time of non-movement" that is without momentum, direction, or continuity.[45] Calling attention to the state of "passive awareness" in which the dissolution of psychological time becomes possible, he advocates nothing less than "the ending of time."[46] This is not an apocalyptic narrative but a tentatively posited "new beginning" by which we can begin to reinvent and sustain our inner selves on a different "ground" of being.

If I choose to inscribe "the ending of time" at the end of my essay, it is not because I see it as some kind of solution. Indeed Krishnamurti would not want us to believe in solutions, because that would imply a progression in time, which is the very source of our pain. He would be skeptical of our attempts to articulate this "ending," as indeed he was frustrated by his own attempts to put vision into words: "We are using words to measure the immeasurable, and our words have become time."[47] I use Krishnamurti as a provocation because in a

---

42 Jiddu Krishnamurti, "On Time," *Mind without Measure* (Madras: Krishnamurti Foundation India, 1983), p. 87.

43 Krishnamurti, "Time and Transformation," *The First and Last Freedom* (London: Victor Gollancz, Ltd., 1986), p. 134.

44 Krishnamurti, quoted in Pupul Jayakar, "Is There a Time of Non-Movement?" *Fire in the Mind: Dialogues with J. Krishnamurti* (New Delhi: Penguin Books, 1995), p. 250.

45 Ibid., pp. 250–51.

46 *The Ending of Time* is a series of thirteen dialogues that Krishnamurti conducted with the quantum physicist David Bohm. The keyword here is "dialogue," the kind of which there is very little evidence in political and social forums, even as "dialogue" is prioritized by nongovernmental organizations, truth commissions, and activist groups. Countering the seemingly apocalyptic resonance of its title, *The Ending of Time* reflects a tentative yet rigorous process of questioning that moves from abstract subjects like "Ground of Being, Mind of Man," "Mutation of the Brain Cells?" and "Ending of 'Psychological' Knowledge" into a very fundamental question: "Can Personal Problems Be Solved and Fragmentation End?" There is a humbling process of "truth and reconciliation" here that is explored through active thinking – and listening. See Krishnamurti and David Bohm, *The Ending of Time* (Chennai: Krishnamurti Foundation India, 1996).

47 Krishnamurti, quoted in Jayakar, "Is There a Time of Non-Movement?" p. 254.

sense he works against the premises of this essay – he complicates the agenda. He makes us want to requestion its priorities. Most decisively, he infiltrates the conjunction "and" that separates (and links) "truth" and "reconciliation." He breaks the causality by collapsing these terms. And in that sense he fills us with profound unease. Should it be otherwise?

Visual Arts Gallery, India Habitat Centre, New Delhi, May 7–21, 2001

A House in Jerusalem
Israel 1998 / 98 min. / Director: Amos Gitai
Twenty years after Amos Gitai shot *Bait* (House), which shed light on the difficulties of the young nation of Israel, he returned to the same house featured in
that film. Through its owners past and present *A House in Jerusalem* examines
the country's new situation. As the film describes a series of concentric circles
around the house and its neighborhood, each of its successive residents becomes
a metaphor for the conditions in Israel.

A Season Outside
India 1997 / 30 min. / Director: Amar Kanwar
A Season Outside is an analytical essay on the ambivalent dimensions of the
border conflict between India and Pakistan. A personal and philosophical
journey through borders, time zones, conflicting positions, and the shadows of
past generations, the film wanders nomadically through lines of separation,
examining the scars of violence and the dreams of hope scattered among name-
less people.

Bait (House)
Israel 1980 / 50 min. / Director: Amos Gitai
A house in Jerusalem, previously owned by a Palestinian, undergoes reconstruction for a Jewish proprietor. This documentary for Israeli television examines in
microcosm the relations and conflicts between Jews and Arabs.

Borders
Israel 1999 / 52 min. / Directors: Nurit Kedar and Eran Riklis
Nurit Kedar and Eran Riklis bring to light several emotionally charged stories
across the borders of Israel, the Palestinian National Authority, Syria, and Jordan. *Borders* records poignant personal accounts from people whose lives have
been changed forever by these barriers as well as harsh realities of their lives: the

shell-shocked veteran who visits the place of his affliction, the "shouting fence" that is the meeting point and only form of communication.

Chronicle of a Disappearance

Palestine 1996 / 85 min. / Director: Elia Suleiman

Chronicle of a Disappearance is a journey in search of what it means to be Palestinian. A compilation of possible truths, it transgresses genres, blending fact with fiction to explore the intertwined boundaries of naming, storytelling, history, and autobiography. The film depicts a situation of deprivation, disillusionment, and inaction, its characters wandering in an attempt to break free from their ghettoized existence. The character E. S. – Elia Suleiman, the filmmaker himself – moves in a social and political labyrinth, experiencing the rift between his native place and himself. Beginning to inquire into his sense of belonging and his role as simultaneous insider and outsider, he moves between the roles of actor and observer, mediator and storyteller – a storyteller who finds himself without a story.

Der Nürnberger Hauptkriegsverbrecherprozess (The Nuremberg Trial)

Three parts: *Die Anklage* (The charge), *Die Verteidigung* (The defense), *Das Urteil* (The verdict)

Germany 1967 / 3 x 100 min. / Director: Bengt von zur Mühlen

This documentary on the Nuremberg Trial (which ran for 218 days between November 20, 1945, and October 1, 1946) is presented in three installments: The Charge, The Defense, and The Verdict. The film tries to reflect the atmosphere of the trial: the prosecutor's attempt to establish the truth; the witnesses who report the atrocities in the concentration camps; the appearances and voices of the accused.

Deutschland im Herbst (Germany in Autumn)

Germany 1977–78 / 116 min. / Directors: Alf Brustellin, Hans Peter Cloos, Rainer W. Fassbinder, Alexander Kluge, Maximiliane Mainka, Beate Mainka-Jellinghaus, Edgar Reitz, Katja Rupé, Volker Schlöndorff, Peter Schubert, Bernhard Sinkel

Eleven leading filmmakers collaborated on this protest against fascist tendencies in West Germany. The film reflects on the tragic events of autumn 1977, when the industrialist Hanns-Martin Schleyer was kidnapped and murdered by the Red Army Faction (RAF). Shortly afterward, the leaders of the RAF died mysteriously in the high-security prison of Stammheim, outside Stuttgart. The contributions to the film range from an elegiac sequence of the burial of the RAF prisoners, through newsreel clips of the funeral cortege of Field Marshal Erwin

Rommel, to a fictitious argument among TV executives about a controversial production of Sophocles's *Antigone*.

Dissidência (Dissidence)
Angola 1998 / 56 min. / Director: Zézé Gamboa
Civil war continues to ravage Angola. This documentary project is the result of a collaboration among filmmakers from across Europe trying to understand the causes of one of the longest and most violent conflicts in history. The directors are four men and one woman: Rui Ramos (Lisbon), Manuel Lima (Lisbon and Paris), Manuel Jorge (Paris), Gilberto (Anvers), and Lurdes Miranda (Lisbon). All are Angolans, black, white, and *métisse*, and each in his or her own way reveals something about Angola, its history of resistance, and its civil war. Theirs is also an account of exile.

Informe general sobre algunas cuestiones de interés para una proyección pública
Spain 1975 / 153 min. / Director: Pere Portabella
Taking into account his occupation with political-witness documentaries in earlier years, Pere Portabella here discusses questions of politics and militancy, portraying the political panorama after the death of the Spanish dictator General Francisco Franco. In the film, returned exiles speak about that period, and about the fate of Spain's democracy after a long dictatorship.

La Commission de la verité (The Truth Commission)
France 1999 / 140 min. / Director: André Van In
Before 1994, South Africa had never known a democratic government, and that year, when the country adopted majority rule, it had to invent its own model of democracy. One of Nelson Mandela's first decisions upon becoming president was to set up the Truth and Reconciliation Commission, an attempt to enable social reconciliation, healing, judgment, and exorcism of the past. The evolution of the Commission was an integral part of the making of this film. Like South Africa itself, the characters in the film are undergoing a process of transformation.

Landscape of Memory
Four parts:

1. From the Ashes
Mozambique 1999 / 26 min. / Director: Karen Boswall
This film portrays the attempts of a community to resolve the traumas of civil war. Three veterans try to purify themselves through different rituals.

2. I Have Seen

Namibia 1999/26 min./Director: Richard Pakleppa
The film tells of war crimes committed by Namibia's former liberation move-ment, which came to government in 1990. Now its members urge that the past should be forgotten and forgiven.

3. Soul in Torment

Zimbabwe 1999/26 min./Director: Prudence Uriri
A former soldier of President Robert Mugabe's brigades, a former dissident, and a victim of torture by the opposition at the dawn of Zimbabwe's independence discuss the frustrations of the past and the desire for forgiveness.

4. The Unfolding of Sky

South Africa 1999/26 min./Directors: Antjie Krog and Ronelle Loots
Through a dialogue between a white journalist, an Afrikaaner, and a black woman involved in the Truth and Reconciliation Commission, we decipher the meaning of the concepts of truth, reconciliation, and forgiveness.

Long Night's Journey into Day

USA 2000/90 min./Directors: Deborah Hoffmann and Frances Reid
As apartheid rule began to disintegrate in South Africa, so did the "truth" of the regime. In the bitter ashes of apartheid, the impulse for revenge on the part of the victims and their families moved from the vigilantism of the previous forty years into the community halls and gathering places visited by the Truth and Reconciliation Commission. This film documents four major incidents that had occurred under the apartheid regime, following the sometimes inspir-ing, sometimes overwhelming, but always gripping personal struggles of the participants.

Nous ne sommes plus morts (We Are No Longer Dead)

Belgium, France, Rwanda 2000/126 min./Director: François L. Woukoache
Long-planned and meticulously prepared genocide is carried out in Rwanda. Africans become guilty of crimes against humanity. More than a million men, women, and children are murdered in the space of 100 days. *Nous ne sommes plus morts* focuses on a central question: in the face of such events, how do you carry on with your life? The film describes a journey across the country in search of symbols and signs of remembrance – signs between words and everyday ges-tures, between bodies and space – to grasp the movement of life, to be present, to testify to the continuing hope for a future to open up, for a dream to believe in, for life to continue in Rwanda today.

Nuba Conversations

Britain 1999 / 55 min. / Director: Arthur Howes

This film about the Nuba people, who live 700 km (over 400 miles) from Khartoum, the capital of Sudan, points to a little-known human disaster. Ten years after he lived in Sudan, teaching English and shooting the film *Kafi's Story*, Arthur Howes returns to show his film and to track down some of the villagers he met on his earlier visit. Some of them he finds eking out an existence as refugees, victims of the government's policy of Islamization. Others have been forced into the army to act against their own people.

Return to Ngu Thuy

Vietnam 1997 / 28 min. / Directors: Le Manh Thich and Do Khanh Toan

The girls' artillery company in Ngu Thuy was renowned during the Vietnam War for sinking five American warships. In 1971, Lo Minh's film *Girls of Ngu Thuy* won several prizes. *Return to Ngu Thuy* documents the director's return to the village after nearly thirty years, revisiting the characters in the earlier film to see them in their present civilian life.

Shoah

France 1986 / 566 min. / Director: Claude Lanzmann

Claude Lanzmann's epic film is an attempt, however impossible, to create an intimation of the totality of the Holocaust and its origins. Instead of using archival footage, Lanzmann intercuts interviews both with survivors who bear witness to their time in the camps and with Nazi functionaries who appear unable to comprehend the process of which they have been part.

The Specialist

Austria, Belgium, France, Germany, Israel 1999 / 128 min. / Director:
Eyal Sivan with Rony Brauman

On May 11, 1960, the Israeli secret service captured the Nazi leader Adolf Eichmann in Argentina, where he had been living under the alias Ricardo Klement. One year later he was put on trial in Jerusalem. Inspired by Hannah Arendt's book *Eichmann in Jerusalem*, *The Specialist* uses original footage from Eichmann's trial to present a devastating portrait of what Arendt called "the banality of evil." The title of the film derives from Eichmann's specialty – the transportation of freight by railroad.

Videogramme einer Revolution (Videograms of a Revolution)

Germany 1992 / 106 min. / Directors: Harun Farocki and Andrei Ujica

Using footage documenting the Romanian revolution in late 1989, this film writes and reflects on a minute-precise chronology of the days between December 21 and 26 of that year. It shows that videogram recordings are to be seen as an audiovisual writing of history.

Ye Wonz Maibel (Deluge)

USA 1997/61 min./Director: Salem Mekuria

A personal essay on history, conflict, loss, and reconciliation as told through a first-person narrative, *Ye Wonz Maibel* explores the momentous events that took place in Ethiopia between 1974 and 1991. The film is a tale of love and betrayal, of idealism and the lure of power; a memorial to a brother who disappeared and to a best friend who was executed; and a story of Ethiopian students, their "revolution," and its aftermath.

The Witness Archive

This program of eleven documentaries features videos from Algeria, Bosnia, Congo, East Timor, Haiti, Kosovo, Nigeria, Northern Ireland, Rwanda, Sierra Leone, and Zaire, all produced or distributed in conjunction with Witness, a project of the Lawyers Committee for Human Rights based in New York.

A Massacre Remembered

Witness, 2000/226 min./Narrator: Michael Stipe/Music: Philip Glass

Guatemala's thirty-six-year civil war claimed the lives of over 200,000 citizens and displaced millions more, many of them Mayan. *A Massacre Remembered* tells the story of Jesus Tecu Osorio, one of the few survivors of the Rio Negro Massacre, which took place on March 13, 1982. After witnessing the massacre of more than 100 children and nearly 80 women by members of the Guatemalan army and civil patrols, Jesus and 17 other children were put to work as servants in the houses of the men who had killed their families. Jesus lived in captivity for three years until he was freed by his only surviving sister, Laura.

Expelled

National Coalition for Haitian Rights and Columbia University Human Rights Law Clinic, 2001/10:40 min.

Expelled documents the Dominican government's practice of illegally expelling people of Haitian descent who live in the Dominican Republic. In March 2001 the video was screened for the UN Human Rights Committee, which was assessing a report by the Dominican government on human rights.

Going Home

Guinea 1997 / 31 min. / Director: Emily Marlow

In 1997, Guinea hosted an estimated 430,000 refugees – 190,000 from Sierra Leone and 240,000 Liberians escaping the eight-year civil war there. Focusing on a ten-year-old boy named Mohammed, who had been forced to fight alongside rebel forces in the jungles of Sierra Leone, *Going Home* evaluates the success of the Guinean government and the UN High Commission for Refugees in protecting the rights pledged to this huge African refugee population under the Organization of African Unity Convention.

If Hope Were Enough

Women's Caucus for Gender Justice in association with Witness, 2001 / 38 min.

If Hope Were Enough captures the historic importance of united actions by women to affect the structure and substance of the International Criminal Court, working to make it into a mechanism for addressing violations of women's human rights on an international level. Through the voices of female survivors of both historical and ongoing violence, whether in conditions of armed conflict or of peace, the video documents the inspiring struggle toward justice and an end to the ability to commit violence against women with impunity.

Kosovo & Beyond

Witness, 2000 / 388 min.

This film demonstrates how future victims of human-rights abuses like those perpetrated against ethnic Albanians in Kosovo could be served by the establishment of the International Criminal Court (ICC). It includes testimony from a Kosovar Albanian who witnessed a massacre by Serb forces, as well as depicting recent efforts by NGOs and human-rights advocates around the world to promote this institution. The feature fuses footage shot by Witness partner organizations with a Witness public service announcement calling for the ratification of the ICC.

Mirror to History

Cristian DeFrancia and Witness, 2000 / 52 min.

In Bosnia, a country of remarkable beauty and cultural richness, the experience of the kind of war crime unseen in Europe since the concentration camps of World War II continues to plague people's efforts to rebuild their lives. Is it possible to break the cycles of revenge? Witnesses to the most recent Bosnian war explain and demystify the conflict through compelling testimony of demoralization, resistance, and the struggle to achieve a tolerant and multiethnic Bosnia.

Judges and prosecutors explain and discuss, the law is confronted, and the initiators are exposed in this look inside the legacy of the war crimes in Bosnia.

Policing the Police

Committee on the Administration of Justice in Northern Ireland and Witness, 1997/18 min.

This video shows police brutality during the marching season in Northern Ireland.

PSA for the Campaign for a Permanent International Criminal Court

Coalition for an International Criminal Court, Asphalt Films, and Witness, 1999/1:33 min.

This brief public service announcement uses footage of atrocities committed throughout the twentieth century to convey the need for the creation of a permanent International Criminal Court to prosecute war crimes, genocide, and crimes against humanity.

The Diamond Life

Guerrilla New Network in association with Witness, 2000/408 min./ Commentary: Aroun Rashid Deen

The attack of the Revolutionary United Front (RUF) on Freetown, Sierra Leone, in January 1999 was the culmination of a bloody decade-long struggle between the RUF and the national government. In the continuing war over control of the country's rich diamond fields, the rebel forces, bolstered by the former Sierra Leonean Army, which had turned on the government, swept into the city, killing, mutilating, and raping thousands. Since 1990, half the country's population of five million has been displaced. Today, Sierra Leone produces more refugees than any other country in Africa.

The Drilling Fields

Catma Films and Witness, 1994/51 min./Director: Glenn Ellis

This video describes the struggle of the Ogoni people to combat the environmental damage caused by oil production in the Niger Delta. The Ogoni's peaceful actions to inform the world about their plight, and the sympathetic outcry that their activism engendered, led to continuous interference and violence from the Nigerian military, abuses for which the government denies responsibility. *The Drilling Fields* focuses on the late Ken Saro-Wiwa, the president of the Movement of the Survival of the Ogoni People (MOSOP), as he describes the group's efforts to promote human rights.

Triumph over Terror

Television Trust for the Environment (TVE) in association with Witness, 1998, 6 x 30 min.

Triumph over Terror, a series of six half-hour films from Bangladesh, Guinea, Nepal, Nigeria, South Africa, and Thailand, is one of four series and three individual documentaries on human-rights issues that TVE is offering broadcasters and nonbroadcast educational and campaigning organizations worldwide on the occasion of the fiftieth anniversary of the Universal Declaration of Human Rights.

Witness Video for Change

Witness 2000 / 25 min.

Witness Video for Change is the second training video produced by Witness. Using footage shot by human-rights activists from around the world, it illustrates various strategic ways in which video and Internet technology can be used to further human-rights advocacy efforts. The video is accompanied by a written manual used to train human-rights activists in video documentation.

Contributors

Shahid Amin is Professor of History and Dean of the Faculty of Social Sciences, University of Delhi. A Rhodes Scholar at Balliol College, Oxford, he has been a fellow at the Stanford Humanities Center; the Shelby Cullom Davis Center, Princeton University; and the Wissenschaftskolleg, Berlin, and a visiting professor at the University of Chicago. Among his publications are *Sugarcane and Sugar in Gorakhpur: An Inquiry into Peasant Production for Capitalist Enterprise in Colonial India* (1984), *Event, Metaphor, Memory: Chauri Chaura, 1922–1992* (1995), and, as coeditor, *"Peripheral" Labour? Studies in the History of Partial Proletarianization* (1997). He is a founding editor of the journal *Subaltern Studies*.

Yadh Ben Achour is Professor of Law in the Faculty of Juridical Sciences, University of Tunis III. His research concerns the state and Western political and legal philosophy, particularly in its relationship to the Islamic world. His publications include *Politique, religion et droit dans le monde arabe* (1992) and *Normes, foi et loi* (1993).

Rory Bester is a curator and independent scholar based in Johannesburg. He has curated a number of multimedia exhibitions, including *Democracy's Images: Photography and Visual Art from South Africa* (Umeå, 1998) and *Kwere Kwere/Journeys into Strangeness* (Cape Town, 2000) and was an associate curator of *The Short Century: Independence and Liberation Movements in Africa, 1945 to the Present* (Munich, 2001). He teaches cultural and media studies in the Wits School of Arts at the University of the Witwatersrand.

Rustom Bharucha is an independent writer, theater director, and dramaturge based in Calcutta. He is the author of several books, including *Theatre and the World* (1990), *The Question of Faith* (1993), *In the Name of the Secular* (1998), and *The Politics of Cultural Practice* (2000). One of the foremost interlocutors of intercultural theater, he has directed, lectured, and conducted workshops in different parts of the world, attempting to strengthen dialogue at the grassroots level with underprivileged communities and minority cultures. As an advisory member of the International Council of the Prince Claus Fund for Culture and Development, he has been involved in policy-making decisions for the exchange of cultures that pay close attention to issues of social equity and ecology.

Boris Buden is the editor and publisher of the political journal *Arkzin* (Zagreb) and the editor of *Springerin* (Vienna), a magazine on culture. He regularly contributes articles on philosophy, politics, and cultural criticism to periodicals in the former Yugoslavia, Western Europe, and the United States. He has also translated two works of Sigmund Freud into Croatian, and has published two collections of his own essays, *Barikade* (Barricades) *I* and *II* (1996–97).

Urvashi Butalia is a cofounder of Kali for Women, India's first and only feminist publishing house. She has been involved in the women's movement in India for more than two decades, and has published widely on issues relating to women, fundamentalism, sectarian strife, feminist historiography, and media. Butalia's works include *The Other Side of Silence: Voices from the Partition of India* (1998), *Making a Difference: Feminist Publishing in the South* (cowritten with Ritu Menon, 1995), and several edited volumes, two of which are *In Other Words: New Writing by Indian Women* (coedited with Ritu Menon, 1992), and *Women and the Hindu Right: A Collection of Essays* (coedited with Tanika Sarkar, 1995).

Manthia Diawara is Professor of Film and Comparative Literature at New York University, where he directs the Africana Studies Program. He is the editor-in-chief of *Black Renaissance/Renaissance Noire*, a journal of art, culture, and politics, and an author and filmmaker whose areas of specialization include Africa, the United States, and the Black Diaspora in Europe. His published works include *African Cinema: Politics and Culture* (1992), *Black American Cinema* (1993; a classic in black studies and film studies), and *In Search of Africa* (1998). Diawara's films include *Sembene Ousmane: The Making of African Cinema* (codirected with Ngugi wa Thiong'o, 1993), *Rouch in Reverse* (1995), *In Search of Africa* (1997), and *Diaspora Conversation* (2000). He is currently working on a book on African immigration in France, entitled *We Won't Budge*, to be published by Harvard University Press, and on a documentary film on art and democracy entitled *Bamako Sigi-Kan*.

Vojin Dimitrijević is director of the Belgrade Center for Human Rights. Until 1998 he was Professor of International Public Law and International Relations at the University of Belgrade School of Law. He has been a visiting professor at the universities of Virginia, Oslo, Lund, Split, and Sarajevo. Dimitrijević is a member of the Institut de Droit International and was a member and vice-chairman of the UN Human Rights Committee. His published works include *The Insecurity of Human Rights after Communism* (1993), *The Fate of Non-Members of Dominant Nations in Post-Communist European Countries* (1995), and *Human Rights in Yugoslavia* (2001).

María José Guembe is a practicing lawyer and a law professor at the University of Buenos Aires. She also works as a project coordinator at the Center for Legal and Social Studies (CELS), where she investigates the topic of memory and the struggle against the impunity of state terrorism. For the past four years she has overseen the publication of *The Annual Report of Human Rights in Argentina.* She is a member of various committees of the Ombuds Office and City Parliament of Buenos Aires.

Alfredo Jaar is an internationally renowned artist who was born in Santiago, Chile, where he studied architecture and film. Important solo exhibitions of his work have been held at the New Museum of Contemporary Art, New York; the Museum of Contemporary Art, Chicago; the Whitechapel Art Gallery, London; the Moderna Museet, Stockholm; the Pergamon Museum, Berlin; and the Museum of Contemporary Art, Hiroshima. He has participated in the Venice, São Paulo, Johannesburg, Sydney, Istanbul, and Kwangju biennials, as well as in Documenta 8. Jaar recently completed *The Rwanda Project 1994–2000*, and an exhibition of this work traveled to Spain, the Netherlands, Germany, Switzerland, and the United States. In 2000 Jaar was named a MacArthur Fellow.

Franz Kaltenbeck is a linguist, practicing psychoanalyst, and lecturer in Paris and Lille. He is the president of the Lille Association for the Study of Psychoanalysis and Its History (ALEPH) and contributes to the seminar on the transmission of psychoanalysis at the International College of Philosophy, Paris. He has published widely in French, German, English, Italian, and Spanish journals on psychoanalysis and literature. In 2000 he published *Trauma and Memory* (coedited with Peter Weibel). His next book, *Lacans Nicht-Wissen*, is forthcoming.

Gurjot Malhi was Operations Commander and Deputy Chief of Investigations in the Office of the Prosecutor, UN International Criminal Tribunal for the former Yugoslavia (ICTY) until April 2002. In that capacity he conducted and supervised investigations into violations of international human rights law and has organized, coordinated, and supervised forensic investigative operations in Kosovo, Bosnia-Herzegovina, and Croatia. Malhi has made many presentations on the ICTY's role, mandate, and work. Before joining the United Nations, Malhi worked as a senior police officer in different parts of India, where he holds the rank of Inspector General of Police.

Mahmood Mamdani is Herbert Lehman Professor of Government and Director of the Institute of African Studies at Columbia University, New York. He was the founding executive director of the Center for Basic Research in Kampala (1986–96) and is currently president of the Dakar-based Council for the Development of Social Research in Africa (CODESRIA). Mamdani is the author of many books, including *The Myth of Population Control* (1973), *Imperialism and Fascism in Uganda* (1983), *Citizen and Subject: Contemporary Africa and the Legacy of Late Colonialism* (1996), and *When Victims Become Killers: Colonialism, Nativism, and the Genocide in Rwanda* (2001).

Avishai Margalit is Schulman Professor of Philosophy at the Hebrew University of Jerusalem. He is currently a visiting scholar at the Russell Sage Foundation. In May 1999 he delivered the University of Frankfurt's Horkheimer Lectures, on "The Ethics of Memory." He is the author of numerous articles on a variety of philosophical topics, including the philosophy of language, logical paradoxes and rationality, social and political philosophy, and the philosophy of religion. His books include *Idolatry* (with Moshe Halbertal, 1992), *The Decent Society* (1996), and *Views in Review: Politics and Culture in the State of the Jews* (1998). He is a frequent contributor to the *New York Review of Books* and a founding and active member of Peace Now.

Geneviève Morel practices psychoanalysis in Paris and Lille. She is co-organizer of a seminar at the International College of Philosophy in Paris, and director of the project Knowledge and Clinical Practice (*Savoirs et clinique*) in Lille. Her research interests include testimony, suicide, and gender. Her most recent publication is *Ambiguïtés sexuelles: Sexuation et psychose* (2000).

Lolle Nauta is a former professor of philosophy at the University of Groningen, a former jury member of the international Bertrand Russell Tribunal, and the founder of an institute for philosophy at the University of Zambia, Lusaka. In 1977 he coedited a basic leftist program for the Partij van de Arbeid, the Dutch Labor Party. He has published in the fields of ethics, social philosophy, and theory of science, and his essays are collected in the books *De factor van de kleine c: Essays over culturele armoede en politieke cultuur* (1987) and *Onbehagen in de Filosofie: Essays* (2000).

Albie Sachs, a Justice of the South African Constitutional Court, was a leader in the struggle for human rights in South Africa and a freedom fighter in the African National Congress. Twice detained without trial by the security police under the apartheid regime, he describes his detention in *The Jail Diary of Albie Sachs* (1966), which was made into a play in London. *The Soft Vengeance of a Freedom Fighter* (1990) recounts an attempt by the South African security forces to kill him in a car bombing. He is the author of numerous books on human rights, including *South Africa: The Violence of Apartheid* (1969), *Justice in South Africa* (1973), *Protecting Human Rights in a New South Africa* (1990), and *Advancing Human Rights in South Africa* (1992). As a member of UNESCO's International Bioethics Committee, he helped draft the International Declaration on the Human Genome.

Dilip Simeon is a political activist and historian and Senior Research Fellow with Oxfam India in Delhi, where he directs a conflict mitigation project. In 1988 he was elected to the Academic Council of the University of Delhi on a reform platform. He has worked as a research scholar in the Center for Social Studies, Surat; the Institute of Development Studies, Sussex University; the University of Chicago; and the Institute of Asian Studies, Leiden. He is the author of *The Politics of Labour under Late Colonialism* (1995).

Eyal Sivan is a militant pro-Palestinian whose first film, *Aqabat Jaber/Passing Through* (1987), about displaced Palestinian populations, won the Prix du Cinéma du Réel, awarded by the Bibliothèque publique d'information, Centre Georges Pompidou, Paris. Sivan's writings, lectures, and films concern the politics of memory in Israel, questions of disobedience, and the instrumentalization and representation of genocide. In 1993 he was a resident at the Villa Medici, Rome. His film *The Specialist* (codirected by Rony Brauman, 1999), inspired by Hannah Arendt's book *Eichmann in Jerusalem*, won Germany's Adolf Grimme Gold Prize. He is currently working on an autobiographical film about immigration, identity, and borders.

Susan Slyomovics is the Geneviève McMillan–Reba Stewart Professor of the Study of Women in the Developing World and Professor of Anthropology at the Massachusetts Institute of Technology, Cambridge. Her research and teaching cover the expressive culture of the Middle East and North Africa, gender studies, human rights, and the overlap between oral and written literature. She is the author of *The Merchant of Art: An Egyptian Hilali Oral Epic Poet in Performance* (1987) and *The Object of Memory: Arab and Jew Narrate the Palestinian Village* (1998), and coeditor (with Joseph Suad) of *Women and Power in the*

Middle East (2001). She is currently writing a book about human rights in Morocco.

Barbara Maria Stafford, the William B. Ogden Distinguished Service Professor in the Department of Art History, University of Chicago, and currently the Rudolf Arnheim Professor at the Institute of Art History, Humboldt University, Berlin, specializes in art and imaging theory of the late seventeenth century through the Romantic period, focusing on the intersection between the arts and sciences. She writes criticism on contemporary art and serves as a visiting critic. She is currently continuing her work on analogy and neurobiology. She recently curated the exhibition *Devices of Wonder: From the World in a Box to Images on a Screen* for the Getty Museum, Los Angeles (2001–2). Her latest book is *Visual Analogy: Consciousness as the Art of Connecting* (1999).

Ruti Teitel is the Ernst Stiefel Professor of Comparative Law at New York Law School, where she has taught since 1988. She was the Senior Schell Fellow at Yale Law School in 1996–97 and 1999–2000, and is a member of the Human Rights Watch Steering Committee for Europe and Asia. She has published widely; recent works include *Transitional Justice* (2000), "The Constitutional Canon: The Challenge Posed by a Transitional Constitutionalism," *Constitutional Commentary* 17 (2000), "Vouchsafing Democracy: On the Confluence of Governmental Duty, Constitutional Right, and Religious Mission," *Notre Dame Journal of Law, Ethics, and Public Policy* 13 (1999), and "The Universal and the Particular in International Criminal Justice," *Columbia Human Rights Law Review* 30 (1999).

Susana Torre is an architect, urban designer, and architectural scholar/educator based in New York City. Among her best known projects are the master plan for the restoration of Ellis Island, New York (1981) and Fire Station #5, Columbus, Indiana (1987). She has taught at Columbia University, Yale University, and the University of Sydney, and served as the chair of the Parsons School of Design's Department of Architecture and Environmental Design in New York and as the director of the Cranbrook Academy of Art in Bloomfield Hills, Michigan. Torre's writings on gender and public space have been widely published; they include "Claiming the Public Space: The Mothers of Plaza de Mayo," in *The Sex of Architecture* (1996), and various articles in *Women in American Architecture: A Historic and Contemporary Perspective* (1977).